Comrades and Cousins

Walter Crane's idealistic portrayal of international labour solidarity (1896).
Reproduced by courtesy of the National Museum of Labour History.

Comrades and Cousins

Globalization, workers and labour
movements in Britain,
the USA and Australia
from the 1880s to 1914

Neville Kirk

THE MERLIN PRESS

First published 2003 by The Merlin Press Ltd.
PO Box 30705
London WC2E 8QD
www.merlinpress.co.uk

ISBN: 0850365155

British Library Cataloguing in Publication Data
is available from the British Library

Printed in Great Britain by Antony Rowe Ltd., Chippenham

Dedication

I would like to dedicate this book to the memories of my mother, Norale Kirk (1912-2001), and my brother, Allen Kirk (1949-2000)

Contents

Acknowledgements

The research for this book was carried out in England, the USA and Australia. In the course of my work I accumulated a mountain of intellectual debts and gratitude. Friends and colleagues also generously provided accommodation, hospitality and even a late night 'live' viewing, from Australia, of the 2001 Cup Final between Liverpool and Arsenal.

I am grateful for the time and assistance provided by librarians and archivists working in the following: Manchester Metropolitan University, the University of Manchester, Warwick University (both the university library's Inter-Library Loans section and The Modern Records Centre), Harvard University, the University of Maryland (the Gompers Papers), the University of New South Wales, the Australian National University (The Noel Butlin Archives Centre), Manchester Central Library, the National Museum of Labour History in Manchester, the Institute of Commonwealth Studies in London, the National Library in Canberra and the Mitchell Library in Sydney.

The book owes a great deal to the advice, patience and good humour provided by a truly international collection of colleagues and friends. Leon Fink, Rick Halpern, David Montgomery, Greg Patmore, Paul Pickering, Sean Scalmer, Lucy Taksa and John Walton read and made searching and most helpful comments upon various parts of the text. My publisher, Tony Zurbrugg, and Dorothy Thompson read and commented constructively and encouragingly upon the entire manuscript, Louis Mackay provided the book's wonderful cover and Adrian Howe skilfully and patiently attended to the production of the book.

My research was also helped at various stages by the very useful information and advice given by Stefan Berger, Huw Beynon, Frank Bongiorno, David Coates, Fiona Devine, Roger Fagge, Paulo Fontes, Raelene Frances, Larry Glickman, Sarah Gregson, Phil Griffiths, Barry Higman, David Howell, Karen Hunt, Terry Irving, Pat Jalland, Sue Levine, Marcel van der Linden, Chris Lloyd, Stuart Macintyre, Kevin Morgan, Craig Phelan, Richard Price, Tim Rowse, Mike Savage, Bruce Scates, Shel Stromquist and Ian Syson. Participants' valuable feedback upon papers presented in seminars and conferences in Nottingham, Manchester, Canberra, Sydney and Cambridge, Massachusetts, also helped me to improve and develop aspects of the text.

Generous financial assistance was provided by awards from the British Academy, the Lipman-Miliband Trust, the University of Manchester (election to a Hallsworth Research Fellowship, 1998-9), and the History Program,

Research School of Social Sciences, the Australian National University (Visiting Fellow 2001). The Department of History and Economic History, Manchester Metropolitan University, kindly granted me study leave during the academic year 1999-2000. As an Honorary Visiting Fellow in the School of Industrial Relations and Organisational Behaviour, the University of New South Wales (2000), I was given office space, access to the University's library facilities, its labour historians, and an invaluable introduction, by Lucy Taksa, to that most warm, welcoming and enthusiastic of groups, the Sydney Branch of the Australian Society for the Study of Labour History.

Indebted to all these people and institutions for the opportunity to pursue primary-based research into related aspects of the histories of Britain, the USA and Australia, I am, of course, entirely responsible for the published outcome. However, in this era of the straightjacket imposed upon academic work by the Research Assessment Exercise, I hope that I have repaid at least some of my debts by writing a wideranging and experimental work of comparative history which has something new and interesting to say to the specialist and general reader alike.

Neville Kirk, New Mills, March 2002

Introduction

Since the 1960s labour and social history have established themselves as major fields of intellectual inquiry within Britain and many other countries. However, the impressive advances made in terms of local, regional and national studies have not been matched by similar progress at the cross-national comparative level. The first general aim of this book of three essays is to make a contribution both towards filling the gaps in and further developing comparative areas of study.

All the essays focus upon discrete, but closely related, aspects of workers' and labour movements' politics and ideologies – embracing, *inter alia*, questions of class, race, nation and empire – in Britain, the USA and Australia during the era of 'new imperialism' between the 1880s and 1914. I also pay some, if much lesser, attention to the South African case, with special reference to the 'rule of race over class' within that country (see chapter three). Many white workers and their labour movements in these countries, of course, were bound together, for better or worse, by the powerful forces of common tradition and language, the migratory patterns and influences of immediate family, kin and friends, and their very, if varying and changing, presence in past, present and continuing transatlantic, colonial and imperial systems of exchange, rule and power. Indeed, my second general aim is to plead the case for paying more attention than is commonly the case in the literature to the transatlantic, colonial and imperial dimensions of the history of workers and organised labour.[1]

On a more specific level, I identify, investigate and explain common, similar and different political and ideological responses and initiatives on the part of organised labour in Britain, the USA and Australia to key changes and developments in the political economy of late nineteenth- and early twentieth-century international capitalism. It is accordingly to a brief outline of the key features of this broad politico-economic context that I will now turn.

Between the 1880s and 1914 the international capitalist system displayed a number of common and similar characteristics. Above all, it was increasingly global in ambition and reach. (It was my political interest in the current process of 'globalization' that first excited my curiosity about its past phases and manifestations.) As Ellen Wood has recently argued, 'globalization is not a new epoch but a long-term process, not a new kind of capitalism but the logic of capitalism as it has been from the start'.[2] Part of that logic resides in intensified capitalist competition, both within and beyond nation states, and an extended search for new markets and sources of cheap labour to satisfy the basic imperative of profit maximisation. The period between the 1880s and 1914 was a crucial one in the history of globalization. For it was during these years that the capitalist mode of production extended its influence across much of the globe, and that the 'new imperialist' powers of Britain, the major European countries, the United States and Japan intensified their rivalry and sought to 'carve up' and subject to their formal rule or informal political control Africa, Asia and much of the rest of the world.[3]

In addition to the accelerated pursuit of new markets and 'spheres of influence', capitalist countries also stepped up the search for new and additional sources of cheap labour, especially among 'coloured' workers. As Haden Guest, a British socialist, observed in 1905,

> Railroads, railways and steamship routes, which have already brought all parts of the world closer together, are extending in all directions ... Before twenty years are out ... capital will be hard at work with all its resources, either importing cheap unskilled coloured labour into Europe and America, or exporting all the industries that can be exported to the lands of the cheap coloured man.[4]

For example, between 1880 and 1920 'nearly two-thirds of the 23.5 million immigrants into the American labour market came from outside of north-western Europe'.[5] The latter, of course, had been one of north America's main sources of 'old' and mainly 'white' immigrant labour during the nineteenth century. Now, both 'pull' and 'push' factors drew into the USA massive numbers of peasants and rural dwellers from capitalism's 'rural periphery' in southern and south-eastern Europe. Significantly, these rural immigrants were often portrayed by members of the 'host' society as 'black' or 'non-white'. Attracted to industrial capitalism's core, they provided the raw semi-skilled or non-skilled labour required by the US in its drive for industrial supremacy in the world economy.[6] In addition, 'more than 450,000 African-Americans' migrated from the South to the northern states of the USA between 1916 and 1918 in search of work and improvement and 'to pry themselves loose from racial bondage'.[7]

This was also a period which saw the migration of capital and workers from western Europe and North America 'to develop mines, plantations, railroads and ports' in 'an even larger third world' beyond the rural periphery. Within that third world western capital frequently employed not only local, but also migrant workers. The latter, as seen particularly in the case of the Indians and Chinese, were sometimes 'unfree' workers imported from other parts of that very same third world.[8]

On an even wider canvas there existed a multitude of workers from within the capitalist countries who pursued work and plied their skills and experience according to the *global* logic and dictates of expansionary industrial capitalism. For example, by the end of the nineteenth century United Kingdom emigrants had secured a massive presence in the 'white-settler' colonies of Australasia, South Africa and Canada. In Australia approximately ninety-eight per cent of the population were of British and Irish descent; while those Chinese and other 'non-whites' who had crossed the seas to work predominantly in the gold and cane fields of Australia were soon to be banished from her shores under the terms of the White Australia policy, officially introduced in 1901.[9]

Two further examples of what Frank Thistlethwaite has termed 'proletarian globe-hopping',[10] may serve to secure this point.

First, in 1911 the Redfern branch of the Amalgamated Society of Engineers (ASE), in Sydney, Australia, regretfully reported the death of Brother William Thompson, aged sixty-eight years of age. Thompson, a member of the ASE for forty-six years, had served his time in Wolverhampton, England. He then moved to London. Subsequently he was sent to Egypt, 'to fit up some locomotives; returning to England, he was sent to Canada, thence to Cape Colony, fitting up locomotives; again returning to England, he sailed for Australia, arriving in Sydney in 1881'.

After working in Sydney for fourteen years, Thompson left for the Cape, only finally to return 'home' to 'settle down' in Sydney's Railway Department. Throughout his globe-trotting career, Thompson had shown himself to be 'a staunch trade unionist ... always ready to do his share of work in the branch'.[11] Second, during the 1890s some of the many eastern Australian victims of that country's severe depression, including immigrants from Britain, migrated in search of work not only to the newly-discovered goldfields of western Australia, but also to New Zealand, Paraguay and the seemingly rich pickings offered by the new and booming gold mines of South Africa's Witwatersrand. As Brian Kennedy informs us, the five thousand plus Australians living along the Rand in 1904 had carried with them their passions for drink and sport, 'a strong trade union tradition', and 'marked antipathies to Asian and coolie labour'. Significantly, some of these immigrants from Australia 'came to play an important part in the early history of South Africa's trade unions and Labour Party'.[12]

Expansionary in character, late nineteenth- and early twentieth-century capitalism, nevertheless, was afflicted by serious and closely linked national and international problems. Indeed, these problems amounted to a 'crisis of competitive capitalism' within its core industrial heartlands.[13] For example, although displaying variations in intensity and chronology both within and between the two nations, a common crisis of capital accumulation manifested itself in the USA and Britain between the mid-1870s and later-1890s. This was reflected economically in increased business competition and uncertainty both domestically and internationally, price deflation (most marked in the arable sector of agriculture), downward pressure on money wages combined with rising real wages for those in employment, a decline in the rate of increase of productivity and total output, a general squeeze on profit margins, erratic rates of growth in key economic sectors and seemingly more frequent and threatening periods of recession and depression. Indeed, many contemporary members of the British middle- and upper classes, however mistakenly, characterised the whole period from 1873 to 1896 as one of uniform doom and gloom, or, as some later economic historians exaggeratedly termed it, the 'Great

Depression'. (In fact there were sufficient variations in prices, levels of production and employment to invalidate the notion of uninterrupted depression.) However, there was no mistaking the fact of recurrent downturn in Britain. In terms of the United States, the massive depression between 1893 and 1897 was one of the worst experienced by American workers in the nineteenth century. In sum:

> Rising wages set against falling prices, profit margins and decelerating rates of growth of output and productivity meant ... that many employers faced a battle for continued economic health. That battle would not only align capital against labour, but also test to the limit capital's claim to be the true representative and moral guardian of the public good. There would emerge a profound legitimation crisis.[14]

Indeed, the latter manifested itself throughout society, in politics, ideology and culture as well as economically. For example, there was widespread discontent in both Britain and the USA among small farmers and rural workers, combined with rising expectations and self-confidence among increasingly organised and assertive industrial workers. Many contemporaries in both societies noted, often with alarm, that laissez-faire capitalism had failed to eradicate poverty and bring about social harmony between the classes. They also pointed to the more widespread questioning of 'traditional' and 'normal' patterns of social, cultural and political allegiance and patterns of authority and power. This was reflected in the decline of deference and the growing crisis of landed power in Britain, in growing criticisms of the 'tyrannical', 'monopolistic' and 'un-republican' nature of capital and its allies in the state machinery in the USA, and in political challenges to the 'establishment' and the mainstream parties in both countries.

Above all, perhaps, there was the marked growth of the belief that the allegiances and conflicts of class had entered the centre-stage of political and social life on both sides of the Atlantic. For this was the era in which Britain and the USA, along with several European countries, saw the emergence of recognisably 'modern' mass labour and trade union movements. These were generally more inclusive socially and occupationally than in their more exclusive and 'aristocratic pasts', highlighted their industrial and political *independence*, and often created labour or socialist parties committed for the most part to the gradual reform and eventual transformation of capitalism. There also came into being generally minority-based revolutionary industrial and political alternatives to 'labourism' and evolutionary socialism.[15]

The responses of the various representatives of capital and the state in Britain and the USA to the crisis of competitive capitalism were essentially fourfold in character.[16] First, the 'new imperialist' drive for untapped sources of investment, profit, power and influence across the world was in large measure a response to the interlocking economic, political and ideological crisis of competitive capitalism. Britain and the traditionally more isolationist USA were key players in the 'new imperialism'.

Second, in an attempt *structurally* to resolve the crisis, and especially the economic aspects of that crisis, upon their own terms and in their own interests, large employers and financiers were prime movers in the, albeit long, limited and un-even process of transition from 'competitive' to 'monopoly' or 'corporate' forms of capitalism. The latter was increasingly characterised by large units of production, mass production and semi-skilled labour, and Taylorite or 'scientific management' attacks on the established rights and workplace controls of workers, especially craft and skilled workers. Between the 1880s and 1914 the transition was far more marked in the vibrant and modernist USA than in more traditional Britain. However, of its important initiation and effects upon labour, especially in the United States, there can be no doubt.[17]

Third, many employers and representatives of the state, in both Britain and the United States, sought to find a solution to the crisis directly at labour's expense. This was reflected, albeit to varying national degrees, in intensified employer attacks upon trade unionism, in 'driving' at work, in downward pressure upon wages, in mounting anti-trade union legislation and in the attempts of mainstream parties to present organised labour as the representative of selfish and sectional concerns rather than those of the nation or 'people' as a whole. In the case of the USA, there was a very close connection between the second and third responses.

The fourth response was to suggest that laissez-faire capitalism had become outdated, and that the future health and security of capitalism resided in 'collectiv-ism' rather than in 'individualism'. 'Advanced' social-welfare provision (old-age pensions, unemployment insurance, effective measures against 'sweating' and so on), combined with attacks on corruption, waste and inefficiency in all walks of life were seen as the guarantors of both enhanced economic efficiency, including the improved health of the nation, and the realisation of 'minimum standards', and social stability. The socialist menace was to be repulsed by means of a reformed and more humane form of capitalism which, notwithstanding the greater strength of individualism and voluntarism in the USA, envisaged an enhanced regulatory and interventionist role for the state. This form of liberal 'capitalist collectivism',[18] especially in the case of the United States, had much in common with the 'manage-rialism' of the second, 'Taylorite' response.[19]

Occupying an important and sheltered position within Britain's colonial net-work, later nineteenth-century Australia seemed to have escaped the travails in-creasingly experienced by capitalism in its British and US heartlands. The discovery of gold in Victoria at mid-century, combined with Britain's sustained and massive demand for antipodean sources of wool, meat, dairy produce and minerals, under-pinned Australia's 'long boom' between the 1850s and 1880s. However, the good times came to an abrupt end in the early 1890s when the worldwide depression hit Australia especially hard. The abrupt withdrawal of credit from Britain, Australia's main financier, in 1890 triggered the 'collapse of the urban housing boom' and 'sharp decreases in export prices of wool'. The resulting depression, complete with massive unemployment and poverty, persisted throughout most of the 1890s.[20] To make matters even worse, there occurred a 'terrible series of droughts' in the country districts of eastern Australia.[21] Aided and abetted by the state, Australia's major employers responded, in the name 'freedom of contract', by locking horns with trade unionism per se. Major conflicts in the maritime, dock, pastoral and mining industries resulted in clear employer victories. By the mid-1890s the ranks of the trade-union movement were decimated.

As I will show in chapter two, the Australian economy, still tied heavily to Britain and sheltering behind a protectionist wall, nevertheless largely maintained its 'traditional' character in the period under review. As such, it was not 'transformed' to anything like the US or even the British cases. However, the industrial conflicts of the 1890s did shatter the social and political balance of forces. As we will also observe in chapter two, Australian workers recuperated quickly from the employers' 'counter-attack' of the 1890s to build an extremely impressive movement. Much in the manner of their American and British counterparts, they took the feelings and conflicts of class to the very heart of 1900s Australia's national life and politics.

Before moving to a specific description of the ways in which the chapters of the book address various aspects of labour's initiatives and responses to the changing political economy of capitalism in Britain, the USA and Australia, I would like to make clear to the reader three important general and contextual factors which inform my study.

First, in terms of methodology, it will now be evident that my overriding interest rests with similarities and differences across the three national case studies. (I am cognisant of divisions *within* national labour movements, but these do not constitute my core concern.) Such an interest, however, does not mean that I pursue endless complexities of detail and meaning at the expense of generalisation. Indeed, I argue that we can observe general *patterns* both within and across Britain, the USA and Australia that arise out of the very complexity, contingency and seeming incoherence and uniqueness of experience. Moreover, these patterns are not viewed as being synonymous with 'norms' and 'exceptions'. Contrary to the approach and method of 'exceptionalism' which has traditionally informed much cross-national comparative historical and sociological research, I suggest that there are not 'normal' kinds, stages and routes of working-class consciousness and labour-movement development that move, in mainly linear fashion, towards a largely pre-ordained end. For example, there is not a single, uniform standard, such as socialism, against which all forms of related consciousness and action must be tested or measured. In both theory and practice the method of exceptionalism has shown itself frequently to be teleological, static, and insensitive. All too often, it flattens and schematises the richness, complexity, reverses and downright messiness of historical experience. By way of contrast, close attention to the complex and changing articulation of those factors that united, differentiated and divided cross-national labour movements enables us better to do justice to their multi-faceted experiences and characteristics, and the rich and nuanced nature of the evidence selected for this study.[22]

Second, a brief comment is in order concerning the relative strengths and weakness of the three labour movements. Notwithstanding Britain's premier position among the world's nineteenth-century labour movements, especially as the veritable 'home' of trade unionism, the 'young' Australian movement was seen to move very impressively into the lead between 1900 and 1914. As we will observe in chapter two, whether measured in terms of its powers of recovery and the rapidity of its 'forward march', its trade-union density, the successes of its Labor Party, or influence upon national life and consciousness, the Australian labour movement was increasingly regarded by many domestic and foreign observers alike as the new beacon, the 'hope of the labour world'.

Whether Australian labour constituted a *socialist* beacon was, and still is, a matter of some debate. However, we do know with absolute certainty that a stream of foreign visitors and observers were captivated by the Australian achievement. This, as shown further in chapter two, was part of a wider European and north American fascination with the late nineteenth- and early twentieth-century Australasian 'social experiment' of state collectivism, advanced social-welfare provision and democracy, and the overall 'rule of the people'. On the eve of the First World War, most of our contemporary labour-movement commentators were still highly impressed with the strength of trade unionism in Britain, and especially the organisation of the non skilled into mass 'new' unions. However, the continuing appeals of Liberalism and Conservatism, both to sections of the labour movement and the wider working class, combined with the limited and uneven gains made by the Labour Party at the national level, signified that independent labour politics in Britain were less successful than in Australia.

Finally, and notwithstanding the advances made by the Socialist Party and American labour's main body, the trade-unionist American Federation of Labor (AF of L), American labour was widely perceived to be the weakest of the three movements. As we will observe in more detail below, in contrast to the British and Australian examples, the mainstream US trade-union movement decided not to create an independent labour party. Moreover, the movement's relative weakness reflected the hegemonic power and influence of anti-labour forces within US society.

Third, the more extensive movements of capital and parts of its labour force across the world were paralleled by extended and strengthened international labour-movement links and contacts, both at the formal, institutional level, and in terms of less formal, personal and group contacts. Britain, of course, had supplied much of the personnel and had been a major ideological and institutional model for the formation and development of labour movements in many countries throughout the nineteenth century.[23] Moreover, the fact of growing international institutional links, especially in the form of the Second International, at the end of the nineteenth century, is well established. As such, it is not a concern of this study.[24] However, far less well known and documented is the fact that between the 1880s and 1914 many labour-movement leaders and related radicals both travelled widely across the world and left valuable written records of their impressions of foreign countries, including the latter's workers and labour movements. For example, Samuel Gompers, President of the AF of L, recorded his impressions of his four-month visit to Europe, including Britain, in 1909 in the pages of the official organ of the federation, the *American Federationist*. A succession of British labour movement figures, including Keir Hardie, Margaret and Ramsay MacDonald, Sidney and Beatrice Webb, Tom Mann, Ben Tillett, Dora Montefiore, Henry Champion and Will Crooks, visited, and in some instances resided for a time, in Australia. In turn, Australians such as the Labor Prime Minister, Andrew Fisher, and a group of Labour colleagues visited Britain in 1911. Other, less influential, figures in the British and Australian movements keenly recorded their impressions of their 'cousins', 'comrades', 'brothers' and 'sisters' overseas in the pages of the labour and socialist press.

Such recorded impressions, observations and representations, much neglected, and in numerous instances undiscovered, as a valuable historical source, figure very heavily in the pages that follow. It is true to say that without their existence and 'discovery', this book could not have been written. Do these contemporary views suggest that closer contact across the seas led our labour-movement subjects in the three countries to develop 'customs in common'? Or did they resolutely cling to established or changing national habits and 'peculiarities'? Furthermore, how do we *explain* similar and different labour responses? These three questions centrally inform the essays as a whole.

The book is organised in the follow way. I begin by presenting a table below, *Timetable of Key Events*, which the reader can consult at appropriate points in the text. The rationale of the table is simple. While many readers will be familiar with an outline of the chronology(ies) of labour informing this study in relation to one or even two of the countries covered, it is doubtful that he or she will be equally at home with events in all three countries.

Timetable of Key Events

The increasingly global spread of industrial capitalism and mounting rivalry among the main imperial powers. The crisis of small-scale 'competitive capitalism' and the marked, but limited and uneven, growth of corporate or 'monopoly' capitalism. Mass migration of people across the globe, especially to the industrial economies, in search of work and opportunity. The birth of 'modern' mass labour and socialist movements.

Date(s)	Britain	USA	Australia
1880–1914			
1881	Formation of the Democratic Federation. 1883–4 adopted a socialist programme and changed its name to the Social Democratic Federation. Main organ, *Justice*.		
1883–4	Foundation of the Fabian Society. Main organ, *Fabian News*.		
1886		Foundation of American Federation of Labor, Main organ, *American Federationist*.	
1886–8		Massive growth of Knights of Labor to 750,000. Thereafter, precipitous decline.	
1889–92	Upsurge of 'new' or 'mass' and 'old' or 'craft' unionism.		
Late 1880s–1890s			
1890			End of 'Long Boom', major depression throughout 1890s. Defeat of the Maritime and Pastoral strikes. Publication of the Brisbane *Worker*.
1891			Formation of the Labor Party in New South Wales. Publication of the *Hummer* – became the Sydney *Worker*.
1891	Robert Blatchford's *Clarion* first published.		
1892	Start of the depression and employer and state 'counter-attack' against organised labour in Britain. This 'counter-attack' was more widespread, hostile, persistent and effective in the USA and Australia.		

Timetable of Key Events cont.

Date(s)	Britain	USA	Australia
1893-7		Severe depression.	
1893	Formation of the Independent Labour Party. Main organ, *Labour Leader*.		
1893-4		The AF of L crucially debates its political future. Eventual defeat for advocates of socialism and a labour party 'on the British model'. Triumph of 'pure and simple' trade unionism and political non-partisanship.	
1894			Formation of the Australian Workers' Union.
1895		Formation of Daniel de Leon's Socialist Trades and Labor Alliance.	
1896	Economic recovery.		
1897-1903		Economic recovery. American Federation of Labor becomes the dominant force in the labour movement.	
1898		Spanish-American War. America becomes a particpant in the 'new imperialism'.	
1899-1902	South African War.		
1900	Formation of the TUC-inspired Labour Representation Committee. Marks the beginning of the Labour Party.		
1900-1			Formation of the 'Commonwealth' Labor Party. First shoots of economic and strong labour recovery.
1901		Formation of the Socialist Party of Ameria.	Federation. Creation of the Constitution and the Commonwealth of Australia. Indigenous Australians denied citizenship.
1900s			The New Commonwealth adopts 'White Australia'; protection, arbitration and social

Timetable of Key Events cont.

Date(s)	Britain	USA	Australia
1900s	Further serious judicial blows to trade unionism in the USA. However, a more mixed and generally more favourable legal picture emerges in both Britain and Australia (see references in the text to Buck's Stove, the Danbury Hatters' case, Taff Vale, Trade Disputes Act, the Harvester Case, the High Court, referendum of 1911).		welfare as the basis of 'national settlement', following the acute social and political conflicts of the 1890s.
1902			Women enfranchised for federal elections.
1904-7	British, South African and Australian Socialists debate the 'Chinese labour experiment' – the importation of 'slave' Chinese labourers, under contract, into the mines of the Transvaal.		
1904			Election of the first (minority) Labor government.
1905		Birth of the Industrial Workers of the World.	
1906	The Labour Representation Committee becomes the Labour Party. British and South African socialists debate the 'Bambatha rebellion' in Natal.		
1907			Justice Higgins sets the principle of the 'living wage' in the Harvester case. Formation of the Australian branch of the IWW.
1908-10	British and South African socialists discuss the formation and development of the Union of South Africa.		
1908			Election of minority Labor government.
1910			Election of majorty Labor government.
1910-14	'Labour Unrest': Further Expansion of 'new' and 'old' trade unionism.		
1914	Outbreak of the First World War.		Election of third Fisher Labor government.

Sources: Mark Hearn and Greg Patmore (eds.), *Working the Nation: Working Life and Federation 1890-1914* (London, 2001), 287–90; David Howell, *British Workers and the Independent Labour Party 1888-1906* (Manchester, 1983), 471–484; E.H. Hunt, *British Labour History 1815-1914* (London, 1988), Chs. 8, 9; Richard B. Morris (ed.), *A History of the American Worker* (Princeton, 1983), 'Chronology'.

To proceed to a description of the three chapters comprising this study. Chapter one explores the interplay between national 'peculiarities' and cross-national similarities in relation to the political trajectories of mainstream labour movements and institutions in Britain and the USA during the 1890s and 1900s. Building upon some of my earlier comparative work,[25] I investigate the similarities and differences between the politics of the AF of L and the mainstream British labour movement. I show that AF of L leaders looked to the industrial and political practices and achievements of the mid- and later-Victorian British Trades Union Congress (TUC) as the model for their own movement's practice. I also demonstrate that in important, but not all, respects, organised labour and workers in both these countries drew common class-based conclusions and lessons from their experiences of the crisis of competitive capitalism and state and employer attempts to resolve that crisis at the expense of workers. For example, in both countries, within the AF of L as well as the TUC, loud voices were raised in favour of the creation of an independent labour party better to represent 'the labour interest' than labour's conventional lobbying of the mainstream parties. However, the AF of L decided not to go down the 'new British road' of commitment to independent political *party-ism*, as specifically expressed in Britain in the Labour Representation Committee (1900) and its successor, the Labour Party (1906). Despite its increasingly close ties to the Democratic Party, the AF of L in this period formally opted to stay loyal to its 'traditional', indeed 'British' commitment to the independent labour politics of lobbying and non-partisan party loyalty.

Chapter one is based mainly upon the institutional records of the AF of L, the TUC and the infant Labour Party, sections of the labour press, and the published papers of Samuel Gompers. It sets new comparative questions to these largely well known, but insufficiently worked, sources. It concludes, in opposition to the wisdom of 'exceptionalism', that the decision of AF of L not to go down the new British political path issued mainly from experiential considerations rather than from the supposedly inbuilt and unchanging 'exceptionalist' features and structures of US society (pervasive capitalist individualism and entrepreneurialism, racism, uniquely open, accommodating and largely non-ideological political parties, unmatched levels of occupational and social mobility and so on). Of primary importance to the AF of L leadership was the hard-headed belief that the 'traditional', but contingent, and combined American 'peculiarities' of weak trade unionism, strong and militant state and employer anti-labour sentiment, and a heterogeneous working class rendered the dangers of changing political course far too hazardous. Above all, the AF of L placed a premium upon the survival and the solid, if slow and uneven, growth of trade unionism. This was not to be jeopardized by a political leap in the dark.

The issue of national 'peculiarities' is further explored and geographically extended in chapter two. The latter concerns itself with the history of workers and the labour movement in Australia between 1890 and 1914. This was a crucial period in Australia's history, characterised as it was by the federation of her six colonies and the birth of the New Commonwealth of Australia in 1901. In the 1900s the labour movement recovered quickly from the depressed 1890s to demonstrate precocious development, both politically and industrially.

A key aim of chapter two is to move beyond the predominantly 'top-down' and institutional perspectives of the first chapter. This is achieved in three ways. First, I pay close attention to relevant voices, both 'from below' and 'from above', within Australia. Second, equally close attention is paid to the representations of Australian workers and their labour movement provided by foreign (especially British) and mainly labour-movement visitors and more distant observers and commentators. Third, I set the experience of Australian labour within its wider societal context. The discovery of a wide range and depth of largely untapped and predominantly labour-movement Australian, British and, to a lesser extent, north American and European sources, both greatly eased my task and extended the scope and length of the essay in unanticipated ways.

I engage centrally with the long-established and well-known, but far less thoroughly interrogated, view of Australia as a 'workingman's paradise'. This enables me to explore the nature, position and characteristics of the Australian working class and organised labour. It also facilitates the development of more general comparisons and contrasts between Australian labour and labour in Britain and the USA. Somewhat curiously, domestic and foreign contemporary labour-movement perspectives on Australia as a paradise for workers have been largely overlooked or marginalised in much of the wide-ranging secondary literature. I am thus in a favourable position to fill gaps in the historiography.

My conclusions are in accord far more with those of 'optimistic' contemporaries than with those of predominantly 'pessimistic' (especially recent) historians. I argue that, while by no means perfect, Australia was widely perceived, both within 'the movement' and beyond, to offer working people a much better range of opportunities and prospects than countries in the 'Old World'. The latter was seen to include the prematurely aged 'young' republic of America – broken down by overweening capitalist power, money, and bribery and corruption. Moreover, contemporaries strongly maintained that these opportunities were being translated into practice, and that, notwithstanding some defects, the rapidly expanding, ideologically eclectic, and seemingly all-conquering Australian labour movement constituted, as noted earlier, *the* hope of labour throughout the world.

Set largely within the context of the British Empire, the third chapter invites us further to expand our geographical, descriptive and analytical frameworks of reference. The focus of the chapter rests upon a comparative study of socialist attitudes to class, race and empire between the outbreak of the South African War in 1899 and the 1910 Act of Union in South Africa, as revealed mainly in the pages of the British socialist weeklies, *Justice*, the *Labour Leader* and the *Clarion*. While knowledge of international socialist attitudes towards these matters has traditionally been gained from sources relating to institutions – especially those of the Second

International – the rich and detailed material to be found in the British socialist press has been insufficiently consulted and interrogated, particularly in more recent literature. Most striking, perhaps, has been the general neglect of the fascinating and complex evidence within these socialist weeklies concerning socialist attitudes towards race and racism.

My main point of concentration in this third and final essay rests upon the attitudes of British socialists towards the closely related issues of empire and imperialism, 'non-white' indigenous peoples in South Africa, India and the Far East, and migrant labour, both 'free' and 'unfree' (especially Chinese), in various imperial locations. However, the weeklies also carried much relevant, often troubling, and always engrossing information and opinion about the attitudes of both Australian and South African socialists towards these issues. Significantly, they also convey to the reader a very real sense of socialist debate about the issues of race and racism. Debate was conducted both within and across national boundaries.

In contrast to the prevailing historiographical and sociological wisdom, my essay concludes that, notwithstanding some exceptions, most British socialists writing in the weeklies asserted the supremacy of class over race and racism. Their attitudes to 'race' were complex and multi-dimensional; they expressed strong support for racially inclusive labour-movement and labour-market strategies; and they supported the political and ideological struggles of people of colour. Furthermore, they offered a critique of British imperialism, indeed imperialism per se, as a *systemic* method of class- and race-based domination and exploitation. Moreover, this was a critique which, *pace* the recent and current claims of 'liberal-revisionism', cannot convincingly be subsumed under the framework of seemingly enduring, expansive and accommodating traditions of radical-Liberalism and/or liberal-radicalism.

In shifting our attention to the very different imperial locations of South Africa and Australia we find, among socialists in general, and notwithstanding considerable anti-imperialist sentiment and the presence of some critical and oppositional voices on the 'race' issue, the loud and even proud assertion of race over class. For most white socialists in South Africa and Australia, 'non-white' labour was seen as being necessarily cheap and racially inferior, a resource to be employed by conspiratorial capitalists as an effective barrier to the realisation of the white socialist commonwealth.

The conclusion pulls together the main issues and themes of the book around a question prompted by its title: To what extent did organised workers in the three countries act as comrades, as well as cousins, across the seas? Finally, I briefly consider the implications of labour-movement responses during the era of 'new imperialism' for the practices of international labour in today's more completely globalized world.

Notes

1. For stimulating and challenging forays in these directions see, for example, Peter Linebaugh and Marcus Rediker, *The Many-Headed Hydra: The Hidden History of the Revolutionary Atlantic* (London, 2000); Rick Halpern and Jonathan Morris (eds.), *American Exceptionalism? US Working-Class Formation in an International Context* (London, 1997); Peter Alexander and Rick Halpern (eds.), *Racializing Class Classifying Race: Labour and Difference in Britain the USA and Africa* (London, 2000); Stefan Berger and Angel Smith (eds.), *Nationalism Labour and Ethnicity* (Manchester, 1999);
Sam Davies, Colin J. Davis, David de Vries, Lex Heerma van Voss, Lidewij Hesselink and Klaus Weinhauer (eds.), *Dock Workers: International Explorations in Comparative Labour History* (Aldershot, 2000). See also the unpublished papers by Rick Halpern ('Labour and Empire: Race and Work in the Sugar Industries of Louisiana and Natal, 1870-1910') and Kevin Morgan ('The Other Future: A.A. Purcell, the British Left and America in the 1920s') presented to the 'New Directions in Comparative and International Labour History' conference, International Centre for Labour Studies, Univ. Manchester, March 1999.

2. Ellen Meiksins Wood, 'Labor, Class, and State in Global Capitalism', in Ellen Meiksins Wood, Peter Meiksins and Michael Yates (eds.), *Rising from the Ashes: Labor in the Age of 'Global' Capitalism* (New York, 1998), 6.

3. Eric J. Hobsbawm, *The Age of Empire 1875-1914* (London, 1995).

4. See Guest's article, 'The Coloured Labour Peril', in *Labour Leader*, 21 April, 1905.

5. Gary Cross, 'Labour in Settler-State Democracies: Comparative Perspectives on Australia and the US, 1860-1920', *Labour History*, 70 (May 1996), 6.

6. David Montgomery, *The Fall of the House of Labor: The Workplace the State and American Labor Activism 1865-1925* (Cambridge, 1987), 68-87.

7. Montgomery, *The Fall*, 378-9.

8. Montgomery, *The Fall*, 71.

9. Myra Willard, *History of the White Australia Policy to 1920* (Melbourne, 1923, reprinted Frank Cass, London, 1967).

10. As quoted in Montgomery, *The Fall*, 71.

11. *ASE: Australasian Council Monthly Reports*, 268 (May 1911), 10-11.

12. Brian Kennedy, *A Tale of Two Mining Cities: Johannesburg and Broken Hill 1885-1925* (Carlton, Victoria, 1984), 1-2.

13. Montgomery, *The Fall*, 44-57; Neville Kirk, *Labour and Society in Britain and the USA*, Vol. 2, *Challenge and Accommodation 1850-1939* (Aldershot, 1994), 1-6, 11-14.

14. Kirk, *Challenge and Accommodation*, 14.

15. Kirk, *Challenge and Accommodation*, Chapter One; Montgomery, *The Fall*, Introduction.

16. For a discussion of these responses see Kirk, *Challenge and Accommodation*, 14- 45.

17. Montgomery, *The Fall*, Chapters 4,5.

18. 'Collectivism', of course, was a contested term. For many socialists it signalled the means of transformation, rather than the reform and preservation, of capitalism.

19. Montgomery, *The Fall*, Chapters 5,6.

20. Cross, 'Labour in Settler-State Democracies', 11-12.

21. Charles Manning Hope Clark, *A History of Australia*, Vol. V, *The People Make Laws 1888-1915* (Carlton, Victoria, 1999), 65-6, 90-9.

22. For extended critiques of the method of exceptionalism see chapter one below; Neville Kirk, '"Peculiarities" versus "Exceptions": The Shaping of the American Federation of Labor's Politics during the 1890s and 1900s', *International Review Social History*, 45, I (April 2000), 25-50; Larry G. Gerber, 'Shifting Perspectives on American Exceptionalism: Recent Literature on American Labor Relations and Labor Politics', *Journal of American Studies*, 31,2 (1997), 253-74.

23. See, for example, Ray Boston, *British Chartists in America* (Manchester, 1971); Michael Durey, *Transatlantic Radicals and the Early American Republic* (Lawrence, Kansas, 1997).

24. For the Second International see, GDH Cole, *The Second International* (London, 1956); James

Joll, *The Second International* (London, 1974). For a stimulating study of socialist-feminist Dora Montefiore's institutional and personal links with labour in Britain, Europe and Australia see Karen Hunt, 'The Challenge of Internationalism: The Politics of a British Socialist Woman Before the First World War', paper presented to the 'New directions in Comparative and International Labour History' conference, International Centre for Labour Studies, University of Manchester, March 1999.

25. Chapter one is a revised version of an unpublished paper presented to the 'New Directions in Comparative and International Labour History' conference. See also Kirk, *Challenge and Accommodation*, especially Chapter 3; idem, '"Peculiarities" versus "Exceptions"'.

Chapter One. Transatlantic Connections and American 'Peculiarities': Labour Politics in the United States and Britain, 1893-1908*

Introduction

During the course of a lengthy and increasingly acrimonious debate concerning the relative strengths and weaknesses of non-partisan *independent* versus partisan *party* politics, a delegate to the American Federation of Labor's (AF of L's) 1903 convention accurately reflected the feelings of the majority of delegates in his observation that, 'I think we are all agreed as to the advisability of union men using their voting power to further their cause. The real question is, *what kind of politics* shall we adopt, and who is to decide that question?' (emphasis added).

Delegate White's further observations – that upon that 'real question' 'there is a wide divergence of opinion'; and 'to throw our movement into the political arena would be injecting a firebrand of discord that would soon scatter it to the four winds of heaven'[1] – also reflected majority opinion. The debate ended in chaos and uproar, with President Samuel Gompers clearing the galleries of his opponents and denouncing the socialist delegates who had spoken in favour of their ideology and AF of L commitment to partisan party politics as 'at heart, and logically, the ANTAGONISTS OF OUR MOVEMENT'. 'I want to tell you, Socialists', thundered Gompers, in an oft-quoted passage,

> that I have studied your philosophy, read your works ... I have kept close watch upon your doctrines for thirty years; have been closely associated with many of you, and know how you think and what you propose. I know too what you have up your sleeve. And I want to say that I am entirely at variance with your philosophy ... Economically, you are unsound; socially, you are wrong; industrially, you are an impossibility.[2]

Contrary to the expectations of many delegates and much of the press, delegates to AF of L conventions who advocated socialist and/or independent labour party politics, were not crushed by their defeat in 1903. Bitter exchanges between 'socialists and trade unionists' occurred at the federation's 1904 convention.[3] Furthermore, between 1906 and 1908, the successes of the widespread anti-union endeavours of the National Association of Manufacturers (NAM), the significant influence of NAM upon Congress and the latter's unsympathetic treatment of organised labour's legislative demands, and the frequent, very threatening and often successful resort of employers and the courts to anti-labour injunctions, compelled the AF of L seriously to consider the very nature and concrete results of its 'independent' political commitment. As Julia Greene has observed, during these years the AF of L leadership attempted to mobilise a 'popular uprising' of the rank- and -file membership in support of its 'own', and especially trade-union, candidates for political office. Indeed, in a minority of cases workers formed local labour parties to advance the federation's independent cause. However, in supporting the Democratic Party presidential candidate, William Jennings Bryan, in 1908, the AF of L leadership 'virtually shut down its machinery of popular mobilization'. Thereafter, and notwithstanding its continued formal commitment to non-partisanship, the AF of L moved ever closer to the Democratic Party, and effectively closed its door against any possible allegiance to a labour party.[4]

The years between 1903 and 1908 did not, of course, mark the beginning of political debate inside the AF of L. From its origins in the Federation of Organized Trades and Labor Unions (FOTLU) in 1881, through its Founding Convention in 1886 and during its 1880s and early 1890s conflicts with the Knights of Labor, the AF of L had developed an independent political strategy which, although modelled closely upon the lobbying practice of the Parliamentary Committee of the British Trades Union Congress (TUC), assumed a plurality of institutional forms. In 1881, for example, the FOTLU had as one of its objects the establishment of a Congressional Labor Committee in order to 'secure the passage by the United States Congress of such laws as are needed by the various trades to better their condition'.[5] Five years later the founding convention of the AF of L supported a two-track course 'favorable to independent political action'. State organizations of labour were to be formed to 'secure State legislation in the interests of the working masses', while the AF of L as a whole would set out 'to secure national legislation in the interests of the working people and to influence public opinion by peaceful and legal methods in favor of organized labor'.[6] During these early years there had, however, existed differences of opinion inside the federation between advocates of political non-partisanship and those favouring independent labour, 'people's' and/or 'farmer-labour', or socialist politics.

It was nevertheless during the acutely depressed years of 1893 and 1894 that AF of L conventions witnessed the most intense, prolonged and finely balanced debates concerning its past, present and future political direction.[7] It was agreed at the 1893 convention that socialist Thomas Morgan's proposal or 'political program' – that the federation's unions follow the apparent example of the TUC and both 'adopt the principle of independent labor politics as an auxiliary to their economic action' (ie. form a labour party) and commit themselves to a programme of collective ownership[8] – be considered by the affiliated unions, with a view to the unions' delegates being instructed to vote on the programme at the 1894 convention of the federation. At the latter there was initially considerable, indeed arguably majority, support for the eleven planks of Morgan's programme, including commitments to the 'British road'.[9] However, the 'old guard', in the form of Gompers, Adolph Strasser and their strategically placed allies in the federation's most influential unions, carried the day. From 1894 onwards, and despite Gompers being voted out of office for one year, the AF of L reaffirmed and strengthened its commitments to 'legislative demands', as opposed to a 'legislative program', and to non-partisan lobbying and other forms of 'independent' political action. 'Party slavery' was to be eschewed at all costs.[10]

Wherein lay the causes of the AF of L's non-partisan stance? We may begin to compose an answer by reference to a letter which Gompers wrote to Tom Mann, the celebrated British socialist and trade unionist, in May 1894. In the course of the letter Gompers thanked Mann for writing an article for the *American Federationist*, the recently-formed official organ of the AF of L, and expressed the view that, 'In America we have something peculiar to contend against in connection with the development of an Independent Labor Party movement'.[11] A key purpose of this essay is to identify Gompers' perceived 'peculiarity'.

Gompers promised to 'freely communicate' with Mann in a future letter about the nature of this US 'peculiarity', but this promise was not directly fulfilled, at least in published correspondence between the two men. Nevertheless, there exist sufficient clues, both in Gompers' own verbal and written accounts and in the wider historical evidence as to the nature and crucial importance of such a 'peculiarity' – or, more precisely, 'peculiarities' – fully to justify further investigation. Indeed, given the existence of these clues it is surprising that they have not attracted their full scholarly attention.

While historians such as Kaufman, Kazin, Fink, Laslett and most recently Greene[12] have made important *contextualised* contributions towards enhancing our understanding of the political thinking of key figures in the Knights of Labor and the AF of L, there is still a tendency among some scholars to resort to mainly decontextualised, functionalist, unchanging and one dimensional 'exceptional' structural determinations and explanations of the failures of US socialism and labour party politics. While by no means unimportant, the structural explanations traditionally offered – racism, working-class heterogeneity and division, the 'promise of mobility', the pervasive commitment to liberal individualism, the values of 'citizenship' versus 'class', and the all-consuming embrace of an 'open', cross-class political system and its two main political parties – are sometimes, and especially in some 'social-scientific' accounts,[13] pitched at too general a level to do full justice to the nuances, complexities and contradictions of specific historical conjunctures. For example, even when confronted by major structural obstacles, considerable numbers of American workers and trade union leaders both outside and *inside* the AF of L – and including some supposedly 'aristocratic' and 'conservative' printers, machinists and building trades' workers – did form labour parties and support the Socialist Party of America in its pre-First-World-War heyday.[14]

During the period from the post-bellum years up to the 1920s the problem for those on the American left resided not in the recurring presence of independent labour and socialist movements, but in their failure to sustain and increase their support and momentum. Notwithstanding its limited and uneven progress among both trade unionists and the wider electorate before 1914, the British Labour Party did, in contrast, become a viable and durable mass political organisation. By the mid 1920s the latter had become a national party of government commanding the overwhelming support of the trade union movement, while the AF of L was still officially committed to nonpartisanship.[15]

As a corollary to the identification of 'peculiarities', the essay makes a contribution towards filling substantive gaps in the literature and helping to remedy some of the methodological weaknesses outlined in the previous paragraph. This second purpose is achieved by two means. First, the reader's attention is directed centrally to the thoughts and actions of some of those men active at the very centre of the British and US labour movements, and especially Gompers, who played a crucial role in determining political tactics and strategies. These historical actors have tended to be neglected by the 'new' labour history of the post-1960 decades with its emphases upon the non-institutional and community-based aspects of workers' lives. The reader should thus be clear from the outset that my main focus rests upon the ideas and institutional strategies of labour leaders rather than the structure, culture and politics (including relations with the mainstream parties) of the wider working-class(es) in the two countries.

Second, my focus upon the leadership does *not* suggest that only consciously experiential, as opposed to more impersonal structural, forces informed politics. Rather, I argue the case for engaging structure and agency within a clearly defined historical conjuncture. The nub of the argument is that this process of engagement constitutes a more rounded and satisfactory method of historical investigation than sole attention to either structure (structuralism) or agency (subjectivism and idealism).[16]

A third purpose involves clarification of the issue raised by delegate White: the kind of politics to be pursued by the AFL. Thus, while the *fact* of the AF of L's nonpartisan politics has been extensively and repeatedly noted in the historical literature, the *full character* and *underpinnings* of that non-partisanship, and especially its *independent* and *British-inspired* characteristics, have not, for the most part, been sufficiently, indeed at times accurately,[17] identified and explained.

Finally, since Gompers and other members of the AF of L were consciously seeking to model not only the AF of L's trade union structures and policies, but also its politics upon the lines of the British 'craft' or 'old' unions, and that Gompers viewed American 'peculiarity' in relation to experiences of British labour, this essay adopts an explicitly comparative approach. As part of the latter, I argue that an initial understanding of relevant aspects of the political economy of US and British capitalism during the years in question, enables us far more successfully to get to grips with the issue of US 'peculiarities' than sole concentration on the US material would permit. It is, therefore, to an examination of the comparative politico-economic dimension, absent in most accounts of the AF of L's politics,[18] that I now turn.

THE COMPARATIVE CONTEXT

The late nineteenth- and early twentieth-century US and British labour movements and their respective capitalist systems were characterised by numerous similarities and differences. Indeed, the very presence, magnitude and variety of, and the complex interplay between, these similarities and differences render instant judgements concerning American 'exceptionalism' – in relation to some supposed socialist or class-conscious international labour-movement and working-class 'norm' – most hazardous. Similarly, they invite us to approach with extreme caution the traditional historiographical wisdom that a growing class consciousness constituted the defining characteristic of British, indeed European, labour; a form of class consciousness which allegedly sharply differentiated 'radical and socialist' European labour from its 'business-unionist and conservative' US counterpart.[19] Fortunately, the presence of numerous and varied US and British labour-movement similarities and differences, as opposed to blanket differences and simple, contrasted outcomes, is particularly conducive to interesting and fruitful comparative investigation and explication.[20] What follows below is an overview of those similarities and differences relevant to our study of politics.

Similarities: Experiences and Grievances

Important similarities may be observed in terms of the perceived experiences and articulated grievances, means and objectives of labour movements in the two countries. In terms of the general picture, the period from the 1870s to the inter-war years was one in which competitive or laissez-faire, 'individualistic' capitalism increasingly gave way to corporate, managed or 'monopoly' capitalism.[21] Broadly speaking, the period saw the dominance of the family firm being undermined by the factory and the emergence of trusts, corporations and other forms of oligopoly or monopoly. Corporate capitalism was also widely associated with the methods of Taylorism or 'scientific management' and mass production, complete with an increase in the division of labour, the growth of semi-skilled labour, and intensified threats to craft control over work and trade unionism.

This was, however, a very chequered process of development. For example, contrary to the Braverman thesis, by no means all skilled workers were 'transformed' into a dependent and increasingly passive mass of semi-skilled 'wage slaves'.

Furthermore, monopolies and oligopolies, mass production techniques, 'scientific management' and anti-union attitudes and practices among employers all developed far more rapidly and extensively in the late nineteenth and early twentieth century United States than in Britain. Cushioned to a great extent by the safe markets of Empire and by her continued dominance of the world's financial and trading systems, Britain proved to be far more resilient in terms of her 'traditional' commitment to the diverse structures and practices of competitive capitalism.

Notwithstanding such differences and variations, we can observe the articulation of common and similar grievances on the part of labour leaders and workers in both countries in relation to the processes of capitalist development and transition. There was, for example, the strong and increasingly widespread belief that many British and American employers and their allies in the judiciary, other organs of the state and the mainstream political parties, were attempting to resolve the crisis of late nineteenth-century competitive capitalism, of capital accumulation, largely at the workers' and organised labour's expense. This was a crisis which, as noted in the introduction, manifested itself, both within national capitalist economies and internationally, in increased competition, falling prices, reduced profit margins, declining and erratic rates of growth, the onset of more frequent and, especially during the 1890s, more profound and threatening periods of recession and depression and in mounting working-class and popular 'unrest'.

There was a widespread popular sense of sharply increased employer hostility towards labour. It was claimed that such hostility was evident in the extensive and frequent resort of employers to 'driving' and anti-unionism, in their ready resort to the importation of 'scab' or 'blackleg' labour during labour disputes and in their strong assertion or reassertion of their formal and informal controls over the labour process. As J.N. Bell, Secretary of the National Amalgamated Union of Labour, declared in 1903 at the Third Annual Conference of the Labour Representation Committee (LRC),

> ... the tone and temper of the employing class has undergone a change for the worse within recent years, and ... there is a more aggressive tone and spirit among them. British capitalism has of late grown alarmed at the discovery that it has formidable competitors in the world's markets, and in its efforts to account for the success of these competitors, and its own loss of prestige and monopoly, it has sought a scapegoat in the person of the British working-man, who is accused of nothing more or less than organised laziness ...
>
> ... The power of organised capital seems to be increasing, while the power of organised Labour has, relatively at least, decreased ... Some good people who so piously object to what they call our class movement, may yet find in that movement the best safeguard against a power more subtle and dangerous than that of monarchy or aristocracy.[22]

Many labour leaders also maintained that judges and courts were adopting an increasingly anti-labour stance. In Britain, the employer 'counter-attack' of the

1890s, directed especially against the 'new' mass unions, took place alongside a series of adverse legal decisions which culminated in the Taff Vale decision of 1901 to award damages against the Amalgamated Society of Railway Servants. These decisions were widely perceived to put the very existence of trade unionism at risk, thus threatening to negate the substantial gains in official government and legal recognition and protection for unionism achieved during the 1870s. As W.J. Davis, President at the LRC's 1902 Conference, protested, 'We have now class legislation and class exclusion with a vengeance'.[23] In the United States, judicial anti-unionism – seen most notoriously in the damages awarded against the Danbury Hatters' Union (for 'restraint of trade': 1903-1908) and the injunction obtained by the Buck's Stove and Range Company against the AF of L's attempted 'boycott of its products' (1907-8) – was more rampant and successful than in Britain, as were acts of violence and repression against the labour movement.

There was, furthermore, a growing chorus of labour criticism directed at the mainstream political parties. The latter were portrayed as being insufficiently sensitive and responsive to labour's grievances and demands. During the second half of the 1890s there was, for example, mounting frustration within the TUC at organised labour's lack of effective lobbying pressure upon parliament. In 1896 the report of the Parliamentary Committee noted that, 'the past year had been almost barren of progressive legislation for the workers', and that measures promised by mainstream politicians during the general election of 1895, concerning employers' liability, reduced hours of work and old age pensions, 'had been grossly neglected'.[24] Some of this neglect was attributed, especially by the traditionally dominant 'old' unionist and Lib.-Lab. element within the TUC,[25] to the fact of Conservative victory at the 1895 general election. But criticism was more widely targeted, often, but not exclusively, by 'new' unionist and socialist voices in the TUC, against the unresponsiveness of parliament as a whole, including, of course, many of the 'old' unionists' staunch political allies in the Liberal Party. In 1898, for example, the American fraternal delegates to the Bristol TUC, held in September, reported back to the December AF of L convention that there was growing dissatisfaction inside the TUC with the policy of independent, 'non-partisan' lobbying. The report of the Parliamentary Committee itself had conceded that little had been gained from parliament during 'the last two or three years'. Furthermore,

> it was useless to expect any measures of industrial reform from the House of Commons *as at present composed*, for it was plain that any measure having for its object the improvement of the working classes, the strengthening of trade-union principles, or the prevention of monopolies, however fair and reasonable the proposal might be, was summarily dealt with and defeated in the end.[26] (emphasis added)

During the crucial Plymouth Congress – held in the following year and declaring in favour of 'a better representation of the interests of labour in the House of Commons' – W.J. Vernon, the President of the TUC, complained that trade unionists had voted into parliament,

> a host of gentlemen who had no sympathy whatever with your movement, who were
> diametrically opposed to your views … These gentlemen … are ever ready to legislate
> when their own interests, or those of their friends, are concerned. But their interests
> are not yours; they live and move in quite another world. Occasionally one of the par-
> ties is *condescending* enough to dole out a 'sop' to you, and that very often to 'dish' the
> other party so that legislation in favour of the worker is very small indeed.[27]

Similarly independent-minded and anti-deferential sentiments were expressed
in the early and mid 1900s. For example, at the LRC's 1901 and 1902 Annual
Conferences there was widespread agreement with the sentiments expressed respectively by delegates Hodge, Davis and Curran that 'Trade Unionists must look
after themselves in politics. It was getting almost impossible to find anything in either party for intelligent Trade Unionists to support'; that working men 'must see
that they have made a great mistake' in sending to Parliament 'too many landhold-
ers and capitalists, and too few to represent their own principles and wants'; and
that 'Our aim should now be to organise Labour apart from Capitalist politics'.[28]
In 1904 miners' leader, James Wignall, one of the British fraternal delegates to the
AF of L's annual convention, declared that,

> We long ago became tired of going cap in hand to those we have given our votes to,
> and have come to the conclusion that the Almighty did not give all the brains to the
> rich people.

Wignall urged support for the parliamentary candidature of Tom Richards,
Secretary of the Miners' Association, 'against all the wealth and power that can be
brought against him'.[29]

A year later, another fraternal delegate, David Gilmour, told his AFL audience
that,

> For our own self-preservation the time has come when we cannot depend upon the
> capitalists, the men of the class whose interests are opposed to the interests of the
> workers.[30]

In sum, there was a growing current of opinion in the British labour movement
that trade unionists should strengthen their resolve to elect to political office 'true'
representatives of their own class and their own movement. Furthermore, these
representatives would, unlike the Lib.-Labs., be fully independent of ties to the existing parties. As 'Miss' (Margaret) Bondfield, a delegate to the 1899 TUC declared,
'there were many grievances which could only be remedied by legislative enactment', and 'they were not likely to get any redress in the House of Commons until
the labour members formed an appreciable party in that assembly'.[31]

Five years earlier – at a time of serious depression, complete with mass un-employment and suffering, the march of Jacob Coxey's 'Commonweal Army' of the poor on Washington, acute class conflicts, such as the coal and Pullman strikes, and the 'Great Debate' within the AF of L concerning Morgan's political programme – Gompers had turned his thoughts to American labour's political grievances. In January he expressed the view that 'the people are now beginning to see how insincere and shallow the protestations of friendship from the old parties and politicians are'.[32] Indeed, not only politicians and parties, but also large sec-tions of the press, the courts, indeed the entire machinery of government, were, he argued, becoming daily the pawns of the Pullmans, Carnegies and other 'pluto-crats'. Lacking 'human sympathy or apparent responsibility', these 'tyrants' sought to subvert the rights of 'the people', the 'toiling masses', the 'working class' in the interests of the 'selfish' and 'monopolistic' 'capitalist class'. Republican America, rooted in wide citizenship, 'producerism' and 'Equal Rights', was now in grave danger of passing, notwithstanding her continued formal (male) political equality and civil and religious freedoms, into 'plutocratic power' and 'corporation (sic) rule', 'class oppression', 'wage slavery' and 'economic thraldom'. The values and practices of unfettered 'self-interest' and 'avaricious tyranny' were visibly asserting their domination over those of 'human sympathy' and social responsibility.[33]

In his July communication to the 1894 Convention of the National Alliance of Theatrical Stage Employees Gompers fulminated,

> On every hand we see the capitalist class, the corporate and moneyed interests concentrating their efforts for the purposes of despoiling the people of their rights, encroaching upon our liberties and endeavoring to force the workers down in the social, economic and political scale. Allied with them are the governmental powers, national, state and municipal. Their efforts are concentrated, their actions united. Nothing is allowed to interfere with the full development of the protection and ad-vancement of their interests.[34]

One month later he wrote to Eugene Debs, enclosing a check for $670.10 to sup-port Debs and the officers of the American Railway Union in their fight against contempt of court charges brought during the Pullman dispute, and conveying, 'more eloquently than I can find words to express',

> our unqualified disapproval of the attempts on the part of governmental officials and the courts in throwing the weight of their influence in favor of corporate wealth and against the most necessary, useful and liberty loving people of the country – the wage workers.

In an attempt to stop the disruption of rail traffic, almost 2,000 troops and 4,000 militia were despatched to Chicago, the Pullman strike centre, over 5,000 deputy marshals and sheriffs were sworn in locally and injunctions issued against the strikers. Victims, according to Gompers, of 'class justice' and 'the violation of rights guaranteed by the Constitution and the Declaration of Independence', Debs and his co-defendants were nevertheless found guilty of violating the injunction against strikers interfering with trains carrying the US mails and sent to jail for terms varying between three and six months.[35]

In 1896, in the course of advocating the establishment of a Department of Labor, Gompers bemoaned the decline of the republican tradition:

> The founders of the republic and their immediate successors did not anticipate an era of money power, with giant corporations in control of the production of the earth and of transportation ... They did not contemplate that it would become necessary for American citizens to unite in order to protect themselves and oppose attempted control and regulation of skilled and unskilled labor by centralized wealth ... They did not intend that the regular army should be massed and state troops mobilized at industrial centers wherever and whenever a corporation suggested that 'life' and 'property' were in danger ... They spurned aristocracy, classes and military rule when independence was achieved, and they legislated for a republican form of government in accord with the definition of democracy.

A Department of Labor would provide a counterweight to 'the aggrandized possessors and directors of corporate power', and as such, be 'effective in perpetuating the purposes and intentions of the founders of the American republic'.[36] Gompers observed at the AF of L convention in 1899 that 'the state has always been the representative of the wealth possessors'. Legislation designed to regulate trusts, such as the 1890 Sherman Antitrust Act, had in fact far more frequently been used against trade unions. This had been the case in the interracial general strike in New Orleans of 1892 and during the Pullman dispute itself. In effect such legislation had 'simply proved incentives to more subtly and surely lubricate the wheels of capital's accumulation'.[37]

Intensified US attempts more effectively to 'lubricate the wheels of capital's accumulation' were perceived to be taking place externally as well as internally. Just as British socialists and trade unionists mounted vigorous opposition to the South African War and other examples of British 'new imperialism',[38] so Gompers and many others within the 1890s American labour movement, including socialists, radicals and 'conservative' trade unionists, were 'alarmed by the growing strength of pro-imperialist sentiments within the US'.[39] While the 1898 war against Spain was justified on account of that country's 'barbarism and cruelty', American labour activists were determined to ensure that the Cubans and other nationalities liberated from Spanish 'tyranny', be afforded a genuine opportunity to achieve self-determination rather than becoming 'the "slaves" or subject people of a newly imperialistic US'. It was for this reason that the AF of L opposed US designs on Hawaii, Cuba, the Philippines and Puerto Rico, and actively supported campaigns in those countries for trade union recognition and wider civil and political rights.

The 'new imperialism' was seen to be not only 'fundamentally at odds with the self-determining tradition of American republicanism', but also a capitalist ploy to exploit 'cheap' and 'servile' labour abroad. In turn, American capitalists would, if at all possible, import 'cheapness' and 'slavery' into the United States in order to undermine 'the American standard' and the cherished '"independence", 'manhood' and 'freedom"' of the domestic worker.

In relation, therefore, to both domestic and foreign affairs Gompers and others were expressing the unambiguous view that the state and to a great extent the mainstream political parties had become the effective tools of a corporate power hostile to the interests of both organised labour and the wider democratic 'people'. Moreover, class feeling and class conflict were increasingly perceived to be rooted not simply in the actions of one or two 'dishonourable' or 'rogue' employers, but in the very nature of a *system* in which capital purchased labour 'as cheaply as it can', sold 'in the dearest market' and stimulated competition 'so that wages shall go down and the condition of the laborer become deteriorated'.[40] The preamble to the AF of L's constitution thus referred to,

> A struggle … going on in all the nations of the civilized world, between the oppressors and the oppressed of all countries, *a struggle between the Capitalist and the Laborer*, which grows in intensity from year to year …[41]

Placed within this hostile productive and wider socio-political environment, workers were urged to organise themselves collectively. Inclusive trade unions, recruiting workers 'irrespective of creed, color, sex, nationality or politics', were seen by Gompers to constitute the *natural* and, *ipso facto*, most important or *primary* form of collective working-class organisation. Whereas party politics were associated with ethnocultural and other *divided* allegiances among workers, trade unionism was perceived as being rooted in the mass and potentially *unifying* fact of wage earning in capitalist society. As Gompers declared in 1898,

> The trade unions are the legitimate outgrowth of modern societary (sic) and industrial conditions. They are not the creation of any man's brain. They are organizations of necessity. They were born of the necessity of the workers to protect and defend themselves from encroachment, injustice and wrong. They are the organizations of the working class, for the working class, by the working class …[42]

As organisers of wage earners in 'the class conscious struggle against all profit mongers', the trade unions would, in Gompers' view, engage in a daily struggle to improve the workers' immediate conditions in the workplace and sometimes have a necessary resort to strike action.[43] Yet during the 1890s and 1900s the AF of L leaders attributed to trade unionism goals which transcended the search for material gain or 'more'. For example, the unions would cultivate a spirit of 'manly independence'. They would extend the helping hand of organisation to the 'lower depths'. They would forge ties, by means of the fraternal delegate system, confer-ences and written correspondence, with their 'brothers' in Britain and elsewhere overseas in the interests of internationalism, peace and opposition to war and imperialism. And through the enforcement of standard rules at work and labour market regulation more generally, they would deliver 'order' out of 'capitalist dis-order', and 'civilize' the 'soulless', 'brutal' and 'inhuman' unfettered market-place. In sum, trade unionism was, at least in principle, nothing less than *the* vehicle of an alternative 'moral' vision of mutuality, cooperation, 'fairness', 'common human-ity' and even 'the gradual and natural elimination of all classes and the emancipa-tion of man'.[44]

To be sure, the 'lessons' of experience played a crucial part in sometimes modify-ing and changing these radical ideas and at times revealing the tensions and con-tradictions between rhetoric and action. For example, the significant improvement in workers' living standards and the substantial membership advances made by the AF of L between 1897 and 1904 (from 272,000 to 1,682,000) did induce a more moderate and accommodating stance. This was the period in which Gompers and the more progressive employers, organised in the National Civic Federation, laid stress upon the newfound harmony between labour and capital and their joint goals of binding contracts, industrial peace and social harmony and progress. It was also a period in which many AF of L unions became more cautious in their attitudes to mass and sympathy strikes, more exclusively white, male and 'skilled' in their composition, and in which their fear of many African-American workers and loathing of the Oriental 'other', became particularly marked. In articles in the *American Federationist* and elsewhere, Gompers expressed serious reservations about the 'limited' trade-union capacities of women, African-Americans and some of the 'new' immigrants from southern and eastern Europe.[45] Moreover, Philip Foner argues that after 1901, 'when imperialist annexation was no longer the major aspect of American imperialism', so anti-imperialist activity within the labour movement 'gradually receded'. The AF of L became far less concerned with the broad principles of imperialism than with narrowly pragmatic question of how best to avoid 'competition from labor in the colonial possessions'.[46]

However, even during these years Gompers continued to see 'militant trade unionism' as an essential factor in bringing employers to a more widespread ac-ceptance of organised labour's 'just' and 'reasonable' demands. The 'inevitable' rivalry among 'the social elements' had only been 'raised to a humane plane' rather than eradicated.[47] Furthermore, declining membership and the renewed, indeed greatly intensified, employer and judicial attacks against organised labour between 1904 and 1908 once again brought radical language to the fore. For example, at the AF of L's 1907 convention, Gompers' report variously referred to 'the continuous struggle of labor against tyranny, brutality and injustice', the 'shortsightedness and greed of industrial captains', the 'machinations of financiers' and 'the cupidity ... of the worst elements of the capitalist class'.[48] In April 1908 he declared that the 'application by the Supreme Court of the United States of the Sherman anti-trust law', had resulted in 'the most grave and momentous situation which has ever confronted the working people of this country'. Unionised workers had become liable for financial damages and unable to advocate, in print, the boycott of the products of anti-union employers. In addition, workers now 'enjoyed' the 'rights' to be 'maimed and killed without liability to the employer', to 'be discharged for belonging to a union' and to 'work as many hours as employers please'.[49] To compound labour's misfortunes, Gompers and other officers of the AF of L were sentenced to prison in 1909 for being found in contempt of an injunction successfully brought against the AF of L by Van Cleave's anti-union Buck's Stove and Range Company.[50]

Finally, although less outspoken in its anti-imperialism in the post-1901 years, the AF of L did continue actively to support the development of trade unionism and political and civil rights in Puerto Rico, Cuba, Mexico and other US 'spheres of influence'. Such support frequently brought the federation into conflict with the policies of big business and its allies in the state machinery. In sum, to argue, in the manner of many critics, that the AF of L became preoccupied with competition from cheap labour from abroad and the compliant tool of corporate US foreign policy interests is 'greatly to oversimplify a more complex picture'. There continued to exist 'a "classed" "dialectic of conflict and consensus"' at the heart of the federation's stances on US foreign policy and imperialism.[51]

Gompers' and the mainstream US labour movement's challenging, and in many ways class-based, condemnation of corporate capitalism and their expression of a profound sense of worker grievance, invites five observations. First, we have seen that the class consciousness offered by Gompers and the AF of L was primarily of a militant trade-union, as opposed to party-political kind. Second, Gompers' radical language and ideas cannot be interpreted primarily either as 'mere rhetoric' – as 'spin' largely devoid of 'real' substance – or as a tactical and strategic device to consolidate his power within the AF of L. There is no doubt that Gompers was, as demonstrated in his struggles with Morgan in 1893-4 and other socialists in the 1900s, acutely aware of the importance of strategic and power-based uses of language and ideas. But the very fact that his employment of class-based, radical language dated back to the 1870s and extended beyond his 'rise to power' in the AFL, strongly suggests that something more than 'empty rhetoric' or tactics, strategy and power was at work. It is accordingly probable that Gompers believed what he said and attempted, however imperfectly and unevenly, to translate words and ideas into action.[52]

Third, the very continuity and strength of Gompers' and many other US labour activists' class-based, radical critique, resting upon the bedrock of trade unionism, strongly suggest that a serious question mark be set against the general notion of conservative American exceptionalism. This questioning process assumes added urgency when the radical US critique, as sketched above, is set against the seemingly more moderate and conciliatory views of many of the 'old' skilled or craft unionists of Victorian Britain.[53]

Fourth, the continued association of US trade unionism not only with short-term and sectional material gain, but also long-term and expansive radical social change, further compels us to question a closely related form of received historical wisdom. In this case, the historical wisdom – assuming the proportion of self-evident and closed truth – states that the US labour movement underwent a fundamental and largely irreversible transition from transforming 'artisan' or 'producer' radicalism/republicanism to a narrow and defensive 'trade union' or 'wage earner' consumerism during the 1890s and 1900s.[54]

Fifth, it is important to set the mounting grievances of Gompers, likeminded US trade unionists and those articulated by mainstream labour-movement figures in Britain during the 1890s and 1900s within a wider international context of escalating 'labour unrest'. From Russia to Germany to Australia the changing political economy of world capitalism – its combined and uneven development, its impact on 'traditional' societies, its internal contradictions, tensions and crises, and its painful change of character from 'competitive' to 'monopoly' form – set the scene for the growth of recognisably modern labour movements, composed principally of wage earners, in which notions of independent labour and/or socialist politics often achieved positions of unprecedented importance.[55] Notwithstanding patterns of national variation – from 'labourist' Britain and Australia to 'socialist' Germany – labour-movement activists internationally saw their movements during the 1890s and 1900s as being placed under mounting *systemic* attack, as being 'outside' or in serious danger of losing previous advantages gained. Internationally we may observe, therefore, not only economic problems and crises, but also a political and social crisis of legitimation, of how capitalism could continue to command the allegiance of its increasingly discontented 'masses'.

Similarities: Responses

The problem of legitimation was compounded by the fact that the 'masses' not only expressed anger and dissatisfaction, but also began to organise themselves, in mainly unprecedented numbers, in labour movements. In Britain the period from the 1870s to the First World War saw the development of a mass labour movement.[56] Trade union membership grew from approximately 500,000 in the mid-1870s to over four million by 1914. By the latter date the 'new' unionists, largely non-skilled in character and organised mainly in two key periods of labour insurgency (1888-1892 and 1910-14), dominated the trade union movement, both numerically and ideologically. Membership of the Co-operative movement showed a spectacular advance – from about 600,000 in 1880 to over three million by 1914. Socialism also saw a late nineteenth-century revival, albeit of distinctly more modest proportions. None of the three main socialist groups, the Independent Labour

Party (1893), the Social Democratic Federation (1884) and the Fabian Society (1884), enjoyed mass membership. The most important of the three, the ILP, had a dues-paying membership of only 9,556 in 1905-6. But small membership figures were more than offset by the increasingly significant influence of socialists upon the training and ideas of labour movement activists, upon trade-union organisation and work with the unemployed, and more generally upon the mainstream labour movement. During the 1890s, for example, the socialists achieved notable, if chequered, successes in their attempts to move the TUC away from its customary voluntarism and Lib-Labism in favour of the legal eight-hour day, independent labour politics, and various degrees of nationalisation and common ownership.[57]

The United States saw repeated mass insurgencies (1884-6, the early-mid 1890s and at various times between 1912 and 1922) in support of union recognition and improvements in living and working conditions.[58] The establishment of permanent 'new' or 'mass' unions in the US would have to await the New Deal era of the 1930s, but trade unionism as a whole, as represented increasingly by the AF of L, did show significant gains. Between 1892 and 1914 the number of US trade unionists increased , albeit unevenly, from approximately 400,000 to 2,566,000. And in both Britain and the USA there were major gains in trade union membership between 1914 and 1920. By the latter date there were 4,775,000 members in the United States (16.7 per cent density) as compared with a massive 8,348,000 (45.2 per cent density) in the United Kingdom.

Socialism in the United States assumed much greater *numerical* importance than its counterpart in Britain. Between 1901 and the outbreak of the First World War the Socialist Party of America 'vigorously entered the political process', winning control of local government 'in a number of cities' and electing local officials 'in hundreds of other municipalities'. The highpoint of the Party's success at the national level came in 1912 when its presidential candidate, Eugene Debs, received 6 per cent of the popular vote and its membership peaked at 118,000.[59]

If the turn to socialism constituted a minority response, then, as noted, urgent attention to the issue of political *independence* became very much a majority matter for the labour movements of both countries. In Britain, the decision taken at the 1899 Plymouth TUC, by 546,000 to 434,000 delegated votes, to call for 'better representation', found concrete institutional expression in the Labour Representation Conference of February 1900. Convened by the Parliamentary Committee of the TUC, and involving representatives from the trade unions, the Independent Labour Party, the Social Democratic Federation and the Fabian Society (the invited Co-op movement being 'unable to pledge their organisations') the milestone LRC recommended, in the form of socialist ILPer Keir Hardie's amendment, the establishment of 'a distinct Labour Group in Parliament'. While ready, in the words of Hardie, 'to co-operate with any party which for the time being may be engaged in promoting legislation in the direct interest of labour', and while indeed forming an electoral pact with the Liberals in 1903, the formation of the Labour Group was tangible evidence of the ascendant spirit of *independent labourism* within the TUC. As Hardie declared, his amendment,

> left no doubt as to its meaning. It aimed at the formation in the House of Commons of a Labour *Party* having its own policy, its own whips, and acting in all that concerned the welfare of the workers in a manner free and unhampered by entanglements with other parties.[60] (emphasis added)

Furthermore, as Hardie advised delegates to the LRC's Third Annual Conference, the 'common denominator' for Labour MPs was that that, 'when acting in the House of Commons, they should be neither Socialists, Liberals, nor Tories, but a Labour party'.
And,

> ... let them beware lest they surrender themselves to Liberalism, which would shackle them, gag them, and leave them a helpless, discredited, and impotent mass. Let them have done with Liberalism and Toryism and every other 'ism' that was not Labourism ...[61]

Notwithstanding its belief in trade unionism as the main means of labour's emancipation and the misleading 'pure-and-simple-trade-union' emphasis in much of its historiography, the AF of L had, as noted earlier, been determined from its inception to secure, by independent means, 'legislation in the labour interest'. As Gompers declared in his report to the 1898 AF of L convention:

> We want legislation in the interest of labor; we want legislation executed by labor men; we want trade unionists in Congress and more trade unionists in the State legislatures ... We shall secure them, too, by acting as trade unionists rather than turning our trade unions into partisan ward clubs.

And,

> No-one having any conception of the labor problems – the struggles of life – would for a moment entertain the notion, much less advise the workers, to abstain from the exercise of their political rights and their political power. On the contrary, *trade union action upon the surface is economic action, yet there is no act which the trade unions can take but which in its effects is political.*[62] (emphasis added)

The common, and once more misleading, historiographical conflation of independent labour politics and independent labour *party* politics has, furthermore, led to an underestimation of the AF of L's consistent determination to pursue an independent course of action. As Gompers argued in 1894,

> He would indeed be shortsighted who would fail to advocate independent voting and

political action by union workmen. We should endeavor to do all that we possibly can to wean our fellow-workers from their affiliation with the dominant political parties, as one of the first steps necessary to insure wage-workers to vote in favor of wage-workers' interests, wage-workers' questions, and for union wage-workers as representatives.[63]

British influence was much in evidence. In January 1894 Gompers was reported in an article in the *New York Herald* as having said,

The trade unions of England have had the benefit of longer experience and struggle, and their actions are closely watched by the men who are prominent in the Labor movement here. England has been going through for some years what we are beginning to feel here and has been able to figure out what is needed. *We have watched her and are ready to profit by her example.*[64] (emphasis added)

'In that country', observed Gompers in December 1894,

the organized wage-workers avail themselves of every legal and practical means to obtain the legislation they demand. They endeavor to defeat those who oppose, and elect those who support, legislation in the interest of labor, and whenever opportunity affords elect a bona fide union man to parliament and other public offices. The Parliamentary Committee of the British Trades Union Congress is a labor committee to lobby for labor legislation. *This course the organized workers of America may with advantage follow,* since it is based upon experience and fraught with good results.[65] (emphases added)

The precise nature of the AF of L's political independence and the content of its legislative demands will be fully addressed in the *What Kind of Politics?* section below. Three brief observations, however, should be made at this juncture. First, notwithstanding its more marked and persistent opposition than the British labour movement, at least on the national level, to state 'paternalism' or 'charity' (for example, old-age pensions, the legal eight-hour day for non-government workers and municipal housing provision) and its full endorsement of the 'British' system of voluntary collective bargaining and trade-union legal immunities and freedoms, the AF of L as a whole, and especially at the state and local levels, was less committed to the principle of voluntarism, in terms of both its guiding philosophy and legislative demands, than often claimed.[66] Second, the full extent and tenacity of voluntarism among British workers and within the British labour movement is frequently neglected or underestimated by those pro-exceptionalism scholars wishing to contrast US 'voluntarism' and 'individualism' with British 'collectivism'.[67] Third, it is ironic that the kind of political independence espoused by the 1890s and 1900s AF of L was closely modelled upon the 'old' British model of independent lobbying by the Parliamentary Committee of the TUC, rather than upon the latter's post-1899 commitment to the creation of a 'distinct Labour group' or

'Labour Party' in the House of Commons. This third observation invites us to examine the differences rather than the similarities between the US and British labour movements. It is to such an examination that I now turn.

General Differences

The existence of important labour movement similarities and the overall anti-exceptionalism thrust of this essay must not allow us to lose sight of significant differences between the British and US labour movements and the wider working classes in the two countries. These differences, fivefold in character, may be identified in the following manner.

First, and notwithstanding the successful growth of the AF of L and periodic mass upsurges of those black, female and immigrant workers often beyond the reach of AF of L unions, the 'new' union organisation of the non-skilled was, as suggested most recently by Kim Voss, more pronounced and durable in Britain.[68] As a result, and taking into account the large constituency of the friendly society and co-operative society movements, the British labour movement acquired, as noted earlier, more of a mass character than its American counterpart.

Second, the British movement was far more successful than the American in gaining 'official' acceptance and recognition. This success derived, in part, from the less extensive, violent and sustained opposition to trade unionism practised by employers and the state machinery as a whole in Britain as compared with their American counterparts. Notwithstanding its endurance of periods of considerable 'labour unrest' (especially 1910-1914), and areas of persistent employer non-unionism and anti-union violence (especially parts of Scotland and Wales), Britain did not generally experience the sheer scale and chronic nature of US industrial conflict, combined with the latter's high and *often successful* levels of anti-union violence and repression.[69]

Third, the labour movement was, by and large, more united in Britain than in the United States. To be sure, there were enduring conflicts within the TUC between, on the one hand, socialists and 'new' unionists, and, on the other, the 'old guard' of 'craft' unionists and Lib.-Labers. There was, in addition, a tradition of support for Conservatism among organised workers in Lancashire and elsewhere. There was an attack in the 1895 TUC upon the 'hopeless' and 'disruptive' campaign of the ILP during the general election of that year. And opposition was voiced at the crucial 1899 TUC to the 'impracticable' and 'divisive' nature of the (successful) call for 'better representation' in the House of Commons.[70] However, most sections of the British trade-union movement did eventually come to see the benefits of the establishment of the Labour Representation Committee and worked relatively harmoniously together in the 1906 general election and beyond to defend and advance the industrial and political aims of labour.

By way of contrast, and notwithstanding the class-based radicalism of Gompers and the AF of L during the 1890s and 1900s, the common 'moral universality' which had underpinned the various movements which comprised the late nineteenth-century American labour movement splintered during the late 1900s and 1910s. As David Montgomery has crucially observed,

> Monopoly capitalism … fragmented the political ideology of the American workers' movement. By 1920 conflicting groups of workers fought each other, rhetorically armed with different fragments of what had formerly been a coherent vision of redeeming the republic.

By 1920 an AF of L trade union leadership 'explicitly committed not only to reforming American capitalism by strictly trade union means, but also to defending the state against foreign foes and domestic revolutionaries alike' was now set against the Socialist party and 'the direct action movement, most clearly represented by the IWW'.[71]

Fourth, the weaker and more divided US movement was set within a wider working class which, while in many ways inhabiting the same 'classed' and increasingly commercialised culture of its British counterpart, was more divided by racial and ethnic conflicts than was the overall case in Britain.[72]

Finally, and taking into account the necessary cautions of the revisionists concerning the limited influences of socialism and class in Britain, and our identification of considerable support within the AF of L for the creation of a labour party, nevertheless the stark fact remains that the British trade union movement created a Labour Party whereas the AFL remained steadfast in its independent non-partisanship. This was, moreover, a British Labour Party in which both class-based considerations and socialist influence were more influential, in terms of its formation and subsequent development, than the new revisionism would allow.[73] In contrast, Gompers and likeminded spirits were proof of the claim that class consciousness could, and did, take many forms, including an AF of L version which combined a critique of American capitalism, support for trade unionism and independent politics *and* opposition to socialism and the creation of a trade-union based labour party! Indeed, it is now time more directly to address this 'peculiarly American' question of the absent labour party.

Labour Party Absence and the Question of American 'Peculiarity'

Between 1893 and 1908 Gompers' and the majority AF of L's opposition to the formation of a labour party revolved far less around long term structural factors than around questions of relatively short-run experience and a pragmatic and hard-headed assessment of the likely costs and benefits involved in the adoption of a particular political course of action. References to hegemonic US individualism, entrepreneurialism and market-embeddedness, and strong attachments to 'open' political parties as major or insuperable obstacles to the development of independent labour party politics were, at least as reflected in the speeches and writings of Gompers and many other national leaders, conspicuous either by their absence or the relatively low priority afforded to them.

We would, of course, be mistaken to deny the adverse effects of racism, other 'ethnocultural' factors, and the wide social embrace of the two mainstream parties and the Progressives upon the mass *appeal* of socialist and labour party politics in the pre-1914 years and beyond. Similarly, some leaders, including Gompers, maintained that the culturally diverse nature of the American working class, coupled with the (albeit much diminished) influence and material standing of 'the people' in Equal Rights America – as compared with its supposedly more homogeneous, if poorer and less influential counterpart in 'monarchical' and 'aristocratic' Britain – made it correspondingly more difficult to establish common political commitment to a labour party among large numbers of workers.[74] But the overriding tactical, strategic *and* ideological question facing its leaders in the period under review was: how to increase the AFL's membership and advance its wider industrial and political interests in the short- to medium-term in a predominantly hostile climate?

The answer which emerged rested, above all else, upon the AF of L's overriding commitment to the 'primacy of trade unionism' approach. As noted earlier in this essay, Gompers identified the trade unions as the natural, primary and unifying means of working-class defence and advancement. As Stuart Kaufman claimed, Gompers' socialist contacts and readings in the 1870s, and especially with Ferdinand Laurrell and Carl Hillmann, who prized trade union over political means of emancipation, had a profound influence upon his emerging philosophy. Similarly, ensuing disputes within the Workingmen's Party of the United States between 'Marxist' advocates of the primacy of economic organization and Lassallean proponents of the primacy of politics, combined with what Gompers perceived to be the debilitating effects of the Lassallean Socialist Labor Party upon the fortunes of trade unionism, further strengthened Gompers' trade-union resolve.[75] The main task facing labour movement activists was accordingly to establish trade unionism on a firm footing. Anything or anyone which interfered with or detracted from this basic task – including the Knights of Labor with their very broad goals and 'improper' encroachments upon trade-union autonomy, those advocating AF of L commitment to socialism and other forms of potentially divisive partisan party politics, and 'religious differences or race prejudice' – was to be opposed.[76]

As Gompers declared in his 1894 Report to the AF of L that advocated 'first things first':

> It is ridiculous to imagine that the wage-workers can be slaves in employment and yet achieve control at the polls. There never yet existed co-incident with each other autocracy in the shop and democracy in political life. In truth, we have not yet achieved the initial step to the control of public affairs by even a formal recognition of our unions ... Before we can hope as a general organization to take the field by nominat-

ing candidates for office, the workers must be more thoroughly organized and better results achieved by experiments locally. A political labor movement cannot and will not succeed upon the ruins of the trade unions.

In the same report he gave examples of the past mistakes of premature political action and putting politics first:

During the past year the trade unions in many localities plunged into the political arena by nominating their candidates for public office, and sad as it may be to record, it is nevertheless true that in each one of these localities politically they were defeated and the trade union movement more or less divided and disrupted.

And,

I need only refer you to the fact that the National Labor Union, the predecessor of the American Federation of Labor, entered the so-called independent political arena in 1872 and nominated its candidate for the presidency of the United States. It is equally true that the National Labor Union never held a convention after that event.[77]

American labour needed, above all, to heed the lesson of the British movement: to build up the strength of the unions and 'lobby for labor legislation', taking the utmost care in the process not to place the trade union movement at risk by giving too much attention or weight to politics so as to weaken or 'leave behind' trade unionism. (It is significant in this context that Gompers selected as his 'British model' the independent lobbying activities of the Parliamentary Committee rather than the partisan party activities of labour's Lib.-Lab. MPs.) Political lobbying was thus to be employed as an auxiliary to trade unionism. And the 'peculiarity' of the US trade union movement lay in the fact that it had not yet gained the strength, success and influence of its British counterpart, rather than in the adoption of novel or different political tactics and strategies from those employed by the pre-1899 TUC.[78] The wisdom of the AF of L's 'trade unionism first' strategy was to be fully confirmed to Gompers by the fact that, whereas previous depressions had devastated the ranks of trade unionism, the AF of L managed not only to weather the most depressed years of the entire century, between 1893 and 1896, but also to survive the onslaught launched against labour by corporate capital, the courts and the state.

It was within this context of successfully adopting the 'British model', albeit within a 'peculiarly American' context, that Gompers' attitudes to the socialists must be understood. Given his commitment to the primacy of trade unionism, it was more or less inevitable that Gompers and his supporters within the AF of L would sooner or later clash with those socialists who attached the utmost importance to building up the party and the primacy of the political road. It is, however, the case that generally up to the mid 1890s, and in some instances beyond, Gompers displayed a certain amount of ambivalence towards socialists and socialism. In 1894 he declared that, 'until the advent of Prof. De Leon in the socialist movement', the 'different wings in the labour movement' had, much in the manner of the British socialists and Lib.-Labers. and Old Unionists, 'managed matters so that we could at least work together'. Tactical, as opposed to fundamental ideological, differences appeared at that stage to be paramount. 'After all', concluded Gompers, 'it is merely a difference of opinion as to the most practical methods to be employed in securing to the laborer his just rights'.[79]

From the crucial 1894 AFL convention onwards, complete with its renunciation of a labour party and the collectivism of plank 10, relations between Gompers and many socialists did take a turn for the worse. But in the immediate post-1894 period socialists *within* the AF of L were extremely critical of De Leon's policy of 'dual unionism' and his attacks on the federation's leadership. Furthermore, Gompers continued to the end of our period to draw a sharp contrast between 'true' and 'fake' socialists. The former, embracing Keir Hardie, Tom Mann, Karl Marx and Frederick Engels were portrayed as loyal and committed to the mass labour movement, regarding 'the existing trade unions' as 'the basis for all progress of labor', and being or having been prepared to subordinate differences of opinion and, indeed, socialist purity to the causes of mass labour unity and independent political advancement.[80] In contrast, the latter, embracing many American socialists, but especially De Leon and his Socialist Trades and Labor Alliance (formed in 1895), were seen as a divisive 'splitters', as arrogantly dismissive of AF of L 'craft' trade unionism, as foolishly wishing to subordinate trade unionism and independence in politics to the interests of socialist party politics and as intent upon setting up rival unions to, and so undermining, those affiliated to the AF of L.

Throughout 1896 the *American Federationist* was bitterly critical of De Leon's 'professional duty and mission', as witnessed in his activities in New York City's garment industry, 'to destroy every existing trade union ... to besmirch the character of every trade union officer'.[81] De Leon's Socialist Trades and Labor Alliance was described as acting in a manner befitting 'Pinkerton's men' – a society 'to render labor organizations ineffective, or a combination to hand over the workers, shackled hand and foot, to the tender mercies of the capitalist class' which had been condemned by 'many honest socialists' as 'would-be union wreckers'.[82] Similar charges against De Leon – of being a 'fake' socialist, and of being an *agent provocateur* and 'serving the interests of the capitalist class' in his opposition to the miners' leaders and their struggles and in helping to break disputes in textiles and cigarmaking – were to follow in 1897, 1898 and beyond.[83]

In the case of Victor Berger and others who would become leading lights in the Socialist Party of America and who nevertheless remained members of the AF of L, the situation was, at least in theory, more complex. Gompers continued into the late 1890s to welcome 'genuine' offers of assistance to the trade union movement by 'all reform forces, the socialist political party included', and expressed the view that, 'the hope and aspiration of the trade unionist is closely akin to that expressed by the socialist'.[84] But increasingly during the 1900s conflicts between, on the one hand, Berger and his comrades and, on the other, Gompers and his brothers became more bitter, entrenched and personal in character. Charges of 'treachery to the trade union movement', the 'gigantic failure' of AF of L lobbying, and Marx's alleged defence of trade unionism and denunciation of the socialists as 'the worst enemies of the labouring classes' becoming the standard, if debased, currency of exchange at AF of L conventions.[85] In such a context it was obvious that no reconciliation between 'trade unionists' and 'socialists' could possibly take place. The socialist 'partyism' of Berger and Max Hayes and the trade unionism and political 'independence' of Gompers proved to be totally incompatible.[86] There was also a very real sense in which Gompers perceived his worsening relations with the socialists to be 'peculiarly American' in character. As noted earlier, Gompers continued to contrast the actions of British socialists, such as Mann and Hardie, with those of their 'intolerant', 'cowardly' and 'slanderous' American counterparts. British labour leaders, including the socialists, were portrayed as more tolerant and given to compromise in the interest of labour unity, as more open and honest, and as possessing 'true manhood'. Thus, 'though they may differ', yet they 'retain a high regard for the personal welfare and character of their adversaries'; it being 'one thing to differ with a man', yet 'quite another to regard him as dishonest simply because of that difference'.[87] Furthermore, in marked contrast to 'divisive' and 'disruptive' US socialists, the British leaders presented 'a solid front whenever the interests of labor are at stake', so demonstrating 'their honesty, earnestness and devotion to the cause of the wealth producing masses of Great Britain'. And, although 'engaged in the active work of a Political Labor Party', Tom Mann evinced 'no attempt to underrate the importance of the trade union movement'.[88]

In a similar vein, Gompers and the AF of L maintained their seemingly cordial contacts with a wide range of British labour leaders, by means of the fraternal delegate system, visits and written correspondence. And British socialists were invited openly to express their thoughts in the pages of the *American Federationist.* Pete Curran of the Gas Workers' Union and the ILP, Ben Tillett of the Dockers' Union, Mann and Hardie were among those who accepted their invitations. While Curran shared the view of many on the British Left at this time that the outlook for independent labour party and socialist politics in the USA was very bright,[89] in his 1895 article in the *Federationist,* Hardie was keen both to display his own socialism and to put the case for a labour party in the United States. 'It matters not to me at home', he wrote,

whether a man be a Liberal or a Tory. If he is not a Socialist, he is an *opponent,* and as such I treat him; I may respect him for honestly holding his opinions, but I cannot support him.

'It is along this direction', continued Hardie,

> ... that trade unionism must develop. To-day the workers of America are divided
> into republicans and democrats, but both parties support the system which is bring-
> ing American workmen down to the pauper labor of Europe. *Therefore*, were I an
> American, I would support neither but would endeavor to build up a party separate
> and distinct from both ... which would unite the workers under their own banner,
> and enable them to send men as law-makers and administrators, who would repre-
> sent them and their interests, and not the interests of property. And in so doing, I
> would claim to be interpreting the true spirit of trade unionism.[90]

Significantly, there was no response to Hardie's article from the 'true spirit of trade
unionism' in America, Samuel Gompers, the editor of the *American Federationist*!
Indeed, we may speculate that the adoption, by US advocates of a labour party, of
Hardie's commitments to the mass movement and the 'common denominator' of
labourism rather than socialism, would still not have been sufficient to persuade
Gompers and his allies in the AF of L to put at risk their 'trade union first' principles in the interest of independent labour *partyism*. Rather, policies of 'digging in'
and 'incremental gradualism' – by means of trade unionism supported by non-
partisan politics – continued to be seen as less hazardous and more suited to the
'peculiar' American environment.[91]

   Doubts concerning the extent to which the organs of the state could *substantially and fundamentally* be persuaded to support organised labour's cause, and
even more fundamental doubts concerning the extent to which the state could be
'transformed' by a labour or socialist party, also weighed heavily upon the minds
of the AF of L leadership when they pondered which political road to follow. The
primacy afforded by the socialists to politics meant that legislation and the necessary transformation of the state – from an instrument of class oppression to one of
class liberation – constituted the principal means by which the socialist commonwealth would be created. While intent upon securing legislation in the trade-union
interest, the AF of L, however, demonstrated traditional republican opposition to
a large and centralised state machinery, and, as already noted, was nationally more
persistent than the British TUC in its 'voluntarist' attitude towards social-welfare
provision. In addition, in view of their perceived control of the state by forces hostile to the interests of labour and the past susceptibility of labour party experiments
to middle-class carpet-bagging, Gompers and his allies saw the socialist emphasis
upon the primacy of the ballot box and the transformation of the state as so much
'pie in the sky'.[92] By way of contrast there was the marked feeling among British
labour leaders that, notwithstanding its immediate hostility, the state had, since
the mid-century demise of Chartism, generally responded positively to organised
labour's demands. It was widely believed that enhanced labour-movement pressure, especially by independent political means, would persuade the state and the
political parties to give, once again, precedence to a positive rather than a hostile

stance towards organised labour.

Finally, Gompers offered the important argument that the adoption of independent, nonpartisan political means was, albeit slowly and unevenly, bringing rewards to organised labour which the party-political option would, in all probability, not deliver. At first sight this appears to be a curious, indeed contrary argument. At the *national* level the results of lobbying in Washington, by the AF of L's Legislative Committee, and the attempted election to Congress of members with sound trade-union credentials or connections, were, to say the least, far from impressive. In his report to the 1896 AF of L convention, Gompers recorded only 'fair progress, and went on to complain that,

> There are too few members of Congress who are elected upon distinctive labor issues or committed to labor's interests. Hence the members of Congress imagine that the special interests of labor have small need to be considered.[93]

Ten years later, in the midst of the AFL's beleaguered stance against non-unionism, injunctions and claims for damages Gompers observed that, as to Congress 'we have not elected a single trade union member'. Furthermore, while Congress had been very quick to respond to 'the demands of special interests' – by means of 'the prompt granting of charters, franchises, immunities, special privileges and special and class legislation' – it had been very slow to enact measures in favour of the 'toiling masses'.[94] Indeed, the AF of L's 'Bill of Grievances', protesting against 'judicial usurpation and judicial legislation rather than Congressional legislation', and presented to the President of the United States, the President of the Senate and the Speaker of the House of Representatives in March 1906, had not been heeded. Gompers concluded that, 'We present these grievances to your attention because we have long, patiently and in vain waited for redress', the 'toilers'' appeals and petitions being 'treated with indifference and contempt'.[95]

In truth, throughout the period under review, the AF of L had sought in vain to attain the eight-hour day for government employees and the other freedoms and immunities won, partially lost and then successfully regained by legislative means by British labour. As Leon Fink has reminded us, 'Despite the wishes of the AF of L, American trade unionists in the era of industrial consolidation, unlike their British counterparts, *never* got to experience true voluntarism or "collective laissez-faire"'. (emphasis added).

> Statutory restraints on judicial authority proved either internally faulty or were effectively annulled by the power of judicial reinterpretation … Attempts to grant trade unions an implied statutory immunity from legal intervention repeatedly failed as a result of the American (but not English) practice of judicial review.

And 'judicial volleys' against the trade-union movement were by no means confined to the period 1893-1908. 'During the decade of the 1920s', continues Fink, injunctions rose to a new peak ... the injunction power was extended to yellow-dog contracts ... picketing was often judicially restricted, and even the Clayton Act, labor's hoped-for 'Magna Carta', was interpreted to deny the legitimacy of the secondary boycott ...[96]

However, even at the national level, Gompers perceived some brightness in a generally gloomy picture. The provision of the AF of L's 1895 convention 'for the setting up of a permanent lobbying committee' (which became the Legislative Committee), with its members based in Washington DC. as 'legislative representatives of the Federation', and the transference of the Federation's headquarters in the following year from Indianapolis to Washington, signified that the AFL was intent, much in conscious imitation of the TUC, upon maximising its influence within the nation's political capital.[97] Furthermore, by the end of our period limited and scattered, yet clearly perceived and highly prized gains had been secured. For example, in 1898 the *American Federationist* lauded the decision of the US Supreme Court to sustain the Utah eight-hour law. Various AF of L leaders claimed that the federation's growing political power and influence had been instrumental in the more widespread abolition of child labour, in securing improved legislation concerning sanitation and safety, in the more widespread attainment of lien laws (to ensure the payment of wages), in the improved working conditions and work-place freedoms of seamen, and in extending the period of Asian exclusion.[98] As a result of the AFL's 'mass mobilizations' of 1906 and 1908, respectively six and thirteen trade unionists had been elected to Congress. And, notwithstanding congressional deafness to the AF of L's 'Bill of Grievances', Gompers had derived enough satisfaction from the federation's 1906 political campaign to declare in December that,

> We put (the) fear of God into them ... While at this writing no definite results can be predicted, I feel confident that we have enough Congressmen elected and pledged to the rights of Labor and the people as to make it impossible for another 'hostile or indifferent' Congress to treat labor's demands in the future as they have been treated in the past.[99]

Indeed, he was later to claim that 'at no time in the history of our movement was there so much independent voting' as in 1906, and that, mainly as a result of organised labour's campaign, the dominant Republican majority in Congress had been cut in half.[100]

Further major judicial and legislative reverses for the AF of L between the end of 1906 and 1908 may have caused Gompers to temper his optimism somewhat. But the generally favourable response of the Democrats to organised labour's demands in 1908 once again restored a good measure of faith in labour's 'forward march'. The message from the centre was clear: press on in the face of adversity – determination would reap its own rewards.

If the pursuit of politics by independent means was perceived to bring tangible, if limited and uneven, gains at the national level, then the rewards of such a pursuit were believed to be much more substantial at the state and local level. In 1899 the *American Federationist* observed 'a steady and very gratifying gain' in the numbers of 'men from our own ranks' elected, irrespective of party colours, to make laws 'according to the legislative demands' of the AF of L. The *Federationist* continued,

There is scarcely a legislature in the country but which contains a number of sincere, able and honest union men ... What is true of State legislatures is equally true of local and municipal bodies. We hope, yes, have every reason to expect, that the time is not far distant when we shall have the presence of tried and true union men in large numbers, not only in State and local bodies, but also in the halls of Congress and in every department of our political and civil life.[101]

And as a result of the 1906 campaign,

In state legislatures Labor scored a remarkable victory in many cases and the legislation which will be passed in the various states will do much to show that our efforts have not been in vain.[102]

Gompers was securely of the opinion that the strong lobbying presence of organised labour had a profound impact upon the type and extent of local and state legislation secured. In 1899 he declared,

Measures in the interests of labor have been passed by a large number of the State legislatures. The bills are of a widespread character and influence. It is notable that the States in which there are State Federations of Labor affiliated with the American Federation of Labor are those most conspicuous for the progress made in legislatures along all lines of reform.

The spread of factory legislation and lien laws were illustrative of 'the progress made'. In anti-voluntarist vein, Gompers also regarded as 'gratifying' the discovery that 'municipal legislation, establishing a maximum number of hours per day (eight) and a minimum wage, is generally being adopted for municipal work'.[103]

In recent years Gary Fink, Michael Kazin and Julia Greene have demonstrated the very considerable extent of organised labour's political activities at local and state level. Such activities, conducted mainly but not invariably by non-party independent means (in a minority of cases there were 'turns' to labour parties), were often, *contra* Hattam, designed to secure 'legislated social reform approximating the welfare or guarantor state'.[104] But we should note not only the extensive nature of such activities, but also their perceived positive effect in inducing pro-labour overtures, measures and concessions, albeit made unevenly and most markedly in the post-1908 period, by Democrats, Progressives and, to a much lesser extent,

Republicans.[105]

In sum, we may suggest that both Gompers and more recent commentators have identified, in organised labour's attempted entry into, and 'warrening' of, the worlds of local, regional and national politics, profoundly important, if unduly neglected, roots of an American version of 'labourism' – of the achievement of measures in 'the labour, and especially trade union, interest' by predominantly independent, non partisan-party-based means. Here, too, there exist obvious similarities of tactics and strategy, albeit by increasingly different post-1900 methods (non-partisan independent versus partisan-party), with mainstream labour in Britain. Unfortunately constraints of time and space have permitted only the most fleeting and impressionistic treatment of this important and as yet barely researched area of the political and sociological roots of US labourism. Future research will hopefully be moved precisely and extensively to chart the political geography of the AF of L's spheres of influence and their limitations, the responses of external political forces, and the meanings and lessons derived from the whole process (on a par with the detailed map we now possess of the 'rise of Labour' in Britain and its interplay with Liberalism and Conservatism).[106] In such a manner will our knowledge and understanding of the roots and nature of the AF of L's 'peculiar' labourism and the sources of political accommodation and challenge be greatly enhanced.

What Kind of Politics?

In this final section it seems appropriate to return to delegate White's question posed at the very beginning of this essay – 'What kind of politics?' – in order to provide further clarification concerning the nature of the independent political path trodden by the AF of L. Four main conclusions are presented.

First, we have seen that the AF of L's opposition to involvement in party politics did not amount to opposition to political involvement per se. While opposition was registered to what were perceived to be the divisive and debilitating effects of partisan party allegiance upon the trade union movement, strong support was given to independent political action free from party entanglements. Arguing thus, I have accordingly registered strong disagreement with the 'pure-and-simple-trade-union' approach, so prevalent in the 'traditional' historiography of the AFL and still to be found in some of the more recent work. For example, a historian of labour politics, writing in 1997, baldly declared:

> After some initial vacillation the American Federation of Labor (AFL) rejected the arguments in favour of independent labour politics … and opted instead for AFL President Samuel Gompers' vision of *a non-political 'pure and simple' unionism*.[107] (emphasis added)

Second, notwithstanding the primacy of its commitments to trade unionism, the workplace and voluntarism and the unwelcome facts of life of state hostility and the power of the courts to 'strike out' legislation as unconstitutional (the power of judicial review), the AF of L was far more committed to the political road, – in the form of the attainment of favourable legislation – than suggested in recent accounts by Victoria Hattam and William Forbath.[108] To be sure, the voice of delegate Blackmore was raised at the 1902 AF of L convention in support of the adoption of the legislative road in Britain and against its practicability in the United States:

> … conditions in England differ very materially from those which confront trade unionists in America. In England, once an act is approved by Parliament, it is fixed, and no supreme court or other tribunal can declare it unconstitutional or otherwise check its force …
> It will be seen, therefore, that the chief efforts of trade unions in Great Britain, in national matters, must be toward securing the election of their own members or safe friends of their cause as members of Parliament.[109]

However, Blackmore's view was very much a minority, indeed largely isolated view within the AFL. The majority view was to continue, notwithstanding frequently adverse circumstances, to seek 'legislation in the direct interest of labor'. Perhaps the most telling illustration of the latter view was provided between 1906 and 1908 when, in response to the most serious judicial onslaught in its history, the AF of L continued, indeed more actively and concertedly stepped up, the campaign (in the forms of its 1906 'Bill of Grievances' and its 1908 'Protest to Congress') to seek from Congress anti-injunction and anti-damages relief and trade union-exemption from the terms of the Sherman Act.[110] As Gompers remarked at the federation's 1907 convention in relation to the British Trade Disputes Act of 1906 – restoring the pre-Taff Vale situation of union immunity from damages – that was 'a law which we have been trying to get from our Congress in vain for these past several years'.[111] AF of L affiliates, such as the United Mineworkers of America, also continued, *pace* Hattam, very actively to seek political redress for 'workplace concerns', by means of lobbying for safety and other legislation.

We should also take cognizance of the fact that the AF of L's legislative demands, as expressed nationally and on the state and local level, were far from insignificant or insubstantial. For example, the planks adopted *seriatim* at the 1894 AF of L convention embraced compulsory education, direct legislation through the initiative and referendum, a legal work day of not more than eight hours, sanitary inspection of workshop, mine and home, employer liability, the abolition of the contract system in all public work, the abolition of the sweating system, the municipal ownership of street cars, water works, gas and electric plants and the nationalization of telegraphs, telephones, railroads and mines. It was, of course, the case that delegate Pomeroy's subsequent motion that the convention 'endorse the above planks as a whole' was rejected. Thereafter confusion reigned as to the precise nature of the AF of L's formal legislative demands. However, the 1895 convention, while rejecting the notion of a formal political platform and party attachments, did agree that the federation had 'legislative demands'.[112] During the remainder of the 1890s and throughout the 1900s, in addition to AF of L opposition to Asian immigration, competition from convict labour, child labour, sweating, anti-union legislation and 'judicial tyranny', such 'demands' included the eight-hour day for goverment employees, seamen's rights, maximum hour legislation for women and children,[113] free compulsory elementary education, compulsory school attendance and free textbooks for the public schools, initiative, referendum and recall, improved sanitation, factory and mine inspection and safely laws, municipal ownership of public utilities, the national ownership of telegraphs and (on the part of some unions) railroads and coal mines, and women's suffrage.[114]

Furthermore, although less committed at the national level to state-sponsored social reform than the 1900s TUC, the AF of L locally and at the state level cannot be cast as 'exceptional'. Many state federations of labour, the 'crucial agencies' for political action, and central labour unions embraced a wide range of fundamentally anti-voluntarist demands. These included commitments to the substantial elements of nationalisation and municipalisation embodied in Morgan's 1894 'programme', workmen's compensation (the scheme to be administered by the state), unemployment insurance, old-age pensions and health and sickness insurance.[115] Finally, the San Franciscan labour movement, the stronghold of AFL building trades' craft unionism, not only created (albeit unusually for such crafts) a political party of labour, the Union Labor Party, to provide a political shield for the gains of trade unionism, but also supported 'the establishment of an eight-hour day on all public works in California, the setting up of public works to absorb the seasonally unemployed, and public health insurance'. In so acting it was, as Michael Kazin informs us, seeking to create a 'commoners' paradise'.[116]

Third, the AF of L set out to attain its legislative and other political goals by a variety of 'independent' means. The latter ranged from lobbying and voting to, as seen most prominently in 1906 and 1908, the effective screening and nomination of candidates and trade unionists themselves standing for political office. Just as 'the full scope of union lobbying has yet to be examined by historians',[117] so the history of the Legislative Committee of the AFL, from 1896 onwards the federation's official lobbying body, has yet to be written. We do know that at the AF of L's 1895 convention the Executive Council was authorised to appoint such a committee, but it was not until formal approval had been received from the following year's convention that the committee was actually set up. It was based in Washington DC and had Andrew Furuseth, of the Seamen's International Union, as its legislative agent. Consciously seeking to imitate the lobbying activities of the Parliamentary Committee of the TUC within the House of Commons, the Legislative Committee was to target Congress 'to secure the enactment of measures in the interests of labor, or to prevent the passage of measures inimical to its interests'.[118] Regular reports of the Committee's activities are to be found in the *American Federationist*.[119]

'Independent voting' referred to the judicious exercise of the franchise in favour of candidates who, irrespective of their party-political affiliation, were favourably disposed towards the AF of L's legislative and other political demands. This was, in effect, the most common form of 'independent politics' adopted by AF of L members. In the first issue of the *American Federationist*, in March 1894, Gompers wrote,

> In politics we shall be, as we always have been, *independent*. Independent of all parties regardless under which name they may be known. The only interest we shall have in either is their real, not merely their avowed, attitude towards labor. We shall endeavor to aid in exposing the folly of being a Union man 364 days in the year and failing to remember the Union man's duty on election day.[120]

As in Britain, a premium was to be placed, whenever 'opportunity affords', upon the election of candidates who were bona fide union men. In 1898 the *American Federationist* regularly ran an official declaration of the AFL's policies, entitled 'TRADE UNION POLITY', which outlined 'the subjoined resolutions ... adopted at successive conventions of the AF of L' and which '*must be regarded as the practical policy of the trade union movement of America*' (emphasis added).

Under the sub-heading, 'Political Action', the text read,

> That the American Federation of Labor most firmly and unequivocally favors the independent use of the ballot by the trade unionists and workingmen, united regardless of party, that we may elect men *from our own ranks* to make new laws and administer them along the lines laid down in the legislative demands of the American Federation of Labor, and at the same time secure an impartial judiciary that will not govern us by arbitrary injunctions of the courts, nor act as the pliant tools of corporate wealth ... That as our efforts are centered against all forms of industrial slavery and economic wrong, we must also direct our utmost energies to remove all forms of *political servitude* and *party slavery*, to that end that the working people may act as a unit at the polls at every election.[121] (emphasis added)

Significantly, Gompers was at considerable pains to demonstrate that, far from being a new policy, 'independent voting' had been consistently advocated by the AF of L since its inception.[122]

In terms of routine practice, far more votes were cast by AF of L members for supposedly sympathetic middle-class Democrats and Republicans than for 'men from our own ranks'. (Max Hayes offered the quip that 'we have elected corporation lawyers and other capitalists to both branches of Congress'.)[123] However, at times of acute crisis, such as in 1906 and 1908, efforts were considerably stepped up both more carefully to screen and nominate candidates in general and more actively to support trade union candidates. Significantly, following the British example, the instrument created nationally by the AFL in 1906, to realise these purposes, was given the name of the Labor Representation Committee.[124]

Fourth, and notwithstanding our earlier warning against seeing the 1890s and 1900s in terms of uniform closure, there is a very real sense in which we may say that the AF of L's 'independent' political stance had become firmly set by 1908. The latter may be illustrated by the fact that two potentially major shocks to the practice of 'independent voting' failed to bring about a formal change in policy. First, despite the 'mass mobilizations' of 1906 and 1908 and Gompers' endorsement of the Democratic presidential candidate in the latter year, the AF of L refused to abandon its non-partisanship. At the federation's 1908 convention Gompers could still declare,

> I owe allegiance to no political party – The American Labor movement is not partisan to a political party; it is partisan to a principle, the principle of equal rights and human freedom.[125]

Second, early in 1906 the Labour Party was officially formed in Britain. During the general election of the same year the Party put up fifty candidates, twenty-nine of whom were successful (in addition, twenty-four Lib.-Lab. MPs were returned). This result was perceived as constituting a major triumph for advocates of independent political *partyism*. In addition, both the Trade Disputes Bill and a Workmen's Compensation Bill were enacted, and the newly elected Liberals promised the passage of an Eight Hours bill for coalminers in 1907 (in the event it became law in 1908). The American labour movement, suffering under the cosh from the courts, the state and business-dominated political parties, looked with a mixture of envy, fascination, and genuine respect and awe, at the successes of its traditional role model in Britain.[126]

Such perceptions were doubtless compounded, if also somewhat muddied, by the fact that British fraternal delegates to the AF of L conventions of 1906 (JN Bell, National Amalgamated Labour Union, and Allen Gee, Textile Workers) and 1907 (David Shackleton, Textile Workers, and John Hodge, Steel Smelters) were wholehearted in their praise of the Labour Party. Fears concerning potentially debilitating divisions between British socialists and trade unionists working within the new party had not been realised. Both the LRC and the Party had *strengthened* rather than weakened the cause of trade unionism, and especially, as reflected in the legislation of 1906, the successes achieved by trade-union pressure upon parliament. The creation of a new, trade-union based, and independent political presence in parliament had given the trade union leader greater confidence in 'speaking out' on political matters without fear of 'injuring his position as a responsible leader of the men and women in purely trade union work'. Above all, perhaps, in electing its 'own' members, Labour was no longer obliged to go 'cap in hand' to political parties in many instances dominated by anti-labour capitalist interests. Rather, the cause of 'independent' Labour had engendered a newfound spirit of unity, confidence and clarity of purpose within the movement.[127] The AF of L was strongly advised to follow suit. John Hodge, for example, had no reservations in urging his AF of L audience to cast aside their differences and 'nail the colors of Labor Union' to the mast of a labour party, and 'make that your politics'.[128]

The views of the British fraternal delegates met with a respectful response from their American hosts. And David Shackleton was afforded a hero's welcome by Gompers, being presented to the 1907 convention as organised labour's driving force behind Liberal enactment of the historic Trade Disputes Act.[129] However, as in the case of the adverse domestic situation, external advice from the British delegates and the demonstrable successes of the new Labour Party failed to move the AF of L from its chosen 'independent' path. The dominant response from the Federation was one of extreme scepticism concerning 'true' and lasting British commitment to a new form of political independence, rooted in allegiance to a class-based Labour Party, at the expense of the traditional attachment to the independent lobbying of all political parties. Thus Frank Foster and James Wilson, fraternal delegates to the 1906 TUC, viewed 'the future of a class party with unionists forming the bulk of the membership' as 'at least problematical'. And,

> We repeat ... that while the trades union political movement in Great Britain is in a very interesting experimental stage, yet its lines are by no means fixed, nor is the movement by any means committed to the creation of a separate and distinct party machine upon class lines; nor, moreover, in our judgement, will it become so identified.[130]

The attention of AF of L members was also drawn, in 1906 and 1907, to the continued opposition in Britain of 'many of the older and more powerful unions' to affiliation to the Labour Party, to an alleged loss of effectiveness in trade-union matters on the part of British trade union leaders standing as political candidates and to the continued perils of attempting to commit the AF of L's 'many sided and much diversified membership' to a single party-political course.[131] In sum, the risks involved in setting the American labour movement on what was perceived to be an unproven, and in all probability ephemeral, 'new' British course were deemed to be unacceptably high.

Beyond our closing date of 1908, a mixture of old and new structural and experiential factors and arguments informed the AF of L's politics. Gompers drew two crucial conclusions from his four-month trip to Britain and Europe in 1909, undertaken largely to make 'observations of the working people's conditions'; and both conclusions promoted US labour's accommodation to the 'American' system. First, notwithstanding the evils of corporate capitalism and the continued grievances of American workers, the 'trade-union first' and non-partisan independent labour strategies of the AF of L – complete with their emphases upon trade-union autonomy and lack of debilitating entanglement with 'the visionary schemes of the "professoriat"' or 'so-called "intellectuals"' – were perceived to have brought much more substantial gains to workers than those delivered by European and British trade unions and socialist and labour parties. 'In no country in Europe', declared Gompers,

> does there exist a national labor organization of any form better adapted to obtain directly successful results in the interests of the workers than the A.F. of L ... Nowhere have there been greater achievements in advancing wages, shortening the workday, generally improving workshop conditions, or in convincing all ranks of society that the organization of labor is the great contributory and potent power to social peace and general prosperity.[132]

Ironically, Gompers' traditional role model, British trade unionism, was now adjudged to be lagging behind the AF of L in terms of 'rapidity of development' and 'unity and compactness of organization'.[133] The impressive, if uneven, growth of the AF of L between 1900 to 1910, from 869,000 to 2,102,000 members (as compared with an increase of approximately half a million trade unionists in the UK during the same decade) underpinned Gompers' beliefs that the Federation had 'come of age' and that the 'peculiar' weakness of American trade unionism was now largely a thing of the past. Most significantly, in view of this new late 1900s context of the perceived domestic gains and international superiority of the 'trade-union first' American way, it had become both unproductive and unnecessary further to countenance the 'British' road of independent labour partyism.

Second, according to Gompers the social and political will and imprint of 'the people', 'the working class', still prevailed to a much greater extent at home than abroad. Thus,

> In drawing comparisons between certain European and American manners and customs, I have constantly in mind the influence of the people in general upon the development of society in the two worlds. There is always one difference to be kept in mind: in the United States 'We are the people'; in Europe 'the people' are still often regarded by the hereditary dominant classes as mere hewers of wood and drawers of water.[134]

Closer AF of L involvement with the Democratic Party became an increasing fact of political life, notwithstanding continued formal attachment to political 'independence'. This involvement also strengthened labour's accommodation to the mainstream political system. The pro-Labour policies of Progressives and Democrats did much to weaken continued arguments in favour of socialism and the creation of a British-style labour party. The experiences of state repression and wartime, in which socialism increasingly became equated with 'alien subversion', had much the same effect. There continued to be important voices raised within the AF of L in favour of the 'British Road'. For example, John H. Walker, Scots-born ethical socialist of the Hardie stamp, member of the Socialist Party of America and leader of the United Mineworkers of America in District 12, Illinois, was torn between his SPA membership, advocacy of a labour party and pragmatic support for the pro-labour measures of President Wilson and influential Illinois Democrats. Expelled from the SPA in 1916, for supporting the Democratic rather than SPA candidate for Governor, Walker's political career illustrated the enduring hard mixture of experiential and structural choices facing labour party advocates in the 'peculiar' United States. Above all, would support for socialism and a labour party bring rewards greater than those delivered by the mainstream political parties? In the final analysis, Walker, while remaining true to his principles, pragmatically decided that the risks of adopting Keir Hardie's chosen path in America were simply too high and opted for political accommodation and labourism by Gompers' traditional means.[135] Many others on the Left adopted the same course. But, as demonstrated during the early 1920s, the cause of independent labour party politics in America was not dead and buried.[136]

That story, however, must be told another time.

Four main conclusions emerge from our discussion of similarities and differences in the politics of organised labour in the United States and Britain between 1893 and 1908. First, we have seen that, in terms of both shaping influences and characteristics, the politics of the two labour movements were more similar than suggested in many traditional and some recent accounts. In particular, late-Victorian British labour acted in many ways as a role model for Gompers' AF of L. Second, in his own thoughts and actions, Gompers epitomised the enduring strength of transatlantic connections and similarities, the weaknesses of the notion of American 'exceptionalism', and the complex, multi-faceted, and indeed contradictory features of terms such as class consciousness, radicalism and conservatism. Third, however, I have identified and sought to explain a major difference: the absence of a labour party in the United States. Fourth, reference to the speeches and writings of labour leaders, and especially those of Gompers, has suggested that a number of American 'peculiarities', rooted more in experiential than structural factors, and especially the nature, development and strength of trade unionism, underpinned this difference.

* The award of an Honorary Hallsworth Research Fellowship at the International Centre for Labour Studies, University of Manchester, 1998-1999, enabled me to complete the research for this essay. I am grateful to the directors of Labour Studies, Jamie Peck, David Coates and Huw Beynon, for their support. John Bennett and the inter-library loans librarians at Manchester Metropolitan University and at Warwick University have given invaluable assistance. Leon Fink, David Howell, Marcel van der Linden and Craig Phelan have made very helpful comments. David Montgomery has offered his customary enthusiasm, expertise and constructive advice. Versions of the essay were delivered to the 113th Annual Meeting of the American Historical Association, Washington DC, January 1999, and the Autumn conference of the Society for the Study of Labour History, University of Nottingham, November 1999. I am grateful to conference participants for their comments.

Notes

1. AF of L, *Procs.*, (1903), 193.

2. AF of L, *Procs.*, (1903), 196-198.

3. AF of L, *Procs.*, (1904), 185-186.

4. Julia Greene, '"The Strike at the Ballot Box": The American Federation of Labor's Entrance into Election Politics, 1906-1909', *Labor History*, 32,2 (Spring 1991), 165-192; idem, *Pure and Simple Politics: The American Federation of Labor and Political Activism 1881-1917* (Cambridge, 1998)

5. Stuart B. Kaufman (ed.), *The Samuel Gompers Papers*, vol. 1, *The Making of a Union Leader 1850-86* (Urbana, 1986), 211,213.

6. Kaufman, *Gompers Papers*, 468.

7. See Joseph Finn, 'The Great Debate, 1893-1894: A Study of the Controversy on Independent Political Action in the American Federation of Labor in the first half of the 1890s', Unpubd. MA, University of Warwick, 1969; Stuart B. Kaufman and Peter J. Albert (eds.), *The Samuel Gompers Papers*, vol. 3, *Unrest and Depression 1891-94* (Urbana, 1989), 419-422, 435-437, 442-445, 611-661.

8. As revealed in debates during the AFL's 1894 convention, it was highly questionable as to whether the British TUC had actually gone down this road, at least in a sustained and continuous manner. See Kaufman and Albert, *Gompers Papers*, 611-612, 619-620, 634-641 for the views of Gompers, Morgan and Strasser and the acrimonious exchanges between Strasser and Morgan. As we will see in due course, the fortunes of independent labour politics and collectivism within the TUC were mixed during the 1890s.

9. Finn, 'Great Debate', 174.

10. 'Gompers President',95-7, 'Trade Unions and Party Politics', 183-185, 'Excerpts from the Minutes of the Executive Council of the AFL', 241, in Stuart B. Kaufman, Peter J. Albert, and Grace Palladino (eds.), *The Samuel Gompers Papers*, vol. 4, *A National Labor Movement Takes Shape 1895-98* (Urbana, 1991); Finn, 'Great Debate', 206, 224, 226.

11. 'To Thomas Mann', in Kaufman and Albert, *Gompers Papers*, 504-505.

12. Stuart B. Kaufman, *Samuel Gompers and The Origins of The American Federation of Labor 1848-1896* (Westport, 1973); Michael Kazin, *Barons of Labor: The San Francisco Building Trades and Union Power in the Progressive Era* (Urbana, 1987); Leon Fink, *Workingmen's Democracy: The Knights of Labor and American Politics* (Urbana, 1983); John H. M. Laslett, 'Samuel Gompers and the Rise of American Business Unionism', in Melvyn Dubofsky and Warren Van Tine (eds.), *Labor Leaders in America* (Urbana, 1987); Greene, *Pure and Simple Politics*.

13. See, especially, Seymour M. Lipset, *American Exceptionalism: A Double Edged Sword* (New York, 1996) for such a structuralist account of a basically unchanging picture of American 'exceptionalism'. See also Lipset and Gary Marks, *It Didn't Happen Here: Why Socialism Failed in the United States* (New York, 2000). See John H.M. Laslett's *Colliers Across the Sea: A Comparative Study of Class Formation in Scotland and the American Midwest 1830-1924* (Urbana, 2000), for an historically-informed emphasis upon the key importance of 'the logic of the open franchise' and the largely accommodating and pragmatic character of the 'existing two-party system' in shaping the AFL's policy of non-partisan lobbying.

14. Kazin, *Barons*; David Montgomery, 'Machinists, the Civic Federation and the Socialist Party', in his *Workers' Control in America: Studies in the History of Work,Technology and Labor Struggles* (Cambridge, 1986), 48-90; Eric Foner, 'Why is There No Socialism in the United States?', *History Workshop Journal*, 17 (Spring 1984).

15. Kirk, *Challenge and Accommodation*, 244.

16. For the successful application of such a method to the study of Australian history see R.W. Connell and Terry Irving, *Class Structure in Australian History* (Melbourne, 1980).

17. For example, Gwendolyn Mink contrasts the political independence of the post-Taff Vale labour movement in Britain with the movement of its American counterpart 'more deeply into middle-class coalition politics': *Old Labor and New Immigrants in American Political Development: Union Party and State 1875-1920* (Ithaca, 1986), 36-7. In fact, the turn to independent labour politics in

Britain (ie. politics independent of the two main parties) preceded the Taff Vale case of 1901. The AFL leadership did not define their 'independent voting' stance as either 'middle class' or 'coalition politics'. In her book *Labor Visions and State Power: The Origins of Business Unionism in the United States* (Princeton, 1993), Ch. 1, Victoria C. Hattam also exaggerates differences in the political trajectories and legislative demands of the British and US labour movements, especially before 1906 when the Labour Representation Committee had not yet formally assumed the title of the Labour Party. Finally, John Laslett gives the somewhat misleading impression that Gompers and the AFL were opposed to independent labour politics per se, as opposed to independent labour politics *of a party kind*. In so doing, Laslett also tends to exaggerate the political differences between the AFL and the TUC during the period from the 1890s to 1906. See Laslett, 'Samuel Gompers', especially 62, 73-4. For further investigation and substantiation of these points see the material presented below under the headings, **The Comparative Context** and **What Kind of Politics?**

18. Although Henry Pelling, in his *American Labor* (University of Chicago Press, Chicago, 1960), did make brief reference to the importance of the British model of trade unionism and political lobbying for Gompers and the AFL: see 82, 115-116. See also Kirk, '"Peculiarities" versus "Exceptions"'. For consideration of the wider similarities and differences between labour in the United States and Britain see John H.M.Laslett, 'State Policy Toward Labour and Labour Organizations, 1830-1939', in Peter Mathias and Sidney Pollard (eds.), *The Cambridge Economic History of Europe*, vol. 8, *The Industrial Economies: The Development of Economic and Social Policies* (Cambridge, 1989), 495-548; Gary Marks, *Unions in Politics: Britain Germany and The United States in The Nineteenth and Early Twentieth Centuries* (Princeton, 1989).

19. For an effective critique of the thesis of US exceptionalism see Sean Wilentz, 'Against Exceptionalism: Class Consciousness and the American Labor Movement', *International Labor and Working Class History*, 26 (Fall 1984). For the new 'revisionism' which questions 'traditional' class-based arguments in relation to British working-class history, see, Eugenio F. Biagini and Alastair J. Reid (eds.), *Currents of Radicalism: Popular Radicalism, Organised Labour and Party Politics in Britain 1850-1914* (Cambridge, 1991); Duncan Tanner, *Political Change and The Labour Party 1900-1918* (Cambridge, 1990). For a critique of this 'revisionism' see Neville Kirk, *Change Continuity and Class: Labour in British Society 1850-1920* (Manchester, 1998), Intro., Chs. 4,8.

20. See John Breuilly, 'Comparative Labour History', *Labour History Review*, 55, 3 (Winter 1980), 6-9; John H.M. Laslett's review of Roger Fagge's book, *Power Culture and Conflict in The Coalfields*, in *ILWCH*, 53 (Spring 1998).

21. The following section on similarities relies heavily upon Kirk, *Challenge and Accommodation 1850-1939*, Ch. 1.

22. *The Labour Party Foundation Conference and Annual Conference Reports 1900-1905*, Hammersmith Reprints of Scarce Documents No. 3, The Hammersmith Bookshop Ltd. (London, 1967), 98.

23. *Labour Party Foundation Conference*, 65.

24. For a US labour report on the activities of the Parliamentary Committee of the TUC see *American Federationist*, III, 8 (October 1896), 165.

25. From the 1870s onwards the 'labour interest' in the House of Commons had been represented by a 'small, but distinct' group of Lib.-Lab. MPs. Sitting in parliament as labour members, the Lib.-Labs. nevertheless 'sat on the Liberal benches ... and took the Liberal whip', an expression of 'their enduring belief in liberalism as a political faith and in the Liberal party as the means to achieve social and political reform'. Proud of their 'humble origins, lack of formal education, and experience of working at a trade from an early age', Lib-Labs. such as Thomas Burt, Alexander Macdonald, and Sam Woods had been 'professional trade union officials and labour organisers'. Strongly representative of coal mining trade unionism, this group of MPs opposed the move to independent labour representation in the 1890s and 1900s TUC, while simultaneously describing themselves as 'a distinct Labour group' and even as 'the first "Labour Party"'. See John Shepherd, 'Labour and Parliament: the Lib.-Labs. as the First Working-Class MPs, 1885-1906', in Biagini and Reid, *Currents*, 187-213.

26. AF of L, *Procs.*, (1898), 43-4.

27. *Report of The Thirty Second Annual Trades Union Congress: Plymouth 1899*, National Museum of

Labour History, Manchester, England, 45.

28. *Labour Party Foundation Conference*, 37,64-65, 69.

29. AF of L, *Procs.*, (1904), 112, 122.

30. AF of L, *Procs.*, (1905), 138.

31. TUC, *Report*, (1899), 66.

32. 'An Article in the *New York Herald*', Jan. 7, 1894, in Kaufman and Albert, *Gompers Papers*, 445.

33. For examples of Gompers' employment of radical, class-based language see, AF of L, *Procs.*, (1893), 11,14, 15; *Procs.*, (1895), 17,59; *Procs.*, (1899), 15; *Procs.*, (1906), 32; *American Federationist*, 1,6 (August 1894), 120-125, 1,10 (December 1894), 228; Kaufman and Albert, *Gompers Papers*, 514-515.

34. 'To the Delegates at the 1894 Convention of the National Alliance of Theatrical Stage Employes', in Kaufman and Albert, *Gompers Papers*, 518.

35. 'To Eugene Debs', Kaufman and Albert, *Gompers Papers.*, 562-3, 521-525.

36. AF of L, *Procs.*, (1896), 86-87.

37. AF of L, *Procs.*, (1899), 15, 148.

38. See chapter three below.

39. The following section is indebted to Neville Kirk, 'American "Exceptionalism" Revisited: The Case of Samuel Gompers', *Socialist History*, 16 (2000), especially 17-18.

40. 'Excerpts from Samuel Gompers' Testimony before the U.S. Strike Commission', in Kaufman and Albert, *Gompers Papers*, 569-574.

41. See, for example, AF of L, *Procs.*, (1893), for the full preamble.

42. *American Federationist*,V,1 (March 1898), V,3 (May 1898); AF of L, *Procs.*, (1898), 5-6. There is plentiful evidence to suggest that Gompers remained, during the period under review, committed, in principle if much less in practice, to the workplace organisation of women, black workers and many European immigrants, both the 'old' and, far more infrequently, the 'new'. He was, however, exclusive and racist in his attitude towards 'Orientals'. For his views on these matters see, for example, *American Federationist*, VI, 4 (June 1899) for Gompers' letter to Lady Dilke praising her efforts on behalf of the organisation of women workers; AF of L, *Procs.*, (1900), 92, concerning the organisation of women in trade unions *and* the 'domestic ideal'; *American Federationist*, V,7 (Sept. 1898), 138, VIII,4 (April 1901), 118-120, AF of L, *Procs.*, (1900), 12-13, (1907), 207-208 for racialised inclusive and exclusive strategies and tactics.

43. *American Federationist*, IV,6 (Aug. 1897), 115-16; Kaufman and Albert, *Gompers Papers*, 569.

44. For references to these wide or 'noble' trade-union goals see, for example, *American Federationist*, III,5 (July 1896), 90-1, III, 11 (Jan. 1897), 237, III, 12 (Feb. 1897), 259-260, IV,6 (Aug. 1897), 116, IV, 9 (Nov. 1897), 215, V,3 (May 1898), 53, V,5 (July 1898), 93, V,6 (August 1898), 107, V,7 (Sept. 1898), 139, V,9 (Nov. 1898), 179-180, V,10 (Dec. 1898), 203, VII, 3 (March 1900), 56-62; AF of L, *Procs.*, (1899), 16,148-9, (1905), 20-1 (Gompers' report), (1907), 21-3; 'Excerpts from Samuel Gompers' Testimony before the U.S. Strike Commission', in Kaufman and Albert, *Gompers Papers*, 57; David Montgomery, 'Labor and the Republic in Industrial America, 1860-1920', *Le Mouvement Social*, 111 (April-June 1980). The fraternal delegate system between the AFL and the TUC was set up in 1894 and had become firmly established by the turn of the century. For an expression of the 'solidarity of feeling and sympathy' and the 'strong bond of union' existing between the US and British labour movements, see Gompers' speech at the 1895 TUC Conference. TUC, *Report*, (1895), 48-49.

45. For the AFL's and Gompers' attitudes to race and racism see, in addition to the references in footnote 42, *American Federationist*, IV,9 (Nov. 1897), 216-17, V,5 (July 1898), 93-4; AF of L, *Procs.*, (1906), 24,26,142, 179; Kirk, 'American "Exceptionalism" Revisited', 9; Philip Foner, *Organized Labor and The Black Worker 1619-1981* (New York, 1982), Chs. 5,6,10,12; Eric Arnesen, 'Charting an Independent Course: African-American Railroad Workers in The World War I Era', in Eric Arnesen, Julie Greene and Bruce Laurie (eds.), *Labor Histories: Class Politics and The Working Class Experience* (Urbana, 1998), Ch. 11; idem, *Waterfront Workers of New Orleans: Race Class and Politics 1863-1923* (Urbana, 1991).

46. Philip S. Foner, *History of the Labor Movement*, Vol 2: *From the Founding of the American*

Federation of Labor to the Emergence of American Imperialism (New York, 1975), Chs. 26- 7; Kirk, 'American "Exceptionalism" Revisited', 3.

47. AF of L, *Procs.*, (1899), 6 (Gompers). For the languages of accommodation, progress and conflict see *American Federationist*, IX, 2 (Feb. 1902), 70-71,IX,3 (March 1902), 111; AF of L, *Procs.*, (1899), 6-7 (Gompers' report), (1900), 7, 12 (Gompers), (1906), 63 for the treasurer's report on 'marked progress', (1907), 22-4 for trade union gains.

48. AF of L, *Procs.*, (1907), 17, 21-3.

49. *American Federationist*, XV,4 (April 1908), 261-262.

50. *American Federationist*, XVI,2 (Feb. 1909), 101.

51. Kirk, 'American "Exceptionalism" Revisited', 18-20; Gregg Andrews, *Shoulder to Shoulder? The American Federation of Labor The United States and The Mexican Revolution 1910-1924* (Berkeley, 1991).

52. Kirk, 'American "Exceptionalism" Revisited'.

53. However, see Alastair J. Reid's spirited defence of the 'old- unionist' leader, Robert Knight, as being more progressive and radical than suggested by the Marxist or marxisant historigraphical tradition in Britain: 'Old Unionism Reconsidered: The Radicalism of Robert Knight, 1870-1900', in Biagini and Reid, *Currents*, Ch. 10.

54. Lawrence B. Glickman, *A Living Wage: American Workers and The Making of Consumer Society* (Ithaca, 1997). I am grateful to Larry Glickman for a copy of his book.

55. See, for example, Ray A. Markey, 'The 1890s as the Turning Point in Australian Labor History', *ILWCH*, 31 (Spring 1987), 77-88.

56. Kirk, *Challenge and Accommodation*, 62-7.

57. Growing, if far from smooth, socialist influence upon the trade-union movement is revealed in the TUC *Reports* for the 1890s, consulted at The National Museum of Labour History, Manchester, England. Particularly useful is *History of The Congress: The Twenty Seven Previous Meetings*, contained in the *Report of The Twenty-Eighth Annual TUC*, Cardiff, 1895. Reports back to the annual conventions of the AFL by American fraternal delegates to the TUC also provide interesting, if somewhat partial and sometimes inaccurate, reading of an anti-socialist and nonpartisan character. See, for example, AF of L, *Procs.*, (1895), 56-8, *Procs.*, (1898), 44-5. See also *American Federationist*, III,8 (Oct. 1896), 165; Eric J.Hobsbawm, *Labouring Men: Studies in the History of Labour* (London, 1964), Chs.9-14; E. H. Hunt, *British Labour History 1815-1914* (London, 1988), 309-311.

58. The following section on US labour is based on Kirk, *Challenge and Accommodation*, 115-144.

59. See Shelton Stromquist, 'United States of America', in Marcel van der Linden and Jurgen Rojahn (eds.), *The Formation of Labour Movements 1870-1914: An International Perspective*, vol. 2 (Leiden, 1990), 564-567; Kirk, *Challenge and Accommodation*, 231-234.

60. *Labour Party Foundation Conference* 8-9, 12-13.

61. *Labour Party Foundation Conference* 109.

62. See AF of L, *Procs.*, (1898), 6.

63. 'President Gompers' Report', Dec. 10, 1894, in Kaufman and Albert, *Gompers Papers*, 611-612.

64. 'An Article in the *New York Herald*', in Kaufman and Albert, *Gompers Papers*, 444.

65. Kaufman and Albert, *Gompers Papers*, 611-612.

66. See Gary M. Fink, 'The Rejection of Voluntarism', *Industrial and Labor Relations Review*, XXVI, 2 (Jan. 1973). It should also be noted that beyond our period the AFL did, in 1909, 1911, 1912 and 1913, endorse 'a need-based national pension scheme'. See Ann Shola Orloff and Theda Skocpol, 'Why not Equal Protection? Explaining the Politics of Public Spending in Britain, 1900-1911, and the United States, 1880-1920', in David Englander (ed.), *Britain and America: Studies in Comparative History 1760-1970* (New Haven, 1997), 260.

67. For example, Victoria Hattam tends to neglect those British traditions of voluntarism and suspicion of the state pioneeringly reconstructed by Henry Pelling and recently observed by Alastair Reid, and James Hinton. See Hattam, *Labor Visions*, 6-7; Henry Pelling, *Popular Politics and Society in Late Victorian Britain* (London, 1979), Ch. 1, esp. 12-13; Reid, 'Old Unionism', 238-243; James Hinton, 'Voluntarism versus Jacobinism: Labor, Nation and Citizenship in Britain, 1850-1950', *ILWCH*, 48

(1995), 68- 90.

68. Kim Voss, *The Making of American Exceptionalism: The Knights of Labor and Class Formation* (Ithaca, 1993).

69. Kirk, *Challenge and Accommodation*, 57-8, 131-50; Roger Fagge, *Power Culture and Conflict in the Coalfields: West Virginia and South Wales 1900-22* (Manchester, 1996); Montgomery, *The Fall*, 240, 269-275, 288-9, 318-327, 387-399, 407-410.

70. Kirk, *Change*, Chs. 4 and 8 for working-class Conservatism; TUC, *Report*,1895, 27-8, *Report*, 1899, 65.

71. Montgomery, 'Labor and the Republic', 214-215.

72. Kirk, *Challenge and Accommodation*, 51-57.

73. In successfully criticising an *exaggerated* notion of discontinuity, Reid and Biagini, however, underestimate the full nature and extent of changes associated with the rise of independent labour politics. Contrary to the revisionist claim, the birth of the Labour Party cannot adequately be explained solely or even mainly in terms of the narrow issues of the payment of MPs, Liberal failure to select working-class candidates and Taff Vale. Rather, as demonstrated earlier, a range of wider, and often class- based, economic, political and cultural factors was also in evidence. It was a combination of such issues and factors which proved decisive. See Kirk, *Challenge and Accommodation*, 256-259; idem, *Change*, 192-198.

74. See, for example, the comments of delegate MacArthur at the 1894 AFL convention, in Kaufman and Albert, *Gompers Papers*, 620-1; Finn, 'Great Debate', 220; and Gompers' very instructive letter home to the AFL from his European trip in 1909, entitled 'President Gompers in Europe', and published in the *American Federationist*, XVI,12 (Dec. 1909), 1081- 86. This was one of a series of fascinating letters published in the *American Federationist* between August 1909 and March 1910 concerning Gompers' four month trip to Europe. The trip was undertaken 'largely for the purpose of making what observations of the working people's conditions which the time of my visit permits'. Published by Harper and Bros. in New York City in 1910, under the title of *Labour in Europe and America*, these letters constitute an important, but almost forgotten source, for students of comparative US, British and European history. They merit a reprint.

75. Kaufman, *Gompers Papers*, 21-43, 83-4.

76. See, for example, *American Federationist*, V,6 (Aug. 1898), 115, V, 11 (Jan. 1899), 220.

77. 'President Gompers' Report', in Kaufman and Albert, *Gompers Papers*, 611-612.

78. 'To Tom Mann', and 'An Interesting Discussion On A Political Programme', in Kaufman and Albert, *Gompers Papers*, 504, 619-620, 622. See also John Swinton's praise for the achievements of the English movement, reported in the *American Federationist*, 11,12 (Feb. 1896), 217.

79. 'To Henry Lloyd', July 2, 1894, in Kaufman and Albert, *Gompers Papers*, 516.

80. Kaufman and Albert, *Gompers Papers*, 516, 588; *American Federationist*, III,2 (April 1896), 33, III,3 (May 1896), 52, III,4 (June 1896), 71, V,2 (April 1898), 38, V,6 (Aug. 1898), 107-9, V,7 (Sept. 1898), 131, V,8 (Oct. 1898), 153-4, V,9 (Nov. 1898), 175-177; Fred Reid, *Keir Hardie: The Making of a Socialist* (London, 1978).

81. See *American Federationist*, III,2 (April 1896), 33, III,3 (May 1896), 52.

82. *American Federationist*, III,4 (June 1896), 71.

83. See, for example, *American Federationist*, IV,6 (Aug. 1897), IV,7 (Sept. 1897), 132, 139-140, V,I (March 1898), 10-11, V,2 (April 1898), 37-8.

84. *American Federationist*, V,11 (Jan. 1899), 220.

85. At the 1894 convention Gompers had accused some of the socialists of casting doubt upon 'the virtue and honesty' of trade union leaders such as himself and of being a 'disruptive' influence within the labour movement. Strasser labelled the socialists anti-union 'cowards', 'denouncers' and 'splitters' of trade unionism throughout Europe and the United States. See Kaufman and Albert, *Gompers Papers*, 624-6, 639-641. For conflicts between Gompers and the socialists within the AFL during the 1900s see, for example, AF of L, *Procs.*, (1902), 178- 184, (1903), 188-198, (1904), 185-6, 196-198, 240.

86. Gompers, *Seventy Years of Life and Labour: An Autobiography*, 2 vols. (New York, 1967), vol. 1,

381-4.

87. Kaufman and Albert, *Gompers Papers*, 588. Hardie's highly personal, as well as political, attacks on the Old Unionists, Henry Broadhurst and Sam Woods, did not figure in Gompers' somewhat idealised accounts of Britain's labour leaders. See Shepherd, 'Labour and Parliament, 196.

88. Kaufman and Albert, *Gompers Papers*, 504,516.

89. For Curran's views see *Justice*, 2,9 Feb., 1901; *Labour Leader*, 2 Feb., 14 Nov., 1901; 'Industrial Outlook in Great Britain', in *American Federationist*, VIII,7 (July 1901); David Howell *British Workers and the Independent Labour Party 1888-1906* (Manchester, 1983), 114-115. For Tillett and Mann see, for example, *American Federationist*, 1,1 (June 1894), 65-6, IV,8 (Oct. 1897), 196, IV,11 (Jan. 1898), 264.

90. *American Federationist*, II,9 (Nov. 1895), 159-160.

91. Kirk, *Challenge and Accommodation*, 44, 136-139, 246; Christopher L. Tomlins, *The State and The Unions: Labor Relations Law and the Organized Labor Movement in America 1880-1960* (Cambridge, 1985), Ch. 3; Leon Fink, 'Labor, Liberty and the Law: Trade Unionism and the Problem of the American Constitutional Order', *Journal of American History*, 74,3 (Dec., 1987), 914-918.

92. Kirk, *Challenge and Accommodation*, 43-45, 246-247.

93. AF of L, *Procs.*, (1896), 9.

94. AF of L, *Procs.*, (1906), 31-3.

95. AF of L, *Procs.*, (1906), 21-2, 32-3.

96. Fink, 'Labor, Liberty and the Law', 918-919.

97. Marc Karson, *American Labor Unions and Politics 1900-1918* (Carbondale, 1958), 21,30.

98. For examples of such gains see *American Federationist*, V,2 (April, 1898), 23; AF of L, *Procs.*, (1904), 240-241, (1906), 191.

99. AF of L, *Procs.*, (1906), 34, 198, 203.

100. *American Federationist*, XV,5 (May 1908), 341, XV,13 (Dec. 1908), 1065.

101. *American Federationist*, VI,2 (April 1899). For a similar claim see *American Federationist*, V,4 (June 1898), 74.

102. *American Federationist*, XV,13 (Dec. 1908), 1065; Greene, *Pure and Simple Politics*.

103. AF of L, *Procs.*, (1899), 14. See also AF of L, *Procs.*, (1896), 10, (1900), 17-19; *American Federationist*, IX,8 (Aug. 1902), 433.

104. Fink, 'Rejection of Voluntarism', esp. 114 ff.; Kazin, *Barons*, esp. Chs. 6,7; Greene, *Pure and Simple Politics*.

105. Fink, 'Rejection of Voluntarism', 116; Kazin, *Barons*, esp. Chs. 8,9; Stromquist, 'United States of America', 571-577; Laslett, *Colliers*, Chs. 7,8; Kirk, *Challenge*, 44, 140, 142.

106. For a guide to the voluminous literature see Kirk, *Change*, 192-198.

107. Robin Archer, 'Why is there no Labour Party? Class and Race in the United States and Australia', in Halpern and Morris, *American Exceptionalism?*, 57.

108. Hattam, *Labor Visions*, ix, 3-6: William E. Forbath, *Law and The Shaping of The American Labor Movement* (Cambridge, Massachusetts, 1991); Gerber, 'Shifting Perspectives on American Exceptionalism', 261-2.

109. AF of L, *Procs.*, (1902), 129-30.

110. Karson, *American Labor Unions*, 52-5.

111. AF of L, *Procs.*, (1907), 128.

112. For the rather confusing legislative state of play at the 1894 and 1895 AFL conventions see Finn, 'Great Debate', Ch. 6; AF of L, *Procs.*, (1895), 81-82, 99-100; *American Federationist*, 1,11 (Jan. 1895), 254; Kaufman and Albert, *Gompers Papers*, 616-659 n. 9.

113. Notwithstanding considerable local labour-movement support, Gompers remained opposed to minimum-wage legislation for both sexes, believing that the minimum wage might become the maximum wage.

114. Karson, *American Labor Unions*, 43; AF of L, *Procs.*, (1906), 187,190; *American Federationist*, IV,11 (Jan. 1898), 257, V,2 (April 1898), 33-35; David Montgomery, *Citizen Worker: The Experience of Workers in the United States with Democracy and the Free Market during the Nineteenth Century*

(Cambridge, 1995), 148-150.

115. Stromquist, 'United States of America', 557-558; Fink, 'Rejection of Voluntarism', 114- 126. David Montgomery is currently investigating US labour and socialist attitudes to the issue of state social-insurance provision, and especially the transformation in socialist attitudes, from one of seeming neglect in the early 1890s (socialism as the cure for poverty) to one of full endorsement for old-age pensions and the like by the early 1900s.

116. Kazin, *Barons of Labor*, 114-120, 155.

117. Montgomery, *Citizen Worker*, 149, n.76.

118. AF of L, *Procs.*, (1905), 177, 232. Philip Taft, *The A.F. of L. in The Time of Gompers* (New York, 1970), 292; *American Federationist*, V,2 (April 1898), 34-5.

119. See, for example, *American Federationist*, V,1 (March 1898), 17; IX,4 (April 1902), 185, IX,5 (May 1902), 233-4.

120. *American Federationist*, 1,1 (March 1894), 11.

121. *American Federationist*, IV,12 (Feb. 1898), 274, V,3 (May 1898), 55-56, V,5 (July 1898), 94.

122. *American Federationist*, V,3 (May 1898), 55-56, V,4 (June 1898), 73-74.

123. AF of L, *Procs.*, (1904), 187.

124. Greene, 'Strike at the Ballot Box', 170.

125. AF of L, *Procs.*, (1908), 34.

126. AF of L, *Procs.*, (1906), 100-2, 183-204 for extremely interesting observations and debates on domestic and external political and trade union developments during 1906.

127. AF of L, *Procs.*, (1906), 120-4, (1907), 131-2.

128. AF of L, *Procs.*, (1907), 134.

129. AF of L, *Procs.*, (1907), 127-131.

130. AF of L, *Procs.*, (1906), 100-2.

131. AF of L, *Procs.*, (1906), 101.

132. *American Federationist*, XVI,8 (Aug. 1909), 661, XVI,12 (Dec. 1909), 1077, 1086. For the AFL's 'workerist' opposition to 'intellectuals' and 'entangling alliances' see *American Federationist*, XVI,10 (Oct. 1909), 883; 11 (Nov. 1909), 965, 12 (Dec. 1909), 1077.

133. *American Federationist*, XVII,2 (Feb. 1910), 151, XVII,3 (March 1910), 225, 243.

134. *American Federationist*, XVI,12 (Dec. 1909), 1086; XVII,1 (Jan. 1910), 55-61.

135. For Walker's fascinating career see Laslett, *Colliers Across The Sea*, Chs. 7,8.

136. Andrew Strouthous, *US Labor and Political Action 1918-24: A Comparison of Independent Political Action in New York Chicago and Seattle* (London, 2000).

Chapter 2

The Australian 'Workingman's Paradise' in Comparative Perspective, 1890-1914 *

Overview

For the Left and many historians, the nineteenth- and early twentieth-century notion of a 'workers', 'workman's' or 'workingman's' 'paradise'[1] under capitalist conditions of production, distribution and exchange is a contradiction in terms. As members of a subordinate social group within capitalist society, workers – whether black or white, men or women, skilled or unskilled – have been noted in the historical literature far more for their unceasing attempts to 'make ends meet' and to achieve recognition, respect and, where possible, modest advancement, than for the pursuit and attainment of great wealth, status, power and influence. Poverty was both widespread and chronic among nineteenth and early twentieth-century workers throughout the capitalist world. Institutional progress was limited and uneven, with labour movements fighting recurrent battles for survival, recognition and influence.

To be sure, the twentieth century as a whole, and more particularly the period since 1945, has witnessed significant working-class and labour-movement gains. These have been reflected, for example, in improved living standards and general opportunities in life – the expected attainment for many of the 'US standard' in North America and the family-based 'living wage' in Australia, and the onset of 'mass affluence', at least in relative terms, in post-Second World War Britain. In addition, there has been the marked growth and rise to power of mass labour movements and their labour and socialist parties. Yet against such gains we must set the crushing blows dealt to labour movements by European Fascism in the inter-war period and the enduring successes of deep-seated and militant employer anti-unionism endeavours in the United States. Attention must also be drawn to the current ascendancy of neo-liberal ideology – complete with its messianic belief in the necessary triumph of capitalist globalization and its fundamental opposition to organised labour's traditional collectivism – and the dogged and profound persistence within capitalist societies of patterns of absolute and relative poverty, deprivation, and inequality of opportunity. Moreover, the dominant aim of labour and socialist governments, at least in western Europe and Australia, has been, in practice, to 'civilise' or 'humanise' rather than to transform capitalism.

In sum, generally speaking, both labour movements and working classes have constituted far more of a subordinate, if at times challenging and by no means totally passive and incorporated, presence within capitalism rather than a transforming or hegemonic force.[2] A key assumption of much of the historical literature is that this condition of subordination has rendered the attainment of 'real' working-class emancipation, the creation of a 'true' 'workers' paradise', objectively impossible under the conditions of nineteenth- and twentieth-century capitalism, indeed into the foreseeable future. As a corollary, claims to paradisaical status are often said to have rested, and continue so to do, more upon 'myth' and 'rhetoric' than upon 'reality'.[3]

However, the very existence of such claims, made over time and in a variety of places, suggests a case for their further investigation rather than their neglect or summary dismissal. This case is strengthened by the fact that representations of personal and social life, such as the idea of the 'workingman's paradise', constitute as much a part of reality as do people's actions and their structured conditions of experience. It is the *interplay* between, on the one hand, agency, representation and consciousness and, on the other hand, conditioning, structure and behaviour which excites the curiosity and invites detailed historical investigation.[4]

It is with these considerations in mind that this chapter addresses itself to an examination of the notion of late nineteenth- and early twentieth-century Australia as a 'workingman's paradise'. The chapter is structured in the following way. I begin with an outline and evaluation of the ways in which the term 'workingman's paradise' was employed both within and outside Australia. I then turn to a consideration of the Australian case between the onset of the mass industrial conflicts of the 1890s and the outbreak of the First World War. This specific focus in turn opens up more general questions and issues concerning the overall nature, aims and development of labour movements and the working classes in our chosen comparative contexts of Australia, Britain and the United States. On the basis of the evidence examined, I reach six main conclusions. First, while not promising absolute paradise, Australia was widely held to offer workers and labour organisations opportunities for growth and advancement not enjoyed to anything like the same extent in the 'old world' of Britain and western Europe and the increasingly 'moneyed' 'old' New World of the United States. Second, Australian workers and labour movements recovered extremely quickly from the massive setbacks of the 1890s readily to seize their opportunities. As Stuart Macintyre observes, they demonstrated extremely impressive and, comparatively speaking, very *precocious*[5] development – in terms of trade unionism, independent labour politics, working and living conditions and standards and the establishment of a strong and predominantly class-based culture – between the late 1890s and 1914. Third, the reasons for Australian labour's precocity, indeed vanguard position in terms of international labour movement development, resided in that country's 'traditional' economic structure, the largely united, disciplined, well organised and ably led nature of 'the movement' itself, the relative homogeneity of the working class, and the favourable opportunities for labour's growth provided by the political conjuncture of the 1900s (Federation and national settlement or class reconciliation following the conflict-ridden 1890s). Fourth, I argue, on the basis of these advances, that the *national* imprint of workers and their organisations – on state structures and patterns of national culture and consciousness – was far more profound in Australia than in both Britain and the United States. Fifth, the ideological imprint offered by Australian labour was a veritable mixture of pragmatism and 'respectable' labourism, transforming and visionary thought (including socialism), and class and 'populism'. Strong support for the notions of the male breadwinner and separate spheres for men (public) and women (private) existed alongside limited and uneven pragmatic acceptance of a place for women in the labour movement. Australian labour also warmly embraced the notion of progressive and 'classed' nationalism. This notion was combined with opposition to 'coercive imperialism', and yet growing support for Australia's 'mature' and 'independent' presence within the increasingly 'enlightened' British empire.[6] A highly racialized, indeed racist, view of Australia and the world beyond also constituted a core feature of labour's eclectic ideology. Sixth, while recognising the imperfections of their country, many white working-class males, and especially those involved in the labour movement, did believe that Australia in 1914 was truly on the way to becoming 'God's Own Country' and themselves 'God's Own People'.[7]

Questions of Usage

It is a well known fact among Australian historians that resort to the notion of Australia as a paradise for workers was most pronounced during the period of the 'long boom' between the Victorian gold rushes of the 1850s and the mounting financial speculation and material expectations of the late 1880s. During this period labour was generally in short supply and, notwithstanding the harshness and isolation of life in the bush and instances of both rural and urban poverty, insecurity and poor working and living conditions, aggregate working-class living standards in Australia were among the highest, maybe *the* highest, in the world.[8]

Yet references to the notion of Australia as a 'workingman's paradise' both preceded and post-dated the boom years. According to Richard White, Henry Kingsley's novel, *The Recollection of Geoffrey Hamlyn*, published in 1859, contained the 'first recorded use' of the phrase 'Workingman's Paradise'.[9] Indeed it had been during the course of the twenty or so years preceding 1859 that Australia was transformed, in the eyes of British Chartists and other radicals, from a place of 'Horrible Destitution' – a dumping ground for domestic convicts, including radicals, and a source of 'wealth and power which the rich could exploit to boost their ascendancy in the class struggle' – to a land of opportunity, 'virtually a working-class paradise'.[10] As Alan Beever and Paul Pickering have shown, the dominant view of Australia to emerge in the pages of the *Northern Star, Reynold's Newspaper* and other organs of the mid-century British radical press was that of a country possessing 'vast potential' for 'ordinary people', her fine climate and natural resources being accompanied by abundant opportunities for the attainment of highly paid work, social mobility, independence, political democracy and general escape from the stifling class structure of Britain.[11]

During our chosen period of study of the post-boom years between 1890 and 1914, Australians in general, and the labour movement in particular, became far more circumspect and qualified in their references to their country as a 'workingman's paradise'. This mood of circumspection, indeed questioning and doubt, was induced by the chastening experiences of the 1890s, especially mass unemployment and the major industrial defeats in the maritime, pastoral and mining industries. The recuperation, indeed remarkable 'forward march' of the labour movement between 1900 and 1914, combined with a general, if uneven and limited, improvement in living standards, helped to lift much of the gloom of the 1890s. The phrase, 'workingman's paradise', continued to be employed by Australian labour movement activists and some of those in positions of power between 1890 and 1914, indeed beyond our time frame,[12] although far less frequently and uncritically than during the boom years. We will also observe that both reference to, and debates surrounding, the notion of Australia as a workers' paradise concurrently became very marked among a string of foreign labour movement observers and visitors. These included Samuel Gompers of the AF of L, the French socialist, Albert Metin, numerous German middle-class reformers, moderate labour politicians and revolutionary Marxists, leading British labour movement figures such as Sidney and Beatrice Webb, Margaret and Ramsay MacDonald, Keir Hardie, Tom Mann, Dora Montefiore and veteran Irish Republican and land campaigner Michael Davitt. Their interest was part of a wider western European and North American fascination with the Australasian 'social experiment' of advanced social-welfare legislation and enhanced state intervention and regulation either as a proposed cure for the ills of capitalism or as a means of socialist transformation.[13]

Beyond the shores of Australia, the term 'workingman's paradise' was used with reference to other current and former 'settler colonies'. For example, labour movement activists in South Africa both corresponded with and shared their Australian counterparts' strong desire to build a 'white' wall around their projected 'workers' paradise'.[14] Notwithstanding the weakness of its labour and socialist movements, late nineteenth- and early twentieth-century New Zealand, with its regulatory and social-welfare Liberalism very much to the fore, was quite often claimed to be the most complete 'workingman's paradise' to date.[15]

In related, if generally far more defensive fashion, the desire to preserve or redeem the power and will of 'the workers' and/or 'the people' in the face of the 'monopolistic' and 'selfish' desires and depredations of capital, constituted a key feature of artisan republicanism throughout the nineteenth-century USA.[16] By the

1900s the USA was becoming *the* paradise for corporate capital rather than 'the people', 'the producers' or 'the workers'. Yet claims to instances of a 'people's' and 'workers' paradise and power were still to be found. For example, the powerful building unions in 1900s San Francisco saw themselves as constructing an urban and potentially state-wide 'commoners' paradise' rooted in working-class political, economic and cultural hegemony. In the face of resurgent, united and anti-union capital, this claim proved to be short-lived.[17] Samuel Gompers pitched his claims higher. His four-month trip to study labour movements and working conditions in Europe in 1909 led him to two conclusions. First, that the American Federation of Labor had overtaken its British and European counterparts to become *the* leading trade union power in the world in terms of 'unity and compactness of organization, progressiveness of propaganda, thoroughness and clearness in scope of purpose, militancy of spirit, soundness in finances, adaptability in administration to the ends sought, or continuity and rapidity of development'.[18] Second, that the independent-minded, assertive and relatively well paid and treated American 'people', and especially the organized 'people', still had a much greater influence upon the shape, character and direction of their country than did the generally poor proletarian 'hewers of wood and drawers of water' of Europe and Britain.[19] In actual fact, the power and influence of the late 1900s AF of L would prove to be ephemeral, and hegemony in US society and politics as a whole manifestly rested not with organized labour but with predominantly anti-union capital and its political and ideological allies.

As argued by Richard White in relation to Australia,[20] and as implied in the previous two paragraphs, the term 'workingman's paradise' has not for the most part been employed in a purely neutral, and we may add consensual and objective, manner. Rather general issues of subjectivity and relativity – manifested in the specific areas of power, contestation, self interest and ideology – have been to the fore. For example, during the 'long boom' the term 'workingman's paradise' signified not only good working and living conditions, but also, in the eyes of some, the 'rule' of labour over capital. While this presumed state of affairs was a matter for congratulation in some labour circles, it frequently occasioned dismay and displeasure among those more sympathetic to the claims of capital. Thus in 1886 the *Australian Magazine* opposed 'The insolent demands continually made by the Australian working-man upon his employer, whom he insists upon regarding as his subordinate, if not his slave'. While the 'working-man' had achieved his aims 'of thirty years ago' to 'make labour respectable and respected', yet 'at this moment' he ' is secretly hated by everyone not of his own class; for he is selfish, wilful, narrow-minded, truculent, and, what is perhaps worse than all, generally unintelligent and technically unprogressive'.[21] Writing in the *Nineteenth Century* in 1891 on the subject of 'The Seamy Side of Australia', the Hon. John W. Fortescue agreed: 'The working man is supreme in Australia, and cares for nothing, so his wages, raised to an artificial height in the old days of scanty population and discoveries of gold, remain undiminished'. High wages had been extracted at the expense of the capitalist, and the urban labour unions, although 'admirably organised', were 'very powerful, very rapacious, and very unscrupulous'.[22] By way of marked contrast, the British socialist, Henry Hyde Champion, in the course of his infamous attack upon the 'ass-like' trade-union leadership in his 1891 article 'The Crushing defeat of Trade Unionism in Australia', could not contain his enthusiasm for the opportunities available to, and the power of the worker in the colony. 'Imagine', wrote Champion,

> a society in which there is hardly a man whose father did not work for his living with his hands; where there is practically no leisured class, and the comparative absence of poverty does away with the need for a Poor Law; where there is universal suffrage and payment for members, and every politician trembles at the labour vote.

Champion's glowing, but exaggerated, claims went further: a 'nominal' eight-hour day in the towns and 8-10 shillings as 'a customary daily wage'; employer inducements to scarce agricultural and pastoral labour of 'three meat meals a day and a wage that will allow any single man who does not drink to excess to save £20 per a year'; and shearers' wages 'which in six weeks exceed the yearly income of the agricultural labourer in Dorset or Essex', and which 'if used with moderate care, will in a short time make them wealthy men'.[23]

However, this putative state of affairs could not last indefinitely. According to the *Australian Magazine*, the 'greedy' and 'self-interested' worker, little concerned with anything and anyone beyond 'the attainment of his own material ends', would eventually get his just deserts and 'the much-tried capitalist will have his revenges' (sic).[24] Indeed, it was during the severe depression which blighted the entire decade of the 1890s that the 'revenges' of massive unemployment, want and suffering, employer counter-attacks, labour movement defeats and the 'restructuring' of significant sectors of (especially craft) production took place.

It was in this context of class-based 'reckoning' that the Bristol-born socialist, William Lane, who had arrived in Queensland in 1885 'after a newspaper career in Canada and the United States', published his 'bitter-ironic' novel, *The Workingman's Paradise*, in 1892, under the pseudonym John Miller. Lane's purpose in writing the novel was threefold: to demonstrate the hollowness of Australia's claims to be a 'workers' paradise', with particular reference to living and working conditions in Sydney; to 'raise funds for the families of imprisoned unionists' during the shearers' bitter and unsuccessful fight against the pastoralists' employment of 'free labour' in 1891; and to 'draw out the socialist message' of the 1891 strike.[25] However, the socialist 'message' was to be transplanted elsewhere. Despairing of the situation in 'old' Australia, Lane 'called on the disenchanted to uproot themselves and sail to a new place, where a society based on socialist principles and simple mateship could be founded'. In July 1893 he, along with over two hundred other white Australians, left behind what they perceived to be the failed potential of Australia preposterously to create their socialist paradise in Paraguay, a 'tiny, war-ravaged land where revolutions and dictatorship were endemic, social reforms virtually unknown, the climate inhospitable, amenities of life few, transport difficult and the language incomprehensible to the newcomers'.[26] Some seventeen years later, in the northern aspect of the American 'New World', another socialist, Upton Sinclair, similarly wrote a 'bitter-ironic' piece entitled 'The Workingman's Paradise', for the New York *Call*, which graphically exposed the appalling working and living conditions endured by predominantly 'new' immigrant workers in Sam Gompers' celebrated 'people's America'.[27]

Self-interested and contested usages and meanings of the term, the Australian 'workingman's paradise', were by no means confined to the second half of the nineteenth century. From the beginning of assisted migration from Britain to Australia in the 1830s up to the end of our period, emigration societies, official government recruiting agencies and agents, at times sections of the 'capitalist press' in both countries (to draw off 'excess' labour from the 'mother country'), and colonial and Commonwealth employers, had a strong pecuniary interest in boosting labour emigration.[28] The Australian authorities at least, were also desirous of encouraging emigration from Britain of the 'right type' – 'respectable' and 'industrious' as opposed to 'pauper' labour – and maintaining and extending the 'purity' of the 'British race'.[29] But within these 'moral-economic' and openly racist constraints, the authorities, the press and employers were prone to exaggerate the climatic and socio-economic attractions of the 'workingman's paradise' in order to attract a sufficient supply of labour.

While equally concerned to ensure the 'right' moral-economic and racial flow of immigration, nevertheless large sections of the labour movement consistently and frequently viewed such exaggeration as a cynical device, a prelude to the importation of cheap labour. The latter, it was believed, would undermine the hard-won conditions and gains of Australian labour and erect a barrier against the achievement of the (white) 'workingman's paradise'.[30] For example, in 1908 the main organ of the labour movement in western Australia, the *Westralian Worker*, denounced the 'guarantee' put out by the agent of the New South Wales government to workers in Scotland that Australia offered 'Regular Employment at High Wages', a 'Splendid Climate!' and 'Cheap Living!'. This was at a time when that very government 'cannot find work for its own people'.[31] In the same vein the Sydney *Worker*, in an article entitled 'South Australia: A Workers' Paradise', was critical of the 'capitalist press' for presenting a picture of that state's 'unexampled prosperity' in 1908, a picture which ignored unemployment and insecurity.[32] Three years later Alex McCallum, a leading figure in Perth's labour movement, wrote an article in the *Labour Leader* criticising the unduly favourable impression of employment opportunities in Australia drawn by the British press, and advising British workers to stay at home so as not to depress the Commonwealth's labour market.[33] Similar advice to intending emigrants was increasingly to be found in the journals of Australian printers and engineers in the immediate pre-First World War years.[34]

Strong ideological concerns and predispositions also greatly influenced assessments of whether Australia was or was in the process of becoming a 'workingman's paradise'. As we will see in more detail below, foreign revolutionary-socialist and syndicalist commentators on the Australasian 'social experiment' from Britain and continental Europe, were in agreement that the attainment of a 'workers' paradise', whether in Australia or elsewhere was, notwithstanding temporary improvements for sections of the working class and comparative international advantage, ultimately an impossibility under capitalism. Their negative assessment has become, in large measure, the received historical wisdom identified at the very beginning of this chapter. By way of contrast, reformist socialists and advanced or 'new' Liberals, complete with their gradualist and evolutionary emphases, tended to be far more optimistic about the Australians' chances of permanently resolving class conflict and their progress on the path to 'emancipation', if not a complete paradise on earth.[35] However, some of the more moderate socialists also suggested that the price of comparative international comfort for the Australian worker was the widespread adoption of the habits and values of 'bourgeois respectability', of, as Metin put it, the realization of 'English middle-class ideals'.[36]

From the very different ('British') trade-union perspective of voluntarism, 'free' collective bargaining and deep suspicion of state intervention and regulation, Sam Gompers and his leadership colleagues in the AF of L could not bring themselves remotely to consider Australia as a 'workingman's paradise'. To be sure, decent working and living conditions had been won by Australian workers. However, Australia's state-led arbitration system signalled not freedom but rather 'industrial despotism'. As Gompers concluded in his 1915 article, 'Australasian Labor Regulating Schemes',

> The New South Wales system of regulating industrial relations with all its authority and power makes provision for all industrial problems *except industrial freedom*. The *judicial despotism* which rules over industry maintains many of the principles and practices which the workers of the United States of America have persistently denounced and opposed. *Instead of being a workers' paradise, New South Wales is rather a paradise for lawyers.* There is nothing in the system of governmental regulation of industry as developed in New South Wales that is in conformity with the spirit or the genius of the people of the United States.[37] (emphases added)

To draw the reader's attention to these issues of subjectivity and relativity is to suggest that we must be attentive to the complexities involved in attempting accurately and truthfully to describe and interpret verbal representations of social life. In particular we should be wary of a one-dimensional or 'face-value' reading which argues that words simply and literally 'mean what they say'. As demonstrated in the examples given above, the very words, 'the Australian workingman's paradise', could and at times did carry different and contested meanings for different individuals and social groups. However, I am *not* thereby suggesting the futility of pursuing questions which seek to evaluate the standing of verbal representations as purportedly true and accurate statements about the world. At the same time I do maintain that the truth, accuracy and meanings of verbal representations emerge not in a narrowly self-referential and idealist manner solely from words themselves. Rather they emerge as a result of a tough-minded and contextualised engagement between, on the one hand, the structured conditions of existence of the representer and his or her representations and, on the other hand, the social world represented, of which he or she is a part and a judge or interpreter. This process of engagement involves close attention to an *ensemble* of words, actions and their intended and unintended consequences, structures or 'experience' (both conscious and unconscious), values, ideas, events and processes. In sum, it comprises an evolving dialogue between 'culture' and 'structure'.[38] It is important to identify these guiding and relatively abstract assumptions, procedures and propositions at this juncture because they consistently inform the substantive body of the text.

Sources and Objectives

My substantive concerns are set into dialogue with a body of evidence which draws upon a range of Australian, British and, to a much lesser extent, US sources.

In terms of the Australian material – my main source of evidence – I have relied most heavily upon the labour movement press. Two newspapers in particular, the *Westralian Worker* and the *Worker*, have commanded most of my attention. The former, a weekly, started life in 1900. It billed itself as being, the 'Pioneer Labor Paper of the State', 'Owned by Trades Unions and Conducted in the Interests of Labor'. Experiencing a 'somewhat chequered' early career, the *Westralian Worker* nevertheless gained prominence in the towns of Kalgoorlie, Coolgardie and other parts of the newly-established and mushrooming western goldfields. A strong supporter of socialism, the Labor Party, 'new' unionism and class solidarity, the paper also provided a welcome and lively platform for the discussion of gender-based politics. However, the language of class inclusion was circumscribed by the boundaries of race. For example, the desired emancipation of 'workers of the world' was largely limited to workers 'of our own race'.[39]

The *Worker* began life in March 1890 under the editorship of William Lane. Published as separate editions in Sydney and Brisbane, the paper became the weekly organ of the most important trade union in Australia, the Australian Workers' Union, a 'new union' of 'catch-all' ambitions, formed in 1894 as a result of the amalgamation of the Amalgamated Shearers' Union and the General Labourers' Union. The AWU, in turn, became the dominant influence upon the Australian Labor Party, in terms of leadership, organisation, financial donations, and delivery of the country vote.[40] By the late 1900s the *Worker* had, according to a leading, if partisan, authority, 'the largest circulation of any weekly in Australia'.[41] The tradition of socialist leadership and ideology, combined with outright racism, initiated by Lane, was continued in the editorship of the Brisbane *Worker* (1902-1911) and later the Sydney *Worker* (1914-1943) by the Liverpool-born Henry Ernest Boote, 'the most outstanding Labor journalist in Australia'.[42] The secretary (1894-8) and subsequently president (1898-1917) of the AWU, William Guthrie Spence, had likewise emigrated from Britain to become a veteran trade unionist, *the* driving force behind the creation of the inclusive AWU, a visionary socialist, a committed teetotaller and a fierce advocate of White Australia.[43]

I have concentrated my focus on these two newspapers because of their heavy influence and appeal among organized workers. (Each member of the AWU received a free copy of the *Worker.*) In addition, they are seen to be partly, but by no stretch of the imagination totally, representative of the interests and outlook of organised labour, and especially labour in the pastoral, rural and mining sectors, in the western and eastern parts of Australia.[44] However, whenever possible, I have also consulted other journalistic organs expressive of or sympathetic to 'the claims of labour', for example, the *Bulletin* and the *Champion*,[45] in order to present a more rounded picture. Achievement of this goal has been further aided by the investigation of a range of predominantly urban, eastern and southern, trade union and friendly society sources; and much invaluable and geographically wide-ranging autobiographical and biographical material contained in both primary and secondary sources.[46]

In moving beyond the Australian sources, the labour and socialist press, especially in Britain and to a much lesser extent in the USA, constitutes a very rich source of information on 'movement' attitudes in those countries towards both Australia as a 'workingman's paradise' and the Australian labour movement. When read in conjunction with official labour movement reports, such as those of the British Trades Union Congress (TUC) and Labour Party, and autobiographical and biographical material, organs such as the *Labour Leader*, the *Clarion, Justice* and the *American Federationist* provide many illuminating insights into the Australian experience.

In setting my substantive concerns and questions to these sources, I aim to realise the objective of making an original and worthwhile contribution to arguments concerning Australia as a 'workingman's paradise'. This contribution resides in widening the substantive nature of debate, in bringing new questions, sources and perspectives to bear upon it, and in presenting new findings.

Traditionally, both supporters and opponents of the notion of the Australian 'workingman's paradise' have rested their central claims upon the subject area of working and living conditions. My purpose is further to investigate this area. However, it is also to extend and deepen the nature of the relevant subject area and its terms of debate to include, as contemporary labour movement people did, matters concerning the shifting fortunes of workers, their leaders and their institutions, their individual and collective prospects of recognition and advancement, the nature and claims of workers' cultures, and the impact of 'the movement' upon the life of the nation as a whole.

As noted earlier, the perspectives of a number of foreign observers of the Australasian 'social experiment' are reasonably well known, mainly through the medium of published books. However, their views and those of other foreign labour-movement activists in the socialist and labour press concerning Australia as a 'workers' paradise' – including the characteristics and fortunes of its workers and labour movement – have barely been addressed in the secondary literature. Somewhat surprisingly, much the same can be said about the attitudes towards the 'workingman's paradise' of many contributors to the labour movement press and other labour movement sources *within* Australia. Australian attitudes have mainly been derived, far too narrowly, from a few literary sources, such as Lane's novel, and the, admittedly fascinating and insightful, writings of the famous 'bush' writer and poet, Henry Lawson.[47] This chapter aims both to fill some of the gaps in the literature and to advance our understanding of the issue of the 'workingman's paradise', by duly recapturing and presenting to the reader these important, yet neglected and forgotten, foreign and domestic 'voices of labour'.

I also wish to draw the reader's attention to the crucial importance of carefully listening to and critically evaluating the pertinent views or 'voices' of contemporaries in general. For, in truth, such voices are insufficiently heard in much of the secondary literature on the topic of the 'workingman's paradise'. They are either muffled or even silenced by the preoccupations and prescriptions of the authors themselves. Whether political commentators or academics, these authors have all too often fought the battles of their present – reformism versus revolution, socialism versus pragmatic 'realism', class versus 'populism' or whatever – over the heads and voices of the dead. However, it is with the neglected voices of labouring people and the labour movement, properly set within their own contexts, values and terms of reference, that this chapter specifically concerns itself.

Investigation: Nature and Findings

Due attention to these contextualised voices lends itself to an examination of four substantive areas: Australia's promise as a 'new' country; working and living conditions; labour movement advancement; and organised labour's impact upon national life, including the movement's ideological impact. I will now move to a presentation of the nature and results of my investigation into these respective areas.

1. The Promise of a 'New' Country and Labour's 'Manifest Destiny'

In ways reminiscent of attitudes towards the young American republic in the late-eighteenth and early-nineteenth centuries, there was general agreement among 'advanced' foreign and domestic commentators that, as a 'new' country, Australia offered abundant, and to some extent unprecedented and unparalleled, promises and challenges, both for its workers and its citizenry as a whole. However, as in the north American case, indeed numerous other colonies of white 'settlement', the indigenous peoples, in this instance the aboriginal people who had lived in Australia for thousands of years, were effectively denied citizenship and dispossessed of their land, sometimes very violently.[48] In company with most other Australians, the vast majority of labour-movement people maintained that the 'uncivilised' aboriginals would soon become extinct. The fiction of 'terra nullius' – of an 'empty' continent prior to white 'settlement' – was invoked to justify dispossession. The charge of being 'uncivilised' and 'savage' was used to sanction white brutality, the destruction of aboriginal culture, their removal to reservations and the separation of large numbers of Aboriginal children from their families from 1910 onwards (the 'stolen generations'). Their presumed lack of 'intelligence, interest or capacity' invoked to deny them the vote under Federation. It was within this highly racialized framework of aboriginal separation and exclusion , allied to the official adoption of the White Australia policy in 1901, that Australia's promise was couched.[49]

Perceptions of promise and opportunity were extended to most areas of life. Above all, Australia was seen, unlike the Old World, to be very advanced, indeed increasingly a beacon to the world, in the ways of democracy, openness and mobility (both geographical and occupational); social advancement on the basis of 'industry, merit and worth' rather than 'aristocratic' birth, connection and patronage ; and of the, albeit gendered, egalitarianism of 'mateship'. The snobbery, class-based distinctions, 'patrician visage' and deference of much of Britain and Europe were likewise rejected. As Manning Clark wrote of Australians during this period,

> They prided themselves on their emancipation from the Old World errors and lies about class: they boasted that Australians 'call no biped lord or sir, and touch their hats to no man'. They were New World egalitarians. Yet paradoxically they were not strangers to the vices of domination. They were passionately committed to the domination of the white man over all other people.[50]

In terms of those foreign commentators who also possessed first-hand knowledge of Australian conditions, the views of Tom Mann merit special attention and respect. Already a veteran of the 'new' unionist, socialist and independent labour agitations in Britain during the 1880s and 1890s, and a well respected figure in labour-movement circles worldwide, Mann played a prominent role in the Australian labour movement during the 1900s. In 1902 he became paid organiser for the Political Labor Council of the Melbourne Trades Hall, the forerunner of the Labor

Party in Victoria. Active throughout the state, Mann 'personally organised some fifty country branches of the Labor Party'. However, he was increasingly critical of the limitations of 'labourism' and gave up the organising post in 1905. By the latter date he was urging the necessary and urgent progression from labourism to socialism. Indeed in 1906 he was a key figure in the establishment of the Victorian Socialist Party, becoming in turn editor of its journalistic organ, the *Socialist.* A superb propagandist and inspirational writer and speaker, Mann was very active in a number of working-class 'grass-roots' campaigns, including the fight for 'free speech' in Melbourne in 1906 and 1907 and the Broken Hill industrial dispute of 1908-9. Mann suffered imprisonment as a result of his involvement in both these campaigns. He left Australia at the beginning of 1910 to return to Britain via South Africa. According to Joseph White, Mann's experiences in Australia, and especially the workers' defeat at Broken Hill, had convinced him that 'to aim for political solidarity prior to, and at the expense of , industrial solidarity was doomed to failure'. Henceforward, the way forward would reside 'chiefly in Industrial Unionism' allied to 'Revolutionary Socialism'.[51]

Notwithstanding his growing criticisms of the Australian Labor Party's moderation and racism, and his belief, shared with comrades in the SDF, that a 'workman's paradise' and capitalism were incompatible, Mann continued to argue throughout his 'Australian years' that the country was very, indeed perhaps the most, favourably placed among nations to facilitate and expedite the 'Forward March of Labour' and the triumph of socialism.[52] For example, in 1903 he wrote, 'Young Australia has glorious opportunities of being to the front in this world's struggle', and 'everything worth having is obtainable'.[53] Similarly in the following year: 'Fate has decreed that these Australian states shall be the forerunners in a really triumphant democracy'.[54] As late as September 1909 Mann's criticisms of Australia's unemployment and poverty and the deficiencies of labourism were more than offset by his positive emphases upon the relative abundance of opportunities and paucity of obstacles there. Moreover, 'The Socialists are at work steadily and persistently, and their work is telling, and telling well, too'.[55]

It is also interesting to observe that Mann subscribed to the notion, common among both British and Australian socialists and labourites, that it was Australia's position as the world's most advanced political democracy that augured well for the transition to social and economic democracy, to socialism.[56] Both Ramsay MacDonald and William or 'Billy' Hughes, future Labour Prime Ministers of their respective countries, saw Australia as *the* beacon of political democracy.[57] Despite its criticisms of Australian support for British imperialism and the imperative need to advance from political to the 'full' democracy of common ownership,[58] the Marxist *Justice* was in agreement. Thus, in 1901 the Australian colonies were described as being 'the most democratic ... in the whole world', enjoying 'security of personal and political freedom' and possessing 'neither standing army, nor navy, nor aristocracy, nor Established Church'.[59]

Another socialist schooled in Britain, Henry Champion, was resident in Melbourne and one of Mann's key allies in the Victorian socialist movement during the 1900s. Champion was similarly enthusiastic about the possibility of change of a progressive kind and the opportunities for workers' individual and collective advancement in Australia. Writing in the *Labour Leader* in 1909, he maintained that 'temporary setbacks', such as the defeat of the Australian Labor Party (ALP) at the federal level by the combined forces of Liberalism and Conservatism, could not disguise the fact that Australia offered far more exciting and plentiful, if somewhat fluctuating, opportunities than conservative Britain. 'Imagine', declared Champion,

> a country where there is no 'upper class', as you style it in England – that is to say, none whose great-great grandfathers always lived by drawing on the workers. Imagine fortunes so uncertain that the bankrupts of twenty years ago are the millionaires of to-day ... Imagine a country where amongst the 'news of the day' you read of a boy picking up a bottleful of nuggets worth from £60 to £70. Such a people don't mind changes, and are not afraid of them. Clearly it will be a country worth watching.[60]

The views of Mann and Champion were frequently endorsed by foreign labour-movement and other radical visitors. For example, in 1898 Michael Davitt drew attention to the absence of 'ruling classes' in Australia, and to the fact that, as a result of male universal suffrage, Australian Conservatism 'has to be more democratic in its professions and programmes than an opportunist English liberalism dares yet to be'.[61] In the same year Sidney Webb discovered in Australia 'all the political conditions and institutions which by many people were put down to Radicalism and Democracy', with none of the evils of bribery and corruption 'which accompany them in America'. [62] During his six months visit in 1899 Albert Metin, then a 'brilliant, young, radical-minded student of the Sorbonne', was impressed with the relatively advanced and 'thriving' state of Australia. This was manifested in all the six colonies' legislative assemblies 'made up of paid members elected by universal suffrage'; the vote for women in parliamentary elections in South Australia (achieved in 1894); and the 'translation into reality, [in] more than any other British country, the traditional slogan of English workers: Eight Hours to Work, Eight Hours to Play, Eight Hours to Sleep, and Eight Bob a Day'.[63]

Many of the reformist and revolutionary German socialists turning their gaze upon Australia shared the view expressed in 1906 by Kathe Lux that within the 'new' land of Australia – with 'tradition non-existent, and the absence of conservative elements in the population' – 'factors that tend to retard progress are eliminated'.[64] Certainly Margaret MacDonald, like many other visitors, was impressed with the opportunities presented for women's progress in Australia, as compared with the situation in more conservative Britain. For example, the fact that women were voting in a parliamentary election (having gained the Commonwealth franchise in 1903) moved MacDonald to declare, during a visit to Women's Leagues in

Western Australia in early 1907, 'It really is very refreshing to see adult suffrage in full swing, and we felt very envious of the advanced democratic machinery which Australia has secured'.[65]

In an article published in *Fabian News* in the following year, Sir John Cockham, a former Premier of South Australia, pushed the gender-based claim further. Thus,

> Throughout Australia, the principle of the participation of women in public life was universal, and universally accepted as a necessary and salutary outcome of democracy.[66]

Cockham's claim was exaggerated. After all, many of Australia's 'advanced' social-welfare measures and ideas of this period, including the maternity allowance and the concept of the 'living wage', the latter famously enunciated by Justice Higgins in 1907, were consciously designed largely to confine women to the private sphere of the home as wives and mothers.[67]

Moreover, the continuing practices of plural and property-based voting at the municipal level provided an effective bulwark against the attainment of 'full' local democracy. Conversely, the general attainment of adult suffrage, cheap elections and the payment of members *did* constitute sufficient evidence of the existence of that 'advanced democratic machinery' suggested by MacDonald. (By 1909 women had also gained the vote in all states.) Indeed, both Margaret and Ramsay MacDonald derived 'fresh zest and fresh enthusiasm' for the tasks of building complete democracy and socialism at home from 'our visit to the Antipodes'.[68]

The view expressed by radical foreign visitors – of Australia as a 'new land of opportunity', in conscious revolt against the worst features of the 'aristocratic' Old World – was mirrored in, indeed in large measure derived from, the very strong and continuing tradition of class-based radical nationalism within Australia itself. During the late 1880s, 1890s and early 1900s Henry Lawson played a prominent part in both shaping and expressing this tradition. Lawson was born into the labouring family of Peter and Louisa Lawson (originally Larsen) in the Mudgee hills, west of Sydney, in 1867. His father gained a living mainly from carpentry and building, but also had experience of being a sailor, gold digger and selector (small farmer). His mother, a housewife, left the bush in 1883 after the failure of the marriage. She arrived in Sydney 'to work for the elevation of women', becoming well known in that city as a socialist-feminist.[69] As a boy and young man Henry turned his hand to a variety of rural and urban labouring jobs, including factory work in Sydney, and frequently experienced considerable difficulty and hardship in making a decent living. In Sydney he was also strongly influenced, from 1883 onwards, by republicanism, socialism and humanitarianism.[70]

Two of Lawson's early publications, *A Song of the Republic* (1887) and *Freedom on the Wallaby* (1891), illustrate these influences. In the former the 'Sons of the South' were exhorted to 'awake! arise!' and,

Banish from under your bonny skies
Those old-world errors and wrongs and lies.
Making a hell in a Paradise
That belongs to your sons and you.

They were also given a choice between,

The Land of Morn and the Land of E'en,
The Old Dead Tree and the Young Tree Green,
The Land that belongs to the lord and the Queen,
And the Land that belongs to you.

Victory awaited an activated people:

Sons of the South, aroused at last!
Sons of the South are few!
But your ranks grow longer and deeper fast,
And ye shall swell to an army vast,
And free from the wrongs of the North and Past
The land that belongs to you.[71]

In the latter, Lawson predicted that the struggles of the 'fathers' and the sins of Britain's exploitative and tyrannical past would redound to Australia's freedom and glory:

Freedom on The Wallaby

Our fathers toiled for bitter bread
While idlers thrived beside them;
But food to eat and clothes to wear
Their native land denied them.
They left their native land in spite
Of royalties' regalia,
And so they came, or if they stole
Were sent out to Australia.

They struggled hard to make a home,
Hard grubbing t'was and clearing.
They weren't troubled much with toffs
When they were pioneering;
And now that we have made the land

A garden full of promise,
Old greed must crook his dirty hand
And come to take it from us.

But Freedom's on the Wallaby,
She'll knock the tyrants silly,
She's going to light another fire
And boil another billy.
We'll make the tyrants feel the sting
Of those that they would throttle;
They needn't say the fault is ours
If blood should stain the wattle.[72]

The theme of Australia as being 'uniquely situated' and so bearing a 'unique destiny' for the future wellbeing of mankind as a whole, figured prominently in the pages of the *Worker*. In 1910 the Sydney *Worker* pretentiously expressed the matter thus:

Never before in the history of the world since Athens, the Violet City, made Greece what she was, and is, have a little people and a great problem been so set face to face.

The Australian was,

an old world development faced by new problems; possessing a vast continent as his birthright ... His heart and brain are enriched by the noblest idea since Christ – to correct its social mistakes of the past, to clothe the naked, to feed the hungry, to house the outcast. Born of pioneers, he is a pioneer – a pioneer of Humanity, Justice, Fellowship, Love.[73]

The Brisbane *Worker* was equally effusive in its claims. Thus 'No nation of the past, no Power of the present' could 'vie with Australia in wealth of chances'. The 'old countries', having 'to look backward for their glory', were placed in 'the cruel position of being incapable of reaping the harvests that in blood and tears they have sown'. The 'parasitic growth of centuries' had 'overrun the ground':

Aristocracies have twined tenacious tendrils round the State. Ancient orders, establisht (sic) churches, entrencht (sic) fortunes, racial hatreds, hereditary interests – all these block the way.[74]

By way of marked contrast, Australia was relatively free from these impediments:

No aristocracy of birth, no State chartered clerical order, no military caste dominated

their destinies or marred their advance. The people were practically of one class differentiated only by the possession of a greater or lesser amount of wealth.[75]

Infused by her advanced 'social-reforming' and 'democratic spirit', and her 'people of one race, with thoughts and feelings in common', Australia, 'alone of the
nations of the earth', was thus 'free to avail herself of the world's experience':
Australia 'gazes ahead, to an horizon all effulgent'.[76]

It was true that the way ahead was not completely clear. There remained the task
of removing the remaining 'Old World' features of 'patrician haughtiness' and
'groveldom' *within* Australia. Although lacking 'the genuine article to form a true
blue caste', Australia, according to the *Worker* in 1910,[77] had something worse:
'their butlers and their footmen and their valets', a body of 'flunkeys' who were
'even more exclusive than the lords', more 'aristocratic' than the aristocracy in
Britain, a new 'snobility'. Seeking to 'constitute themselves an electro-plated peer-
age', members of this group,

> are becoming landed proprietors, and are truckling and cringing to the
> Imperial authorities for tinpot titles. And they have their shoddy aristocratic
> customs – their 'smart sets' and their 'bridge parties', and their yachts and
> their motor-cars, and their pet poodles and their racehorses'.

The democratic egalitarianism, embodied in Australian notions of 'mateship' and
'a fair go', were anathema to the 'snobility'. Expressing 'haughty disdain' for the
'multitude', the 'rabble', they were appalled by the swift rise of the class-based
labour movement, especially the ALP, to a position of national power and influence:

> That the workers should rule is a thought that rankles in their hearts. That a Labour
> party should make or dictate laws to which *they* have to submit, is bitterness inex-
> pressible.

Notwithstanding the official standing of the White Australia policy, the continued
desire of the 'snobility' was, in the opinion of the *Worker*, 'to flood the country
with the coloured alien, who doesn't understand the meaning of independence,
and is willing to take many kicks and demand few halfpence!' In such a manner
did the *Worker* (consistently and repeatedly) express that curious mixture of class
consciousness and unrepentant racism, the latter rooted in both economics and
personal 'capacity', highlighted in chapter three below.[78]

Labour thus bore a heavy responsibility to defeat the large pastoralists (the
'squattocracy') and those Liberal protectionists and the Anti-Socialists (formerly
Freetraders) who were combining or 'fusing' politically to check 'the progress of
Australia towards the social and industrial supremacy of the people' in the interests

of 'privilege and monopoly'.[79] Equally, there was a strong duty to safeguard the 'purity' of Australian democracy against the 'bribed leaders and corrupt statesmen', and the 'money power' which were in the process of disfiguring the US 'people's' democratic experiment. Once ruled by the 'money power', declared the *Worker*, 'the Democracy … ceases to be a Democracy and becomes a plutocracy'. Australia, 'having escaped from Monarchy', had to 'base the State on the hopes and needs and aspirations of the people'.[80]

Expressive of the democratic, egalitarian and racist perspective of the Australian labour movement as a whole, the outlook of the *Worker* was also in tune with that of many radicals who had imported the legacy of British radicalism into Australia. To provide one example. In October 1912 the *Clarion* carried a two-part article, entitled 'Australia and its Socialism', by Henry Fletcher.[81] 'Horrified at the ever present and appalling misery', Fletcher had left his native London for Canada, and later Australia, some thirty years earlier. Proud of his Chartist ancestry in the person of his grandfather,[82] Fletcher nevertheless denounced the British as 'conservative' and 'thick-headed'. Australian had exceeded all Fletcher's expectations. It was 'startlingly free' and anchored in the rough equality of mateship. There was an absence of deference, there being 'no reverence for money, position or birth'. The clergy were regarded 'in a genial way' as 'blokes trying to earn a crust at a poor tucker game'. Workers were independent-minded and resourceful, with opportunities for upward mobility, and feared neither the boss nor the sack. Indeed, the main danger to the future advance of socialism in Australia lay in the 'easy-going contentment' of the people.

As in the case of the *Worker*, Fletcher's view was highly racist. Thus,

> So far only the best of the white race have shown that they are so far advanced in mental evolution as to be successful democrats. Coloured men have regularly failed. For these reasons and others, Australia will not admit the coloured man. Our creed is 'The Brotherhood of Race'.

Fletcher urged 'sleepy Britishers' to emigrate. Australians would 'wake you up, and make you worthy citizens of this great land, the 'only all-white continent', destined to become 'the leader of the world'. In turn, the welcoming hand was offered to Canadians and north American 'serfs' of private railroads and trusts.

Finally, both the *Worker* and Fletcher shared the widespread belief that the labour movement constituted *the* means whereby Australia would further advance and fulfil her destiny. For Fletcher Australia's 'Labour Socialists' had 'already done much that you in Britain are trying to do'.[83] 'Summing up the unique chances of Australia', observed the *Worker*,

> it is in her Labour party that they centre. It is by means of this instrument, lying right to hand, that she will be able to convert her opportunities into achievements.[84]

The key question for my purposes is: To what extent had these opportunities *already* been coverted into sufficient achievements to constitute a 'worker's paradise'? To substantively begin to answer this question we must consider our findings concerning living and working conditions.

2. Working and Living Conditions

As seen most dramatically, enduringly and often acrimoniously in the 'classic' British case of the period of the 'Industrial Revolution', generalisations about working-class living and working conditions, standards and experiences during the early period of industrial capitalism constitute a perilous undertaking. The often patchy and incomplete nature of the evidence, the relative strengths, weaknesses and contested claims made on behalf of quantitative and qualitative sources ('hard' versus 'soft', 'objective' versus 'subjective' and so on), and the values and ideological predispositions of the historians involved in debate, have been among the important contributory factors to the longstanding, and still unfinished, nature of the debate in Britain.[85]

While less longstanding, the 'standard of living' debate in Australia, embracing the period from the 1850s to the First World War and, *ipso facto*, the issue of 'the workingman's paradise' at a time of the development of industrial capitalism, has also occasioned, both among contemporaries, historians and other investigators and commentators, considerable heat and dust. It is with the main features of this Australian debate, and the light thrown upon it by our evidence drawn mainly from Australian and foreign labour-movement sources, that this section concerns itself.

Most of the recent historiography has been strongly critical, and at times impatiently dismissive, of the notion of Australia as a 'workingman's paradise', *at least in any absolute sense*, during the period in question. Buckley and Wheelwrights' verdict, as expressed in their *No Paradise for Workers*, may be taken as representative of the current orthodoxy. Thus:

> Despite weaknesses, the ability of the Australian working class to extract a reasonable share of the total output of a highly productive economy in the years of the long boom led to claims of 'a workers' paradise'. These claims were exaggerated ... unemployment was not properly measured, much work was of a casual or seasonal nature, and although there were labour shortages in the countryside, each city had its 'reserve army of labour'. The extent of house ownership by the working class was exaggerated, especially in the cities, where it was costlier – in the countryside many houses owned by workers were of very inferior quality. Public health was neglected; infant mortality was high; the sewering of the cities did not begin until very late in the nineteenth century; even as late as 1900 there was an outbreak of bubonic plague in Sydney.[86]

Evidence selected from the 1890s and 1900s may also be cited in support of the pessimistic case. For example, the severe depression of the 1890s saw unemployment approach twenty-five per cent and, in 1893, 'a generalised banking failure' which 'wiped out the entire savings of most of the population'.[87] In the same decade much of the 'new' and sections of the 'old' trade unionism were decimated by employer attacks, the coercive actions of the state and the effects of the depression. Employers, faced with shrinking markets and declining profit margins, resorted increasingly to 'technological change' and 'productive re-organization'. According to Markey, the skilled and craft sectors were hit particularly hard by this accelerating process of capitalist transformation; while in the primary sector 'it became more difficult to fulfil the Australian dream of independence from wage-earning, on the land or as a miner'.[88] The latter phenomenon occurred in the face of continued agitation for improved access to the land, and the growth of an increasingly self-conscious small-farmer or 'selector' mentality and institutionalized presence.[89] It was also the case that much social mobility on the part of workers was sideways, rather than upward – in Markey's opinion an index more of 'economic insecurity' than real and permanent advancement.[90]

It is true that the period between 1900 and 1914 saw 'striking economic advance'. As Macintyre informs us, this was reflected in an 'almost twofold' increase in the value of Australian production, in the 'growth and diversification of the primary industries', in 'the rapid expansion of manufacturing', a general revival and advancement of wages and an increase in population from 3,825,000 to 4,941,000.[91] Nevertheless, wage standards 'did not make a sustained recovery until the very eve of the First world War', the distribution of personal wealth by occupation and occupational group was 'extreme', and 'the prosperity of the long boom, such as it had been, was not recovered in Australia until the 1940s'.[92] Moreover, at both the state and federal level, the arbitration system, with its bureaucratic procedures and delays, its 'costly legalism' and the appeal or even avoidance of its decisions by disgruntled employers, proved to be no panacea for industrial unrest. Indeed, the revival of serious and protracted industrial conflict between 1908 and 1912 was accompanied by anti-strike legislation, major labour defeats – most prominently at Broken Hill in 1909, among coalminers of New South Wales in 1910, and in the Brisbane general strike in 1912 – and organised groups of employers who were strikingly successful in their anti-labour and anti-reform appeals to the High Court. Justice Higgins's 'living wage' decision in the Harvester case of 1907 immediately met with a successful institutional challenge in the form of an appeal to the High Court on the part of a member of the Chamber of Manufactures against the constitutionality of the Excise Tariff Act. (In 1906 the government had introduced an excise duty on local products 'which would be waived if the Australian manufacturer paid his workers "fair and reasonable" wages'.) 'In short', declares Macintyre, 'the New Protection', guaranteed to render the 'living wage' an actuality, 'could not be institutionalized': the 'Harvester standard was not generally at-tained in awards until after the war'.[93]

The case against the paradisaical standing of both Australia and New Zealand receives strong support from the balance of evidence contained in contemporary labour-movement sources. For example, both activists in the Australasian and British labour movements and the respective labour and socialist publications keenly identified and sought widely to publicise problems in terms of living and working conditions in Australia and New Zealand. Such publicity, of course, was not purely disinterested. Labour-movement sources were concerned to debunk 'exaggerated' 'official' claims concerning favourable standards of life in those countries. As noted earlier, labour viewed these claims as 'false enticements', as a means of encouraging 'excessive' immigration and so undermining the hard-won gains and independence of the Australasian 'working man'. Yet I wish to suggest that the very frequency, depth and widespread nature of labour complaints concerning unsatisfactory conditions in the Antipodes meant that more than special pleading was at work.

Reference may be made to a selection of the numerous complaints contained in the Australian and British labour press in order to convey a sense of their overall character and aims. In January 1911 an editorial in the *Westralian Worker* maintained that the high cost of living in the booming infant goldfields of the West meant that a married man with a small family, regularly employed and taking home, at most, £3/5- per week, 'has no chance to save', his life being 'a miserable struggle to keep out of debt'.[94] This complaint was echoed, and indeed widened to include housing, leisure and environmental issues, in the 'Notes for Women' section and the 'Women's Page' of subsequent issues of the *Westralian Worker*. Fathers, 'as a rule', were thus 'too poorly paid to allow of any spare cash for luxuries'. 'Not more than 5%' of the homes of workers in Kalgoorlie and Boulder were claimed to be 'fit for this climate and for our conditions of life': they were 'unsightly ovens in the summer time and still more unsightly freezing chambers in winter'. 'Very few families' were said to have 'more than four rooms' and 'a bath room is out of the question'. As a result, 'real home life is impossible in these hovels'.[95] Beyond the home, the 'bleak' and 'ugly' environment made scant provision for the needs of women and families, and especially families with children. Elsie D. Emerson drew attention in the 'Women's Page' to the dearth of public 'gardens, lakes, museums, art galleries, amusements and recreations' in Kalgoorlie and Boulder. Even 'picture shows' and 'hand concerts' were 'beyond the means of most families'.[96] Drinking constituted both the main male leisure activity and source of family conflict and breakdown. Women's needs took second place to those of paid male work and male sociability. However, as seen in reports in the *Westralian Worker* on trade unionism, politics and campaigns for improved social-welfare provision, some women were increasingly active in the goldfields in asserting their powers of agency in the public sphere.[97]

Complaints that life was often little more than a struggle for existence in the 'workers' paradise', were to be found not only in the western goldfields, but also throughout Australia and beyond. Writing in the *Worker* in the depressed year of 1892, W. G. Spence noted that, as in Britain, 'thousands' of Australians 'were starving'.[98] Fifteen years later Thomas R. Morgan, General Secretary of the Industrial Employees Union, wrote from Australia to the *Labour Leader* to caution British miners against the 'glowing reports' put out by 'Australian capitalists' concerning 'the constant work and the high wages to be secured' in New South Wales. Those poor, unwitting miners who had recently arrived in the state 'now find that they can scarcely make a living wage, and are practically stranded in a strange land' – the victims of employers whose 'object ... is flooding the country with surplus labour'.[99] Similar cautions and laments – revolving around false promises and inflated hopes and expectations, and the reality of unemployment, poor wages, conditions of work, and restricted access to the land in Australia – appeared frequently in the other organs of the British labour press.[100] *Justice* was particularly scathing of 'exaggerated views' of 'magnificent conditions'. 'Do Not Emigrate!' and 'The Emigration Fraud' were typical headlines in the SDF's newspaper; and, in flat contradiction to the 'lies' of the *Times* in 1910: 'Conditions are as bad, and in many places worse, in Canada and Australia as they are here in England'.[101] For example, in 1899 *Justice* published a highly critical letter from a workman 'who has spent many years in Australia'. In the opinion of the correspondent, there was, in Queensland, much 'tramping' and unemployment, poor wages for navvying, preference shown to 'yellow, black and brindle' labour over 'white', and an unyielding climate that in 'ten years will dry a man up like a dried sheepskin'. In Tasmania women were to be found 'doing men's work', and many workers were 'overworked' and 'underfed'; while in New South Wales acute poverty and low wages were to be found in coalmining and quarrying.[102] Moreover, Australia, a land which promised free speech and freedom of movement, was not averse to banning labour marches, practising police surveillance, passing anti-trade union legislation and imprisoning 'freedom fighters' such as Tom Mann.[103]

Mann, himself, was among a chorus of labour movement figures who refused uncritically to sing the praises of working and living conditions in Australasia. Thus, while Mann held the adverse effects of capitalist industrialization to be less widespread and deep in 1900s Australia than in Britain, nevertheless the evils of unemployment and poverty were 'knocking at her door'.[104] In his lectures in Australia Mann consistently called for political 'realism' – an approach and philosophy constructed upon a full realisation of *both* the absolute and relative advantages and opportunities enjoyed by Australian workers, *and* the very real tasks ahead. Australian comrades were thus exhorted to fight against the continuing poverty, unemployment and oppression within their own country, to transform labourism into socialism, and more effectively to counter reports in the Australian newspapers 'as to statements emanating from London concerning the excellent conditions that exist here for workers'.[105]

In the course of his political and industrial work, Mann developed a close familiarity with, and became a fierce critic of, the specific problems of unemployment and poverty in Melbourne and other parts of Victoria.[106] As a result of their close contacts with Mann and their periods of residence in the city, Champion and Ben Tillett – the latter yet another veteran of British 'new' unionism who was attracted to Australia – also developed keen insights into Melbourne's continuing social problems. In drawing comparisons and contrasts between Melbourne and London in the 1899 May Day issue of *Justice*, Tillett declared:

> Melbourne has its miseries, its hovels, its dirt its bumbledom. The streets are full of the same sights – by night and day squalor and sin and rags ... shriek of the shrew, mad drunk, foul oath and indecent gesture, painted faces, gossip and scandal, an art that would put to shame even Mayfair.[107]

On his visit to Australia in 1908, Keir Hardie drew attention to the problem of youth unemployment in Melbourne and the fact that newly-arrived immigrants to Australia frequently had to 'rough it' for a while before settling into relatively secure employment.[108] Almost one year later, and notwithstanding subsequent ameliorative action on the part of the authorities, there were reportedly 'fully 4,000 men now out of work in Melbourne or working so casually that they do not get 10s a week, and only a small percentage get that'.[109]

Tillett, like Mann, was also critical of the racism of both Australian labour and the wider society. For example, the 'poor aboriginals' who 'had land for centuries', had become the victims of white contact, dispossession and 'European diseases': 'the white man has taken death and desolation, disease ... uncleanliness to these poor souls'.[110]

Finally, critical labour-movement comments were also directed at that other purported workingman's paradise in the southern hemisphere, New Zealand. In a piece in the *Labour Leader*, entitled 'New Zealand: God's Own Country!', Thomas Lowe, former secretary of the Hyde Labour Church, reminded intending emigrants that 'New Zealand has a capitalist Government and a competitive industrial system', complete with surpluses of labour in some sectors and 'much harder' work required in others than in the home country.[111] In *Justice* Fred Raper, a member of the New Zealand Socialist Party, penned a damning article, 'Wake up, New Zealand', in which 'God's Own Country' was equated not with paradise, but with overcrowding, poor labour conditions, anti-unionism and an arbitration system which was seen as a palliative to, rather than a solution for, exploitation at the workplace (a perception of arbitration common in left-wing socialist circles both in Australasia and Britain).[112]

Of consuming interest were the experiences in New Zealand of Mary Walker and her husband, also early recruits to the New Zealand Socialist Party, published in the *Labour Leader* in 1902. The couple had been compelled for most of their first year in New Zealand to 'rough it'. Notwithstanding the existence of the eight-hour day in some sectors of the economy, the Walkers worked hard and long, and for precious little reward. First there was a three months stint on a sheep station. There, Mary worked as a servant to 'the ladies of the house', and endured in the process 'one of the worst experiences I ever had in the way of work'. The couple then moved to become cooks in a hotel in Wellington which 'resembled a corner in Dante's inferno'. At the time of writing, in the early summer of 1902, the Walkers were still 'roughing it', and had come to the sobering conclusion that '"The working-man's paradise" will want the little word 'lost' added to it'.[113] A letter from R. Scott, also published in the *Labour Leader*, was in complete agreement. Formerly a member of the ILP in Edinburgh and now resident in Christchurch, Scott declared in 1903 that 'things in New Zealand are very far from being what they are represented to be', there being 'no signs, to my mind at least, of this country ever having been the paradise that we read of it being at home'.[114]

Yet however critical the labour press and labour leaders in Britain and Australia were of an undiluted picture of antipodean 'workingmen's paradises', it is crucial to record that this was by no means the whole story. For, as we will see below, the full weight of Australian and British labour-movement evidence strongly lends itself to the overall conclusion that, irrespective of their shortcomings, *actual* working and living conditions in Australia (and, we may add, New Zealand) were, on the whole, perceived to be better, and often *much* better, than comparable conditions in the Old World. In this sense Australia's unparalleled opportunities were, to a significant extent, seen to have been, or at least in the process of being, translated into reality. Crucial to this process of translation was the single-minded determination of men and women of the labour movement, whether native-born, well-established or recent immigrants, not to 'quit' in the face of difficulties, but to mould the New World in their own images.

However, before proceeding to a consideration of the primary sources, it is important to note that some of the secondary literature, including the work of many of those authors who have either partially or indeed wholly put forward, 'pessimistic' arguments, would support the thesis offered in the previous paragraph. For example, the foremost critics of the claim that Australia was a 'workingman's paradise', Buckley and Wheelwright, nevertheless make it clear in the text of their book, if not in their misleading title (*No Paradise for Workers*), that they are offering heavy qualification to, rather than an outright dismissal of, the claim. The claim, in its absolute form, is shown to have been 'exaggerated' rather than entirely without foundation. Furthermore, Buckley and Wheelwright concede that, in a relative sense, the claim did possess considerable truth. Thus:

> The formation of the working class is a crucial factor in the development of capitalism, for the conditions under which it is formed tend to set a 'floor' for the wage levels achievable. The conditions in Australia were very favourable. They included a perennial labour shortage, high productivity in rural industry because of abundant land and imported capital, and early trade unionization fostered by the British herit-

age of struggle by the common people. Consequently the wage levels achieved in Australia were amongst the highest in the world.... It is true that the common people were less downtrodden in Australia than was the case in Britain, Europe and the USA ... Average income per head in Australia was one of the highest in the world, so that colonial capitalism was successful in this respect.[115]

While duly recording the negative aspects of Australian living and working conditions, Stuart Macintyre, whose overall perspective and judgement on the 'standard of living' debate is admirably balanced, reaches the conclusion that workers, on the whole, were better off in Australia than in Britain:

The average Australian ate better, was better housed and lived longer than his British counterpart. Both consumed approximately the same amount of staples, bread ... and sugar ... but the Australian was the greater carnivore, putting away twice as much meat as John Bull ... and he had a much wider range of fresh fruit and vegetables. He lived in a house of five rooms, which he had almost a one in two chance of owning and which provided a room for every occupant. His cities contained slum neighbourhoods, but not the vast stretches of tenements and back-to-backs that disfigured Britain.

'Furthermore', continues Macintyre, by the early 1900s 'his lot was improving'.[116]

By way of contrast, Raymond Markey, another important contributor to the debate, reaches a largely negative conclusion. Against the 'optimist' viewpoint of colonial prosperity, expressed by the economic historian, N.G. Butlin, and the Australian New Left's similarly 'optimist' thesis that 'the Australian working class was pampered out of revolutionary socialism by British capital', Markey, much in the manner of Buckley and Wheelwright, strikes a note of 'strict qualification'. He rightly questions conclusions about Australian workers' material conditions largely reached on the basis of *aggregate* data (effectively masking intra- and inter-class differences and inequalities), and the fact that 'the statistics only refer to some aspects of material life, and not at all to the *quality of life*' (emphasis added). Markey agrees that 'Australian workers were more prosperous than the British'. However, 'the comparison takes no account of *expectations*, that is the *standards* by which Australian workers judged their prosperity' (emphasis added). Moreover, in the process of exploring these 'expectations' and 'standards' within the specific context of late nineteenth-century New South Wales, Markey takes his argument beyond that of 'strict qualification'. He arrives at the extremely pessimistic overall conclusion that the short-term depression of the 1890s combined with the longer term 'shift towards industrial capitalism', evident from mid-century onwards, degraded working and living standards and widened 'the gap between material conditions and expectations for many'. Markey maintains that capitalist transformation during the late nineteenth century had profoundly adverse effects upon workers' skills, apprenticeship, security of employment, treatment by employers, wage levels and general expectations and life chances across a range of urban and rural occupations.[117] In sum, Markey chronologically extends the verdict passed by Shirley Fitzgerald and Greg Patmore on the 'boom' period that 'Australia was hardly a 'workingman's paradise'.[118]

However, I offer an opposing viewpoint. Markey's case is greatly weakened, ironically, by his disproportionate concentration on structural changes at the work-place and material conditions at the expense of detailed attention to the qualitative evidence, as expressed in the very contemporary expectations and standards he exhorts us to investigate. As a result, he largely overlooks the most important subjective factor: the majority labour-movement voice continuing to proclaim the virtues of living and working conditions in the 'new' country over those in the 'old'.

To substantiate my thesis, I will recall four witnesses, Mary Walker, Richard Scott, Tom Mann and Keir Hardie who first appeared on behalf of the pessimistic case. Their additional evidence, which points to far more positive and optimistic overall conclusions than hitherto imagined, will then be supplemented with supporting testimony from new witnesses.

The reader will recall the unfavourable initial experiences of New Zealand articulated by Mary Walker and Richard Scott. However, initial misgivings and criticisms signalled neither a desire to return to Britain, nor the belief that conditions were better in that country. Thus Scott,

> Of course, I do not mean to give the impression that things are not better than they are at home, because they are much better. The standard of living is much higher here than at home ... if fortunate enough to get work.[119]

And Walker,

> Although at present we are roughing it, we do not regret coming here, nor do we desire to return home. We both feel that in time we shall arrive at the niche most suited for us, and once there we shall do much better than we could do at home.[120]

Similarly, Tom Mann's verdict in 1904 was that 'speaking generally ... the standard of living is higher than in England'. This was the case particularly for shop assistants and 'many mechanics'.[121] Mann's subsequently developed more intimate knowledge of workers 'in their homes and at work' in both Australia and New Zealand. This experience, combined with his growing disillusionment with the Australian Labor Party, arbitration, and the primacy of the political road to socialism, compelled him to moderate somewhat his earlier enthusiasm. Thus he was reported in the *Labour Leader* in 1909 as concluding that the standard of life in Australia 'is a little higher than in Britain, only a little'.[122] This was a view which also found favour in the eyes of *Justice*.[123]

Yet Keir Hardie, writing a year earlier in the *Labour Leader*, and notwithstanding his caution concerning the immediate difficulties facing new immigrants, waxed lyrical overall about the climate, the environment, and the modern conveniences and provisions for the people in Australia. Thus, of Port Adelaide and its environs:

> It was near the end of November, and I thought of the raw London fogs and Scotch mists as I basked in the sunshine of as perfect a day as it ever fell to my lot to enjoy ... the place looked like a Corner of the Garden of Eden.

Broken Hill was, 'spacious, well lit and lined with streets of handsome shops; the crowd, well-dressed and orderly, showing much less evidence of drunkenness than a mining town at home'.

Indeed, Hardie's praise was extended to many Australian 'mining cities'. They were,

> simply marvellous ... Hundreds of miles from anywhere, situated in the midst of a sandy, rocky desert: they grew up ... to become great centres of population. Handsome buildings, good shops, electric lights, tramways, and all modern conveniences are everywhere in evidence.[124]

Hardie's knowledge obviously did not extend to the serious housing and environmental problems in the western mining towns raised in subsequent years by the *Westralian Worker*. However, his eulogy on Australia's progressive urban modernity was shared by Margaret MacDonald. During her visit to Bendigo and Ballarat, MacDonald was impressed with their fine buildings and gardens. These towns presented a pleasant contrast to the rough-and-ready mining camps many imagined them to be.[125]

Among my new witnesses, we encounter the positive accounts of foreign visitors and observers and resident Australians and New Zealanders. Sir Charles Dilke's *Problems of Greater Britain*, published in 1890, and based upon the author's extensive travels, declared that in Victoria 'workers of all classes' and 'in some degree the worker of all the Australian colonies', now 'possess advantages which make Australia a workers' paradise. High wages are there combined with cheap food and leisure for culture or amusement.'[126]

Michael Davitt's seven months journey throughout the Australian colonies and New Zealand brought forth even more ambitious claims on behalf of the achievements of the Australasian 'experiment'. In 1898 Davitt wrote,

> Speaking generally of all the colonies, I would unhesitatingly say that they give better all-round conditions of existence to the average man than any of the European countries I am acquainted with. A drier and healthier climate, higher wages, and less labouring hours for the worker, with all the prospects and possibilities of young and only partially developed countries added to the solid advantages of the present.[127]

Despite its opposition to the burgeoning state in Australia, even the AF of L found itself compelled, from afar, to afford due recognition to the Australian achievement. In 1898 the *American Federationist*, the federation's official mouthpiece, congratulated organised Australian workers upon the successes of the eight-hour-day movement in their country, and maintained that, in contrast to the USA, Australian workers enjoyed high living standards and property ownership.[128]

The overall impression of working and living conditions provided by our selected resident Australians and New Zealanders – all involved in, or sympathetic to, the claims of organised labour – is also an extremely favourable one. For example, in 1904 Claude Thompson, an Australian delegate to the International Socialist Congress, 'gave a hand' with the socialist educational and propagandistic work of the Clarion Van movement in Middleton and Oldham, urban centres in the vicinity of Manchester. On the basis of his travels, Thompson concluded that there was 'far more ground in England for dissatisfaction with Labour (sic) conditions than there is in Australia'. By British working-class standards, of course, the cotton district of north-west England was 'affluent', with the family-wage in cotton frequently offsetting the relatively low take-home pay for many individual workers, especially girls and women, in the industry. However, Thompson was concerned at the 'low wages' – '£2 being considered very good' – the long hours and the unhealthy living and working conditions of the operatives. His account, published in the *Westralian Worker*, conjured up a uniformly depressing picture of weary and fatalistic operatives, 'existing' rather than 'living' in a gloomy and dispiriting environment. Given the unusual nature of this source – of an Australian socialist reporting on Britain rather than vice versa – it is worth quoting from it at length. 'Coming out of Manchester to Middleton', wrote Thompson,

> I could not help observing how necessary it is that the people living in this particular district should live under better and brighter conditions. The grimy mills, the tall chimneys, vomitting (sic) forth smoke, the dull uniformity of the homes, make up a picture of dismal England which is not pleasurable to look upon.

There was an absence of purpose and enjoyment:

> The operatives in the mills were ceasing work and going to their homes. I was struck with the youth of some, the age of others, *and with the worn, joyless expression on the faces of all*. There seemed to be *no life, no spirit* in them. I have noticed that in the factories which we have in Sydney and Melbourne *the work does not take all the natural vivacity out of the operatives* probably because the hours of labor are considerably shorter, and because more stringent factory regulations render the conditions under which they labor considerably easier. (emphases added.)

Thompson's conclusion signalled Australia's and the Australian workers' rapidly growing maturity and independence:

The Mother-land has taught us many things, for which, perhaps, with our usual
Colonial nonchalance, we are not duly grateful, *but in many things we can teach the
old land useful lessons.* (emphasis added.)[129]

As noted earlier, Henry Fletcher had long since fled the 'present and appalling misery' of London for the welcoming and democratic shores of the New World. While
given to bald assertion and flowery exaggeration, Fletcher, like Thompson, entertained few doubts as to the superiority of living and working conditions in Australia.
Thus,

In these wide lands where the air is pure, the sky always blue, and sordid poverty unknown, the life in London town seems to me, even now, like some horrible
dream.[130]

The introduction of old-age pensions (in New South Wales in 1900, Victoria in
1901 and the whole Commonwealth in 1908), the growing acceptance of wage
fixing by arbitration, the living wage, factory inspection, tariff protection and
other aspects of the 'social-welfarist' state, constituted, for Fletcher, unassailable
evidence of general prosperity. Simultaneously, prosperity, combined with 'excessive' state regulation and interference in Australian's lives, were seen to pose a
serious threat to individual freedom and initiative. 'With general comfort', opined
Fletcher, 'ambition sleeps'. However, on balance, Australia was seen to stand head
and shoulders above 'poor', 'sluggish' and even 'antediluvian' England.[131]

Fletcher's views, published in the *Clarion*, elicited a lively 'Clarion Postbag', with
responses arriving from socialists living in Australia and New Zealand. The prevailing tone – that of relative, but properly guarded optimism – was set by Percy
Ashworth of Melbourne:

The workers, though much better off than at home, find life a tolerably hard propo-
sition, and he is a lucky or a thrifty man who can bring up a family and pay off his
interest and call his little suburban home his own.

Furthermore,

What Mr. Fletcher and others do not see is that in this Promised Land, despite better
conditions of life, Capitalism rules the roost much as it does elsewhere, and brings in
its train a multitude of evils sweating, poverty, ignorance and degradation. No doubt
by-and bye (sic) old Britain will advance as far as young Australia has done ...[132]

Sydney's 'sweating, poverty, ignorance and degradation' had been exposed by
William Lane ('John Millar') in his *The Workingman's Paradise* (1892). Yet a review of Lane's novel soon after its publication by an anonymous 'Sydney women
writer' – described by the *Worker* as 'one of the ablest art critics on the continent'

– was critical of its literary merits and its socio-economic conclusions, while simultaneously praising its 'Zola-like' passion. The reviewer argued that poverty and its associated evils, although 'not unheard of', had been 'the exception not the rule' in Sydney; and that 'John Millar's sketches of the workingman's quarters read more like a description of London slums than of Sydney back streets'. 'New world cities', continued the reviewer, did have 'a dire tendency to drift towards old world wretchedness'. This 'contingency' had to be 'avoided at all risks'. However, as matters stood Lane's dire picture of Sydney was greatly exaggerated:

> But as yet the first thing that strikes the 'new chum' on arrival is the apparent comfort, the decent clothing, the generally debonnair air of the so-called destitute classes, even when 'times are bad'.

Favourable comparisons were drawn with conditions in London and Europe:

> If John Millar doubts my word let him take a trip across seas and walk through the back streets of the fashionable parts of London when 'times are good' … In Sydney – 'our gutter children' – may be foul mouthed but 'are not foul bodied; they are straight of limb, vigorous and muscular in action, not shrunken. ricketty (sic), deformed as is the child of the European large town; our men, even when out of work, carry themselves with an independent air, be they unionists or blacklegs; our women, even those with an empty cupboard on their minds, are not to be seen, tattered and unkempt, reeling outside the ginshop.[133]

Dora Montefiore, having lived in both London and Sydney, was in agreement. In her report of an interview with Andrew Fisher in 1911, Montefiore wrote: 'I quite agreed with him that one does not see the mass of misery here that one does in the Old Country'.[134] The secondary literature has tended further to endorse the 'optimist' urban case: while Sydney and other urban centres in Australia certainly had their poor, their unemployed and their casual workers, yet the scale and severity of urban poverty and destitution were probably less pronounced than in Britain.[135]

The absence of comparative British and Australian regional studies, means that it is impossible to draw meaningful comparisons concerning the standard of living at this level. However, and taking full cognizance of those contemporary complaints noted earlier in relation to the financial, domestic and environmental costs involved in living and working on the western goldfields, it is important to remember that, unlike Britain, the regional 'frontier' in Australia was still expanding rapidly in the period in question. As such, it continued to provide a magnet for new opportunities, adventures and independence, especially for young, single and enterprising men, and, at least in the immediate term of tight labour-market conditions, high wages.[136] For example, there was a mass exodus from Victoria in the early and mid 1890s to the newly-discovered goldfields of Western Australia. Soon to be labelled 'the richest goldfield in the world', the mines around Kalgoorlie (and Coolgardie) offered migrants a veritable mixture of costs and benefits. However, for many men the latter often outweighed the former. As 'Veritas', writing in the *Champion* from the 'Western Wilds', declared to his predominantly Melbourne-based readership in 1896: 'There is an abundance of work for able-bodied men all over the field, wages from £3 to £4 a week, hard manual labour and plenty of discomfort.' Labourers were arriving in trains 'packed like sardines'. Carpenters, in great demand to construct rudimentary accommodation, could earn up to '17/6d per day'. Lots of mining towns were 'now springing up in this barren wilderness'. Snakes, scorpions and the absence of a water supply constituted obvious deterrents. 'But', declared 'Veritas', 'any man who will earn his tucker by the sweat of his brow is sure to get a living on the field, and to save enough in a year or two 'to go on his own'. For, 'to be his own boss is every man's ambition here, and wages are only taken with the object of gaining goldfields experience and a little capital'.[137]

In the event the western goldfields did not prove to be a 'diggers' paradise'. The substantial capital costs involved in the mechanised deep-shaft mining around Kalgoorlie and Coolgardie meant that by the early 1900s proletarian, as opposed to small-operator, standing, had become the lot of most of those who worked the mines and rented their homes from the companies. North American influence, in terms of both engineering and ownership, was marked.[138] Yet, as we will observe in due course, there were compensations. For it was under such booming frontier conditions that a strong and independent labour movement would grow extremely rapidly in the 1900s West.

Finally, T.A. Black's view, expressed in 1901, that his country, New Zealand – complete with its old-age pensions, female franchise, conciliation and arbitration services, a 'magnificent' system of public education, and other progressive features – had successfully avoided the 'old world' problem of 'enormous wealth and abject poverty', was one widely shared by progressives and socialists both within New Zealand and abroad.[139] Two years earlier, and notwithstanding its infant socialist party and its relatively weak labour movement, Sidney Webb had similarly commended New Zealand upon its very wide diffusion of wealth', its lack of 'ostentation', and its Liberal government which, 'if not ... Socialist', was 'at least more advanced than our own'.[140] In 1902 an article in the *Westralian Worker* entitled, 'New Zealand As a Workers' Country', went so far as to claim that New Zealand was 'far ahead' of Australia 'politically and socially':

> Wages are higher, work is more regular, the hours of labour are shorter, the sweating of women and children is restricted, the voting power of the people is wider and more effective ...[141]

While in the pages of *Labour Leader* in 1905, New Zealand was further praised for being 'the richest country in the world': 'This fact is doubtless due to its Socialistic legislation, which tends to the greater production as well as equalisation of wealth'.[142]

In moving from the general picture to a more specific concentration upon the fortunes of occupational groups within the Australian working class, it is, once again, the generally positive and 'optimist' judgements of contemporary labour-movement participants and observers that strike one most.

It is true, as claimed by Markey, that the 1890s depression did accelerate mechanization, employer 'driving', unemployment, general worker insecurity, and threats to skill, apprenticeship and craft control in the workplace. There was also a hardening of class divisions and consciousness. The latter development was partly reflected in the 'turn' to independent labour and socialist politics, and partly in the shift from the language of the 'moral economy', complete with its tenets of the 'producing classes' and 'fair play' between 'honourable' 'masters' and 'men', to a more *systemic* notion of conflict and struggle between 'capitalists' and 'workers'. As highlighted by Markey, this more class-based language was rooted within the new industrial-capitalist political economy of profit maximisation, cost minimisation ('buying cheap and selling dear') and unfettered individualism and competition.[143]

However, as the recent studies of John Shields, Raelene Frances and Chris Wright have shown, the Braverman-inspired accounts of Markey, Fitzgerald and others have clearly exaggerated the *actual extent* of the 'transformation of labour', and the general 'degradation of working and living conditions' in Australia during this period. For example, industrial capitalist development was limited and uneven, and the methods of mass production, Taylorism and 'transformed' (ie. de-skilled and dependent) labour generally awaited a future date. The undoubted threats to craft control, skill and apprenticeship, however, were limited, differentiated and cyclical in practice rather than pervasive, uniform and unilinear. And worker *agency*, as reflected in struggle and resistance, was often more pronounced *and successful* than suggested.[144] Indeed the reverses of the 1890s gave way to a period of remarkable and sustained labour-movement *advances* between 1900 and World War One which commanded international attention and fascination. Moreover, widely felt and articulated advancements in living and working conditions during the same period hardly lend themselves to an overall conclusion of doom and gloom.

The case histories of engineers and printers illustrate the general points made in the previous two paragraphs. Both printing and engineering witnessed increased mechanization in the period under review and the growth of more specialised 'operatives'. (A similar trend was evident in the construction industry as seen in the specialised factory production of doors and windows.) However, as emphasised by Shields, the expansion of engineering and the introduction of new machine tools created a range of new skills and correspondingly expanded opportunities for upgrading within the workforce. In engineering, as in the building trades, 'hand skill remained the focus of trade activity', with fitting and turning continuing, for the most part, to be the preserve of highly skilled males. Shields draws an instructive comparison with Britain:

> Unlike his British counterpart, the archetypal colonial engineer remained basically an 'all-round' craftsman who not only furnished his own tools of trade but exercised job knowledge and manual ability across a wide range of tasks, tools and products.[145]

In printing the widespread introduction of the linotype machine and its specialist operator into the newspaper industry in the 1890s, did result in a large increase in unemployment, especially among older hand compositors. It also occasioned much bitterness within this traditionally 'aristocratic' and 'respectable' craft. For example, while emphasising the fact that it was *not* opposed to mechanization per se, the Melbourne Typographical Society strongly criticised the *Argus* employers' action in failing to consult the union in their unilateral and 'unmanly' introduction of the linotype, and the substitution of machine for hand labour, into the newspaper's production.[146] In March 1897 the *Australasian Typographical Journal* sounded a dire warning:

> if ever the printing trade was in danger, it is at the present time. *Machinery has blasted its prospects in every direction*, and no man's billet is worth a month's purchase. Old and young are turned adrift without a passing care for their future prospects. *Capital is rampant*, and millionaires who court cheap popularity by lavish and grovelling gifts ... pitch their unfortunate wealth-earners out into the gutter on the quiet.[147] (emphases added)

In addition to the adverse effects of technological change, the 'curses of the trade' were seen by the journal to include the growing presence of 'cheap' women and 'inferior workmen', the poor state of union organisation among printers in the country districts, and the attempted resort to an unlimited number of apprentices by employers.[148]

Some printers in the 1890s saw 'the nationalisation of land and machinery' as the only truly effective solution for the ills of their craft. However, these broad panaceas increasingly took second fiddle to the realisation of a number of more limited goals in order to 'assert their manhood'. These included gaining control of the new machinery and its rates of pay, advancing and widening the embrace of the union, seeking out and establishing good relations and agreements with 'honourable' employers in order to establish and police the 'market rate', and setting up new printing ventures 'upon co-operative lines and truly democratic principles'.[149]

What is most impressive is the extent to which many of these goals were in fact realised. During the 1900s most of the new linotype operators – in practice 'the new elite of the trade' whose job entailed 'speed, accuracy and knowledge paralleling that of hand compositors' – were in fact unionised 'ex-hand compositors'.[150] In contrast to the devastation of the 1890s, employment, wage rates and earnings picked up nicely, if unevenly, from around 1906 onwards and showed a marked improvement from 1911 onwards. While critical of the 'highly-coloured picture of a land of promise and good things' which had appeared in the *British Printer* as an inducement to British printers to emigrate to Australia, nevertheless, the *Australasian Typographical Journal* confidently declared in November 1911:

> For some time past the printing trade in Australia, in comparison with other trades and occupations, pastoral, commercial, and, in fact, every other line, *has been at the high-water mark of prosperity*, with the result that the workers have been able to se-cure better rates and conditions throughout the Commonwealth than had existed for a considerable time. *The wave of prosperity* is not confined to any particular part, but has *swept through the whole continent*. The result to the employers has been of great value, and they have gathered a large crop of gold.[151] (emphases added.)

In the immediate pre-war years wages for printers were among the highest, and in some cases *the* highest, in Australia. According to the *Australasian Typographical Journal*, the wages paid to printers in jobbing offices in the capital cities were about £3 per week and between £2/10- and £3 in provincial and country towns in 1911. Newspaper linotype operators, 'in the leading offices', were said to 'average £6 per week of 40 hours', while £5 per week 'is the average in newspaper offices of lesser importance'.[152]

Between 1900 and 1914 printing also recovered its reputation as a strongly unionised craft. This recovery was greatly aided by the new system of arbitration which, by its process of registration, institutionalised recognition of both unions and employers' organisations. In addition, efforts, albeit limited and uneven, were made to organise new grades of workers. As in so many other occupations, women workers in printing met with a mixture of hostility and grudging, pragmatic ac-ceptance on the part of the unions.[153] Notwithstanding the formal 'no politics' rule, an increasing number of typographical societies also increasingly lent their support to the Labor Party. The industrial turbulence of the 1890s had taught, for many in the trade, two important lessons: the necessity of a political shield, in the form of an independent party of labour, to protect and advance their occupational and material interests; and the newfound reality, however undesirable it might be, of a structured conflict of interest between employers and workers. Hard-headed realism, given a sharp experiential edge by the conflict surrounding the introduc-tion of the linotype, dictated that, however friendly and 'honourable' some master printers had been in the past and might continue to be in the future, it was at all times imperative for the unions to be *vigilant* and *prepared* actively to defend their members' interests. Resort to strike action, if necessary, was seen as an integral part of this pragmatic realism.[154]

However, the unions also strongly believed that the *institutionalisation* of indus-trial relations, in the form of regular negotiations and formal agreements between strongly organised and 'responsible' employers and unions, would keep industrial conflict to a minimum and advance the interests of 'the trade' as a whole. 'Where the employer and employee are well organised', argued the *Australasian Typographical Journal* in 1911, 'there is always an opportunity to discuss trade problems and be mutually helpful'.

Moreover:

> With journeymen who have a knowledge of business, and employers who have the courage to ask good prices, we can develop a *community of interests that will place our trade on a higher plane,* and make it a pleasant and profitable occupation for all concerned'.[155] (emphasis added.)

During the 1880s many of the typographical associations had enjoyed 'amicable relations' with those 'fair' employers who recognised the union, paid the negotiated rate, and attempted to regulate or 'police' the market against the intrusion of 'unfair', 'cheap and nasty' competitors. Indeed, there had been instances of printing associations accepting wage reductions in 'the interests of the trade'.[156] The experience of the 1890s undermined this trust and mutuality. However, there is much evidence to suggest that by the end of the 1900s, and up to the outbreak of war, the desired 'community of interests' had made a very strong resurgence. For example, the pages of the *Australasian Typographical Journal* for these years contain numerous references to the revival of a spirit of 'fairness' and generally 'good relations', as manifested especially in the successful conclusion of industrial agreements, between printing employers and workers.[157]

The *Journal* also cited, as an example of 'good relations', the numerous occasions on which representatives of management accepted invitations to attend printers' picnics, presentations and other 'respectable' social and leisure activities. Such occasions invariably involved expressions of the 'good feeling' prevailing between workers and employers or, albeit less frequently, 'masters' and 'men'. For example, in December 1911 the *Australasian Typographical Journal* carried a report of the annual waygooze[158] of the employes of the *Adelaide Advertiser*. E. A. Dowe, the father of the chapel, was in the chair. The principal toast was made to 'The Proprietor of the *Advertiser*', and the main speaker 'referred to the cordial relations which existed between the proprietor and the *Advertiser* staff'. There was also a report in the same issue of the annual picnic of the printers of H.J. Diddams and Co. of Brisbane. The principal of the firm, Alderman Diddams, and his wife and two children were the 'honoured guests'.[159] Two months later the employees of the 'old-established' printing firm of W.E. Smith, of Sydney, which had recently changed hands, decided that it would be 'fitting to inaugurate the first of what is hoped will be a series of annual outings'. Accordingly, on a sunny Saturday morning three hundred people left Fort Macquarie in the S.S. 'Halcyon' for the Parramatta River. On reaching their destination a picnic was held, athletic events organised, including the obligatory 'tug of war', and toys and sweets distributed to the children present. Mr. R. Venning Thomas, the general manager, toasted 'The

King' and 'The Firm'. In turn the chairman of the firm expressed his pleasure at,

> the remarkable growth of good feeling and *esprit de corps* among the employees ...
> The desire of the directors was that there should be absolutely fair treatment for every
> employee, and a square deal to every customer.[160]

Occasions to promote the virtues of technical education, prizegivings for printers attending the Melbourne Working Men's College, funerals of old printers and
union officials, union socials and presentations to long-serving colleagues also saw
overseers and employers and employees standing side by side.[161]

There were also several instances of paternalist practices. Paternalism, of course,
was by no means a new phenomenon in the Australian printing trades. During the
nineteenth century there were a number of, often large, firms committed to intri-
cate, high quality printing. It was among these 'model employers' that paternalism
had been most pronounced.[162] The 1890s depression struck paternalism extremely
hard. But the ten or so years preceding the First World War saw a significant revival. Most significant from my perspective was the fact that, at least in the cases cited
in the *Australasian Typographical Journal*, paternalism was closely associated with
the 'fair' employer who recognised the union.[163] In return, due employee gratitude
and moderation were expected and received. For example, in June 1912 Mr. J.S.
Toohey left work 'in the shop' to take up the post as the paid assistant secretary
of the Melbourne Typographical Society. He was congratulated upon his new
appointment by Mr. Colley, the manager, who presented him 'with a handsome
marble clock'. Toohey and the executive of the Melbourne Typographical Society
reciprocated by stating their commitment to 'the betterment of the trade' rather
than to the pursuit of narrow, sectional goals. Furthermore, 'the aim of the executive was to always legislate between employer and employed without resorting to
unpleasant actions or using force'.[164]

In sum, industrial relations in printing were characterised by a mixture of conflict and conciliation. Printers and their unions exhibited *both* a hard-headed appreciation of the political economy of class *and* attitudes of responsibility, moderation and conciliation towards capital. Which aspect predominated depended very
much on their experience of events and processes rather than upon predetermined
ideology. However, on balance, the conflicts and antagonisms of the 1890s had
eased greatly by the immediate pre-First World War years, to be overshadowed by
feelings of progress and good relations with employers. In the process printers had
recovered their self-esteem and their 'respectable', 'labour-aristocratic' standing
within the Australian working class. This was rooted in the continuing fluidity of
the social, financial and occupational lines between, on the one hand, themselves
and, on the other, their overseers and small masters;[165] and in the traditional 'craft'
virtues of industry, thrift, sobriety, independence and 'clean living'. As the historian of the printing unions concluded,

Technical change and industrial development combined to renew the need for highly skilled men; the societies responded by emphasising once more the pride of the craft that set them aside from the unskilled.[166]

Much the same conclusions can be drawn in relation to the position of the engineers. In addition to the preservation of their skills and job control, most engineers survived the ordeals of the 1890s to recover their 'aristocratic' standing and 'respectable' way of life between 1900 and 1914. The limited size and differentiated character of the home market, the lack of long continuous runs characteristic of standardised mass production, and continued reliance upon Britain for many manufactured goods, placed severe limitations upon the rate of threatening technological advance in Australia, both in industry as a whole and engineering in particular.[167] The bad trade, serious wage cuts and unemployment of the Depression gave way to short-lived improvement in the early 1900s, but then to more sustained and general expansion and prosperity between 1906 and 1914. During the latter period wage rates and earnings showed impressive powers of recovery and advancement. They also compared very favourably with Great Britain, with the standard minimum daily rate for ASE (Amalgamated Society of Engineers) fitters and turners in Australia around 1910 standing at 10/- as compared with the 6/- to 7/6d of their counterparts in the Old Country. In practice, as observed by Ken Buckley, the great demand for skilled engineers in pre-war Australia often meant that rates and earnings above the minimum 'was very common'.[168] Buckley also notes that 'a considerable proportion' of Australian ASE members bought their homes through membership of building societies, while the prospects of upward occupational mobility for engineers remained strong, both as foremen and as small employers requiring little capital to set up shop within the industry itself.[169]

Between 1891 and 1895 the ASE had lost approximately one third of its Australian membership. However, between 1900 and 1914 the union, aided by the growth of government railway workshops, compulsory arbitration and wages boards (notwithstanding their limited occupational and trade-union embrace)[170] and the more widespread institutionalization of industrial relations, recovered well and extended its organisational reach to new grades of workers. Standing at the modest figure of under 3,000 in 1907, ASE membership in Australia advanced to 6,000 in 1911 and almost doubled again by the outbreak of the First World War.[171] As in the case of the printers, 'respectability' and the welcome presence of managers and proprietors characterised many of the engineers' social and leisure activities.[172]

To conclude this section, on the eve of the First World War claims to material progress and institutional advancement, rather than immiseration and retreat, figured most prominently in the publications of Australian printers and engineers. It was in response to the more favourable conditions prevailing in Australia in this period that emigration from Britain and Europe, which had declined greatly during the 1890s, picked up considerably among printers, engineers and other workers.[173] Concurrent with the growth of industrial capitalism in their country, skilled Australian workers prided themselves upon their assumed premier place in the industrial world's hierarchy of labour. In relation to their British counterparts, Australian printers had thus become by the end of 1911, 'more than their peers in capacity and workmanship'. Furthermore, 'taken altogether', Australian workmen 'have no superiors in any other part of the world'.[174] Indeed, many of the intending immigrants from Great Britain were deemed to be 'not of a class to improve Australia's stock of *virile humanity*'[175] (emphasis added). Finally, so pronounced had the mood of contentment with the present and confidence in the future become that the *Australasian Typographical Journal* could, in the same year, offer a warm welcome both to Frederick Winslow Taylor's scheme of 'scientific management' and mechanization: they 'could be applied with great advantage alike to master and man'.[176]

It is, of course, extremely difficult to ascertain the extent to which the generally positive experiences and expressions of the printers and engineers prevailed among the wider Australian working class. After all, printers and engineers, along with many craft workers in the construction industry, were part of a privileged minority of 'labour aristocrats'. As William Morris Hughes observed in his *The Case for Labor*, published in 1910, 'in every industry' there were 'at least three grades of employees'. These were listed as 'the aristocrats of the labor army' – the regularly employed who formed 'the nucleus of the employer's industrial army'; those in 'regular employment, interspersed with irregular, but usually short, periods of idleness'; and the remaining 20 to 33 per cent who worked 'intermittently' in 'normal seasons', in 'bad seasons not at all', and were 'constantly employed only in good seasons'.[177] To which I may add that even labour aristocrats were, as we have seen in reference to the 1890s, by no means permanently free from bouts of unemployment, poverty and threats, both potential and realised, to their superior standing and security. It is also worth noting that the patchiness of the extant data and the very selectivity at the heart of the historical enterprise, mean that it is extremely difficult, and in all likelihood impossible, to recapture in any definitive way either the 'average' or 'typical' contemporary working-class experience or subjective evaluation in relation to trends in living standards.

However, while keeping these cautions in mind, certain conclusions may still be advanced. First, reference has earlier been made to Stuart Macintyre's considered view that 'The average Australian' enjoyed a higher standard of living than his or her British counterpart. Fully alive to the facts that 'the citizen conforming to the golden mean remains a statistical construct offering only an imperfect measure of welfare' and that there was 'a high degree of inequality' in early twentieth-century Australia, Macintyre, nevertheless, concludes that 'the relative short supply of labour enabled all but the lowest income earners to participate in a broad-based consumer market'.[178] The shortage of labour in Australia also meant that the earning differential between the skilled and non-skilled was usually less pronounced than in Britain.[179] In spite of its defects and critics, arbitration and its associated notion of a 'basic' or 'living wage', increasingly proved to be particularly beneficial to the living standards of 'non-aristocratic' workers. Thus Macintyre is surely correct in his assessment that, despite its successful institutional challenge in the High Court, Higgins' decision in favour of the New Protection for labour rapidly gained widespread popular acceptance and support:

> If Higgins's decision was a myth, it was an extremely powerful one. Within five years of his judgement Labor governments in three states had legislated for the judicial determination of a basic wage.[180]

Moreover,

> As measured by its effect on pay packets, wage fixation and compulsory arbitration were of greatest benefit to the weaker, unskilled workers who had been largely at the mercy of their employers.[181]

Significantly, the growing, if limited, safeguard against chronic poverty and the 'free flow of market forces' provided by New Protection and the 'living wage' in Australia did not figure in the thinking of most male British trade unionists at that time. The latter, while providing some support for a selective and largely gender-based legislated minimum wage (largely in sweated industries), were more committed to 'voluntarism' in industrial relations and the market-based determination of a 'decent family wage' than their more judicially-inclined Australian counterparts. However, in both countries growing protection was also afforded by trade unionism. For, as in Britain, the period between the late 1890s and 1914 in Australia witnessed, in addition to the revival and advancement of 'old' unionism, the remarkable growth of 'new' unionism.

Aided in many cases by the formal registration, and in effect recognition, required by the system of compulsory arbitration, the 'new' unions made rapid advances. For example, the Australian Workers' Union, the 'largest and wealthiest' and increasingly most powerful union in the country, took full advantage of the Commonwealth Arbitration Court's 1907 award to spread the wage increases won 'in districts where the union was strong' to 'areas where union influence had been negligible'. Largely as a consequence, membership of the AWU increased by 9,000 during 1907 alone, whereas it had risen by 10,000 during the whole of the previous five years.[182] In the following year W.G. Spence, the president of the AWU, and a seminal figure in late nineteenth-century 'new' unionism in general, remarked that, 'We have grown till we have reached proportions which few of us would have guessed possible years ago'.[183] In 1908 the total membership of the AWU stood at around 40,000. A further award in 1911 brought substantial improvements in pay, working conditions and protection from unscrupulous employers. By that date membership had risen to a very impressive 47,000.[184] Similarly, in the mush-rooming goldfields of Western Australia another 'new' union, the Amalgamated Workers' Association, had as one of its founding principles, the organisation of 'any worker of either sex'. The union grew very rapidly among mining, timber and urban workers to become by 1902 'the largest union in the state' and 'one of the three leading unions in Australia'.[185]

'New' unionist advances took place within the general context of a dramatic increase in trade unionism as a whole. Greg Patmore thus informs us that union membership in Australia 'among wage and salary earners grew from 9 per cent in 1901 to 33 per cent by 1914'.[186] Whereas Australian trade union membership had stood at an estimated 55,900 in 1891 and 97,200 in 1901, it increased to 302,100 in 1910 and to a remarkable 523,000 by 1914. The period 1910-1914, of course, was one of rapid trade-union growth in a number of countries. For example, in the United Kingdom, the veritable home of trade unionism, membership increased from 2.5 million in 1910 to 4 million in 1914, largely among 'new' unionists. Gains in Britain, however, could not disguise the sheer magnitude of the Australian achievement. As against Australia's union density of 33 per cent in 1914, the British figure stood at 23 per cent. Further evidence that Australia was outstripping Britain as the trade unionists' paradise was supplied in 1919, when it was revealed that 50 per cent of potential recruits were members of Australian trade unions, as opposed to 43 per cent in the Old Country.[187]

I have argued so far that the balance of the evidence, with reference to general Australian working-class living standards and experiences, rests more with the 'optimist' than the 'pessimist' case. Finally, we should remember that such standards and experiences were framed within the wider context of the largely 'traditional' nature of both the political-economy of Australian capitalism, and in its place and role in the wider imperial and world networks.

As suggested earlier, the overall growth of industrial capitalism in Australia during the period in question was limited and uneven. We have already presented some of the relevant evidence with respect to the issue of the 'transformation of labour'. More generally, and taking full account of the rapid growth of Australian manufacturing between 1900 and 1914, there was the continued, if somewhat reduced, dominance of pastoralism and agriculture within the national economy. Australia also continued to rely heavily, albeit less markedly than in the past, upon Britain for exports, capital and manufactured goods. Several additional factors – the 'limited size and segmented character' of the national market; the fact that 'most everyday needs were satisfied locally'; the small size of the great majority of units of production and their heavy dependence upon hand methods; and the low productivity of labour – constituted further convincing testimony to the limited strides made by industrial capitalism.[188]

The continuing 'traditionalism' of the Australian economy had important implications for the fortunes of organised labour. Above all, the relative lack of *sweeping* and *sustained* economic change detrimental to the interests of labour, combined with the post-1890s economic revival and the strong development of a system of instutionalised collective bargaining, meant that workers and their unions had the opportunity to secure a place in the post-depression economic system which could form the platform for future growth. To be sure, there were continuing instances of workplace conflict and struggle which bred some disillusionment with the arbitration system and stimulated the rise of the IWW (Industrial Workers of the World) in the post-1907 years.[189] As seen at Broken Hill in 1908-9 and in Brisbane in 1912, these could sometimes take the form of mass battles in which organised labour suffered greatly from the power and coercive actions of anti-union employers, judges and politicians. However, such instances must not be allowed to obscure the great extent to which labour's early twentieth-century fortunes had improved since the crisis-ridden and conflict-strewn decade of the 1890s.

The changing *political* context of the 1900s, characterised by federation, the creation of the New Commonwealth and national settlement, further served strongly to promote organised labour's development. Rooted in the policies of White Australia, arbitration, advanced social welfare, and protection for both capital and labour, the process of national settlement sought to create social and political stability and ordered economic growth.[190] It promoted social and political compromise, class reconciliation and afforded both labour and capital an important voice and presence in the emerging New Commonwealth.

In sum, Australia's political economy of 'traditionalism', combined with the emergence in the 1900s of what Christopher Lloyd has aptly termed the 'labourist-protectionist' state,[191] created a context which was highly conducive to organised labour's advancement. Simultaneously, as we will observe in the final section of this essay, this new context posed a number of ideological dilemmas for labour. Most crucially, was primacy to be attached to the pragmatic 'realism' of labourism – to the achievement of power and the attainment of concrete, if limited and piecemeal, reforms – or to the 'revolving of the whole system' demanded by some socialists within the ranks of the Labor party?

Some similarities can be observed between this context and the situation facing working-class movements in mid-Victorian Britain. In the latter case, the acute and bitter class conflicts of the Chartist years were similarly followed by accelerated attempts at class reconciliation and the accommodation of some of organised labour's demands and interests. These attempts took place within the context of economic expansion within a predominantly traditional framework. Furthermore, labour activists widely debated the merits of 'revolutionary' versus 'reformist' strategies and tactics, with the latter increasingly taking precedence over the former.[192] However, major differences outweigh these similarities. For example, notwithstanding the enfranchisement of many skilled male workers under the terms of the 1867 Reform Act, the mid-Victorian compromise did not take place either within a fundamentally changed political context on the scale of that of federation, or with reference to the acute immediacy given by federation and national settlement to the issues of state building and the construction of national consciousness. Furthermore, the mid-Victorian British labour movement was far more limited in its social composition, and far more limited and sectional in its consciousness than its early twentieth-century Australian counterpart. As we will see below, labour in Australia also had a far more influential imprint upon the form and content of national consciousness, upon what it meant to be an Australian, than it did upon ruling definitions of Englishness and Britishness in mid-Victorian Britain.

By way of conclusion, reference to the comparative factor also helps us to highlight three other important contextual issues. First, as implied throughout this section, the growth of industrial capitalism in Australia in the period in question was far less profound, enduring and widespread in its disruptive effects upon the lives of labouring people, than it had been in Britain during the period of the Industrial Revolution. Second, as seen above in references to trade unionism and as will be demonstrated in the next section in relation to politics, Australian labour's powers of recuperation and heady advancement in the wake of the 1890s depression certainly matched, and indeed soon outstripped, those demonstrated by British labour in response to the problems posed by 'The Great Depression' (1873-1896) and the employer 'counter-attack' of the 1890s. Third, to widen the comparative point of focus, the very rapid and profoundly disruptive nature of the transition from competitive to monopoly capitalism in the late nineteenth- and early twentieth-century USA, allied to the militantly anti-union sentiments of most employers and the judiciary, ensured that, notwithstanding Gompers' claims to the contrary, both the American trade union movement and independent labour politics were in a much weaker state than in either Britain or Australia.

3. The Advancement of the Labour Movement

As suggested at various points in the previous section, workers' strong sense of wellbeing and progress in Australia was closely related not only to the perceived wealth of opportunities present in the 'new' country and generally favourable living and working conditions, but also to the impressive progress and influence achieved by the labour movement. Reference was made at the beginning of this chapter to Macintyre's view that between the 1890s and 1914 the Australian labour movement demonstrated a degree of precocity largely unmatched in other countries. Indeed, as Macintyre notes, it was not only, or even mainly, the 'patchwork quality' of the Australian Labor Party's platform and 'the pragmatism of its policies, the eclecticism of its doctrine and the sheer indifference to questions of theory', but, above all, that very 'precocity' that 'struck the observers who came from Europe and North America to study the antipodean labour movement'.[193]

The reader has been alerted in the previous section to the remarkable growth of Australia's trade union movement between 1900 and 1914. Yet it was the very rapid and seemingly inexorable advance of *independent* labour politics in Australia which most fascinated and impressed foreign and domestic observers alike. The Australian Labor Party was established first in New South Wales in 1891. It was the forerunner of many subsequent 'turns' to labour politics in the face of the adverse effects of the depression upon workers and the defeats, at the hands of employers and the state, of their collective organisations. The party assumed a national existence in 1900. As Markey notes, the 'early successes' of both the Labor Party and the labour movement as a whole, 'were far in advance of any other in the world'. For example,

> In 1891, the year it was formed, the Labor party held the balance of power in the NSW parliament, and in 1901, in the first Federal Australian Parliament ... By 1910 it was in government in NSW and federally, where it remained for most of the time until 1917.[194]

In addition, Labor enjoyed minority power at the national level in 1904 and 1908-9; and 'by the outbreak of the First World War there would have been a Labor government in every state'.[195] By the end of the war Australians lived in 'the most unionised country in the world, and in the only country where the Labor party had formed majority governments'.[196]

The Labour Party's record in Britain was far less impressive. The year 1900 saw the establishment of the TUC-inspired Labour Representation Committee, which in turn formally became the Labour Party in 1906. However, the current historiographical consensus is that it was not until the era of World War One, and in all probability not until the election of 1918, that the Labour Party in Britain became a major independent political force at the national level.[197] The pre-war Labour Party had certainly been very much the junior partner in the Lib.-Lab. alliance set up in 1903; and its electoral performance, at least at the national level, did not induce the same degree of anticipation and excitement or fear and dread among contemporary observers as was the case in pre-1914 Australia. In addition, within the pre-1914 TUC such key players as the coalminers and many 'old' trade unionists, retained much of their traditional allegiance to Liberalism; while among the highly unionised cotton spinners in Lancashire there was continued support for Conservatism. It was, of course, not until 1924 that the Labour Party formed a minority government. Within the pre-1914 British working class as a whole Liberal sentiments were still pronounced. Furthermore, building upon its support in its traditional heartlands of rural Britain, Lancashire and parts of the Midlands, the inter-war Conservative Party enjoyed widespread and substantial support among workers.[198]

In the United States repeated attempts to create an independent labour party fared very badly. As highlighted in chapter one, the AF of L retained its allegiance to 'non-partisan' politics. Ethnicity, religion, race and various other ethnocultural and material factors continued to divide American workers. Moreover, the

American Socialist Party failed to fulfil its early promise. Labour parties were in fact formed in a number of places where they enjoyed varying degrees of success in the short term. However, generally speaking these parties enjoyed only a short-lived existence and immediate local gains were not translated into substantial and sustained regional and national advances.[199]

Finally, while socialism was in many cases more pronounced in continental European countries than in Australia, and while 'Continental socialists could trace a lineage of more than half a century for their workers' parties', yet, as noted by Macintyre, 'they remained on the margin of politics'. In marked contrast, 'in Australia Labor had achieved office while still in its adolescence'.[200]

The bare outline of the Australian Labor Party's undoubted aggregate level and record of success over Britain, the USA and Europe presented above, requires qualification and refinement at a number of points. Above all, it gives to the reader an exaggerated picture of unilinear progress and party unity, of a new and *independent* political force sweeping all before it. In truth, 'independent' Labor struck deals, formed alliances and faced internal difficulties, squabbles and splits in various places throughout Australia. There were also national, regional and local fluctuations and variations in its levels of support, influence and power.

During the 1890s and early 1900s Queensland and New South Wales were 'the states of greatest strength, with an established record of independent electoral activity'. In fact Queensland 'achieved the first Labor government in the world in 1899, albeit a minority one lasting less than a week'.[201] The alliance formed with radical liberals in Queensland eventually resulted in bitter differences of opinion and a major split within the ranks of Labor. As Patmore informs us, 'tensions heightened' when the Queensland Labor Party allowed two of its members to participate in a non-Labor cabinet from 1903. Indeed, one of those members, William Kidston, a leading advocate of a Lib.-Lab. alliance, became Queensland's Premier in 1906. Furthermore, the Queensland Labor Party's adoption in the mid 1900s of 'tighter controls over parliamentarians' behaviour and a socialist objective', moved Kidston and twenty of the thirty-six Labor parliamentarians in Queensland to leave the party in 1907.[202] From late 1908 onwards Kidston and his newfound conservative allies 'fused', to campaign against the 'socialism' of Queensland Labor. For its part, the Brisbane *Worker* denounced Kidston and his 'splitters' and 'wreckers'. Throughout the 1900s the *Worker* consistently counselled the Labor Party, at both the state and federal level, to be resolute in its commitment to *independent* politics. Coalitions and alliances, per se, were seen as a sign of weakness, of compromise and a prelude to the dilution of Labor's 'true' socialist goal.[203] By 1910, the year when Labor 'secured the first electoral majority in federal politics', the bedrock support of shearers and miners had once again brought the Labor Party in Queensland 'close to political power'.[204]

In its place of its birth, New South Wales, the Labor Party consolidated its forces to become, by 1900, 'one of the major political forces' in that colony.[205] Between

1898 and 1910 Labor increased its vote in New South Wales from 11.4 per cent to a winning 48.9 per cent. During that period of time the New South Wales party played 'an important role in bringing workers' grievances to the attention of the government', and was arguably successful in bringing its pressure to bear upon the state legislature's enactment of old age pensions, votes for women and industrial arbitration.[206] Markey observes that the ALP nationally derived its character and ideology largely from the New South Wales party's commitment to a strict system of internal discipline revolving around the pledge and the caucus, and its synthesis of 'most of the policies which became part of the national settlement'.[207] He also contends that it was from New South Wales that the national Labor Party inherited its 'dominant' characteristic of 'populism'. The latter, defined as 'an ideological phenomenon' produced by 'intermediate social strata and the dream of independence for small men', is said to have developed out of the New South Wales party's alliance of urban socialist intellectuals, such as its future parliamentary leaders William Hughes and W.A. Holman, and the 'populist' leaders of the Australian Workers' Union.[208]

At the time of the first election to the New Commonwealth, in 1901, the Labor Party was weaker in Victoria and South Australia where it existed 'only under the wing of the Protectionist liberals'.[209] In Victoria, according to Frank Bongiorno, the continued influence of colonial Liberalism and 'liberal' ideas – of respectability, active citizenship and community, independence, moderation, and good relations between 'fair' masters and men – upon the colony's labour movement ensured, in contrast to New South Wales, that 'the Labor Party's journey to political independence was long and troubled'.[210] Weak in the rural areas of Victoria, and suffering from conflict between Catholic and Protestant workers, the Labor Party in that state nevertheless gradually expanded its support in the countryside in the post 1905 years, largely as a result of the efforts of the AWU.[211] Relatively strong in Adelaide, Labor also fared badly in the early 1900s in the predominantly rural state of South Australia. However, the party increased its appeal to small farmers and formed a majority government in that state in 1910.[212]

In Western Australia the Scaddan Labor Government took office in 1911. This triumph followed a decade of fluctuating fortunes for Labor in this new and booming state. It was the prior growth of trade unionism on the goldfields, especially the Amalgamated Workers' Association and its creation in 1899 of the first Trades Union and Labor Congress, which underlay the emergence of independent labour politics. As in the field of trade unionism, impressive political gains were soon in evidence. As Patmore observes, 'A fledgling Labor Party won six seats in the Legislative Assembly in 1901'. Three years later Labor's star was in the ascendancy. The party became the largest group in the Assembly following the June election, and its leader, Henry Dalglish, became Premier. The *Westralian Worker* declared that 'the Labor gain is one of the greatest known in the history of the movement'.[213] However, growing disillusionment with Dalglish's moderation, and the ability of

Labor's opponents successfully to organise and combine their forces kept the party out of office between August 1905 and 1911.[214] The operation of a local property franchise and plural voting accounted for Labor's relatively poor showing in municipal elections on the goldfields during these years.[215]

In contrast to Western Australia, the Labor Party in Tasmania 'preceded widespread union organisation'. In Tasmania the late introduction of male suffrage, in 1901, combined with the overall weakness of trade unionism in this predominantly rural state, meant that the Labor Party's growth was slow and uneven. However, as in Victoria and Western Australia, the spread of 'new' unionism to the rural areas of Tasmania, this time in the form of the AWU, provided the base 'for the Labor Party winning twelve out of thirty seats in the April 1909 state elections'. However, as Patmore notes, ' This success and the brief establishment of a Labor minority government in October 1909 forced the non-Labor parties to unite and successfully delay a majority Labor government until April 1914'.[216]

The picture at the federal level was also was more mixed than might be imagined at first glance. The inability of any of the three competing parties – Labor, the Freetraders and the Protectionists – to win an outright majority in the New Commonwealth parliament between its inauguration in 1901 and Labor's majority success in 1910, was a source of both political strength and weakness to Labor. On the one hand, it meant that the Labor Party often held the balance of power in its hands and could, in return for support to the ruling party, expect to receive concessions. The latter was partly the case following the elections of 1901, 1904 and 1905 when both the Freetraders and Protectionists conceded some ground to the Labor Party on the issues of White Australia, the tariff and arbitration. Furthermore, the sympathies of the Protectionist liberal leader, Alfred Deakin, as opposed to the anti-statist and increasingly anti-socialist conservative Freetrader George Reid, rested to a significant extent with those of Labor. Thus Deakin's second Liberal ministry, which retained power with Labor support from 1905 to 1908 was, as Macintyre observes, 'at one with Labor in its commitments to social justice and willingness "to seek those ends by a free use of the agencies of the state". Moreover, 'Old-age pensions, anti-monopoly legislation, higher tariffs and accompanying legislation intended to guarantee domestic living standards were the principal means'.[217]

On the other hand, there were limits to the concessions granted. For example, Deakin consistently registered his opposition to Labor Party demands to extend the jurisdiction of the Arbitration Court to railway workers and other state employees. Indeed, it was on this issue that he both resigned, in April 1904, and allowed Labor to fall in August of the same year. More generally, Deakin came to realise that his brand of regulatory and collectivist Liberalism, however 'advanced', would not and could not satisfy the Labor Party's insistent demands for *more* Commonwealth regulation and collectivism in general: 'for further instalments of social reform by extending federal powers, strengthening the Arbitration Court and regulating living standards'.[218] It was with this realisation to the fore, combined with the declining electoral fortunes of his party and its organisation and growing support for the Labor Party and the Anti-Socialists (the erstwhile Freetraders) that, upon the fall of his government in late 1908, Deakin was 'to join forces with the other non-Labor elements'. This combined Fusionist force of anti-socialists and anti-Laborites, largely representing the interests of property, drove Labor from office in 1909 and became the Liberal Party. The Labor Party would have its revenge in the following year. However, in 1911 the failure of the referenda on Labor's plans further to enhance the powers of the Commonwealth, with reference to trade, industry and commerce and the nationalization of monopolies, constituted a setback to hopes for 'the movement's' untroubled Forward March.

In addition to the threat presented by the formation of the Liberal Party to Labor, there was also evidence of growing anti-labour 'farmer consciousness' in many country areas. This manifested in opposition to Labor's Land Tax of 1910, in plans to extend the coverage of arbitration to rural labourers, and in strong anti-nationalization sentiments especially among the more prosperous freeholding farmers. These sentiments underlay the formation of Country parties in the pre-war years.[219] By the 1920s both the Liberal Party and the Country Party would present formidable challenges to Labor. Finally, although marked in a number of mining, manufacturing and pastoral communities, Labor's support varied across a range of urban and rural communities in the late nineteenth- and early twentieth-centuries.[220]

Qualifications and refinements, however, should not mask the impressive range and magnitude of the young Labor Party's achievements. It had achieved national office, on a majority basis, within ten years of its birth. In the form of Andrew Fisher's government, it would continue to hold power for the next three years. Having decided that there was nothing else to be gained from Deakin's Protectionist Liberals in 1908, it had severed previously close connections and cast them out of office in a most unsentimental, confident and decisive manner. From that moment onwards, the Labor Party, both nationally and regionally, was the concrete embodiment of what could be achieved by a disciplined, pragmatic and clearly focused *independent* party of the left. Above all, as demonstrated even in the Lib.-Lab. heartland of Victoria, by 1910 both the Labor Party and the labour movement had acquired very strong notions of their *own* interests, loyalties, 'understanding of social relations and the economic system', and their 'own rituals, customs' and 'interpretation of the past and vision of the future'.[221] As Deakin realised, Labor's class-based sense of independence and confidence and its insistent and seemingly unlimited collectivist horizon could no longer be accommodated within Protectionist Liberalism. Notwithstanding the strong revival of class in British politics, Liberalism was more successful in retaining its influence upon the British labour movement than upon its Australian counterpart. Similarly the 'fusion' of non-Labor forces in post-1908 Australia had signally failed to prevent

Labor's 'rise', both nationally and at state level.

It was thus as a beacon to the independent labour forces of the world, its seeming ability to deliver on the promise that 'the working classes ... become the ruling classes',[222] that the Australian Labor Party attracted so much fascination and generally warm praise from labour activists both at home and abroad.

However, as noted earlier, the Webbs – so often the exceptions to the general rule – were not impressed. During their late 1890s visit to Sydney they were 'struck with the backwardness of politics here' and the 'uncivilised' nature and 'bad manners of all classes'. Much like the rich Sydneysiders, the 'working men' appeared to be 'also largely non-political'. Their political leaders, having 'no ideas of their own', were merely content to 'propose the legislation of England or New Zealand'. And even the 'so-called radical politicians' had 'no conception of collective ownership'.[223] However, not only were the Webbs' 'expert' observations inaccurate, but they were also way out of line with the contemporary labour-movement consensus that Labor politics in Australia were markedly in advance of those in Britain.

This consensus certainly manifested itself very strongly in the sources that I consulted. For example, western-Australian socialist, Claude Thompson's 'dismal' impressions of the working and living conditions of workers in the Manchester area, recorded earlier, were accompanied by equally dismal, and somewhat bewildered, conclusions concerning the state of their political consciousness. As Thompson recorded in the *Westralian Worker* in September 1904,

> At Oldham, on a Saturday night, we had a smaller meeting than many of the ordinary week night propaganda meetings on the gold-fields. The parliamentary borough of Oldham is as populous as the whole of W.A., the people are all workers or tradespeople dependent on workers, yet the borough returns Winston Churchill to the House of Commons. It is no wonder that Blatchford addressed his 'Merrie England' to stupid 'John Smith, of Oldham'.

Moreover, working-class political 'stupidity' was by no means confined to Oldham. 'Throughout the whole of the Lancashire towns that I visited', wrote Thompson,

> I noticed a great indifference towards the struggle for Labor representation and its consequent improvement in the conditions of Labor. *Everywhere there was the disposition to take things as they were and to whoop for Liberal or for Tory at election time.* (emphasis added)

In sum, while there were some 'sincere workers for reform', 'the vast majority were almost hopeless'.[224]

In an editorial asking why there were so few Labour men in the British House of Commons in 1903, the *Westralian Worker* had likewise pointed to the deleterious effects of tradition, resignation and blindness as to their 'true' interests on the part of the British labour movement. Thus,

> The huge Labor Societies have been content to vote, decade after decade, for one or
> other of the Capitalistic parties who were, broadly speaking, equally contemptuous
> of the desires and aspirations of the workers.

The 'slow-moving' British 'brethren of ours', were exhorted by the *Westralian
Worker* to cast off their support for Conservatism and Liberalism and follow the
LRC's commitment to *Labour Party independence*.[225]

The confidence to be gained from successfully making that commitment was am-
ply demonstrated in the interviews given to the *Labour Leader* by Australian Prime
Minister Andrew Fisher and his ALP colleagues during their visit to London in
1911. Fisher, a former Ayrshire miner, and according to his interviewer, A. Fenner
Brockway, 'distinguished looking, tall, broad shouldered ... erect ... refined and
his manner cultured', expressed both great pride in his party's attainment of national office and unbounded hope for the future.[226] The Labor Party's historic victory of 1910, set against the background of 'the steadily growing popularity of the
Labor cause' in the face of the opposition of the Liberal Party, 'as a whole', meant
not only that the young Australian movement had come of age, but also that it now
held important lessons for the older movements of Britain and Europe from which
Australian labour had often taken its cue.

Much in the manner of many British Labour leaders, Fisher's political thought
was eclectic in character, a mixture of 'labourist' pragmatism and ethical socialism.
Commitments to 'responsible Government' and 'realism' – 'We are ... attacking
practical problems, and are not immediately concerned with Utopian ideas' – mingled with the desire to 'have the power to nationalise monopolies', and a firm belief
in the eventual triumph of a socialist society – 'a brotherhood of free souls, where
men and women shall be free, not only in name but in reality'. Fisher expressed
due solidarity with his British and European brothers and sisters. Yet his internationalism was tinged with a belief in the growing superiority of the Australian
movement and the 'Australian way'. Thus he asserted that the labour movements
of the Old World had not 'gained the position we now occupy'. Fisher highlighted
the specific importance, 'both to the Commonwealth and to the women', of the
early enactment of women's suffrage in his country. More generally,

> We feel, also that the time has come when some of your men and women should take
> a trip our way. There are other parts of the world besides Europe and America.

Fisher's sentiments were fully endorsed by McGowen, Bowman and Jones, the
other Australian leaders interviewed in the pages of the *Labour Leader*.[227]

Leading figures in the British movement were duly impressed by both Fisher and
his colleagues and the advances registered by their movement. At a dinner held by

the British Labour Party in honour of Fisher, Ramsay MacDonald expressed the prevailing sentiment in his party when held up Australia and her Labor leaders as 'the hope of the coming democracy'. He continued, 'We have come from all quarters of the land to do honour to men who, springing from the common people, have risen to the highest positions that the Australian democracy can offer.'[228]

MacDonald's praise was by no means unprecedented. The accession of the Australian Labor Party to minority office in 1904 had occasioned heartfelt praise and congratulation, indeed awe and inspiration, among important sections of the British labour movement. Notwithstanding its opposition to Australian Labor's growing protectionism, this was very much was the case in the British Labour Party. As Stefan Berger has observed,

> The successes of the ALP were keenly followed in the British Labour Party. At the 1905 Labour Representation Committee ... Isaac Mitchell, the fraternal delegate of the Amalgamated Society of Engineers, referred to the Australian party's success as a model for the Labour Party ... In organisation and outlook the ALP came to be an inspiration for the Labour Party.[229]

Similarly, the Ninth Annual Conference of the Labour Party, held in Portsmouth in 1909, sent a cable congratulating Fisher upon his (albeit short-lived) governmental victory of 1908.[230] The latter's resounding victory in 1910 brought forth further, and more effusive congratulations from the British party upon the 'magnificent results'.[231]

Many ILPers followed suit. As early as 1902 the *Labour Leader* had confidently proclaimed that, 'Labour is coming (into) its own in Australasia and no mistake'; and that 'Labour in this enlightened part of the world does not cringe and bow to merely inanimate things – such as capital'.[232] Two years later the *Labour Leader* published a two-part article entitled, 'The Australian Labour Party: The History of its Growth' ('By An Australian'), celebrating the more 'advanced' state of the movement in the 'Workman's Paradise'.[233] In 1905 the newspaper declared that, 'Labour is going ahead in Australia. Election after election sees it increasing its power in the Legislatures'.[234] In the following year, Margaret MacDonald, in Queensland, proudly,

> watched *our* band of Labour stalwarts at the opening of Parliament ... strolling into the House, and knew that Labour at last was beginning to take possession of what belonged to it. Here the process has gone further, and the Labour men captured higher game. (emphasis added.)

Many of MacDonald's Queensland 'stalwarts' had spent their formative political years in socialist and labour movements in Britain and were personal friends or acquaintances.[235] In looking back upon his visit to Australia in 1908, Keir Hardie had no hesitation in pronouncing Australia to be superior to the rest.

Thus, 'I regard it ... as certain that Australasia will be the first country in the world to come under the rule of the working class'.[236]

Even most of those British socialists, in the SDF and elsewhere on the Left, who shared Tom Mann's growing criticisms of Australian labourism, nevertheless also endorsed Mann's view that, on balance, labour's 'forward march' and the inevitability of socialism, respectively, were more pronounced and more likely to be achieved sooner in Australia than elsewhere in the world. In his 1905 pamphlet, *Socialism*, Mann conceded that 'it would not be right' to describe all Australia's 'Labor Men' as 'definitely Socialist' – 'it can only be said of some of them that they are Socialistic in trend'. Yet he went on to argue that, 'no one can doubt that the GUIDING OR DRIVING FORCE IS SOCIALISM PURE AND SIMPLE'.[237] Dora Montefiore, while condemning Australian labour's 'isolation from the international movement' and the 'half-heartedness of their leaders', nevertheless, concluded in 1911 that, 'Practically, the many thousands in the Labour Party of Australia have accepted the interpretation that the world must, in the near future, belong to the workers'.[238] Furthermore, 'the world moves; and even in Australia it is moving towards socialism'.[239] Similarly, and notwithstanding his claim that 'the workers of Australia are not class conscious', at least in a 'socialist sense', Ben Tillett saw the ALP's victory in 1910 as a potential stepping stone to a socialist future. Accession to and the experience of political power within the confines of a capitalist state carried with it the dangers of 'compromise', 'opportunism' and 'party flunkeyism'. (By 1912 Montefiore and other contributors to *Justice* would routinely describe the ALP in office as 'a capitalist party in flimsy disguise'.)[240] But it also constituted 'a start' which could be translated into a real 'gain'.[241]

Australian Labor Party activists, of course, shared, and often surpassed, British observers in their praise and delight at the ALP's growing list of achievements. In 1903 the *Westralian Worker's* report on the Commonwealth Labor (Union) Congress recorded the 'marvellous strides' forward made since the last comparable inter-state gathering of union delegates, in March 1891. At that date, there had been 'no recognised Labor Party in any one of the Australian Parliaments'. Now, 'despite the ravings of every daily newspaper throughout the Commonwealth', there was 'no Australian Parliament without its recognised Labor Party'.[242] Moreover, the uneven and limited progress of the party in Queensland and some of the other states, could not disguise the rise of *independent* Labor as a major national force. In sum, 'a great and glorious future awaits'.[243]

Australia's first Labor ministry, in 1904, was hailed as 'A World's Record' by the *Worker*. 'Behold', declared the newspaper, 'a wonderful thing has happened! Labor sits upon the throne of Power, with the sceptre of government in its hand!'.[244] Labor's even more impressive electoral success of 1910 moved the *Bulletin* to enthuse, 'Between them, Labor and Australia last week won the most brilliant victory that has been recorded since first the flag of the Commonwealth waved over a united people'.[245] While the *Worker* pronounced the 1910 victory to be 'without parallel in the history of the working class'.[246] Even before the election the Labor Party had 'accomplished so much as to make Australia an object of the deepest interest to the entire world'. Without its 'preventive agency', Australia would 'rapidly have sunk to the level of Europe'.[247] ' Such a Movement as this' could not 'be defeated'.[248] In the opinion of the *Worker*, the ALP's impressive organisation and tight self-discipline, allied to the strength of its working-class support, rendered Labor's victory at the polls more or less inevitable. Thus: 'We had only to shout, and the walls of Privilege fell down. We had only to raise an arm, and the forces of Capitalism fled in dismay'.[249]

Moreover, 'IF THE PEOPLE WERE READY FOR IT, WE COULD HAVE SOCIALISM TOMORROW'.

However, as matters stood, the *Worker* believed that the further education of the 'public mind', and the immediate realisation of a land tax (to 'free the soil to the people'), the nationalisation of monopolies, and more extensive NEW PROTECTION to the workers were necessary forerunners to the realisation of the ultimate goal, the creation of the 'Co-operative Commonwealth'.[250] Even the defeat of the referenda in 1911 could not stem the *Worker's* enthusiasm. It was henceforth imperative to redouble efforts, to perfect organisation and end divisions within the party, to create a daily labour press more effectively to counter the false propaganda of the 'Fat press', and to broaden the party's appeal to women and the 'great unattached army of workers'.[251] In such ways would normal progress to socialism quickly be resumed.

The Roots of Labour's Advance

Before proceeding to our final section – a discussion of the overall impact of the labour movement on the national life of Australia – it is worth pausing at this stage in an attempt to pinpoint the main reasons for both the trade unions' and the ALP's precocity in the period under review.

I have earlier established the wider politico-economic framework – federation, national settlement, arbitration, protection, Liberal weakness in the face of Labor's rise, the creation of the 'labourist-protectionist' state and the limited development of industrial capitalism – so crucial to organised labour's rapid growth in 1900s Australia. I will now turn from this wider determining framework to concentrate specifically upon favourable factors within the labour movement and the wider working class.

First, to a degree unmatched in either Britain or, especially, the United States, both the 'new' and 'old' unions provided bedrock support for the ALP. As noted earlier, while it was the TUC which brought the British Labour Party into being, there was by no means total trade union backing for the Labour Party in the pre-1914 period. Trade union allegiance to the Liberal Party, in particular, remained strong. In the United States most unions did not lend their support to independent labour politics. As in Britain, it was the trade union movement which provided the main impetus for the birth and development of independent labour politics in Australia. However, in marked contrast to the United States and to a lesser extent Britain, and taking into account the presence of a few dissenting voices,[252] the overwhelming majority of Australian trade unions soon rallied behind 'their' creation, the Labor Party.

Significantly, the largest and most powerful representatives of *both* 'old' and 'new unionism in Australia, respectively the ASE and the AWU, were involved in the 'turn' to independent labour. Indeed, the AWU rapidly became the dominant influence upon the Labor Party not only in New South Wales and Queensland, but also nationally.[253] Notwithstanding its formal 'no politics' rule, there is also clear evidence that the ASE increasingly committed itself to the cause of the ALP. As the Australasian Council of the ASE declared in April 1904,

> A matter of great importance took place in the political arena last month which is worth mentioning, although politics, pure and simple, are tabooed from our branch meetings, and that is the advent of the Federal Labor Ministry to power. Such a position has been the dream of many an enthusiast of the Labor Party ... it is to be hoped that all of the party will assist Mr. Watson by showing the utmost confidence in him and his colleagues.[254]

While this commitment did not mean that all ASE members were 'weaned away from allegiance to traditional political parties', it did signify the development of an increasingly partisan approach to politics on the part of both the official union and its wider membership.[255] Labor's victory in 1910 was warmly welcomed within the ASE, as it was among most other craft bodies, including the 'aristocratic' printers.[256] More generally, the national, regional and local leadership of the ALP, as in Britain, had extremely close trade-union origins and continuing ties.[257]

As a consequence of the unions' rapid and overwhelming support for the ALP and the inextricable links between the industrial and political arms of the labour movement, the labour movement as a whole in Australia enjoyed an enviable degree of solidarity and unity of purpose. In the Australian case, the fragmentation and divisions characteristic of US labour were conspicuous by their weakness. The rise of a mass trade union movement and a mass Labor Party went hand in hand.

Second, considerable importance must be attached to the part played by Australia's predominantly male labour leaders in advancing the cause of their movement. By the 1900s Australian labour was extremely fortunate to possess a group of very able and committed leaders at all levels. Tough-minded, independent, determined and resourceful, the leadership group comprised two main sections: the pioneers and veterans of 'the movement' who were predominantly British in origin; and younger, mainly native-born, men, often in their twenties and early thirties, highly mobile geographically and full of energy, enterprise and initiative. Both sections were adept at the 'trade of agitation'.[258]

The veterans, most prominent in the skilled and craft unions, had often been introduced at an early age, and duly served their apprenticeship, to a variety of radical working-class movements in Britain. For example, in late 1901 a 'complimentary smoke concert' was held by the Melbourne South branch of the ASE to present Brother John Davies, 'The Australian Father of the ASE', with a certificate of merit – in recognition of his 'pioneer services' to the union movement. A 'faithful member of 57 years', Davies had been among those pioneers 'blacklisted' by the employers in Britain for their part in the formation of the ASE. (Davies was one of the three delegates who had drafted the ASE's first set of rules.) Davies refused to sign 'the document' (a renunciation of trade unionism) and, with financial help from the Christian Socialists, set sail from England 'for some foreign shore where such tyranny did not exist'. Even before his ship, the *Frances Walker*, had reached Sydney, Davies and other brothers had formed 'the first Australian branch of the ASE', the union which now enjoyed 'the longest continuous history in Australia'. The first president of the Sydney branch of the union, Davies left Sydney to establish the Melbourne branch of the ASE in 1859. Symptomatic of the close bond between trade unionism and the infant Labor Party, the 1901 presentation to Davies was made by John C. Watson, the leader of the party and the future Premier of the Commonwealth.[259]

Less prominent than Davies, many other pioneers of the ASE in Australia, nevertheless, shared the very important experience of transporting their trade unionism from the Old World to the New. Four brief examples may be cited in support of this general point. First, George Newton, one of Davies's companions on the *Frances Walker*, became secretary of the Sydney branch of the ASE. He later took his trade unionism to Newcastle, a leading industrial centre in New South Wales. Newton was still a member of the society in 1920 when it became the Amalgamated Engineering Union.[260] Second, in 1901 the ASE in Melbourne paid tribute to David Webster for his long service to the society. Webster had been one of the representatives of the ASE at its first Delegate Meeting in Leeds, England. A veteran trade unionist, he had recently become a trustee of the Melbourne branch.[261] Third, in 1911 Sydney's Redfern branch of the ASE recorded the death of Brother William Thompson, aged sixty-eight years of age. Thompson, a member of the ASE for forty-six years, had served his time in Wolverhampton. He had reached Australia via spells of work in Egypt, Canada and the Cape Colony of South Africa.[262] Finally, in 1912 the Newcastle branch honoured William Millar, a 'prominent trade unionist' for fifty-six years. A member of the Glasgow ASE in the 1850s, Millar emigrated to Australia in 1863. Upon his arrival in Sydney, he immediately involved himself in the work and struggles of trade unionism. Secretary of the Sydney and, later, Newcastle branches of the society, his name had become a 'household word' in Sydney, not only because of his trade-union work, but also 'because of what he had done for humanity'. Millar had eventually become a foreman patternmaker.[263]

British-born veterans and pioneers, were also very prominent in the typographical societies. In 1912 the *Australasian Typographical Journal* mourned the death of 'one of the oldest printers in Victoria', Thomas Boreland McKnight, aged 86. Born in Scotland in 1826, McKnight had served his seven year printing apprenticeship on the *Dumfries Herald*. He then moved to London where he worked on the *Morning Post*. A journey to the United States in search of work was followed by a return to Scotland. However, in 1853 McKnight left Scotland to become a gold digger in Victoria. Unsuccessful in that endeavour, he eventually found his way to Melbourne where he worked on the *Argus* and in various jobbing offices. In later life he became an employer 'in comfortable circumstances'. Yet his commitment to trade unionism did not waiver. The tribute to McKnight ran,

> He was an excellent workmen (sic), with literary attainments, a congenial companion, and good unionist, ever ready to assist a fellow-workman.[264]

In the same year the *Journal* carried the obituaries of several other British-born printers who had remained faithful both to their trade and their union. For example, Thomas Miles, who died aged 87, had been born in London. He, too, had left Britain at mid-century unsuccessfully to try his hand at gold digging in Victoria. As in the case of many other long serving printers, the firm was represented at his funeral.[265] Some years after serving his apprenticeship to the famous Chambers Company in Edinburgh, Sam Mackie decided to try his luck in Australia. He joined the *Ballarat Star* and became a founding member of the Ballarat Typographical Society in 1857.[266] Joseph Watson had also been associated with the *Star* – 'for over twenty five years'. Born in Durham, England, Watson eventually graduated from printer to overseer. He had long been active in a Methodist Sunday School and his local brass band.[267] Similar tributes to long serving British-born printers appeared regularly in the pages of the *Journal* throughout the period under review.[268]

Prominent in craft and skilled trade unionism, British-born 'old hands' were also to be found in important positions in most, and perhaps all, other parts of the labour movement throughout the length and breadth of Australia. The friendly society movement, in both Australia and New Zealand, counted among its leaders numerous widely travelled, 'self-made' and public-spirited men (active as JPs, councillors, on hospital and charitable boards and in a range of educational institutions) who had started life in humble circumstances in Britain.[269] In terms of 'new' unionism, William Spence, probably the most important national figure, had been born the son of a stonemason on the island of Eday, Orkney, in 1846. Arriving in Victoria at the tender age of six, Spence's many talents were reflected in his wide-ranging career. At various points in his life he was a shepherd, butcher boy, member of the Ballarat Rifle Rangers, and mining 'shift boss' and manager. Autodidact and social visionary – 'Abolish Commercialism, abolish Capitalism and Competition, and peace will come' – Spence was also a committed teetotaller and nonconformist preacher. 'New' unionism was 'simply the teachings (sic) of that greatest of a social reformers, Him of Nazareth, whom all must revere'.[270] The *Worker* frequently drew attention to the prominence and ubiquity of British-born men among the industrial and political leaders of the labour movements of New South Wales and Queensland.[271] Margaret MacDonald observed in 1906 that the Queensland movement had been,

> started by men coming out who had been active in the British Socialist and Trade Union movement of the eighties … we met 'old warriors' from England and Scotland and Wales who spoke of Hardie and Hyndman and Burns and Sam Woods as old friends, and who take their LABOUR LEADER or 'Clarion' every week, and know our present-day movement quite as well as many of our home Socialists do.[272]

By the 1900s these and similar 'old warriors', of course, were enjoying considerable public prominence and well-earned respect after lifetimes of hard work and struggle, often for small reward. Whether as politicians or union leaders and negotiators, their jobs involved considerable knowledge and ability, persistence, skill and a willingness to travel long and often lonely distances for the sake of 'the cause'. For example in 1912, S.J. Elston, Organising Delegate for the ASE, reported in the following way upon his efforts to secure, by means of arbitration, extra money for the overtime worked by his members in the mines of Western Australia:

> I proceeded to Perth on 7th December … returned to Kalgoorlie on the 12th. The court sat in Kalgoorlie on the 18th, and I really had only five days to collect evidence and prepare my case. I acted as representative for the Society, and conducted the case. As applicant, I had to open the case and address the Court, which occupied about twenty minutes. Then I commenced to call my witnesses … examining them and they were cross examined by the Respondent Secretary of the Chamber of Mines, who represented the mining companies.

Manifestly able, Elston later accepted nomination for the job of organiser for the whole of Australia.[273]

Upward social mobility was also much in evidence among the British-born veterans. Born into the working class, committed to education, self-help and often nonconformist religion, and with long years of service to trade unionism and politics, many enjoyed advancement primarily through the medium of the labour movement itself. Such was the 'career pattern' of two of the most famous early ALP leaders, Andrew Fisher (Ayrshire collier) and William Arthur Holman (London cabinetmaker).[274] Future Labour Prime Minister, 'Billy' Hughes, born in London and reared in north Wales, was a pupil-teacher who had turned to a variety of labouring jobs upon his arrival in Australia in 1884.[275] Born in Chile rather than Britain, John Christian Watson travelled the hard road from compositor to Labour Premier.[276] As noted above, William Spence was born in Scotland, the son of a stonemason. While the life and career of Henry Boote, the editor of the *Worker*, had embraced the childhood slums of Liverpool, apprenticeship as a compositor at age ten in the same city, artistic training at the Royal Academy in London and work as a compositor in Brisbane upon his arrival in Australia in 1889. Already a committed trade unionist and socialist, Boote put his considerable talents as 'a socialist propagandist and writer' to work in the Queensland labour movement.[277]

Others achieved career advancement more directly as a result of their experiences in the work-place. This was particularly the case in the craft and skilled sectors of the economy. There, as suggested earlier, the dividing line between worker and employer often remained fuzzy and the capital requirements to 'set up shop' were frequently not great. This was certainly the case in printing and engineering. Significantly, the union journals of the printers and engineers contained numerous references to former workers who had become overseers, managers and (usually small) employers.[278] Of equal significance were two further factors. First, these upwardly mobile men, at least in the cases consulted in the union and friendly society journals,[279] had retained their firm allegiance to the labour movement. Second, it was in the craft sector, and especially in 'aristocratic' parts of printing, engineering and construction, that the notion of 'producerism' – rooted in respectability, moderation, and the predominantly shared interests of 'master and man' – was most pronounced.[280]

The first group of labour leaders brought a wealth of experience and knowledge to the Australian movement. The second, comprising enthusiastic, enterprising, relatively young and predominantly native-born men, infused it with new blood and a renewed sense of urgency and purpose at a crucial moment in its history. There is some evidence, albeit limited and scattered in character, to support my argument that the presence of this new, younger generation of labour leaders made a major contribution to the marked growth of the movement in a number of localities between 1900 and 1914.[281] While a vast amount of new evidence is required to substantiate this argument at the national level, the particular case of the goldfields of Western Australia certainly bears it out. In the latter case, young male migrants from Victoria and New South Wales were to the fore, as leaders and activists, in creating the trade unions and the independent labour political organisations which, as noted earlier, grew very rapidly in the new mining centres.

For example, in 1902 the *Westralian Worker* drew attention to the career of James Lockard. Born in New South Wales, Lockard had been 'a grafter all his life'. From the age of eleven he had been involved in 'storekeeping, brewery work, surveying, dam work, wharf lumping, mining and condensing'. A member of the Sydney Lumpers' Union, Lockard had decided to try his luck in the expanding west. In 1897 he arrived in Bulong 'by which democratic little township he swears'. Lockard helped to transform the Bulong Alluvial Rights Association into the inclusive and radical Amalgamated Workers' Association. A.J.P. Lockard had been nominated for the presidency of the AWA.[282] Tom Beasley, recently appointed General secretary of the AWA, had also migrated west from New South Wales, where he had been 'intimately associated with labor in politics'.[283] Another prominent AWAer, Thomas Heitman, a native of Bendigo, had arrived in the west in 1897.[284] E. Fleming, only twenty-one years of age, had left South Australia in 1895. He became a miner on the North Murchison and secretary of his AWA branch.[285] Finally, the thirty-two-year-old Jack Holman, twice elected general president of the AWA, and secretary of the Western Australia Labor Party, had migrated west from Victoria. A miner, Holman had won his spurs in the Arbitration Court. 'As a grafter', observed the *Westralian Worker*, 'Holman's record would be hard to beat, as in organising and propaganda work he has addressed more meetings and compassed more mileage than any of his fellow members'.[286]

The founding fathers and early leaders of the other unions on the goldfields had similar profiles. Although born in Durham, England, in 1877, J.B. Coatham, had arrived in Ballarat as a young boy. Apprenticed to his stepfather, a tailor, Coatham 'had a longing to strike out on his own'. He arrived in Western Australia in 1899 'where he has been striking out on his own more or less ever since'. He had become a leading figure in the Tailors' Society, a crusader against sweating and secretary of the May Day Demonstration Committee.[287] In October 1902 the *Westralian Worker* announced the sad death of John Reside. Only thirty-three at death, Reside had arrived from Bendigo in 1897. A miner and engine driver, he had been one of the founders and leading figures in the Engine Drivers' Association.[288] EJ, 'Ned', Hogan was born in Ballarat in 1884. Raised on a farm and enduring chronic poverty, Hogan won a reputation as a 'great battler'. Upon his arrival in Western Australia in 1905, he worked on the Kanowna wood line, a notorious centre of non-unionism and 'a system of exploitation ... which probably outdid anything in Australia'. Undeterred, Hogan was at the centre of the 'unique struggle', in 1908, which successfully stopped supplies of timber being transported to the mines. Later in 1908 Hogan was one of the founders of the Firewood Workers' Union. A student of 'economics, philosophy and sociology', Hogan had become 'something of a hero with the rank and file of the Labor movement'.[289]

Henry Glance, long an advocate of amalgamation between the AWA and the Amalgamated Miners' Association, had been elected first general secretary of the federated union. Glance was born in Melbourne in 1876. At the age of fifteen he started work in a warehouse. However, three years later he 'threw up his billet and came West'. A few months work on the goldfields was followed by employment at Fremantle in harbour construction work. There, Glance helped to form a union, but was sacked for his efforts. He moved to Kalgoorlie, started mining and was elected president of the Kalgoorlie and Boulder branch of the AWA. Already a union veteran by the age of thirty-five, Glance had also served as a JP for eight years, a Labor councillor for five, given evidence before a Royal Commission and stood as a Federal Labor Party candidate at Boulder.[290]

As seen in Glance's example, there invariably existed very close links between trade unionism and Labor Party politics among labour leaders on the goldfields.

Thus C.E. Frazer, Federal Labor candidate for Kalgoorlie in 1903, had been heavily involved in the Engine Drivers' Association, 'one of the largest unions of this State', and secretary of the Goldfields Trades and Labor Council. A native of Victoria, Frazer had 'come west' in 1895.[291] Paddy Lynch, 'the first Laborist to win municipal honors (sic) on these fields', as a municipal councillor in Boulder, was also a member of the Engine Drivers' Association and, as a trade unionist in the east, had been involved in the Maritime Strike.[292] An important figure in 1900s Labor politics in Fremantle, W.H. Carpenter, a forty-year-old English-born boilermaker, had impeccable trade-union credentials. Chafing against 'the restricted conditions of English factory life', Carpenter had left for Australia. In Ballarat he had been involved in the labour struggles of the early 1890s and was sacked from the foundry where he worked. Carpenter travelled once again and found work in a locomotive shop in Fremantle. He had since become president of the Fremantle Trades Hall Association.[293]

As these examples demonstrate, the second group of labour leaders, in very much the same way as the first, were characterised by their mobility and toughness, their independence and enterprise, their ability to pick up work when and where necessary – to 'turn their hands' to almost anything in order to survive. Like many 'bush' workers, they had led predominantly nomadic lives. Above all perhaps, they transcended, to a great extent, the rural-urban divide and spread the notion of working-class 'mateship' throughout a variety of communities across Australia.[294] In the manner of the British-born veterans, they nurtured *a moving frontier of radicalism*, the transnational radical migrations of the former being complemented by the intra-continental radical movement of the latter. In sum, they made a vital contribution to organised labour's precocity.

Three characteristics of the *combined* group of labour leaders merit further note. First, it will be manifest to the reader that both social/occupational and geographical mobility were associated in the minds of the leaders far more with personal independence, freedom and the opportunity to build the collective institutions of 'the movement' than with 'bourgeois individualism'. These leaders aspired to a 'living wage' rather than great wealth, and sought to 'emancipate' the workers by means of the chosen instrument of the labour movement rather than to escape from the working class. Moreover, the independence often conferred by mobility meant that, as, for example, a publican, small master, shopkeeper, and, at least in some cases, independent digger and selector/shearer, one was in a better position to speak and act more freely in labour's interest than as a pure 'wage slave' subjected to the close supervision and strict control of the boss.

Second, many labour leaders prided themselves upon their respectability. However, the kind of respectability espoused and practised was, for the most part, and in opposition to the view expressed by Metin, McQueen and Clark, far less that of the aspirant, status conscious, individualistic and exclusive bourgeois, than that of the working-class activist seeking to develop self-respect, class pride and the advancement of the labour movement.[295] The cornerstone of their respectability was, once again, *independence*, both personal and collective in character, complete with its fundamental antipathy to deference or 'groveldom'.

Third, the leaders consciously attempted to build a movement-based culture rooted in white working-class unity, in 'mateship'.

The institutions of the labour movement were to be placed at the very core of this culture. Notwithstanding their racialized and gendered boundaries, these institutions were to be the means of promoting the virtues of tolerant and inclusive class-based solidarity. The potentially divisive effects of different economic, political, religious and socio-cultural experiences and beliefs, including the stark contrasts between life in 'the bush' and in the mushrooming urban centres, were to be avoided or overcome by a successful appeal to the common interests of *organised workers* and their allies as the 'true' democrats and producers, the 'true' people, the 'true' backbone of a progressive nation. *Their* movement, the labour movement, was the ascendant force which would 'tame', 'civilise', 'warren' and eventually 'transform' capitalism.

It was this egalitarian and democratic vision, allied to the pragmatic daily requirements of 'movement building', which led labour activists to attempt to construct communities in their own image. They busily set about the establishment of Workers' Halls, Trades' Halls, Workmen's Clubs and Miners' Institutes, branches of the Women's Labour League and socialist clubs, variously equipped with reading rooms, 'running billiard tables' and other recreational facilities.[296] From the new goldfields of Western Australia to the more established rural and urban centres of the East, they organised a wide range of activities appealing to a cross-section of tastes and interests. These embraced, *inter alia*, dances, all manner of 'trips and treats', sports events for all members of the family (often organised by Eight Hours Demonstration Committees) socials (including 'smoke socials'), picnics, lectures, brass bands, retail and producer co-operatives, singing clubs, maternity beds, homes and baskets for 'distressed mothers', and food and clothing for needy sisters.[297] They established a labour press which catered not only to the political and trade-union interests, but also to the sporting and leisure tastes of its readership. For example, the *Westralian Worker* ran a regular sporting column carrying the latest news of boxing, cricket, billiards, horse racing and whippets. It also ran adverts for 'UNION BEER', made at the Union Brewery, Kalgoorlie, from 'Jones and Sons' Best English Malt, the Colonial Sugar Co's very finest Colonial Sugar, the most perfect blend of English, American, New Zealand and Tasmanian Hops, and from the Condensed Water supplied by Mr. James Ryan'.[298] In 1909, in response to 'several requests', the *Westralian Worker* also initiated its 'Woman's Column' by 'Jeanette'. This column defined 'woman's sphere' as being 'as wide as the whole world'. It devoted articles and letters to a wide variety of topics, ranging from 'the woman wage slave', equal pay, and women and electoral politics.[299]

In some instances, as in western Australia, the labour movement was breaking new cultural ground. In the more established labour centres of New South Wales, Queeensland and elsewhere it was building upon relatively strong foundations. However, in all cases we are witnessing the more intensive and extensive efforts of labour leaders to construct an inclusive, eclectic and potentially hegemonic culture. Notwithstanding some exceptions to the general rule, men and women (the latter in both their supportive and independent roles)[300] and their families and friends, both 'abstinent' and 'non-abstinent', (preferably) 'respectable' but also some 'rough' (especially if 'rough diamonds') and 'honest plain speakers' with 'no edge' to them, Catholics and Protestants, urban and rural, and skilled and non skilled were invited to become a part of this 'movement culture'.[301]

To be sure, labour's cultural project by no means met with unqualified success in the period in question. All manner of divisions – 'respectable' versus 'rough', 'locals' versus 'outsiders' and 'foreigners', Catholics versus Protestants and so forth – continued to inform Australian working-class life as a whole, and were by no means totally absent from its labour-movement mainfestations.[302] Furthermore, labour's cultural influence over community life was limited and uneven. It might 'rule' in some mining communities. However, even the outstanding national example of a 'truly union town', Broken Hill, did not attain that status until the inter-war period.[303] Moreover, as Terry Irving has reminded us, research to date has only scratched the surface of 'the rich particularities of working class culture in the mobilising period between the 1880s and the 1920s'.[304]

Taking on board these necessary qualifications and refinements, nevertheless, it is indisputable that the labour movement made remarkable strides forward during our period, that a group of able and influential leaders was to the fore and that they attempted, much like the British Chartists in an earlier period, to build a 'movement culture' rooted in class.[305] Moreover, they met with a very positive and sharpened response from across the working class.[306] In the very midst of their diversity, Australian workers, to borrow Stuart Macintyre's apt phrase, began to 'cohere as a class'.[307] In sum, I advance the tentative and provisional thesis that organised labour's remarkable institutional advance was rooted in the probable 'making' of the Australian working class culturally and socially. At the very minimum, the cultural and sociological roots of the ALP's and the trade unions' 'coming of age' nationally, merit urgent and detailed historical investigation.

4. Labour's Impact on National Life

The three findings presented so far in this essay lend themselves logically to the fourth conclusion that organised labour's impact on Australian national life by the end of the 1900s was considerable. It was considerable rather than hegemonic for the reason stated by Christopher Lloyd – that the process of national settlement represented a compromise between the major forces of capital (including rural capital) and labour rather than the 'triumph' of the one over the other[308] At the same time, however, we must take full account of the popular contemporary view, as articulated by Spence in 1909, that 'The Labor Movement in Australia has now become an almost dominant factor in the political life of the community'.[309] As a corollary, organised labour and the working class were manifestly not the 'subordinate' and 'incorporated' creatures depicted by the Left historiography, respectively, of McQueen and Markey.[310] The work of these two scholars suffers from an exaggerated political pessimism and sociological functionalism, as reflected in the theses that a 'labourist' or 'populist' labour movement had little to offer in the way of 'real' change for the working class, and that it assumed its ideological colouring largely from its capitalist environment. In fact, the 'rise of Labour' demonstrated that there was far more change and conflict in Australian society, and that labour leaders possessed much greater powers of agency, choice and influence upon the character of that society, than is suggested above. As David Palmer, Ross Shanahan and Martin Shanahan have recently argued, a 'fundamental aspect of Australian society that has distinguished it from other countries', resides in the fact that, 'the Australian "state" itself has embedded in it, in its institutions, laws and ethos, 'labourist' values that are widely accepted in the national culture'.[311] Furthermore, as I will show below, organised labour's ideological character continued to be more mixed than suggested by one-dimensional labels, such as 'labourist' or 'populist'.

Reference to our British and American comparative framework underscores the major and unusual impact on national life and consciousness exerted by Australian labour. Despite its impressive trade-union and growing independent political strength, the labour movement in Britain certainly did not possess anything like the same power and influence over national policy and the future direction of the country as did its Australian counterpart. Labour in Britain, of course, had its own core values and vision revolving around labour, class, nation and empire. However, in terms of the national picture and national consciousness as a whole, it still remained very much a subordinate player or 'estate', largely reacting to decisions made by hegemonic 'gentlemanly' capitalists drawn from landed, commercial, financial and manufacturing sources of wealth. *Pace* Gompers' claims to the prevalence of 'people's power' in the United States, noted earlier, there is absolutely no doubt that organised labour exerted even less power and influence in that country. Both the dominant definition of what it meant to be an American and effective social, economic and political power rested firmly with the forces of 'monopoly capital' and its allies. Organised labour was very much a minority, if at times oppositional, voice in the nation's affairs.

One major question remains to be addressed. What kind of *ideological* presence did labour bring to bear on Australian life? This question has elicited a voluminous body of literature which may be roughly broken down into four schools of thought.

First, Robin Gollan and others presented the 'classical' view that the infant ALP embodied a mixture of class consciousness, radical, egalitarian nationalism and, to a lesser extent, socialism. However, the push for and the early acquisition of office very quickly brought about a narrowed focus and more limited ambitions. A concern with short-term, pragmatic and piecemeal labourist demands was held, in practice, to have taken precedence over the goal of social(ist) transformation. In sum, there occurred a rapid 'fall from grace'.[312]

From the 1960s onwards the 'original sin' thesis, associated most closely, but not invariably, with the New Left, challenged that of the 'fall from grace'. This second approach appeared in its most extreme form in McQueen's A New Britannia, first published in 1968. McQueen set out to 'expose' Labour's 'radicalism' and 'nationalism' as being, from the very outset, inherently racist, imperialistic, deferential to monarchy, reformist, militaristic, and 'petit bourgeois'.[313] Despite his identification of elements of visionary idealism, including socialism, within the infant ALP, the 'radical nationalist', Manning Clark, also subscribed largely to the view that there had been no 'fall'. Rather the 'aspirant respectability', characteristic of the bourgeoisie, combined with racism, timid pragmatism, moderation and loyalty to the empire and its royal trappings were the dominant features of the ALP and much of its constituency from the outset.[314]

Third, much of the more recent work has both signalled a return to the 'fall from grace' perspective and emphasised the enduring nature of the ALP's labourist 'closure' of the 1900s. Thus for Bruce Scates, 'The "true" republic Lawson wrote of was nothing less than a total transformation of state, society and culture'. Moreover,

> the New Australia envisaged by the radicals of the1890s was a totalising critique, it challenged class, gender and (less convincingly) racial inequalities. At its centre was a new notion of citizenship – not *just* that Australians were no longer to be the subjects of a distant foreign Queen, but that every aspect of our political life should become open and participatory. The community politics of the 1890s, with its street rallies, open-air meetings and unruly public forums, offered an unaccustomed liberty. It raised the 'political architecture' on which to imagine new forms of society.

However, federation and the rapid growth and triumph of the ALP's 'representative, parliamentary politics' effected 'political exigencies' and a 'cynical regime of compromise'. The labour's movement's politics were increasingly tamed, sanitized, institutionalised, narrowed and, in effect, 'closed'. From the 1910s onwards it became the ALP's guiding mission to 'civilise' and 'manage' rather than transform Australian capitalism'.[315]

Fourth, for some, especially Markey, labour's narrowed vision marked the triumph by 1900 of 'populism' over 'class'. The projected warrening and taming of capitalism was to be conducted mainly in the interests of the 'anti-monopolistic' 'people' rather than specifically those of the manual workers.[316]

In turning to an evaluation of these viewpoints, I would like to offer six main observations. First, all four schools of thought agree that, whether in the form of a 'fall' or 'original sin' and whether rooted in 'the people' or 'the class', the labour movement, and especially the ALP, by 1910 was characterised primarily by its pragmatic 'realism', as manifested in its piecemeal gradualism, moderation and limited ambition. Second, judgements cast upon this 'realism' have been heavily influenced by the politics of the commentators themselves. For example, while the verdict of the New Left has been unfavourable, that of the 'pragmatic reformists' and 'new realists' celebrating the ALP's impressive electoral successes of the 1980s has been far more positive.[317]

Third, interrogation of those predominantly labour-movement sources upon which this essay is heavily based, has led me to the conclusion that the ideological character of both the ALP and wider labour movement continued to be far more mixed, less closed and with far more potential for conflict and even transformation than suggested by the largely accommodating and integrating schools of thought outlined above.

For example, many leaders continued to embrace, at least at the level of conscious intention, a *mixture* of 'realistic pragmatism', piecemeal labourism *and* a willingness to struggle both for labour's immediate 'just' and 'reasonable' demands and for a longer term socialist future. As Terry Irving has rightly reminded us, a commitment to evolutionary socialism has often been a vital, if largely secondary, aspect of the broad and eclectic characteristics of Australian 'labourism'.[318] This fact was recognised in the 1900s by a wide range of experienced and informed politicians and commentators who can hardly be dismissed as suffering from collective 'false consciousness'. As seen earlier in this essay, despite their criticism of 'labourist' and 'reformist' tendencies of the ALP, Tom Mann, Dora Montefiore, and other British revolutionary socialists agreed that the ALP, or at least important parts of it, were *socialistic*, if not 'fully socialist' in character.[319] We have also seen that Keir Hardie and other prominent evolutionary socialists within the British Labour Party strongly believed that their Australian comrades were at the forefront of the worldwide advance towards the Co-operative Commonwealth. 'It is to socialism', declared Hardie on his visit to Sydney in 1908, 'that the active spirits are turning for the coming of the light'.[320] Reference has been made to the fact that Andrew Fisher and other ALP leaders continued to pride themselves upon their commitment to both the pragmatic and ethical aspects of socialism.

Similarly, Australian labour-movement publications routinely identified pragmatism, patience, piecemeal advancement *and* socialism as integral characteristics of a movement which sought both to achieve and hold power *and* to transform society. For example, in 1904 the *Worker* could declare unambiguously that, 'The Labour party stands for Socialism all the time'. The 'masses' were not yet 'ready' for socialism, but 'No Labour candidate worthy of the name is afraid of the Socialistic issue'.[321] The *Worker* viewed measures such as arbitration and old age pensions, not as ends in themselves, but rather as palliatives, 'necessary' as 'stages on the way to the FINAL GOAL'. 'But one day', continued the *Worker*, the grim humour of conciliating and arbitrating with a system of organised plunder will be recognised, and the ultimatum then will be short and sharp – 'Disgorge'![322]

The minority Labor ministry, although defeated, was congratulated upon its adherence to a principled independent political stance, rather than feeling obliged to 'beg or borrow' a majority from the 'representatives of Capitalism' in the opposition parties. Yet at the same time Watson and his ALP colleagues were deemed to have gained valuable experience and competence in the practical business of government. Thus,

> Labor may indulge in one or two gratifying reflections. Absolutely inexperienced, it has held office for four months and has demonstrated in that time an administrative capacity unequalled by its immediate predecessor, and unexcelled even by the Ministry of all talents led by Sir Edmund Barton.[323]

In the same year the *Westralian Worker* could 'take it for granted at this stage that the Labor Party is the Socialist Party'.[324]

Just as 'practical politics' and socialist aspirations were far more closely entwined in the labour movement than often suggested in the historiography, so too were 'class' and 'populism'. The languages of class and populism were often used interchangeably and in mutually supporting ways rather than as discrete, univocal and mutually antagonistic categories. If we follow the logic of Markey, then the *Worker*, as the official mouthpiece of the selector-shearer dominated, 'populist' AWU, should have been the mouthpiece of 'populism' par excellence. However, in practice the newspaper expressed a mixture of sentiments rooted in the assumed interests of 'the workers', 'the people' and 'the producers'. For example, according to the Sydney *Worker*,

> The Labor Party stands for effective legislation in the interests of the Australian *people*. The *workers* of Australia know no political boundaries within the Commonwealth.[325] (emphases added.)

Similarly, the Brisbane *Worker* saw the interests of 'the workers', 'the people', 'the producers' and the 'New Nation' as being largely synonymous.[326] The AWU, 'the pioneer of the political Labor movement', had 'taught the *workers* of the State to concentrate their powers on the legislatures' in order to secure 'an amelioration of their lot and the bringing about of those social conditions under which every worker shall enjoy the full fruits of his industry'. The *Worker* looked forward to the 'gradual nationalising of the means of life, and the ending of a system that is based on the robbery of the *producer by the non-producer*'.[327] In turn, socialism was equated with the 'Kingdom of the Sovereignty of *the People*', '*the People* triumphant'.[328]

The practice of the *Westralian Worker* likewise illustrated the fluidity and interchangeability of labour's linguistic concepts and usages. The paper sought habitually to speak on behalf of 'the worker', 'workers of our own race', and even 'workers of the world' in opposition to their 'capitalistic opponents'.[329]

Yet the eventual, if inevitable, triumph of 'the workers' would also be the triumph of the majority 'people' over the minority 'rich', 'capitalists' or 'upper classes'. In effect, 'class' would be abolished. And 'the workers'/'people's' victory would signal the forward 'march of civilisation'. Thus, 'the rule of the proletariat is certain to encourage morality, science and culture to blossom as never before'. It would rid the world not only of 'the excesses' and the 'vanities and frivolities' of 'the rich', but also 'most of the vices of the poor'. Simultaneously, socialist society would retain all that 'which is good and commendable in either class', 'upper' or 'lower'.[330]

Labour's eclectic resort to the discourses of 'class', 'the people', 'the producers' and 'the nation' served two very useful purposes that were, at one and the same time, practical (i.e. tactical and strategic) and abstract (ideological). It facilitated *both* the ALP's attempt successfully to appeal to as large a constituency as possible, and the labour movement's attempted rebuttal of the charge, made increasingly by its opponents, that it represented the interests of a narrow, sectional and selfish interest group rather than those of the majority of the people. It should also be noted that the variety of languages adopted by organised labour was closely related, but not totally reducible, to its mixed occupational composition and the multiple and shifting identities of its constituents. For example, many of those fiercely independent-minded, yet threatened, insecure, and in some cases downgraded diggers, selector-shearers and craft and skilled workers responded enthusiastically to the transforming, visionary and even millenarian socialist, populist and class-based appeals of Spence, Lane and Bellamy.[331] As noted earlier, more secure and upwardly mobile 'labour aristocrats' tended to adopt the language of moderation, respectability and class conciliation. Yet both linguistic usage and ascribed identity could change in response to the pressures of experience. For example, the conflicts of the 1890s transformed many moderates into militants and many 'aloof' 'aristocrats' into class-conscious workers. Simultaneously these workers often employed highly gendered and racialised views of themselves and their social world.

Fourth, labour's linguistic eclecticism, nevertheless, was underpinned by the dominant structuring influence of class-based independence and collectivism. I have earlier demonstrated the centrality of this influence to the values, habits, ideas and languages of 'movement culture'. I do not need to rehearse or elaborate upon the demonstration at this point. However, I must add that just as the hegemonic influence of class negates the purported dominant power of populism, so does it also invalidate the view that organised labour's ideology and linguistic constructs can be subsumed under the framework of an expansive and enduring 'liberalism'.[332] As observed earlier, while liberal ideas and values formed part of organised labour's rich cultural and ideological inheritance, organised Liberalism, as a political force, signally failed to prevent the rise of an independent labour movement during the 1900s. Moreover, we have seen that this rise was rooted in the experiences of class, involving conflict and struggle, and independence, rather than in the consensual and all-embracing liberal notion of 'community'. The final word on this matter lies with the *Worker*. In 1904 an editorial, outlining the dangers of coalition, ran:

> The greatest of all possible achievements for Labour is the awakening of the (sic) class feeling in the breasts of the unthinking multitude. And that can be accomplished only by maintaining the class line in politics, by class propaganda in the country and class action in Parliament, by vigorously declining, for a mess of palliative pottage, to lower the drawbridge and surrender the 'splendid isolation' of the Movement. CLASS CONSCIOUSNESS IS AN ESSENTIAL CONDITION TO ECONOMIC PROGRESS.[333]

Fifth, organised labour's ideology also embraced the important issues of nation and empire. During the 1890s Britain's ready agreement to Federation under the Crown played a large part in defusing pro-republican and anti-imperialist sentiment in Australia. Mark McKenna has claimed that,

> By the time the Australian colonies federated, the republican fire of the *Bulletin* and the majority of the radical press had been extinguished. All that remained was occasional grumbling about the pomposity of imperial culture. The *Bulletin*, like the Labor Party, had come to see that the imperial connection was appropriate for the new nation, at least for the time being.[334]

However, as we will see in detail in chapter three, much recent historiography has overlooked the fact there did continue to exist a socialist voice within the 1900s international labour movement which remained fundamentally at odds with imperialism per se. Within Australia both the *Worker* and, albeit in a more qualified and selective manner, the *Westralian Worker*, epitomised this voice.

The *Worker* saw imperialism and self-government as 'irreconcilable terms'. Imperialism, as a *necessary* system of capitalist exploitation, involved 'robbery under arms', and 'the robbery and murder of the wealth producers of the Great Empire'.[335] British imperialism involved the 'superstitious' worship of 'false gods', especially the 'decadent' aristocracy and the monarchy, kings being 'the State gods in whom Capitalism consolidates its power'.[336] The whole 'rotten' structure of the British Empire was built upon 'the poverty of the millions of Indian ryots ... of the oppressed Irish peasants ... and of the toiling masses in the heart of the Empire itself'.[337] In terms of the latter,

> On that fetid mass of wretchedness is founded Britain's throne, and Britain's old nobility, and Britain's Holy Church ...
> 'The land where Edward reigns is like a palace with a midden in the cellar, the stench of which has to be drowned in costly perfume and the scent of exotic blooms'.
> 'Britain is a vast sewage farm, and millions of its people are mere refuse and garbage utilised for the profit of the well-to-do'. And Socialism is 'The Australian Peril!'[338]

Imperialism, jingoism and militarism went hand in hand. 'Imperialism is a curse. It is Capitalism in khaki uniform, with a halo of 'patriotism' round its head, and the weapons of murder and assassination in its hands.'[339]

Moreover, the 'active citizenship' and 'independence' of Australian 'mateship' were, in the opinion of the *Worker*, totally incompatible with the deference and the cringing sycophancy demanded by imperial Britain. The 'absurd and entirely useless' function of the Coronation ceremony, complete with its 'ridiculous pretension', 'ostentation' and 'barbaric gaudiness', symbolised, above all, the 'vices', 'parasitism' and 'decadence' of the Old World in the face of the democratic advancement and progressivism of The New.[340]

In more restrained fashion, a contributor to the *Westralian Worker* admitted, albeit with probably more than a touch of irony, that the British Empire was 'a splendid concern, no doubt'. However, in common with the British socialist press and the *Worker*, both the contributor and the *Westralian Worker* as a newspaper were highly critical of Britain's pursuit of 'cheap labour' in the name of 'freedom' in the South African War. Pursuit of the latter suggested that the British Empire 'seems ... to be getting into a bad state of repair – needs patching up a bit, and possibly a few radical alterations'.[341] The death of Edward VII in 1910 occasioned the *Westralian Worker's* to express sympathy for 'the man' rather than 'his office'.[342] In February of the following year an article in the newspaper dubbed the forthcoming coronation of the new monarch, George V, 'A Farcical Survival of Ancient Foolery'. The coronation was described as 'one of the most glaring shams of modern history', occasioning 'one of the most disgraceful wastes of the people's wealth'. It also involved 'barbarous pomp and medieval splendour', the 'flaunting of wealth' on a monstrous scale, and 'all the flummery and flunkeyism so dear to the heart of the average Briton'.[343]

In the way of bitter irony, the *Worker*, in particular, also based its critique of British imperialism on explicitly racial and racist grounds. The newspaper unambiguously condemned, on the basis of a fervent belief in the supremacy of the 'white race', the formal commitment of the British authorities to the principle of equality before the law for all their imperial subjects, irrespective of race, colour and creed. The *Worker* likewise denounced the alleged plot of British capitalist-imperialists to undermine both the wages of 'white' workers and their socialist goal by setting them into competition and conflict with 'cheap coloured labour'. As we will observe in more detail in the next chapter, this issue assumed acute importance in the early and mid 1900s when, with the blessing of the imperial authorities, Chinese contract labourers were imported into the gold mines of South Africa. In the opinion of the *Worker*, the outcome of the South African 'experiment' was crucial to the wider conflict between capitalism and socialism. For there existed throughout the British Empire a racialized class struggle:

On the one side the Capitalistic classes, commanding the docile hordes of the Empire, of Asia and of Africa; opposing them the ranks of White Labour in revolt, disciplined and determined, fired with the sense of Justice, and the Red Flag of Socialism over all.[344]

On a smaller scale, the *Westralian Worker*, while welcoming into the goldfields 'small numbers' of 'new' immigrants from Italy and other parts of southern and south-eastern Europe, nevertheless, believed that preference should be afforded to the employment of 'men of the English-speaking race'.[345]

While representative of the racist views of the labour movement as a whole, neither the *Worker* nor the *Westralian Worker* spoke for the majority labour-movement voice in relation to the issue of empire. As Neville Meaney has recently observed, 'The evidence that Australians in this era thought of themselves prima-rily as a British people is overwhelming'.[346] Meaney goes on to detect among most Australians *both* a strong sense of nationalism, even national destiny, *and* close and continued attachment to the Empire.[347] This is a conclusion which fits the main-stream view within the Australian labour movement.

Many within that movement could oppose the specific instance of Britain's 'ag-gressive imperialism' as manifested in the South African War, while supporting the general view that, for the most part, Britain's 'enlightened imperialism' had responded well towards the aspirations and demands of its 'white-settler' colonies, including Australia. (The subject of 'civilised' or 'enlightened' British imperial-ism is considered in chapter three.) 'The King' and 'The Empire' were commonly toasted at the various functions held by the engineering, printing and many other unions, as well as by the friendly societies.[348] While opposing the payment of a subsidy to the British government for the British navy to defend Australian waters, Andrew Fisher strongly denied any intention of 'hauling down the British flag when the mother country was beset by enemies'. Fisher believed that the best way for Australia 'to assist the Empire' was 'to provide men, money and machinery for her own defence'. In building up her own navy, Australia would 'keep the flag fly-ing', and defend both her own and the Empire's 'honour'.[349] Fisher called Edward VII 'our great and peace-loving Sovereign', while 'Billy' Hughes 'hailed him as a true man'.[350] Australian labour leaders, including Fisher, were conspicuous by their presence at the 1911 coronation celebrations in London.[351]

In truth what the mainstream Australian labour movement increasingly sought was not the severance of the cherished ties with 'home', but rather full recogni-tion from London that both Australia and the labour movement had 'come of age'. The attainment of 'manhood' and the considerable achievements of the New Commonwealth demanded due recognition and respect. In 1911 the demand was raised within the Australian body of the ASE for greater domestic independence and control, but not severance 'from the home body'.[352] Similarly in the same year Fisher informed the *Westralian Worker* that a powerful and prosperous Australia now merited admittance to the 'inner family circle' of the Empire rather than to be kept waiting on the 'verandah'.[353] As Ramsay MacDonald prophetically declared at the dinner in London to honour Fisher in June 1911,

> The problem of Empire ... was how to develop nationality within the bonds of internationality; that would be the great problem that would characterise twentieth century democracy.[354]

In conclusion, I fully endorse Bongiorno's argument that labour adopted a 'genuine' and 'self-reliant' Australian nationalism which 'most sections of the labour movement regarded as consistent with continued loyalty to the empire'.[355] This form of nationalism, fundamentally rooted in the notions of 'mateship' and democracy, symbolised the oneness of the proud and progressive concerns of 'the movement' and 'the people'. In turn, as emphasised by Meaney, in Australia, probably more so than in Britain itself, 'the monarch became the symbol of the historic British race or people, rather than the head of a hereditary class system'.[356] In this way the Empire, in opposition to the view of the *Worker*, became a potent symbol of the unity of the 'white British race' across the globe. It also highlighted the way in which the class interests of the labour movement in Australia were inextricably tied to those of race.

My sixth conclusion will, by now, be self-evident. Labour's purportedly inclusive ideological embrace was, in practice, limited and fractured. Above all, we have seen that it was heavily limited, disfigured and diminished by racism. This subject area receives detailed treatment in the following chapter. At this point I will accordingly restrict myself to some brief comments. Above all, Australians were seen to practise an introspective and defensive form of racialized 'mateship', and to adopt a siege-based mentality. Their close racialized and emotional ties to geographically distant Britain, their assumed separation from and hostility towards the people of Asia and, apart from contacts with New Zealand, their general isolation in the southern hemisphere strongly promoted feelings of being apart and of a beleaguered 'whiteness'. As the contemporary American visitor, Victor Clark observed,

> The labour movement of Australasia is a manifestation of national introspection – a centring inward of the life of the people. It has nothing to do with wider world interests. The Australasians are not exactly a hermit nation, but they are in some respects a shepherd nation. Remote from other communities of their own kindred ... thrown upon themselves in the isolation of the southern ocean, they have pondered upon the phenomena (sic) of their peculiarly separate social existence. They have a trifle of the idealism sometimes generated in the solitude of the bush. They are aiming – whether wisely or not – at national self-perfection.[357]

Furthermore,

> *Protection* and *exclusion* are the means they advocate to maintain what some of their

opponents call a 'White and Vacant Australia'. Something of a Chinese jealousy of the outside world, of the parochial spirit extended to a continent, conditions the labour movement and weakens its moral basis.[358] (emphases added.)

Up to the 1890s Australian workers' fear of being 'swamped' by 'coloured' labour resulted in 'nearly fifty years of agitation, directed solely against the Chinese'. However, exclusionary sentiment was intensified and extended during the 1890s to embrace all 'non-white' groups, including the Japanese who, while classed as 'civilised', were feared for their efficiency and their potential economic and political threats to Australia. Notwithstanding the presence of a minority of cautionary and dissenting voices, organised labour provided overwhelming support for the Immigration Restriction Bill of 1901. The latter required intending immigrants, 'when asked to do so by an officer', to 'write out a dictation and sign in the presence of the officer a passage of fifty words in length in an (sic) European language directed by the officer'.[359] The successful passage of the bill marked the official onset of the policy of White Australia. Henceforth, the 'paradise' sought by organised labour was to be exclusively and officially 'white' in character, an embodiment of the 'fact' that Australians were bound together 'by blood and kinship' rather than by 'fire and sword'.[360] As the *Worker* put it, it became a matter of national concern to impress on all Australians, and especially Australia's schoolchildren, that 'they are of one race, of one family; with one history behind them, and one destiny before'.[361]

However, it was not only the Chinese and other intending immigrants who were excluded from the Australian 'family' or 'race'. For the truly native Australians, the aboriginal peoples, were also consciously excluded from labour's 'paradise'. It is true that the labour movement press was by no means wholly hostile towards aborigines. Ben Tillett, W.G. Spence, Andrew Fisher and many other labour leaders saw the aboriginals as victims of both white racism and the class-based oppression of the 'squattocracy'. Spence could combine outright racist opposition to the 'cheap' and 'coloured' Chinese and the 'Kanakas' (the latter working in the sugarcane fields of Queensland), with sympathy for the plight of the aboriginals. Thus, upon his arrival in Australia, the 'white man' gave 'no consideration to the black man's rights', and especially the rights of 'the aboriginal squatter', but 'drove him off, took up enormous areas, and stocked them with cattle and sheep'.[362] Fisher, too, roundly condemned 'the hideous evils rampant all over Northern Australia', as manifested especially in 'the fevered wishes of a brutalised squatter gang to prey upon the labour of the blacks'.[363] The *Westralian Worker* was in total agreement. In 1904 it called upon the ALP to give 'the very earliest attention' to 'the amelioration of the conditions of servitude under which the blacks in the nor-west exist'.[364] 'In this state', concluded the newspaper, 'the aborigines are as truly slaves as were the negroes in America before the (sic) emancipation'.[365] The *Westralian Worker* also differentiated between 'improvident' and 'intelligent' aboriginals in and around the western goldfields.[366]

Yet organised labour's 'solution' to 'the aboriginal problem', however well intentioned, was, in effect, patronising and exclusive. Both within the labour movement and the wider society, aboriginal people were mainly stereotyped as lacking the independent 'character' or 'manliness' – closely associated with 'whiteness'[367]– successfully to resist their squatter oppressors. References in the labour press to the 'helpless niggers' of the Northern Territory were commonplace.[368] On a general level aboriginals were overwhelmingly depicted by whites as 'primitive', 'child-like', 'uncivilised', and morally 'deficient', being 'given' to drink, sexual excess and 'loose living'.[369] As a 'race', they were deemed by whites either to be on the point of extinction, or, to have a decent chance of survival, in urgent need of the paternalist care and protection of the states and the Commonwealth. The form this 'care and protection' took under Fisher's ministry was the appointment of a 'chief protector' and the creation of separate 'land sanctuaries' for aboriginals in the Northern Territory 'so that 'the natives could develop their capabilities under skilled supervision'.[370] Unfortunately, history would record a short, and all too predictable, step from aboriginal 'separate development', under 'appropriate' white 'care and protection', to the enforced removal of the children of mixed marriages to 'parentage' in white households.

Just as the much neglected subject of labour and aboriginal people requires urgent attention,[371] so does that of labour and women. In terms of the latter, research to date suggests that powerful gendered limitations and boundaries accompanied those of race. However, while strong patriarchal assumptions undoubtedly informed the 'world of labour', white women were not to be totally excluded from active, if limited, participation in either the labour movement or the society of the 'workers' paradise' as a whole. Women, and especially unmarried women, had a significant presence in the tailoring, clothing and 'caring' sections of the economy and society. Within these spheres women displayed a capacity for involvement in trade unionism and campaigns for improved pay and conditions, including the demand for equal pay, sufficient to negate an undifferentiated picture of female passivity at the work-place.[372] Women's attempts to organise unions in the notoriously difficult area of domestic service were even in evidence. Thus in 1911 the *Westralian Worker* reported 'A meeting of those interested in the formation of a Houseworkers' Union'. One speaker at the meeting declared,

> That the great majority of union men are ignorant of the outrageous conditions imposed on domestic workers is largely due to the silent endurance of the latter.[373]

Furthermore, as noted earlier, pragmatic self interest sometimes overshadowed the hostility of printing and other craft and skilled workers to the employment of women in 'their' sectors and women's involvement in 'their' trade unions.

Beyond the world of the work-place, there is evidence of women's involvement in a range of labour-movement and related activities in the public sphere. These embraced, for example, social-welfare work, political campaigns, free speech fights, unemployed struggles, and work for the ALP, the Women's Labour League and socialist societies.[374] From the mid 1890s the labour movement had strongly supported the successful campaign for votes for women.[375] Moreover, there is evidence within the contemporary labour-movement press of, perhaps growing, feminist influence upon women's activities. For example, the 'Women's Page', edited by Mary Gilmour in the *Worker* from 1908 onwards, both offered 'practical advice for wives and mothers on limited budgets', and covered a wide range of subjects in an attempt to enable women to fulfil their 'all-round destiny'.[376] In support of the demand for more active and widespread women's involvement in politics, especially in leadership roles, 'LSH' argued in the *Westralian Worker* that it was now time to redress the balance for the fact that,

> for many centuries women who have homes and women who have none have endured injustices, inequalities and slavery at the hands of men.[377]

However, as in numerous other countries, women's involvement in the world of organised labour in Australia was primarily supportive and secondary in character. It was women who prepared the picnics and other 'treats' held by the various bodies of the movement, and who 'gave help' at union socials.[378] Although women were at times organisers,[379] the vast majority of labour movement leaders were, as seen above, men. Reference was also made earlier to the fact that the very notion of Justice Higgins's 'living wage', widely supported within the labour movement, was based upon the assumption of the male head of the household as the 'natural breadwinner' and 'the wife' as the primary 'carer and supporter' within the home. It is also crucial to recognise the ubiquitous importance of the household to working-class life, complete with its key notion of *mutuality*, however unequally shared, between males and females. In Australia, as elsewhere, all active members of the working-class household were expected to 'pull together' to ensure the family's survival and advancement. Within this tightly-knit unit, at times loving and affectionate at others cruel and violent, women did *negotiate* with men and did exercise some power as household managers, carers and providers. However, matriarchy rarely extended beyond the immediate environment of home and neighbourhood. In the 'wider world' and even in terms of many of the family's leisure pursuits, gender segregation and patriarchy seemingly ruled the roost.[380] Finally, what we urgently require in order further to illuminate the relationship between women and labour is the more extensive reconstruction of Australian women's 'voices', of the values, habits and expectations of women themselves, as both the agents and subjects of their times and places.

Conclusion

On the basis of the overall balance of the evidence considered, and especially the evidence provided by contemporary labour movement sources both within and outside Australia, I offer a comparatively favourable response to the question as to whether Australia was a 'paradise' for workers in this period. While by no means perfect, in any absolute sense, Australia was widely perceived, unlike many 'aristocratic' countries of the Old World and the relatively new republic of the United States disfigured by the triumph of 'monopoly' and the 'money kings',[381] to offer unparalleled opportunities for workers' social, economic, cultural and political advancement. Furthermore, both workers and the labour movement were seen to be eagerly grasping those opportunities and profoundly influencing the course of national life and consciousness. From 1914 onwards the onset of war, labour's fratricidal conflict concerning conscription, and the largely barren years of the 1920s suggested that the movement's continued progress would no longer be so easy and untroubled as in the 1900s. That decade did appear, both at the time and in retrospect, as something of a 'golden age'. As Mr. Somerville declared in proposing a toast to 'The Commonwealth of Australia' at the ASE's 'jubilee picnic and social' in 1901,

> Those whose privilege it was to reside in Australia lived under conditions which could not be excelled in any other country.[382]

Similarly, for twenty-three-year-old H. Dawson, a British emigrant to the West Australian bush, who experienced both rapid upward occupational mobility – from wage-earning to land ownership – and continued commitment to the socialist cause – riding six miles once a week to collect his copy of the *Clarion* – Australia was indeed 'God's own country', at least for 'the man with a bit of go in him'.[383]

Notes

Much of the inspiration for this chapter developed in the course of conversations with Sean Scalmer of Macquarie University, Sydney. I am very grateful to Sean for his support and for permission to consult some of his own source material. I am also grateful to Paul Pickering for his advice and his reading of the chapter. I am further indebted to colleagues in the History Program, Research School of Social Sciences, the Australian National University, for their encouragement and support. Most of the research for this chapter was conducted at the Noel Butlin Archives Centre, the Australian National University. I am extremely grateful for the advice, guidance and warm hospitality provided by the archivists at the Noel Butlin – Tatiana Antsoupova, Emma Jolley, Sigrid McCausland and Pennie Pemberton. Research was also conducted at the National Library, Canberra, and the Mitchell Library, Sydney.

1. Contemporaries used all three descriptions, although in the Australian case the explicitly gendered 'workingman's paradise' was most commonly employed. See Richard White,
Inventing Australia: Images and Identity 1688-1980 (Sydney, 1981), Chapter 3. For an evaluation of

Australia as 'the paradise of the workman' see Tom Mann, *The Political and Industrial Situation in Australia* (Melbourne, 1904), 475.

2. In this context it is important to remember that terms such as 'subordinate', 'labourist' and 're-formist' convey historical messages not only of accommodation, but also points of challenge, conflict and opposition. Moreover, reforms gained for workers and the wider 'people' under capitalism have often followed periods of conflict and struggle. See Terence H. Irving, 'The Roots of Parliamentary Socialism in Australia, 1850-1920', *Labour History*, 67 (Nov. 1994), 97-109; idem, 'Labourism: A Political Geneology', *Labour History*, 66 (May 1994), 1-10; R. Neil Massey, 'A Century of Laborism, 1891-1993: An Historical Interpretation', *Labour History*, 66 (May 1994), 45-71. For the famous debate concerning patterns of working-class hegemony, subordination, reformism and incorpora-tion see Perry Anderson, 'Origins of the Present Crisis', *New Left Review*, 23 (Jan.-Feb. 1964), 26-53; idem, 'Socialism and Pseudo- Empiricism', *New Left Review*, 35 (Jan.-Feb. 1966), 2-42; Edward P. Thompson, 'The Peculiarities of the English', in Ralph Miliband and John Saville (eds.) *Socialist Register* (1965), 311-62.

3. For an extended discussion see Ken Buckley and Ted Wheelwright, *No Paradise for Workers: Capitalism and the Common People in Australia 1788-1914* (Melbourne, 1988).

4. Neville Kirk, 'Postmodernism, History and Class', in Phil Griffiths and Rosemary Webb (eds.), *Work Organisation Struggle,* Papers from the Seventh National Labour History Conference, Australian National University, Canberra, April 19-21, 2001 (Canberra, 2001), 10-17.

5. Stuart Macintyre, *The Oxford History of Australia,* vol. 4, *The Succeeding Age 1901-1942* (Oxford, 1997), 86-7.

6. For Australian labour's opposition to coercive imperialism see Chapter three. See also Charles Manning Clark's sweeping and provocatively brilliant *A History of Australia,* Vol. V, *The People Make Laws* (Melbourne, 1999), 170-76 for labour leaders' opposition to the South African War in the face of massive public support and 'patriotic fervour' in Australia.

7. For usage of these terms see, for example, the editorial in the *Australasian Typographical Journal,* 470 (Dec. 1912), 12.

8. Francis Castles, 'Welfare and Equality in Capitalist Societies: How and Why Australia was Different', in Richard Kennedy (ed.), *Australian Welfare: Historical Sociology* (Melbourne, 1989), 70; Macintyre, *Succeeding Age*, 42-3; Greg Patmore, *Australian Labour History* (Melbourne, 1991), Chapter 3; Buckley and Wheelwright, *NoParadise*, 10; Christopher Lloyd, 'Economic Policy and Australian State-Building: From Labourist-Protectionism to Globalisation', in A. Teichova and H. Matis (eds.), *Economic Change and the Building of the Nation State in History* (Cambridge, 2001).

9. White, *Inventing*, 15-16.

10. Alan Beever, 'From a Place of Horrible Destitution to a Paradise of the Working Class: The Transformation of British Working Class Attitudes to Australia, 1841-1851', *Labour History*, 40 (May 1981), 1-15.

11. Beever, 'From a Place', 11-12; Paul Pickering, '"The Finger of God", Gold and Political Culture in Colonial New South Wales', in Ian D. McCalman (ed.), *Gold: Forgotten Histories and Lost Artefacts of Australia* (Cambridge, 2001); idem, 'From Reading Room to Rifle Club: Sydney's Democratic Vistas, 1848-1856', unpublished paper presented to the Seventh National Labour History Conference, ANU, Canberra, 19-21 April, 2001.

12. For example, in 1917 Judge Powers, Deputy President of the Commonwealth Arbitration Court, described Darwin as a 'working man's paradise'. This followed the Court's policy of awarding high wages to applicants not only to compensate for Darwin's geographical isolation and high cost of living, but also to incorporate the Northern Territory into the nation. Unions continued to be fa-vourable to the Court partly as a result of the latter's concern 'for extending "White Australia" to the "empty" north'. See Bernie Brian, 'Vesteys and the Single "White" Man's Wage: The First Award in the Northern Territory', in Griffiths and Webb (eds.), *Work*, 65-9.

13. See, for example, Jurgen Tampke (ed.), *Wunderbar Country: Germans Look at Australia 1850-1914* (Sydney, 1982); Albert Metin, *Socialism Without Doctrine* (1901 edition, Alternative Publishing Cooperative Limited, Sydney, 1977); W. Pember Reeves, *State Experiments in Australia*

and New Zealand, 2 vols. (London, 1902); Samuel Gompers, 'Australasian Labor Regulating Schemes', *American Federationist*, XXII,4 (April 1915), 253-263; Sidney Webb, 'Some Impressions of Australasia', *Labour Leader*, 26 Aug., 1899; A.G. Austin (ed.), *The Webbs' Australian Diary* (1898, Pitman, Melbourne, 1965); D.A. Hamer (ed.), *The Webbs in New Zealand 1898: Beatrice Webb's Diary with Entries by Sidney Webb* (Price Milburn for Victoria University Press, Wellington, 1974).

14. For the close ties between the labour movements of South Africa and Australia in the 1900s see Kennedy, *A Tale of Two Mining Cities*, Chapter 1. Kennedy highlights the strong racist presence and influence of migrant Australians upon South Africa's trade unionism and Labour Party. Note, for example, the career and views of Australian-born Peter Whiteside who became a leading trade unionist and Labour politician in South Africa. See Kennedy, 21-2; *Worker* (Sydney), 12 March 1908.

15. The Webbs were particularly enamoured of New Zealand's collectivist advances. See Webb, 'Some Impressions'; Hamer, *The Webbs*, especially 54-5. By way of contrast, they were 'struck with the backwardness' of politics in Australia in the late 1890s. According to the Webbs, the 'rich people' in Sydney 'take no part' and 'actually pride themselves on their contempt for public affairs; money-making and racing being their only concerns'. Remarkably, in view of the strong growth of Labor politics in Sydney and New South Wales during the 1890s, Sydney's 'working men' were also considered to be 'largely non-political'. The Webbs concluded that Australia lacked the 'charm' of New Zealand and that Australian 'people' were 'gambling profit-makers; keen on realising the Individualist ideals' of the British 'lower Middle Class of 1840-70'. See Austin, *The Webbs*, especially 31-2, 107-8, 115-6. For claims in favour of New Zealand's paradisaical standing see, for example, *Westralian Worker*, 24 Oct., 1902; *Labour Leader*, 8 June, 1901, 28 July, 1905; Miles Fairburn, *The Ideal Society and its Enemies: The Foundations of Modern New Zealand Society 1850-1900* (Auckland, 1989), Ch. II.

16. Sean Wilentz, *Chants Democratic: New York City and the Rise of the American Working Class 1788-1850* (New York, 1984), Introduction, Chapter 2, Epilogue. Early nineteenth-century British radicals and socialists increasingly adopted the view that the 'logic of capitalism', involving inequality and exploitation, had 'defied republican virtue' in America. See Gregory Claeys, 'The Example of America a Warning to England? The Transformation of America in British Radicalism and Socialism, 1790-1850', in Malcolm Chase and Ian Dyck (eds.) *Living and Learning: Essays in Honour of J.F.C. Harrison* (Aldershot, 1996), 66-80

17. Michael Kazin, *Barons of Labor: The San Francisco Building Trades and Union Power in the Progressive Era* (Urbana, 1987), 119,155.

18. 'President Gompers in Europe', *American Federationist*, XVII,2 (Feb. 1910), 151.

19. 'President Gompers in Europe', *American Federationist*, XVI,12 (Dec. 1909), 1086; XVII, 3 (March 1910), 243

20. White, *Inventing*, 35-6.

21. *Australian Magazine*, no author listed (August 1886), 183, 190.

22. *Nineteenth Century*, CLXX (April 1891), 529, 530. Located in the bound volume, *Nineteenth Century: Australasia*, Mitchell Library, Sydney.

23. H.H. Champion, 'The Crushing Defeat of Trade Unionism in Australia', *Nineteenth Century*, CLXIX (March 1891), 225, 227. Located in the same bound volume, Mitchell Library.

24. *Australian Magazine* (August 1886), 186, 190.

25. See the excellent introduction by Michael Wilding to Lane's *The Workingman's Paradise* (1892, Sydney University Press, 1980), especially page 15. For the shearers' disputes see Clark, *A History*, Vol. V, 44-52, 83-9.

26. Anne Whitehead, *Paradise Mislaid: In Search of the Australian Tribe of Paraguay* (St. Lucia, Queensland, 1998), 1,3, 43.

27. See the *Clarion*, 21 Jan., 1910.

28. White, *Inventing*, 36.

29. See, for example, *Sixth Annual Report of the British Immigration League of Australia*, 1910-11, pp. 4, 26. Mitchell Library, MSS 302, Box 6.

30. For the racist dimension of labour thought and fears see Chapter three and Clark, *A History*, Vol.

V, 131-2.

31. *Westralian Worker*, 5 June, 1908.

32. *Worker* (Sydney), 5 March, 1908.

33. *Labour Leader*, 11 Aug., 1911.

34. See, for example, the *Australasian Typographical Journal*, 469 (Nov. 1911), 18, 470 (Dec. 1911), 12; *Amalgamated Society of Engineers: Australasian Council Monthly Reports*, 283 (Aug. 1912), 5-8. Both of these journals were consulted at the Noel Butlin Archives Centre (respectively, S179 NB and S35NB).

35. For the sharp differences of opinion towards Australia among revolutionary and reformist social-ists see Tampke, *Wunderbar*. Although see note 15 above for the Webbs' view that New Zealand was far more politically and socially advanced than Australia.

36. Metin, *Socialism*, 188-191. It is interesting to note that Metin's turn-of-the century characteriza-tion of Australian workers and their culture, labour movements and leaders as predominantly re-spectable, defensive, aspirant and bourgeois has subsequently found a strong echo in the influential work of both the New Left Humphrey McQueen (*A New Britannia: An Argument Concerning the Social Origins of Australian Radicalism and Nationalism* (Ringwood, 1970), Introduction, 18-20, Chapters 16, 17) and the nationalist Charles Manning Clark (*A History*, Vol. V, 186-191, 238- 241).

37. Gompers, 'Australasian Labor', 263. See also *American Federationist*, XVIII, 11 (Nov. 1911), 912; David Palmer, 'Misunderstanding Australian Labour: Samuel Gompers, Billy Hughes and the Debate over Compulsory Arbitration', in Griffiths and Webb (eds.), *Work*, 318-324.

38. Kirk, 'Postmodernism', 14-15.

39. *Westralian Worker*, 28 March, 16 May, 6 June, 1 Aug., 26 Sept., 1902, 2 Sept., 1904.

40. Patmore, *Australian Labour*, 76-7; Raymond Markey, *The Making of The Labor Party in New South Wales 1880-1900* (New South Wales University Press, Kensington, 1988), 6; Clark, *A History*, vol. V, 40-1; Bruce Scates, *A New Australia: Citizenship Radicalism and the First Republic* (Cambridge, 1997), 113-116.

41. William Guthrie Spence, *Australia's Awakening: Thirty Years in the Life of an Australian Agitator* (The Worker Trustees, Sydney, 1909), 53.

42. Clyde R. Cameron, 'Henry Ernest Boote: "It's Wrong to be Right"', *Labour History*, 80 (May 2001), 212; Ian Syson, 'Henry Ernest Boote: Putting the Boote into the Australian Literary Archive', *Labour History*, 70 (May 1996), 77-9.

43. Spence, *Australia's Awakening*; the entry on Spence by Coral Lansbury and Bede Nairn, in Bede Nairn (general editor), *Australian Dictionary of Biography*, Vol. 6, *1851-1890 R-Z*, edited by Geoffrey Serle and Russel Ward (Melbourne, 1976), 168-70.

44. Both papers, especially the *Westralian Worker*, provided a useful forum for the expression of diverse interests and viewpoints. However, it would obviously be very dangerous, and in all prob-ability foolhardy, to presume that, for example, the socialist message conveyed by both papers, and the fierce anti-imperialist and anti-monarchical stance of the *Worker* (Brisbane), dovetailed perfectly with the consciousness of their readers in their predominantly rural, pastoral and mining settlements or with the increasingly labourist leadership of the AWU. See Mark Hearn and Harry Knowles, *One Big Union: A History of the Australian Workers Union 1886-1994* (Melbourne, 1996). An attempt to develop a more detailed and comprehensive picture of the development of the Australian labour movement and the patterns of thought and action of its many constituencies would necessarily consult a much wider range of labour newspapers and journals than is done in this chapter. In addition, careful attention would be paid to a range of urban- and rural commu-nity-based case studies, complete with their socio-economic and cultural characteristics and political trajectories, throughout Australia. The present chapter is intended to lay the bare foundations for the future construction of this more ambitious and comprehensive project.

45. The Sydney *Bulletin*, noted, above all, for its republican and anti-monarchical sentiments dur-ing the 1880s and 1890s, characterised politics as 'a struggle between evil capitalists and virtuous workers'. See Mark McKenna, *Captive Republic: A History of Republicanism in Australia 1788-1996* (Cambridge, 1996), 135. See also Scates, *A New Australia*, 1- 4. *The Champion*, edited by the quixotic

and 'gentlemanly' socialist, Henry Hyde Champion, in Melbourne between 1895 and 1897, was a supporter of women's suffrage, co-operative production and the 'real' interests of workers as opposed to those determined by the 'fake' trade union leaders in Melbourne's Trades Hall Council. See, for example, the *Champion*, 18 April, July 4, 1896 (copies held in the Mitchell Library). During the 1900s Champion worked with Tom Mann in the Victorian socialist movement, contributed to the *Socialist* and, notwithstanding his continued involvement in political faction-fighting, 'retained the affectionate esteem' of Mann. Beyond 1910 he devoted most of his time to his longstanding literary pursuits. See Geoffrey Serle's entry on Champion in Bede Nairn and Geoffrey Serle (eds.), *Australian Dictionary of Biography*, Vol. 7, *1891-1939* (Melbourne, 1979), 603-5; and the entry on Champion by Andrew Whitehead in Saville and Bellamy (eds.), *Dictionary Labour Biography*, VIII (London, 1987), 24-32.

46. For example, see 112-120 below, for the wealth of material contained in the engineering, printing and Oddfellows journals and in the labour press on the leaders of working-class and popular movements in Australia.

47. For Lawson see Brian Kiernan (ed.), *Henry Lawson: Stories Poems Sketches and Autobiography* (Univ. Queensland Press, St. Lucia, Queensland, 1993). Lawson's 'Freedom on the Wallaby' (84-5) and 'Some Popular Australian Mistakes' (128-30) present starkly contrasting attitudes towards the 'workingman's paradise'.

48. Unlike Australia, the USA was also deeply scarred by chattel slavery. For the US see David Montgomery, *Citizen Worker*, Introduction.

49. Clark, *A History*, Vol. V, 190-1, 217-18; Robert Manne, 'In Denial: The Stolen Generations and The Right', *The Australian Quarterly Essay*, 1 (Melbourne 2001); Henry Reynolds, *The Other Side of The Frontier: Aboriginal Resistance to the European Invasion of Australia* (Harmondsworth, 1995).

50. Clark, *A History*, Vol. V, 131. For a contrasting view of Australia and the other British dominions – as expressed by 'gentlemen emigrants', 'colonial aspirants' and 'proconsular regimes of signal grandeur', and championing adherence to Britain's traditional hierarchical social order and values as against New World egalitarianism – see David Cannadine, *Ornamentalism: How the British Saw Their Empire* (London, 2002), 40. Notwithstanding some subsequent qualification to this view (see pp. 136-7), Cannadine, complete with his reliance upon a narrow and selective range of sources 'from above' and his corresponding neglect of views 'from the middle' and 'from below', greatly exaggerates deferential attachments to British 'traditionalism' among Australians between 1890 and 1914. Much the same can be said in relation to the experiences of the other dominions.

51. For Mann in Australia see Graeme Osborne, 'Tom Mann: His Australian Experience 1902-1910', unpublished PhD thesis, Australian National University, November 1972; Joseph White, *Tom Mann* (Manchester, 1991), Chapter 5; John Laurent (ed.), *Tom Mann's Social and Economic Writings* (Spokesman, Nottingham, 1988); *Justice*, 12 Jan., 25 May 1907 (for the 'free speech' fights in Melbourne); 15 May, 25 Sept. 1909, 14 May, 1910 for Mann's growing disillusionment with solely or primarily political means of working-class advancement. Frank Bongiorno, *The Peoples Party: Victorian Labor and the Radical Tradition 1875-1914* (Melbourne univ. Press, Carlton, Victoria, 1996), 147-157. I have also consulted relevant Australian material in the Tom Mann Papers, Modern Records Centre, University of Warwick, esp. MSS 334/7/1, 334/7/3, 334/12.

52. An excellent summary of Mann's overall position is to be found in his article, 'Conditions in Australia', in *Justice*, 25 Sept., 1909.

53. Tom Mann, *The Labour Movement in Both Hemispheres* (J.J. Miller Printing Co., Melbourne, 1903), 21-2.

54. Mann, *The Political and Industrial Situation in Australia* (1894), 491.

55. *Justice*, 25 Sept., 1909.

56. See Mann's articles in *Justice*, 11 May, 22 June 1907.

57. For Macdonald see Andrew Fisher's reported speech in *Labour Leader*, 2 June 1911; William Morris Hughes, *The Case for Labor* (The Worker Trustees, 1910, Sydney, 1970), 26, 85-90.

58. *Justice*, 16, 23 May, 1903.

59. *Justice*, 7 Sept., 1901.

60. *Labour Leader*, 20 Aug., 1909.

61. Michael Davitt MP, *Life and Progress in Australia* (Methuen, 1898).

62. *Labour Leader*, 26 Aug., 1899.

63. Metin, *Socialism*, Translator's Foreword (Russel Ward), 8- 10,76.

64. Tampke (ed.), *Wunderbar Country*, 8.

65. Margaret E. MacDonald, 'A Week in West Australia', *Labour Leader*, 8 Feb., 1907. For further support for women's suffrage in Australia see *Justice*, 2 Aug., 1902.

66. 'Social Progress and the Empire', *Fabian News*, XIX,3 (Feb. 1908).

67. Macintyre, *Succeeding Age*, 111: 'The very concept of the living wage was intended to enable a man to support a wife and children'. Higgins 'assumed that working women were either single or else part of a larger family unit and making only a supplementary contribution to the family income … Female workers were awarded a wage sufficient to keep a single person'. The family wage was set at 7s per day – 'the very sum that had been regarded as a minimum standard before the depression of the 1890s' (idem, 103).

68. *Labour Leader*, 8 Feb., 1907.

69. Clark, *A History*, Vol. V, 53-4; Henry Lawson, 'A Fragment of Autobiography', in Kiernan (ed.), *Lawson*, 3-65.

70. Clark, *A History*, Vol. V, 5-6. However, upon his return, in 1902, from a highly successful literary trip to London, Lawson, now separated from his family, an alcoholic and at times suicidal, became increasingly jingoistic, racist, and 'in middle age a loyal imperialist bristling with military metaphors'. See Kiernan (ed.), *Lawson*, xxiii.

71. Kiernan (ed.), *Lawson*, 69; Clark, *A History*, Vol. V, 5.

72. Kiernan (ed.), *Lawson*, 84-5; Clark, *A History*, Vol. V, 86.

73. *Worker* (Sydney), 17 March, 1910.

74. *Worker* (Brisbane), 29 Jan., 1910.

75. *Worker* (Brisbane), 5 Jan., 1901, 7 May, 2 July, 1910. See also *Westralian Worker*, 21 July, 1911; ASE, *Australasian Council Monthly Reports*, 264 (Jan. 1911), 12, 267 (April 1911), 10-11 for the views that in contrast to Britain, members in Australasia were 'surrounded by a freer life (and) greater opportunities of initiative and experiment'; and that their brothers in Britain were characterised by 'deep-seated conservatism'.

76. *Worker*, 20 Feb., 1908 (W.G.Spence), 29 Jan., 1910 (editorial).

77. *Worker* (Brisbane), 15 Jan., 1910.

78. *Worker* (Brisbane), 15, 22 Jan., 1910.

79. *Worker* (Brisbane), 29 Jan., 1910.

80. *Worker* (Brisbane), 5 Jan., 1901.

81. *Clarion*, 18, 25 Oct., 1912. Fletcher had also published a piece on Australia in the *Clarion* 16 Dec., 1910.See also the important work of Paul Pickering: 'The Finger of God'; 'From reading Room to Rifle Club'; idem, 'A Wider Field in a New Country: Chartism in a New Country', in Marian Sawer, *Elections: Full Free and Fair* (Sydney, 2001), 28-44. I am grateful to Paul Pickering for a copy of his chapter.

82. Possibly Alexander Fletcher, a boilermaker and London Chartist. I am grateful to Paul Pickering for this suggestion.

83. *Clarion*, 16 Dec., 1910.

84. *Worker* (Brisbane), 29 Jan., 1910.

85. For the British case see Pat Hudson, *The Industrial Revolution* (London, 1992), 29-32; Martin J. Daunton, *Poverty and Progress: An Economic and Social History of Britain 1700-1850* (Oxford, 1995), 420-46.

86. Buckley and Wheelwright, *No Paradise*, 10.

87. Lloyd, 'Economic Policy'.

88. Markey, *The Making of the Labor Party*, Introduction, 19-26

89. B.D.Graham, *The Formation of the Australian Country Parties* (ANU Press, Canberra, 1966), Ch. 3. Above all, the selectors or smallholders chafed against the many obstacles placed by the 'squattoc-

racy' against the break up of their large estates in order to facilitate the more equitable and democratic selection, distribution and settlement of the land. See Markey, *The Making*, 89-90

90. Markey, *The Making*, 20; Patmore, *Australian Labour*, 51; Shirley Fitzgerald, *Rising Damp: Sydney 1870-1890* (Oxford Univ. Press, Melbourne, 1987), Ch. 4.

91. Macintyre, *Succeeding Age*, Ch. 2.

92. Macintyre, *Succeeding Age*, 104; Martin Shanahan, 'No Paradise for Workers: The Personal Wealth of Labourers prior to World War I', in David Palmer, Ross Shanahan and Martin Shanahan (eds.), *Australian Labour History Reconsidered* (Adelaide, 1999) 132-144; Markey, *The Making*, 23.

93. Macintyre, *Succeeding Age*, 104; Markey, *The Making*, 316; Buckley and Wheelwright, *No Paradise*, 238.

94. *Westralian Worker*, 20 Jan., 1911.

95. *Westralian Worker*, 27 Jan., 3 Feb., 1911.

96. *Westralian Worker*, 3 Feb., 1911.

97. *Westralian Worker*, 11 July, 1902, 2 Oct., 1903, 22 July 1904, 1 May 1908, 2 July, 13 Aug., 24 Sept., 22 Oct., 1909, 3,10 Feb., 1911. For women's issues and campaigns see also 131-2 below.

98. *Worker*, 4 June, 1892.

99. *Labour Leader*, 19 July, 1907.

100. See, for example, the letter from John Dixon, resident in Victoria for two years, to the *Clarion*, 20 Dec., 1912; *Justice*, 29 Sept., 1906, 11 May, 22 June, 1907.

101. *Justice*, 29 Sept., 1906, 11 May, 22 June, 1907, 28 Nov., 1908, 9 July, 1910.

102. *Justice*, 12 Aug., 1899.

103. *Justice*, 20 Aug., 1898.

104. See Mann's lecture, 'Social Economics' reported in the *Westralian Worker*, 22 July, 1904.

105. *Justice*, 25 Sept., 1909.

106. Laurent (ed.) *Tom Mann's Social and Economic Writings*, 19- 21; Mann, *Political and Industrial Situation; Justice*, 11 May, 1907; 'The Socialist Movement in Australia', *Labour Leader*, 3 Sept., 1909.

107. *Justice*, 1 May, 1899.

108. *Labour Leader*, 10 April, 1908.

109. *Labour Leader*, 1 Jan., 1909. For the role of the authorities in providing some work for the unemployed see idem, 20 Aug., 1909.

110. *Justice*, 1 May, 1899.

111. *Labour Leader*, 23 April, 1909. But see Fairburn's emphasis (*The Ideal Society*, Ch. II) upon New Zealand's good living standards and plentiful opportunities for workers' upward social mobility into the ranks of the propertied classes.

112. *Justice*, 30 Nov., 1912. For a statement in favour of the virtues of arbitration in New Zealand see the interview with W.Pember Reeves, one of the architects of New Zealand's collective progressivism, in *Labour Leader*, 2 Dec., 1904. For an opposing view see C.H. Chapman, late of Clapham ILP, and resident in New Zealand in idem, 17 Jan. 1908. For a sense of the range of Australian attitudes towards arbitration in their own country see, for example, *Labour Leader*, 3,10,17 Jan., 1908.

113. *Labour Leader*, 12, 19 July, 1902.

114. *Labour Leader*, 9 May, 1903.

115. Buckley and Wheelwright, *No Paradise*, 10.

116. Macintyre, *Succeeding Age*, 42-3.

117. Markey, *The Making*, 19-23.

118. Fitzgerald, *Rising Damp*; Patmore, *Australian Labour*, 48.

119. *Labour Leader*, 9 May, 1903.

120. *Labour Leader*, 19 July, 1902.

121. Mann, *Political and Industrial Situation*, 477.

122. *Labour Leader*, 3 Sept., 1909.

123. *Justice*, 29 Sept., 1906, 11 May, 1907, 25 Sept., 1909.

124. *Labour Leader*, 16 March, 10 April 1908.

125. *Labour Leader*, 20 Jan., 1907.

126. Sir Charles Wentworth Dilke, *Problems of Greater Britain*, 2 Vols.(Macmillan, London, 1890), Vol. 1, 252. See also Vol. 2, Ch.II, Pt. VI, 284, 289-90, 295.

127. Davitt, *Life and Progress*, 29, 41, 408.

128. *American Federationist*, Vol. V, 4 (June, 1898), 67-8.

129. *Westralian Worker*, 16 Sept., 1904.

130. *Clarion*, 18 Oct., 1912.

131. *Clarion*, 18, 25 Oct., 1912. See also idem, 16 Dec., 1910.

132. *Clarion*, 7 April, 1911. See also idem, 14 April, 1911.

133. *Worker*, 9 April, 1892.

134. *Justice*, 22 April, 1911.

135. Robin Walker, 'Aspects of Working-Class Life in Industrial Sydney in 1913', *Labour History*, 58 (May 1990), 36-47. Janet McCalman, *Struggletown: Public and Private Lives in Richmond 1900-1965* (Melbourne, 1984).

136. For a stimulating study of the moving frontier of opportunity for western railway workers in the United States see Shelton Stromquist, *A Generation of Boomers: The Pattern of Railroad Labor Conflict in Nineteenth Century America* (Urbana, 1987).

137. *Champion*, 21 Nov., 1896. See also *Westralian Worker*, 26 Feb., 1904.

138. Clark, *A History*, Vol. V, 159-60.

139. *Labour Leader*, 8 June, 1901.

140. *Labour Leader*, 26 Aug., 1899. See also John E. Martin, 'Labour in a New World: Labour Movement Origins and the State in Nineteenth-Century New Zealand' (paper presented to the Labour and Empire conference, Amsterdam, May 1996) for the crucial role of progressive Liberalism in the social, economic and political development of nineteenth-century New Zealand. I am very grateful to John Martin for a copy of his suggestive paper.

141. *Westralian Worker*, 24 Oct., 1902.

142. *Labour Leader*, 28 July, 1905.

143. Markey, *The Making*, Introduction, Chs. 1, 2. For the similar, if far more marked, development of the new political economy of industrial capitalism in Britain during the period of the Industrial Revolution see Neville Kirk, 'In Defence of Class', *Int. Rev. Soc. Hist.*, Vol. XXXII (1987-1), 2-47.

144. John Shields, 'Deskilling Revisited: Continuity and Change in Craft Work and Apprenticeship in Late Nineteenth Century New South Wales', *Labour History*, 68 (May 1995), 1-29; Raelene Frances, *Politics of Work: Case Studies of Three Victorian Industries 1890-1940* (Cambridge, 1993); Chris Wright, 'Taylorism Reconsidered: The Impact of Scientific Management within the Australian Workplace', *Labour History*, 64 (May 1993), 34-53.

145. Shields, 'Deskilling Revisited', 8.

146. *Australasian Typographical Journal*, 311 (May 1896), 312 (June 1896).

147. *Australasian Typographical Journal*, 321 (March 1897).

148. *Australasian Typographical Journal*, 468 (Oct. 1911), 470 (Dec. 1911), 9.

149. *Australasian Typographical Journal*, 312 (June 1896).

150. Shields, 'Deskilling Revisited', 8.

151. *Australasian Typographical Journal*, 469 (Nov. 1911), 18.

152. *Australasian Typographical Journal*, 465 (July 1911), 18-20; J. Hagan, *Printers and Politics: A History of the Australian Printing Unions 1850-1950* (Canberra, 1966), 187.

153. *Australasian Typographical Journal*, 474 (April 1912), 25-6; Hagan, *Printers*, 145.

154. See, for example, the editorial in the *Australasian Typographical Journal* for February 1912 (12-13) and idem, no 474, April 1912 (12-13, 17-21) for the importance of union preparedness, determination and solidarity in the face of 'the persistent aggressiveness' of the Employers' Federation in the Brisbane general strike.

155. *Australasian Typographical Journal*, 465 (July 1911), 12-13.

156. Hagan, 53; *Australasian Typographical Journal*, 293 (Nov. 1894).

157. See, for example, *Australian Typographical Journal*, 468 (Oct. 1911), 12, 16, 470 (Dec. 1911), 8, 472 (Feb. 1912), 8-9; Hagan, *Printers*, 138, 187.

158. The waygooze was the 'ancient chapel custom of celebrating St Bartholomew-tide, marking the time in the year when men could use candles to work by'. See Patrick Duffy, *The Skilled Compositor, 1850-1914: An Aristocrat Among Working Men* (Aldershot, 2000), 219.

159. *Australasian Typographical Journal*, 470 (Dec. 1911), 3, 14- 15.

160. *Australasian Typographical Journal*, 472 (Feb. 1912), 15-16.

161. *Australasian Typographical Journal*, 468 (Oct. 1911), 14, 470 (Dec. 1911), 3,8, 474 (April 1912), 21, 478 (Aug. 1912), 18.

162. Hagan, *Printers*, 59.

163. See also Hagan, *Printers*, 188. By way of contrast, of course, employer paternalism in nineteenth-century Lancashire had often been anti-union in character. See Patrick Joyce, *Work Society and Politics: The Culture of the Factory in later Victorian England* (Harvester Press, Brighton, 1980), Ch. 4; Neville Kirk, *The Growth of Working Class Reformism in Mid Victorian England* (Univ. Illinois Press, Champagne, 1985), 291-300.

164. *Australasian Typographical Journal*, 476 (June 1912).

165. For the continued importance of upward occupational mobility among printers see 114-116 below.

166. Hagan, *Printers*, 188. For moderate and sectional 'aristocratic' consciousness among printers in Britain see Duffy, *Skilled Compositor*, Chs. 3,5.

167. Ken D. Buckley, *The Amalgamated Engineers in Australia 1852-1920* (Dept. Econ. Hist., Research School Social Sciences, the Australian National University, 1970), 134, 153,155, 163.

168. Buckley, *Amalgamated Engineers*, 155,193. See also *ASE: Australasian Council Monthly Reports*, 276 (Jan. 1912), 2, 283 (Aug. 1912), 5-8.

169. Buckley, *Amalgamated Engineers*, 94-6,164-5.

170. During the 1900s the trade unions and the Labor Party were concerned to extend the benefits of compulsory arbitration to cover all state and commonwealth employees, the less well organised, and effectively to negate the practice of appointing non-unionists to represent the interests of workers on wages boards. See, for example, *ASE: Australasian Council Monthly Reports*, 257 (June 1910), 7, 259 (Aug. 1910), 5, 263 (Dec. 1910), 5; Macintyre, *Succeeding Age*, 89, 92.

171. Buckley, *Amalgamated Engineers*, 206-8.

172. *ASE: Australasian Council Monthly Reports*, 276 (Jan. 1912), 9.

173. Buckley, *Amalgamated Engineers*, 163; *ASE: Australasian Council Monthly Reports*, 276 (Jan. 1912), 278 (March 1912).

174. *Australasian Typographical Journal*, 469 (Nov. 1911), 18.

175. *Australasian Typographical Journal*, 470 (Dec. 1911), 12; *ASE: Australasian Council Monthly Reports*, 283 (Aug. 1912), 5-8.

176. *Australasian Typographical Journal*, 466 (Aug. 1911), 12-15.

177. William Morris Hughes, *The Case for Labor* (The Worker Trustees: Sydney and Melbourne, 1910), 13.

178. Macintyre, *Succeeding Age*, 42-3.

179. Buckley and Wheelwright, *No Paradise*, 132.

180. Macintyre, *Succeeding Age*, 104.

181. Loc. cit. For debates about the strengths and weaknesses of arbitration see Stuart Macintyre and Richard Mitchell (eds.), *Foundations of Arbitration: The Origins and Effects of State Compulsory Arbitration 1890-1914* (Oxford Univ. Press, Melbourne, 1989), especially Introduction; Buckley and Wheelwright, *No Paradise*, 14-15, 232-9; Patmore, *Australian Labour*, Ch. 5.

182. John Merritt, *The Making of the Australian Workers Union* (Oxford Univ. Press, Melbourne, 1986), 341, 354-7.

183. *Worker* (Sydney), 20 Feb., 1908.

184. Merritt, *The Making*, 357, 363; Hearn and Knowles, *One Big Union*, Ch. 5.

185. See *Westralian Worker*, 11, 25 April, 6, 13 June 1902 for the AWA's precocious development.

186. Patmore, *Australian Labour*, 120.

187. Neville Kirk, *Labour and Society in Britain and the USA*, Vol. 2, *Challenge and Accommodation*

1850-1939 (Aldershot, 1994), 64-5.

188. Macintyre, *Succeeding Age*, 27-35, 41-4; Patmore, *Australian Labour*, 46.

189. Verity Burgmann, *Revolutionary Industrial Unionism: The Industrial Workers of the World in Australia* (Melbourne, 1995).

190. Raymond Markey, 'The 1890s as the Turning Point in Australian Labor History', *International Labor and Working Class History*, 31 (Spring 1987), 77-88.

191. Lloyd, 'Economic Policy and Australian State Building'.

192. Kirk, *Working Class Reformism*, Ch. 4.

193. Macintyre, *Succeeding Age*, 86-7.

194. Markey, 'The 1890s', 79.

195. Patmore, *Australian Labour*, 80; Macintyre, *Succeeding Age*, 86.

196. Terry Irving, 'Early views of Industrial Democracy: Australia, 1914-1921', paper presented to the conference on Work and Workplace Democracy, University of Sydney, 1 June 2001. I am grateful to the author for permission to cite.

197. Neville Kirk, *Change* Ch. 8; Tony Adams, 'Labour Vanguard, Tory Bastion, or the Triumph of New Liberalism? Manchester Politics 1900 to 1914 in Comparative Perspective', *Manchester Region History Review*, Vol. XIV (2000), 25-38.

198. Kirk, *Change*, Ch. 8; Jon Lawrence, *Speaking for the People: Party Language and Popular Politics in England 1867-1914* (Cambridge, 1998); Ross McKibbin, 'Class and Conventional Wisdom: The Conservative Party and the "Public" in Inter-War Britain', in McKibbin, *The Ideologies of Class: Social Relations in Britain 1880-1950* (Oxford, 1990).

199. Neville Kirk, '"Peculiarities" versus "Exceptions": The Shaping of the American Federation of Labor's Politics during the 1890s and 1900s', *International Review of Social History*, Vol. 45, Part 1 (April 2000), 25-50; Andrew Strouthous, *US Labor and Political Action*.

200. Macintyre, *Succeeding Age*, 87.

201. Macintyre, *Succeeding Age*, 85.

202. Patmore, *Australian Labour*, 78. I am heavily indebted to Greg Patmore for much of the following material on the fortunes of the Labor Party at state level.

203. For its resolute support for political independence and socialism in the 1900s see, for example, *Worker* (Brisbane), 23, 30 April, 20 Aug., 1904, 22, 29 Jan., 19 March, 16, 23 April, 1910. See also Spence, *Australia's Awakening*, Ch. XXVII.

204. Clark, *A History*, Vol. V, 339.

205. Markey, *The Making*, 171.

206. Patmore, *Australian Labour*, 77.

207. Markey, *The Making*, 2.

208. Markey, *The Making*, 2, 13-15. Populist ideology, according to Markey (page 14), idealizes 'the people', 'asserting their welfare and capacity against corrupt ruling elites, such as "monopolists", financiers or the "Money Power", who "establish and maintain their power by conspiratorial cunning". In this sense it cuts across class divisions'. Central emphasis rests upon divisions between 'producers' and 'non-producers' or 'parasites' rather than workers and employers. For a discussion of the role and place of 'populism' in the ideology of the Australian labour movement See 124-126. See also Patmore, *Australian Labour*, 76.

209. Macintyre, *Succeeding Age*, 85.

210. Bongiorno, *Peoples Party*, 22, 29. It should, of course, be remembered that Liberalism did not have a monopoly on the cluster of 'respectable' ideas identified by Bongiorno. Such ideas were often prominent among working-class Chartists and socialists as well as Liberals. Working-class 'respectability' was not univocal and unchanging. See Kirk, *Working Class Reformism*, Ch. 5.

211. Patmore, *Australian Labour*, 79.

212. Patmore, *Australian Labour*, 77-8.

213. *Westralian Worker*, 22 July, 1904.

214. Patmore, *Australian Labour*, 79.

215. *Westralian Worker*, 24 Nov., 1911.

216. Patmore, *Australian Labour*, 79-80.

217. Macintyre, *Succeeding Age*, 92. My account of Labor's record at the federal level is greatly indebted to Macintyre's work.

218. Loc. cit.

219. Graham, *The Formation of the Australian Country Parties*, 61-2, 76, 293.

220. This subject area merits far more extensive and intensive comparative research. For some of the useful studies already undertaken see the essays listed under the heading of 'Labour History and Local History' in *Labour History*, 78 (May 2000).

221. Bongiorno, *Peoples Party*, 103,114.

222. *Westralian Worker*, 23 Oct., 1903.

223. Austin (ed.), *The Webbs*, 31-2.

224. *Westralian Worker*, 16 Sept., 1904.

225. *Westralian Worker*, 24 April, 1903.

226. For Fisher's views see *Labour Leader*, 2 June, 1911.

227. *Labour Leader*, 9,16, 23 June, 14 July, 1911.

228. *Labour Leader*, 2 June, 1911. See also John Hodge's favourable impressions of the progress made by the Australian Labor Party in the *Labour Leader*, 28 April, 1911.

229. Stefan Berger, 'Labour in Comparative Perspective', in Duncan Tanner, Pat Thane and Nick Tiratsoo (eds.), *Labour's First Century* (Cambridge, 2000), 313. For the LRC's opposition to economic protectionism, see Ramsay MacDonald's letter to John Christian Watson, the Australian Labor Prime Minister in 1904, in the *Labour Leader*, 14 Oct., 1904.

230. *The Labour Party: Annual Reports 1904-1911*, Ninth Annual Report (National Museum of Labour History, Manchester), 20.

231. *The Labour Party: Annual Reports*, Eleventh Annual Report, 19.

232. *Labour Leader*, 5 April, 1902.

233. *Labour Leader*, 10 June, 1904.

234. *Labour Leader*, 2 June, 1905. See also 13 Jan., 1905.

235. *Labour Leader*, 23 Nov., 1906.

236. *Labour Leader*, 10 April, 1908.

237. Laurent (ed.), *Mann's Social and Economic Writings*, 122.

238. *Justice*, 6 May, 1911.

239. *Justice*, 29 April, 1911. See also 22 April, 1911.

240. *Justice*, 19 Oct., 1912. See also 22 June, 1912.

241. *Justice*, 23 April, 1910.

242. *Westralian Worker*, 16 Jan., 1903.

243. *Westralian Worker*, 28 March, 1902. See also 7, Oct., 1904.

244. *Worker* (Brisbane), 30 April, 1904.

245. *Bulletin*, 21 April, 1910.

246. *Worker* (Brisbane), 16 April, 1910.

247. *Worker* (Brisbane), 29 Jan., 1910.

248. *Worker* (Brisbane), 16 April, 21 May, 1910.

249. *Worker* (Brisbane), 23 April, 1910.

250. *Worker* (Brisbane), 7 May, 1910.

251. *Worker* (Brisbane), 29 April, 1911.

252. For example, the Melbourne Typographical Society remained apolitical for much of this period. See Hagan, *Printers*, 105-7

253. Patmore, *Australian Labour*, 80-1; Hearn and Knowles, *One Big Union*, 55-7, 84-7.

254. ASE: *Australasian Council Monthly Reports*, 185 (April 1904), 2.

255. Buckley, *Amalgamated Engineers*, 143-8.

256. ASE: *Australasian Council Monthly Reports*, 256 (May 1910), 4-5, 265 (Feb. 1911), 5; *Australasian Typographical Journal*, 451 (May 1910). The *Typographical Journal* had also congratulated Watson in 1904. See 379 (May 1904), 8.

257. See, for example, *Westralian Worker*, 16 Jan., 1903; Markey, *The Making*, 6-7.

258. See Paul Pickering, 'Chartism and the "Trade of Agitation" in Early Victorian Britain', *History*, 76 (1991), 221-37; idem, 'A Wider Field'.

259. See *ASE: Australasian Council Monthly Reports*, 146 (Jan. 1901), 157 (Dec. 1901); Buckley, *Amalgamated Engineers*, 1.

260. Buckley, *Amalgamated Engineers*, 1, Ch. 8.

261. *ASE: Australasian Council Monthly Reports*, 149 (April 1901).

262. *ASE: Australasian Council Monthly Reports*, 268 (May 1911), 10-11.

263. *ASE: Australasian Council Monthly Reports*, 284 (Sept. 1912), 13-15.

264. *Australasian Typographical Journal*, 477 (July 1912), 16-17.

265. *Australasian Typographical Journal*, 478 (Aug. 1912), 18.

266. *Australasian Typographical Journal*, 479 (Sept. 1912), 2.

267. Loc. cit.

268. See, for example, *Australasian Typographical Journal*, Dec. 1890 (Beckett); Sept. 1891 (Sayers); Oct. 1895 (Creak); May 1896 (Middleton, Macnee); Jan. 1897 (Jeffery).

269. See, for example, 'Oddfellowship Beyond the Seas', in *Oddfellows Magazine*, XXXVI, 364 (April 1905). Also *Oddfellows Magazine*, XXXVI, 367 (July 1905), 224, XXXIX, 397 (Jan. 1908), 21-2, XLII, 436 (April, 1911), 134.

270. William Guthrie Spence, *The Lesson of History* (The Worker Print, Bathurst, Sydney, 1908); Lansbury and Nairn, *Spence*, 168-70; *Worker*, 4 June, 1892; Patsy Adams-Smith, *The Shearers* (Thomas Nelson, Melbourne, 1982), 115, Ch. 15

271. See, for example, *Worker* (Brisbane), 12 Aug. 1893 (Glassey); 16 Feb. (Page), 2 March (Stewart) 1901; 23 April (Airey), 30 April (Mahon, McGregor) 1904; 8 Jan. (Stewart), 15 Jan. (Turley), 22 Jan. (Givens), 12 March (Finlayson) 1910; *Worker* (Sydney), 20 Jan. 1910 (Farrar).

272. *Labour Leader*, 23 Nov., 1906.

273. *ASE: Australasian Council Monthly Reports*, 276 (Jan. 1912), 18-20.

274. Clark, *A History*, Vol. V, 270-1, 284, 327-8 ; *Labour Leader*, 13 March, 1908; Herbert Vere Evatt, *Australian Labour Leader: The Story of W.A. Holman and the Labour Movement* (Sydney, 1954).

275 Clark, *A History*, Vol. V, 116-20.

276. *Westralian Worker*, 29 April, 1904.

277. Syson, 'Boote', esp. 71-7.

278. See, for example, *Australasian Typographical Journal*, 311 (May 1896), 312 (June 1896), 319 (Jan. 1897), 434 (Dec. 1908), 477 (July 1912); Hagan, *Printers*, 58; Buckley, *Amalgamated Engineers*, 164-5; *ASE: Australasian Council Monthly Reports*, 160 (March 1902), 162 (May 1902) 279 (April 1912), 284 (Sept. 1912).

279. *Oddfellows Magazine*, XXXVI, 364 (April 1905), XXX, 373 (Jan. 1906); *ASE: Australasian Council Monthly Reports*, 162 (May 1902).

280. See above, 93-96.

281. See, for example, the essays in *Labour History*, 78 (May 2000) by Greg Patmore, 'Localism and Labour: Lithgow 1869-1932', esp. 60-4; and Bradley Bowden, 'A Time "the like of which was never before experienced": Changing Community Loyalties in Ipswich, 1900-12', esp. 72, 79- 80; Connell and Irving, *Class Structure in Australian History*, 133-139.

282. *Westralian Worker*, 28 Feb., 1902.

283. *Westralian Worker*, 21 March, 1902.

284. *Westralian Worker*, 6 June, 1902.

285. Loc. cit.

286. *Westralian Worker*, 15 July, 1904.

287. *Westralian Worker*, 14 March, 1902.

288. *Westralian Worker*, 3 Oct., 1902.

289. *Westralian Worker*, 7 April, 1911.

290. *Westralian Worker*, 17 Feb., 1911.

291. *Westralian Worker*, 9 Oct., 1903.

292. *Westralian Worker*, 6 June, 1902.

293. *Westralian Worker*, 9 Oct., 1903.

294. For the classic statement concerning the ethos of 'mateship' among 'bush' workers, which assumed the status of 'the national *mystique*' in the later nineteenth- and early twentieth centuries, see Russel Ward, *The Australian Legend* (Melbourne, 1984); idem, 'The Australian Legend Re-Visited', *Historical Studies*, 71, Vol. 18 (Oct. 1978), 171-90. Note also the racialised observation of W.G. Spence, appointed the first president of the Amalgamated Shearers' Union of Australia in 1886, that bush unionism 'had in it that feeling of mateship which ... always characterised the action of one "white man" to another'. Spence, *Australia's Awakening*, 53.

295. Metin, *Socialism*, 191; McQueen, *New Britannia*, 18-20, 204; Clark, *A History*, Vol. V, 248. These three writers unproblematically, and falsely, identify respectability, comprising industry, thrift, sobriety and so on, as *ipso facto* 'bourgeois' or, in McQueen's case (page 20), 'petit bourgeois'.

296. See, for example, Patmore, 'Localism and Labour', 61; Lucy Taksa, 'Like a Bicycle, Forever Teetering between Individualism and Collectivism: Considering Community in Relation to Labour History', *Labour History*, 78 (May 2000), 22; *Westralian Worker*, 9 Oct., 27 Nov., 1903, 26 Feb., 22 April, 1904, 10 June, 1910; *Justice*, 22 June, 1912 (interview with Montague O'Dowd, 'father of the socialist movement in Perth').

297. Duncan Bythell, 'Class, Community and Culture – The case of the Brass Band in Newcastle', *Labour History*, 67 (Nov. 1994); *Westralian Worker*, 1 May, 1902, 2 Jan., 6 May, 1904, 24 Sept., 12 Nov. 1909; Bongiorno, *People's Party*, Ch. 6.

298. *Westralian Worker*, 7 March, 1902, 16, 30 Oct., 1903.

299. *Westralian Worker*, 24 Dec. 1909, 7 Jan. 1910, 27 Jan., 1911 (Dora Montefiore).

300. See *Westralian Worker*, 13 Aug., 22 Oct., 1909 for women's help at union socials. However, see *Westralian Worker*, 11 July, 1902, 2 Oct., 1903, 22 July, 1904, 1 May, 1908, 2 July, 1909, 11 Feb., 1910, 3, 10 Feb. 1911 for the more independent activities of labour-movement women.

301. *Westralian Worker*, 11, 18, 25 April, 1902. It is interesting to note in this context that the ASE in Australia was increasingly critical of the failure of the British ASE to move beyond its narrow craft membership. Some Australian ASE members argued that their organisation 'was not ... aristocratic ... as many people thought'. See *ASE: Australasian Council Monthly Report*, 264 (Jan. 1911), 12, 267 (April 1911), 10-11, 16.

302. For such divisions see, for example, Macintyre, *Succeeding Age*, 48, 67-8; Ward, 'Australian Legend Re-Visited', 179, 185-6; Patmore, 'Localism and Labour', 67; Erik Eklund, 'The "Place" of Politics: Class and Localist Politics at Port Kembla, 1900-1930', *Labour History*, 78 (May 2000), 111; Kiernan (ed.), *Lawson*, xvii, 14, 82, 129. See also the article by A.A. Mills in the *Westralian Worker*, 20 March 1908: 'if we wish to keep our workers from the race track and the beer shops we must supply opportunities for social intercourse in other directions'.

303. Bradon Ellem and John Shields, 'Making a "Union Town": Class, Gender and Consumption in Inter-War Broken Hill', *Labour History*, 78 (May 2000), 116-140.

304. Irving, 'The Roots of Parliamentary Socialism', 102; Connell and Irving, *Class Structure*, Ch. 4.

305. For the Chartists' 'movement culture' see James Epstein, 'Some Organisational and Cultural Aspects of the Chartist Movement in Nottingham', in James Epstein and Dorothy Thompson (eds.), *The Chartist Experience: Studies in Working Class Radicalism and Culture 1830-1860* (London, 1982), 221-268.

306. As Spence observed, workers' heightened sense of class resulted, in part, from the mean-minded and exploitative anti-labour policies of employers' organisations. For example (*Australia's Awakening*, p. 37), 'The Pastoralists' Union is without doubt the most bitterly unscrupulous organisation in the world'; and (p. 53) 'Unionism came to the Australian bushman as a religion. It came, bringing salvation from years of tyranny'.

307. Macintyre, *Succeeding Age*, 48-9.

308. Lloyd, 'Economic Policy'.

309. Spence, *Australia's Awakening*, 11.

310. McQueen, *New Britannia*, 17-20; Markey, *The Making*, Introduction, Epilogue. However, it

should be noted that Markey is heavily critical (*The Making*, p. 8) of McQueen's 'ludicrously histori-cist extreme of arguing that no working-class actually existed, in the Marxist sense– only a "peculiarly Australian petit (sic) bourgeoisie".

311. Palmer, Shanahan and Shanahan, *Australian Labour History Reconsidered*, 3.

312. Bongiorno, *Peoples Party*, 2, 189; idem, 'Class, Populism and Labour Politics in Victoria, 1890-1914', *Labour History*, 66 (May 1994), 14-29; Markey, *The Making*, 7-8.

313. See Stuart Macintyre, 'Who Are the True Believers? The Manning Clark Labour History Memorial Lecture', *Labour History*, 68 (May 1995), 155-167, esp. p. 161.

314. Clark, *A History*, Vol. V, 186-9, 191, 199, 237-248.

315. Scates, *A New Australia*, 3-11, 207-8.

316. Markey, *The Making*, 13-15. See also Patmore, *Australian Labour*, p. 96, for the view that the 'Federal Labor governments did not seek to end the existing economic system, but pursued *populist* causes and tried to minimise the worst excesses of Australian capitalism'. (emphasis added). While I am in agreement with Patmore's first and last claims, I think that the nature of the second claim requires much closer contextualisation and precise definition of populism. Similarly, Markey's 'pop-ulism' (*The Making*, pp. 13-15) is too uncritically borrowed from the very different context of the late nineteenth-century USA and its own Populist Movement. In fact, 'class' was present in American populism to an extent not acknowledged by Markey, but recognised in some of the relevant American literature. As a corollary, 'class' and 'populism' in the United States were by no means *necessarily* mu-tually exclusive and antagonistic. For these matters see Kirk, *Labour and Society*, Vol. 2, 124-131.

317. Bongiorno, *Peoples Party*, 3.

318. Irving, 'The Roots of Parliamentary Socialism'; idem, 'Labourism: A Political Geneology',

319. See especially Tom Mann, 'Socialism in Australia', *Labour Leader*, 5 Aug., 1904.

320. *Labour Leader*, 20 March, 1908. See also the view of the visiting American, Victor S. Clark *The Labour Movement in Australasia: A Study in Social Democracy* (London, Archibald Constable and Co., 1907, p. 281), that while the 'rank and file' of the ALP 'hardly look beyond their own day and generation', nevertheless 'many leaders of the labour party, and even a select band of their follow-ers, are inspired by the unselfish idealism of reformers', seeing 'in the labour movement a phase of a world-wide progress towards socialism, economic equality, the abolition of poverty by collective ac-tion'. Clark, 'an agnostic in social creeds', visited Australia and New Zealand in 1903 and 1904, 'under a commission from the Government'.

321. *Worker* (Brisbane), 27 Aug., 1904.

322. *Worker* (Brisbane), 16 April, 1904.

323. *Worker* (Brisbane), 20 Aug., 1904.

324. *Westralian Worker*, 29 July, 1904.

325. *Worker* (Sydney), 13 Feb., 1908.

326. *Worker* (Brisbane), 5 Jan., 1901. For an instructive comparison with the Chartist identification of 'the people' with the 'working class', see Dorothy Thompson, 'Who were "the People" in 1842?' in Chase and Dyck (eds.), *Living and Learning*, 118-132.

327. *Worker* (Brisbane), 22 Jan., 1910.

328. *Worker* (Brisbane), 29 Jan., 1910.

329. *Westralian Worker*, 28 March, 1902.

330. *Westralian Worker*, 23 Oct., 1903.

331. Clark, *A History*, Vol. V, 57, 60-2, 80-7, 159.

332. Bongiorno, 'Class, Populism', 17, 29; Peter Beilharz, 'The Labourist Tradition and the Reforming Imagination', in Kennedy, *Australian Welfare*, 132-153; Tim Rowse, *Australian Liberalism and National Character* (Malmsbury, Victoria, 1978).

333. *Worker* (Brisbane), 30 April, 1904; John Rickard, *Class and Politics: New South Wales, Victoria and the Early Commonwealth 1890-1910* (Canberra, 1976), Ch. 11.

334. McKenna, *Captive Republic*, 199-204, 205; Gavin Souter, *Lion and Kangaroo: The Initiation of Australia* (Melbourne, 2000), esp. Ch. 6. Luke Trainor, *British Imperialism and Australian Nationalism: Conflict and Compromise in the Late Nineteenth Century* (Cambridge, 1994).

335. *Worker* (Sydney), 11 Nov. 1908; *Worker* (Brisbane), 22 Jan., 1910.

336. *Worker* (Brisbane), 9 July, 1910.

337. *Worker* (Brisbane), 14 Dec., 1901.

338. *Worker* (Brisbane), 27 Aug., 1904.

339. *Worker* (Brisbane), 2 April, 1904.

340. *Worker* (Brisbane), 27 May, 1911.

341. *Westralian Worker*, 28 March, 1902.

342. *Westralian Worker*, 13 May, 1910.

343. *Westralian Worker*, 17 Feb., 1911.

344. *Worker* (Brisbane), 2 April, 1904.

345. *Westralian Worker*, 6 June, 1 Aug., 26 Sept., 1902, 6 Feb. 1903.

346. Neville Meaney, 'Britishness and Australian Identity: The Problem of Nationalism in Australian History and Historiography', *Australian Historical Studies*, 32, 116 (April 2001), 76-90, esp. p. 79. See also the other valuable contributions to the Symposium on 'Britishness and Australian Identity' in the same issue of *Australian Historical Studies*.

347. Meaney, 'Britishness', *passim*.

348. See, for example, *Australasian Typographical Journal*, 475 (May 1912), 24; *ASE: Australasian Council Monthly Reports*, 189 (Aug. 1904), 6-7, 276 (Jan. 1912); *Oddfellows Magazine*, XXXVIII, 393 (Sept. 1907), 470, XL, 415 (July 1909), 465, XL, 417 (Sept. 1909), 521.

349. *Worker* (Brisbane), 12 Feb., 1910; *Australasian Typographical Journal*, 467 (Sept. 1911), 22.

350. Clark, *A History*, Vol. V, 322.

351. For a critical view of their proposed attendance see *Westralian Worker*, 17 Feb., 1911.

352. *ASE: Australasian Council Monthly Reports*, 268 (May 1911), 8-10.

353. *Westralian Worker*, 22 Sept., 1911.

354. *Labour Leader*, 2 June, 1911.

355. Bongiorno, *Peoples Party*, 196.

356. Meaney, 'Britishness', 81.

357. Clark, *The Labour Movement*, 290.

358. Clark, *The Labour Movement*, 291.

359. Andrew Markus, *Fear and Hatred: Purifying Australia and California 1850-1901* (Sydney, 1979), xi-xii.

360. *Worker* (Sydney), 25 June, 1908.

361. *Worker* (Brisbane), 12 Feb., 1910.

362. Spence, *Australia's Awakening*, 9, 178. For Tillett see *Justice*, 1 May, 1899.

363. *Worker*, 20 May, 1911.

364. *Westralian Worker*, 3 June, 1904.

365. *Westralian Worker*, 27 Jan., 1911.

366. *Westralian Worker*, 13 June, 1902.

367. Spence, *Australia's Awakening*, 54.

368. See, for example, *Westralian Worker*, 3 June, 1904.

369. *Westralian Worker*, 25 July, 1902.

370. *Westralian Worker*, 20 March, 1903; *Worker*, 20 May, 1911.

371. In addition to the references listed in note 49 above and note 10 for Chapter three below, see Patmore, *Australian Labour*, Ch. 8; Ann McGrath and Kay Saunders with Jackie Huggins, *Aboriginal Workers* (Sydney, 1995). The latter appeared as a special issue of *Labour History*, 69 (Nov. 1995).

372. *Westralian Worker*, 11 July, 1902, 2 Oct., 1903, 22 July, 1904; Frances, *Politics of Work*; Bradon Ellem, *In Women's Hands? A History of Clothing Trades Unionism in Australia* (Kensington, New South Wales Univ. Press, 1989).

373. *Westralian Worker*, 3 Feb., 1911.

374. Bruce Scates, 'Socialism and Manhood: A Rejoinder', *Labour History*, 60 (May 1991), 121-4; Joy Damousi, 'Socialist Women and Gendered Space: The Anti-Conscription and Anti-War Campaigns of 1914-1918', *Labour History*, 60 (May 1991),1-15; *Westralian Worker*, 2 July, 13 Aug., 22 Oct., 12

Nov., 1909.

375. Bongiorno, *Peoples Party*, Ch. 5; *Westralian Worker*, 29 Nov., 1907 (reception at Fremantle for Keir Hardie).

376. Hearn and Knowles, *One Big Union*, 102-4; Whitehead, *Paradise Mislaid*, 382.

377. *Westralian Worker*, 10 Feb., 1911.

378. *Westralian Worker*, 2 July, 13 Aug., 24 Sept., 1909.

379. Damousi, 'Socialist Women', 5.

380. Marilyn Lake, 'The Politics of Respectability: Identifying the Masculinist Context', *Historical Studies*, 22, 86 (April, 1986), 116-131; idem, 'Socialism and Manhood: A Reply to Bruce Scates', *Labour History*, 60 (May 1991), 114-20. For the English context see Andrew Davies's excellent *Leisure Gender and Poverty: Working Class Culture in Salford and Manchester 1900-1939* (Buckingham, 1992).

381. McKenna, *Captive Republic*, 203.

382. *ASE: Australasian Council Monthly Reports*, 147 (Feb. 1901).

383. Dawson contrasted the opportunities of the bush with unemployment of the towns. He saw socialism as the solution for the latter, particularly for those less 'strong and fit' than the likes of himself. See his letter to the *Clarion*, 13 May, 1910

Chapter 3

The Rule of Class and the Power of Race: socialist attitudes to class, race and empire during the era of 'new imperialism', 1899-1910.*

'But if we are to begin to comprehend the British Left since 1880 we must take very much more seriously the international and imperialist context.' E.P.Thompson[1]

'With regard to the labour movement and the legacy of empire ... it is vital to emphasize that any account of that history needs to take account of the fragmented nature of these influences.
While that legacy clearly does involve the construction of racialized stereotypes and hostility ... there are also examples of positive images and of a recognition of common interests'. Kenneth Lunn[2]

'To think Imperialistically is to think Capitalistically ... Imperialism has all along been a high sounding name for Capitalism'. H.T.Muggeridge[3]

Overview

Traditionally, and notwithstanding important examples to the contrary, most histories of the British labour movement have concentrated their attention far more upon labour's policies and attitudes towards domestic than foreign matters. This point of concentration has frequently been justified on account of the fact that it accurately reflects organised labour's, especially the trade unions', historic preoccupation with immediate 'bread and butter' issues, 'at home' or 'close to home', rather than with a more distant and seemingly more cerebral commitment to full engagement with 'world affairs'. It has also 'traditionally' been the case that the question of class – of the extent to which modern British workers have felt and expressed common interests, ideas, values and norms *as workers* – has dominated the labour and much of the social history written between the 1960s and 1980s.[4]

The past two decades, however, have witnessed shifts in terms of both focus and emphasis, as reflected in the increased historiographical attention given to international/comparative as opposed to purely domestic/national affairs, and to the identities of gender, race and place over those of class.[5] I subscribe to the view that the latter shift has been occasioned by, *inter alia*, the decline of socialism, the accelerated movement of globalisation, the rise of 'new' feminist, black, ethnic, national and environmental movements, and the important challenge mounted by postcolonial and 'subaltern' studies to Eurocentrism.[6] I also suggest that there has emerged a new, if at times contested, historiographical consensus in which it is the serious limitations of both labour's 'traditional' class consciousness and socialism's 'universal' message of emancipation – weakened, indeed often fractured, by support for racism, sexism, nationalism, imperialism and colonialism – which figures most prominently.[7] Moreover, in a wider political context these traditional aspects of organised labour and its working-class constituency are increasingly presented as embarrassing, if not doomed, obstacles to the further development and spread of the 'liberal progressivism' of Blair and Clinton.

This essay takes its cue from the appeals of Edward Thompson and Rick Halpern for the adoption, respectively, of an international framework of reference and the closer integration of imperial history and comparative labour history.[8] The overriding aim is critically to engage with the new historiographical consensus with specific reference to the subject matter of socialist attitudes to the closely linked areas of empire and imperialism, and 'non-white' indigenous peoples and migrant workers, both 'free' and 'unfree', between the outbreak of the Boer War, in 1899, and the 1910 Act of Union in South Africa. These two events, of course, took place within the era of 'new imperialism' (1880-1914), characterised by the colonial empire of 'formal conquest, annexation and administration'; and the partition of 'most of the world outside Europe and America' into territories under 'the formal rule or informal political domination' of 'mainly Great Britain, France, Germany, Italy, the Netherlands, Belgium, the USA and Japan'.[9]

Given the vast and potentially unmanageable nature and scope of my concerns, certain limits have, of necessity, been placed upon the chosen field of enquiry. Thus, while references are made to labour movement and indeed popular attitudes to class, race and empire, my primary concern rests with the attitudes of socialists. I refer mainly to socialists in Britain. However, due reference is also made to socialist, and to a lesser extent and in some instances overlapping trade-union, voices in the 'white-settler' South African and Australian locations of the British Empire. Indeed, an important aim of the essay is to highlight the sense of an active and lively flow and interchange of personnel, ideas and debate among socialists in Britain, South Africa and Australia. Furthermore, on account of the fact that events in South Africa, as opposed to the 'aboriginal question' in Australia,[10] commanded so much of the attention of British socialists in this period, my focus on socialist attitudes to 'non-white' indigenous peoples rests specifically upon black South Africans rather than Australian aborigines. At the same time, however, the text does address both British socialists' interest in, and portrayals, of 'non-white' indigenous peoples in India and the Far East, and wider British, South African and Australian socialists' concerns with 'non-white', most prominently Chinese, migrant labour.

The views of key British socialist leaders and the wider socialist movement, as expressed in the pages of the socialist weeklies, *Justice*, the *Labour Leader* and the *Clarion*, constitute my main object of enquiry and source of evidence. The many voices to be heard within these socialist organs are, wherever and whenever possible, rendered more complete and comprehensive by reference to biographical, autobiographical and other sources. These weeklies were, of course, the organs, respectively, of the Social Democratic Federation (SDF), the Independent Labour Party (ILP) and Robert Blatchford's educational and propagandistic Clarion movement.

The other British socialist group of national significance, the Fabian Society, published a monthly journal, *Fabian News*. However, when set against the three socialist weeklies, *Fabian News* offered a paucity of material dealing with the themes of class, race and empire. Moreover, any such material took the form mainly of factual reports of Fabian Society lectures, or of brief and matter-of-fact accounts of the Society's attitudes towards the Boer War. In marked contrast to *Justice*, the *Clarion* and the *Labour Leader*, *Fabian News* did *not* provide a vibrant forum for wide-ranging and intensive *debate* and *discussion* of socialist, and on occasion non-socialist, attitudes and policies towards a range of issues and events pertaining to our concerns.[11] Rather, it tended to be a much more controlled, 'top-down' and dry publication, intended for consumption, by a largely passive membership, of the predominantly domestic ideas and policies of the Webbs and other mainly London-based national leaders. For these various reasons, and notwithstanding references at various points in the essay to the attitudes of Fabians relevant to the subject matter, *Fabian News* does not constitute one of my main sources. Finally, in view of my concentration upon the *socialist* press, I have not examined the views to be found in the very interesting, yet democratic and republican rather than socialist, *Reynold's Newspaper*.[12]

As hinted in the previous paragraph, although the organs of different socialist groups or tendencies, none of the three weeklies under review pushed a narrow and sectarian 'line', designed to exclude all but 'true believers'. Rather they encouraged open and active debate on a wide range of matters affecting the Left. There was also considerable fluidity and personnel and ideas among them. Thus prominent ILPers penned articles for the *Clarion* and *Justice*, as well as the *Labour Leader*. In addition to those of emergent Labourism, the active voices and agents of provincial Fabianism were to be heard and represented in their columns.[13] Writers and correspondents included members of the 'rank-and-file', as well as leaders of the stature of Hardie, Henry Hyndman and Blatchford. And all three publications published numerous letters and, albeit less frequently, articles by socialists and trade unionists living abroad which closely linked the issues of class, race and empire. In sum, much in the manner of the Chartist *Northern Star*, the socialist weeklies provide the reader with a close, unrivalled and representative 'feel' for the character and main issues and debates activating 'the movement'.[14]

The considerable amount of time, attention and lively debate given by the *Labour Leader*, the *Clarion* and, especially, *Justice*, to the chosen subject matter between 1899 and 1910 effectively negates the charges of parochialism and marginal interest in colonialism on the part of British socialists.[15] Furthermore, while the pages of these socialist organs confirm the well-documented fact of socialist and labour opposition to the 'aggressive'[16] and, according to the new orthodoxy, 'aberrant' imperialism of the South African War,[17] they also contain much other material directly relevant to my purposes which, for the most part, has hardly figured in the written historical record, let alone penetrated historical debate. As I will observe in more detail below, this material addressed issues such as opposition to the 'race and class domination and exploitation' which was widely seen in socialist circles to be a *necessary* feature of capitalist empire itself rather than a peculiarity confined to the South African case. There was also considerable interest in, and positive portrayals of, the attitudes, habits and anti-colonial struggles of 'native' peoples. And support for the principles of political independence and self determination derived, *pace* the new orthodoxy, far more from a tradition of independent popular republican and revolutionary internationalism, rather than from a predominantly middle-class, radical-Liberal or 'Manchester' perspective of largely self-interested, anti-imperialist 'Little Englandism'.[18] Moreover, there were serious attempts to apply the socialist principles of international brotherhood (sic), mutuality and common struggle in wide-ranging and non-racist ways; and fascinating and important debates concerning class, race and racism both between and among British- and white settler-based socialists.

An important function of this essay is to acquaint the reader with this much neglected material. However, my sights are ultimately set higher. Late nineteenth- and early twentieth-century British socialist and labour movement attitudes towards empire and imperialism were, as documented in much of the established historiography, undoubtedly characterised in part by differences and divisions, ambiguities and contradictions. Pro- and anti-imperialist sentiments, for example, were to be found not only among middle-class, but also working-class supporters of Liberalism and socialism. As observed in much of the history written between the 1960s and the 1980s, the great majority of organised workers and leaders were, at least with respect to the South African War, strongly anti-imperialist, while the wider working class displayed a mixture of indifference, opposition and support towards the question of empire.[19] However, an emphasis upon differences, divisions and complexities by no means tells the whole story. Indeed, in opposition to the view found in much of the more recent and current historiography – a view which, I suggest, amounts to a new consensus – I present the thesis that an increasingly class-based, internationalist, anti-imperialist and in many, if by no means all, ways anti-racist perspective predominated or 'ruled' in the views of the British socialist weekly press towards the questions of empire and our selected groups of 'non-white' indigenous peoples and migrant workers during this period. In the opinion of the most prominent British socialists, writing in the most important socialist journals, class took precedence over race, and racism was denounced as the enemy of socialist international brotherhood (sic) and class consciousness. I offer the related thesis that, notwithstanding the very powerful, indeed arguably hegemonic, influence of racism within both their societies, the attitudes of contemporary socialists in South Africa and Australia were characterised by a greater sense of debate and diversity than the conventional picture of pervasive and largely unchanging white working-class racism in those two countries would suggest.[20]

Simultaneously, this is not to argue that racialized, gendered and other limitations, boundaries and exclusions were absent from socialist discourse. They were indeed present among socialists in all three imperial locations, with racism being far more pronounced among, often migrant British, socialists in the 'settler colonies' than in Britain itself. However, I conclude with an endorsement of Kenneth Lunn's prefatory quotation to this essay that, on balance, the 'legacy of empire' – at least with respect to our chosen socialist organs and the views expressed therein – has been with much richer and far more complex than an emphasis upon blanket and unchanging 'racialized stereotypes and hostility' would suggest.[21]

The essay is organised in the following way. First, the key features of the new consensus are outlined. Second, I move to a critique which occupies the main body of the text. The critique proceeds in the first instance by considering socialist portrayals of indigenous peoples and migrants. It then moves to an investigation of socialist attitudes to empire and imperialism, both generally and with respect to the specific period in question. In the course of this investigation the reader's attention is drawn centrally to the socialist critique of *actually existing* capitalist imperialism of the 'new imperialist' era, as a crucial and *necessary* system of continued race and class domination. Furthermore, socialists saw this system as involving increasingly *global* ambitions and processes, embracing parts of the Far East as well as India, Africa, the western world and the Caribbean and Latin America. Accordingly, socialists sought to develop a class-based response with global application, and not to be 'misled' into the adoption of divisive, defensive, sectional, parochial and racist responses. The third part of my critique examines in more detail the nature of this 'class-based response'. This involves discussion of socialist and, to a much lesser extent labour, attitudes to the specific issues of the employment of Chinese 'slave labour' in South Africa , to 'alien and pauper labour' in Britain and, more generally, to 'free' labour. I observe that leading British socialists, such as Hyndman of the Social Democratic Federation, rejected the charge of 'socialist racism'.

Particular attention is focused upon the predominantly inclusive response of Dr. Haden Guest, of the Independent Labour Party. Widely endorsed by British socialists, Guest's strategic response was designed effectively to counteract capitalism's worldwide, and increasingly 'racialized'[22] drive for 'class domination', by means of the creation of a propertyless proletariat and a surplus of cheap labour, both 'free' and 'unfree', and predominantly 'coloured' in character. Guest exhorted

British socialists to demonstrate understanding and support for the struggles of indigenous peoples in South Africa and elsewhere against proletarianisation, and to endorse the notions of enhanced 'capacities' and equality of status, rights and opportunities irrespective of colour. His strategy was thus political and cultural as well as economic in character, and, as such, merits attention in its totality. As will now be evident, parts two and three of my critique raise a number of issues which continue to inform current political debates about globalization and the adoption of appropriate and effective labour strategies.

Guest's strategy of inclusive socialist internationalism, however, was neither un-qualified nor unlimited. For he concluded that, in certain circumstances, organ-ised workers would be forced to insulate themselves against 'unfair' competition in the global market of a mushrooming 'residuum' of irredeemably cheap, and often 'forced' or 'unfree', workers. This protection would be achieved by *excluding* the 'residuum' from labour markets inhabited by the 'regular' and 'independent-minded' or 'manly' workforce.

Both Guest's and the wider socialist responses to the problem of 'cheap labour' were, in principle, colour blind. However, in terms of concrete practice, class and race were often inextricably connected, with labour movements in many countries practising varying degrees of racist restriction and exclusion.[23] Within this context the final section of part three demonstrates some of the ways in which, supported by the state,[24] many white workers, including emigrant British socialists, in South Africa and Australia *were* 'misled' into invoking negative racist stereotypes, as well as moral-economic objections to 'cheapness' and 'slavery', to justify both their ex-clusionary attitudes to 'non-whites' and their 'white internationalism'.[25] This dem-onstration is conducted with specific reference to socialist attitudes to the 1906 'Bambatha rebellion' in Natal and the background and emergence of the Union of South Africa, 1908-1910, and Australian labour and the introduction of the 'White Australia' policy in 1901. However, even this final section of the essay does not lend itself to a conclusion of uniform racism or, as one recent writer has claimed, 'white labourism', affecting the entire 'imperial working class'.[26] Rather, there emerged a much more complex pattern of socialist debate, both between and among social-ists in Britain, South Africa, and, to a much lesser extent, Australia in which class consciousness both mingled and vied for supremacy with racism.

The conclusion summarises my main findings and indicates some of the ways in which future research into the subject of class, race and empire might usefully de-velop. However, the present task is not further to dwell upon hypotheses and find-ings, but to attend to the substantive and methodological evidence upon which the case is built. I turn in the first instance to an examination of the main features of the 'new consensus'.

The New Consensus: Characteristics

Proponents of the new consensus have expounded a number of interrelated theses. These may be summarised in the following way. Inheriting and sharing many of the assumptions and ideas of Cobdenite and Gladstonian nineteenth-century radical-Liberalism, turn-of-the century British socialists and labourites offered only a 'limited' critique of British imperialism. While they objected to the 'new' 'aggressive' imperialism of the naked force, conquest, predatory adventurism and barbarism of the South African War, and while few agreed with George Bernard Shaw that imperialism constituted a necessary stage in human progress, many on the progressive Liberal, Labour and socialist Left, including Robert Blatchford, John Burns, Edward Carpenter and Hyndman, were *not* opposed to the idea of empire per se, rooted as the latter was in the notion of 'true' or 'enlightened' imperialism. As Miles Taylor has observed in comments that well illustrate the new orthodoxy,

> The imperialist creed which developed after 1895 was regarded by virtually all critics of empire as an aberration. Many drew a distinction between … responsible and 'true' imperialism … and the reckless and self-interested pursuit of territory represented by, for example, Cecil Rhodes. 'True' imperialism recognized the right of all colonies to constitute themselves as self-governing republics based on the British model …'True' imperialism also recognized … 'a special obligation to act with self-control and moderation' when dealing with less powerful people and states. By contrast, the new imperialism showed no allegiance to these principles. In the first place it valued the acquisition of territory for its own sake … Secondly, the new imperialists abdicated all sense of moral responsibility … Rhodes' schemes in southern Africa were motivated by purely venal considerations and Joseph Chamberlain's plans for managing the empire amounted to creating an irresponsible dictatorship. The new imperialism, in other words, was imperialism without liberty.[27]

However, there was more than an altruistic love of humanity, fairness and liberty at work. According to Taylor, most radical Liberals and socialists were more anxious about the possible *domestic* consequences of the 'new imperialism' – militarism and conscription, the swollen and parasitical state, the suppression of dissent, the 'growth of executive power', the 'weakening of party government' and the 'undermining of the independence of the electorate' – than about its external threats to the rights of self-government in the white settler colonies and to responsible 'tutelage' or 'trusteeship' in the 'benevolently administered dependencies'.[28]

The limited nature of the anti-imperialist critique furthermore, meant that, while there was 'moral indignation at exploitation in the colonies', there was, according to Stephen Howe, 'very little attempt to trace the causes of such evils or to propose strategies for their removal', apart from the adoption of Ramsay MacDonald's 'Imperial standard' of 'human liberty and the administration of justice'.[29] It is true, observes Howe, that the white Dominions were to be afforded self government and encouraged 'to form an ever-closer Commonwealth in association with Britain'. However, the widespread adoption of a 'racial hierarchy with white settlers at the top and Africans at the bottom' largely excluded 'non-whites', at least in the foreseeable future, from full membership of the Imperial family. Thus, Howe notes that Keir Hardie, 'whilst expressing sympathy for the demands of Congress in India, stopped far short of urging complete independence for India or for any other tropical colony'. According to MacDonald, 'India was to be "nursed" towards self-government within an unspecified time scale', and 'the tropical colonies' to be 'maintained and developed' by 'enlightened' rulers and administrators with a due sense of responsibility to both the national and imperial interest. Indeed, so 'responsible' did the Labour Party become in the full course of time that, according to Attlee, by 1937 Labour 'was a more trustworthy guardian of imperial interests than its opponents'.[30]

The Left's attitudes, we are informed, also 'incorporated and mirrored basic imperialist ideological assumptions' such as 'racism and anti-semitism as well as … more deep-seated patterns of thought like evolutionism and the dualism between "civilisation" and "barbarism"'.[31] For example, Preben Kaarsholm strongly argues that, so deeply enmeshed in the prevailing ideas of cultural chauvinism, Eurocentrism, racism, and social Darwinism[32] were most European as well as British socialists, that, notwithstanding isolated examples to the contrary, they were unable both to relate their own struggles to, and to understand and support, the anti-colonial revolts of indigenous peoples in South Africa and elsewhere. Kaarsholm bleakly claims in relation to the latter that, 'These varieties of anti-imperial struggle were either not known at all, or they were repudiated in the name of 'civilization".[33] Many other historians have similarly accused European and British socialists of a mixture of ignorance, neglect and racist arrogance and superiority towards 'uncivilised' and 'barbaric' 'natives" and 'non-white' migrant labour.[34] In sum, the new consensus argues that racism further prevented the development of a full or 'true' Left critique of imperialism, and that 'race' triumphed over 'class' and internationalism, not only in terms of the imperial working class, but also in terms of its socialist and labour leadership.

The New Consensus: Critique

1. Portrayals of 'Non-White' Indigenous Peoples and Migrant Workers

In terms of the central concern with socialist attitudes towards people of colour in South Africa and migrant Chinese labour and other 'Asiatics', evidence indeed exists to support the view that British and white-settler socialists did at times regard these indigenous people and migrant workers, in addition to other 'native' and 'non-white' peoples, as uncivilised, child-like, and even savage and barbaric, and themselves and many Europeans as infinitely more superior and cultivated beings.

The language of aggressive and unapologetic racism was most pronounced among white-settler socialists, often of British origin. For example, in 1904 F.S. Wallis, Secretary of the United Trades and Labour Council of South Australia, forwarded to Keir Hardie a resolution from that body, 'for use in the House of Commons', protesting against the introduction of Chinese labour into the mines of the South African Transvaal. Protest was registered not only on economic grounds – the Chinese as 'cheap' and their importation productive of 'industrial strife' – but on explicitly racial and imperial grounds – the 'introduction of this class of aliens' being seen as 'a menace to the British race and a disgrace to the flag under which we live'.[35]

Indeed, as noted in chapter two, a wider concern with 'race (sic) purity', as well as with the creation of a 'workman's paradise', was frequently quoted by Australian socialists and labourites in support of their 'White Australia' stance. Thus in 1904 the *Worker* proclaimed that only the 'prospect of an Australian rebellion' on the part of 'an enfranchised people', had prevented Australia being 'swamped with the sweepings of Asia'. 'Cheap Jap (sic) labour', 'the amiable cannibal of Polynesia' and 'turbaned hordes of Hindustanes', declared the *Worker*, 'would have been let loose upon us'. Blending that curious mixture of strident anti-capitalism and aggressive, contemptuous and yet insecure and fearful racism characteristic of white-settler socialist consciousness,[36] the *Worker* opined that 'Capitalism's greatest hope of overturning the Socialistic forces lies in the myriad masses of servile coloured labour', the 'docile hordes' of 'the Empire, of Asia and of Africa'. The concluding message was clear: immediate and concerted action on the Australian model was required on the part of socialists in South Africa to prevent the impending Chinese 'invasion', and to preserve hopes for improved white living standards and, ultimately, white socialism.[37]

Among South African socialists similarly racist portrayals and sentiments were commonplace. For example, in 1905 an article in the *Labour Leader*, entitled 'Towards Socialism in the Transvaal', expressed the views popular among indigenous white socialists and labour movement activists that, 'The life of the country from a poor man's standpoint depends on the exclusion of the Asiatics', and that, in the event of their opposition to Asian exclusion from South Africa, the socialists of Great Britain would be 'playing the capitalists' game'. In supporting 'equal rights for Asiatics with whites', declared 'Kopjes', the author of the article,

the L(abour) R(epresentation) C(ommittee) and the Radicals will support a policy which will hand over the country to the coloured man. Asiatics are the blacklegs of the Orange River Colony and the Transvaal, not only as regards whites but natives. Living on rice, and clothed in calico, they will work for a mere song, and if the Transvaal is not allowed to pass the most stringent laws the white man must leave, and the native seek his kraal or become the servant of the Indian and Chinaman. Naturally, some of the big capitalists recognise the economic value of pitting the

Asiatic against the white man because of their increased dividends. This is supported in England as British fair play. But there is no fair play in such a policy, any more than there would be in flooding Lancashire towns with Indian operatives because they can live cheaper and therefore sell their labour for less. The Boer and British proletariat in the Transvaal and Orange River Colony are absolutely united against the invasion of the Asiatic, unfettered and unhindered, to engage in cut-throat competition with the whites who have made this country their home, and if the Imperial Government refuse much longer permission to colonials to legislate, the very gravest situation is possible. The United States of America had their origin through a dispute of much less importance.[38]

In the same year 'Hugo', the *Labour Leader*'s socialist correspondent from Johannesburg, dismissed the idea of calling a conference between the 'native leaders' and the leaders of the labour movement to discuss the extension of the vote to 'the natives' in the following manner:

In considering the native question one must never forget that the native of South Africa – Zulu, Basuto, Swazi, Hottentot, anything you like – is a savage, a mis-grown child, centuries behind the white. He is not a white man with an accidental black skin; he is a savage.[39]

Moreover, in the following year, Alex M. Thompson, deputy editor of the *Clarion*, attempted to discover the causes, but not to condone, the racism of 'former friends and comrades' who had gone to live in the United States and South Africa. Thompson believed that the facts of such a discovery, while hardly pleasant to reveal and read, constituted a necessary prerequisite to the formulation of an effective anti-racist socialist policy which would not amount to 'pretentious, sentimental bunkum'. Making specific reference to the openly and aggressively racist letters to the *Clarion* of 'Pufff', a South African correspondent, Thompson declared,

Colonials like Pufff and the other South African Socialists ... base their consideration of the Black's 'rights' on the theory that he is, essentially and irretrievably a lower animal, little more superior to the race of the anthropoid apes than he is inferior to the Caucasian. They believe that a mixture of Whites with coloured races would lead to degradation of the species. They believe that the interests of Whites and coloured races are not common, but conflicting; and that unless Whites maintain the upper hand, 'inferior' races will overpower, as they already vastly outnumber, them'.[40]

While not usually subscribing to the kind of unabashed racism so marked among 'white-settler' socialists, British socialists, nevertheless, did on occasion adopt superior, chauvinistic and paternalistic attitudes towards the 'coloured' Other. For example, Robert Blatchford's 'Impressions of a Very Foreign Country', published in the *Clarion* in 1906, typically combined western images of Morocco as fasci-

nating and exotic – as 'intensely interesting, strangely foreign, marvellously pic-
turesque' – with sharp criticisms of the cruelty, ignorance, dirtiness and despotic
intolerance of 'traditional' societies, and a steadfast belief in the innate superiority
of modernising, clean and tolerant 'Englishness'. Thus Blatchford,

> ... it fills one with wonder to find this people still living, dressing, and believing today
> just as their ancestors did a thousand years ago. But I for one was not sorry when the
> gaunt African hills grew dim along the horizon, and the clean English ship glided
> out into the azure loveliness of the great Gulf Stream. The land of the setting sun is a
> land of dreams – but they are bad dreams, I fear. The despotism, the fanaticism, the
> cruelty, the vice of the bad old days are there for all to see. For my part I do not like
> them. These picturesque Moors beat their donkeys and camels, and use their women
> as slaves and cattle and beasts of burden ... The people need soap and science ... It
> was good to get back to the clean English ship, and the free air, and to talk with men
> who love dumb animals and honour women, to listen to dear old Bach's fugues ...[41]

It was, furthermore, commonplace for leading figures in the socialist movement
to employ the evolutionary language of 'stages of development' and 'higher'
and 'lower' forms of civilisation. For example, Blatchford himself referred to
the Australian aboriginals as possessing the 'low intellect and moral standards'
of a 'primitive' people.[42] Haden Guest, who prided himself upon his first-hand
knowledge of the conditions of the African 'natives' – having served in the Boer
War and practised medicine in South Africa, mainly in the Orange River colony
between 1902 and 1905[43] – and who had considerable empathy and support for
their cultures and aspirations, nevertheless routinely described them as 'primitive',
as lacking in 'capacities' and 'civilised needs'.[44]

While the attitudes of most British socialists towards the peoples of Asia were not
generally characterised by the racist hostility and venom prevalent among turn-of-
the century white-settler and US labour movements,[45] they could be rather mixed.
Alex Thompson, writing in the *Clarion*, observed that some people associated the
Chinese, comically, with 'pantomime representations of the Widow Twankey',
or, in more sinister vein, with 'Willie Edonin's presentment of the Heathen'.
Thompson himself was by no means himself immune from racial stereotyping. He
described the eating habits of Chinese labourers as 'uncivilised', 'disgusting' and
'abhorrent'. However, his overall portrayal was far more varied in character. Thus,
while the mass of the Chinese were 'terribly overcrowded, miserably fed, and subject to horrible diseases', yet they were also members of an old and distinguished
civilisation, inhabitants of great cities, and displayed great knowledge and ingenu-
ity, especially with regard to the cultivation of food and 'the finest system of inland
navigation ever known'.[46]

Thompson's mixed portrayal invites us, in turn, to consider the complexities and
nuances of British socialists' representations of indigenous and migrant peoples.
And, in truth, and notwithstanding instances to the contrary, a balanced consider-

ation of the sum of relevant evidence contained particularly in the pages of *Justice* and the *Labour Leader* and, to a lesser and more ambiguous extent, in the *Clarion*, does not lend itself to an overall conclusion of representational racism.

Before further attending to this evidence, however, it is necessary to strike a cautionary methodological note. In approaching such an emotive subject as race, we must be careful to heed John Mackenzie's advice to avoid 'presentism': the 'reading back of contemporary attitudes and prejudices into historical periods'.[47] As a corollary, due attention must be paid to historical context and the full complexity of, and shifts in, attitudes, representations and meanings. As Colin Holmes concluded in his 1988 study of 'host' attitudes to immigration into Britain between 1871 and 1914,

> ... it is necessary to guard against the blanket categorisation of hostility where it did arise, as racism, before paying careful attention to *context*. Those who stroll back into history and assess it from the vantage point of the 1980s illuminate nothing of the past.[48] (emphasis added.)

The advice offered by Mackenzie and Holmes acts as a useful corrective against the adoption of a one-dimensional and ultimately very misleading reading of socialist portrayals of 'non-white' indigenous and migrant peoples. For common resort to the condescending language of social Darwinism constituted, nevertheless, one part of a far more complex socialist response in which factors in a changing social environment were held to take precedence over those of a fixed notion of biology. Thus, the dominant contemporary notion of white European superiority over non-European 'coloured' civilisations was frequently interpreted by socialists as being relative, open to debate and question, subject to the full force of societal change and in some respects contradictory and false, rather than absolute, uncontested and fixed or 'natural' in character. For example, while routinely referring to 'the savage' and 'the civilised' as states of human existence, Sydney Olivier, the respected Fabian-socialist writer on race, neither implied 'the dogmatic assertion of any essential or final Human type', nor assumed an automatic and absolute association between whites and civilisation and people of colour and savagery. Matters were, in fact, far more contingent, shifting and relative than that. Thus Olivier,

> ... it is noticeable that more than one of the races of which we habitually speak as inferior, and which appear to be effete or decaying, are far in advance of the commercial Caucasian who is our own type and standard, not only in some of the most desirable and pleasant human qualities, but in artistic, poetical, and other of the higher spiritual forms of genius or faculty.[49]

In questioning the claim made by 'Pufff' concerning the 'natural' inferiority of black Africans and white superiority, 'Chufff', a letter writer to the *Clarion*, argued that existing white advantage in terms of 'culture, in art, in industry, in economic development' by no means constituted the end of the matter. Equally important was reference to, and understanding of, total social context and immediate and relative experiences and perceptions. 'They may not know (educational) Standard VI', declared 'Chufff', 'but they know more about animals, plants, rivers, and such things as concern them directly than Pufff will ever learn'. Similarly, while the black people of the Transvaal might be seen to be superstitious, they were,

> not more (so) than are the majority of Europeans, who sprinkle "holy water" on dead people, and drink port wine and eat bread under the pretension that wine is blood and the bread flesh. And whose, ye gods, whose?[50]

Many other socialists took such arguments further. Alongside portrayals of the 'primitive' black 'native', there were frequently to be found in the British socialist press positive images of some of the existing aspects of indigenous peoples' lives and their unlimited future 'capacities'. For example, notwithstanding his references to 'primitive barbarians', Haden Guest was among the prominent British socialists who identified the 'mutual aid' institutions and practices of black Africans as standing in opposition to the rampant individualism of western capitalism and, as such, a necessary building block in the construction of black socialism and an 'Entente Cordiale' between black and white leaders.[51] Guest's experiences had taught him that the 'natives of Natal' were 'peaceful, sweet and kindly men and women living in friendship'. 'This is, in the main', observed Guest, 'the character of all primitive people'.[52] Thus, there were 'in South Africa south of the Zambesi over 6,000,000 coloured people, very intelligent, and capable of every advance in culture and civilisation'.[53] Yet white capitalist imperialism had created 'the race problem'. The desire for white racial domination and the economic exploitation of the 'coloured people' had 'largely destroyed the primitive peace and brotherliness of the barbarian mind'.[54] Black 'ferocity ... sanguninariness ... outrage and horror', such as were to be found in Natal during the 1906 Rebellion, were, according to Guest, the 'products of the military organisation of white men and of white men's ideas'. Once again western 'civilisation' was indicted for its hypocrisy and brutality towards indigenous peoples.[55]

Yet Guest's overall view of both the present and future prospects concerning 'race relations' was far from bleak. The spread of 'culture' would 'dissipate the stage of primitive superstition' and ensure equality between black and white.[56] Socialists, with their beliefs in progress, materially-driven change allied to the constitutive power of human agency, and their message of *universal* liberation – rooted in 'fundamental humanity', the 'solidarity of labour', 'the brotherhood of man' and the 'equality' of 'all races and all classes'[57] – had a crucial role to play in this unfolding process of human emancipation. But, equally – and contrary to the one-dimensional, static and hostile depictions of white responses to the black 'other' portrayed in much of the current literature[58] – indigenous black people in Africa and elsewhere were afforded a very positive role as key *agents* in the construction of a socialist future. 'Because his contact has been less' than that of British people with the 'contaminating' influence of capitalism, declared Guest of the black African, 'we shall need his help in building world socialism'.[59] In turn, white socialists were strongly advised to 'get in touch with the leaders of coloured opinion all over the world, and consider with them what should be done'. They must also insist their 'black brethren' be afforded 'a fair and equal chance of cooperating in the development of Natal and the rest of South Africa'.[60]

Moreover, there were encouraging signs that positive changes were already underway. Guest observed that, 'in addition to exceptional leaders such as Dr. Abdurahman and Tengo Jabaru', there were 'very many educated and thoughtful natives all over South Africa'.[61] In the Cape Colony, where 'the Negro, the European, the Malay, the Indian' had mixed 'to produce a race sometimes very handsome, and always very capable', the 'spirit of socialism' was spreading. Dr. Abdurahman, of Indian and Dutch descent, had been elected a member of the Cape Town Council, 'the first coloured man elected on to any elective body in South Africa'. There was a pressing need to preserve and advance such representative gains, and more generally the principles of equality of opportunity and democracy, throughout southern Africa.[62]

Guest's views were representative of the opinions socialists expressed more generally in the pages of the *Labour Leader, Clarion* and *Justice* and elsewhere. Notwithstanding their frequent usage of the language and imagery of social evolutionism, these journals presented, on balance, predominantly positive images of 'coloured' people. For example, black Americans' struggle for decency and self-respect, in the face of white oppression and 'foul imaginations, misrepresentations, injustice (and) insult', won the undiluted admiration of H.G. Wells in the *Labour Leader*.[63] Keir Hardie was to be found in the same journal paying tribute to the 'shrewdness and general intelligence' of the South African 'native', with the Basutos in particular being described as 'this splendid race'; while Tom Mann's scrapbooks contained several photographs of fine looking Zulu women and girls.[64] During the turbulent period of the 1906 Natal Rebellion, the *Clarion* published major articles by Alex Thompson, Haden Guest and Ramsay MacDonald and letters by 'Snufff' and other South African socialists in defence of the 'natives', and in opposition both to the obnoxious racist outpourings of 'Pufff' and likeminded spirits and to 'white slave-drivers' and the repressive and exploitative actions of the white state in Natal.[65] In a similar vein, the 'real sympathy' of Hyndman and *Justice* during the South African War 'was with the Zulus', fear being expressed that the independence of the Boers 'would inevitably entail the complete submission of the natives'.[66] Finally, Sydney Olivier, who had been Colonial Secretary to Jamaica between 1900 and 1904 and who later served as Governor for five and a half years, had no doubt that 'race fusion', especially in the form of intermarriage between whites and blacks, and equal opportunities and status, combined with the 'abandonment of the color line and race differentiation theory' and the more extensive application of the 'vital principle' of 'human equality before God', held the keys to the inevitable advancement of the 'coloured man'. The fruits of such measures were to be seen in the successfully 'blended' society of Jamaica. By way of marked contrast, the pervasive racism and violence of the southern states of the United States of America bore awful witness to Olivier's maxim that 'a community of unmixed white and black is of necessity a combination of masters and serfs'.[67]

Positive images were not infrequently accompanied by idealised depictions of 'native' life and biting, indeed inverted social Darwinist, indictments of urban capitalist 'civilisation'. As a letter from 'A Comrade in Natal', published in *Justice* in 1906, declared,

> To my mind the native is as intelligent a being as one could wish to meet. Let one talk to him even on matters that would puzzle the hard-headed British workman, and he grasps them with apparent ease. Again, physically the native, before he becomes a town dweller and consequently a sort of loafer, *is one of the finest specimens of humanity in existence,* and *to see the women, with their deep chests and whole figures perfectly made, and with a smile of health on their faces* ... one is tempted to curse the civilisation that brought to life *such dregs of humanity as are to be seen in the fashionable towns of Europe.*[68] (emphasis added.)

Six years earlier, in the midst of the War, the 'typical South African native', had been portrayed by *Justice* as 'a creature magnificent to behold', with,

> finely-moulded form, powerful limbs, and well-poised head; with muscular development of just that amount which gives one the idea of a perfect healthful normality.[69]

The socialist press also shared Guest's optimism concerning the growing capacities of 'coloured' people. As a South African socialist, Isipingo, wrote in *Justice* in 1904, the 'natives' or 'niggers' whose 'spirit of manliness' is 'so galling' to 'the whites' or 'governing classes', 'are beginning to know their own power, and the day may become when they will exert themselves'.[70] In 1907, noting that 'Hope Dawns for South Africa' and that 'the political consciousness of the African people is awakening', the *Labour Leader* consistently supported the demands of the 'Ethiopian Movement' for equality of opportunity, the vote 'irrespective of race, creed or colour', abolition of the hated hut tax and improved employment opportunities for black people.[71] Similarly, across the Atlantic the activities of the various Pan African associations, the industry of black West Indians, and the radical consciousness embodied in the work of W.E.DuBois – who 'represents the spirit of Negro revolt' as opposed to Booker T. Washington's 'negro acquiescence' – all met with the *Labour Leader*'s strong support.[72]

As we will see in more detail later, the level and warmth of such support hardly squares with the thesis that, in their assumed western superiority, British socialists barely gave a passing thought to the struggles of 'native' 'coloureds'. In truth, the dominant response on the part of these socialists was to extend the principled hand of friendship and offer inclusion rather than racist hostility and exclusion. 'If the white man pushes the black man down he falls with him', was the persistent claim of the *Labour Leader*.[73] The Australian Labor Party met with British socialist criticism for its support of the exclusion of 'our coloured brothers' from Australia, and its rejection of the principles that, 'all assumptions of race superiority, it is part of our mission as Socialists to remove', and 'brain and ability, as well as character, are not the exclusive possession of the white races'.[74] As 'Chufff' declared in the *Clarion*, 'give the black man economic equality' and 'he will soon be our equal in intelligence, purity, culture and industry'.[75]

British socialists' attitudes towards the peoples of Asia were likewise far more complex and for the most part far more positive than a one-dimensional emphasis upon racist hostility would suggest. Within this context, and notwithstanding its suggestive power, Edward Said's famous notion of 'Orientalism' – 'as a Western style for dominating, restructuring and having authority over the Orient', of 'doctrines of European superiority, various kinds of racism, imperialism and the like'[76] – lacks sensitivity to the full ambiguities and contradictions of the historical record.[77] Many socialists, for example, were quick to debunk the threatening notion of 'The Yellow Peril'. The latter was viewed in the socialist press as a historically constructed, as opposed to natural, form of representation, consciously and hypocritically designed by the ruling forces in the Occident to trumpet the superiority of 'western Christian' over 'heathen oriental' civilisation and thereby to justify, by means of 'cant' and 'cowardice', the former's designs upon, and aggression towards, the latter. R.B. Suthers' representative statement, made in the *Clarion*, is worth quoting at length:

> The Yellow Peril was not by way of being a peril until the Christian Powers, following their spiritual ideals, went to the East with their rifles and guns, and began to steal the yellow man's land. Japan, being a godless nation, resents this action of the Powers with moral checks and spiritual ideals. They did not know we were engaged in our great civilising mission … Being a godless people they mistook us for mere robbers, and having no moral checks they commenced to arm and drill and educate themselves to be able to keep the burglars out …
>
> The Yellow Peril at present is nothing but a fear that the Chinese will follow the Japanese in defending their country from the aggression of the Christian powers.

Observing that 'in the way of morality we can teach the Japanese nothing', Suthers concluded that it would be better to 'cultivate peaceful relations with the yellow man rather than help to bring about a racial and religious war' which the 'appeals to religious bigotry' were calculated to do.[78]

There were instances of popular anti-Chinese feeling in Britain around the 'Chinese slavery' issue of 1904-6, and Beatrice Webb was undoubtedly not alone in Fabian circles in her dismissal of the Chinese as a morally defective, vice-ridden and 'unclean' race.[79] However, most British socialists writing in the pages of the *Clarion*, the *Labour Leader* and *Justice* took care not to construct negative, racist stereotypes of the Chinese and other Asiatics. As will see in more detail below, British socialist opposition to the employment of the Chinese in South Africa was based primarily not upon opposition to the Chinese labourers per se, but upon their employment as *cheap* and *forced*, or 'unfree' and 'slave' labour – the poor and largely unwitting *victims* of the real culprits, the unscrupulous mine owners of the Transvaal and the imperial and colonial governments.[80] As Suthers wrote in relation to the mine owners, 'If they could train monkeys, and they came cheaper than the Chinese, they would deport the Chinese to-morrow'.[81] In keeping with their class-based, inclusive philosophy, British socialists generally offered the hand of friendship to Asiatic labour on the condition that it did not pose a threat to the existing conditions and future prospects of other workers.[82]

As in the case of the black 'native', socialist organs presented generally favourable portrayals of Asian peoples. For example, and *pace* Alex Thompson's racist claims (strikingly similar to those made by American labour activists) that 'barbaric' Chinese labourers were 'passing rich on sixpence per day, and can feed themselves on messes of rice, dogs, cats, dried rats and other convertibles', the *Clarion* took issue with 'the fashion' to mock the Chinese resort to 'pigtails and chopsticks'. Rather, China was commended for its 'tolerably far advanced' intellectual, governmental, scientific and artistic achievements at a time when 'the Britons were mere savages', and 'long before our race emerged from barabarism'.[83] (Many 'heathen' Chinese, of course, were keenly aware of the many and proud achievements of their ancient civilisation, long before the advent of the 'civilising mission' of western Christian imperialism.)[84] H.M. Hyndman, who had employed Chinese labour in a mining venture in California, declared in *Justice* that, 'No one who has ever employed Chinamen can deny that, taken as a whole, they are sober, industrious, good-natured and intelligent'.[85]

Several writers in the *Labour Leader* expressed similarly favourable sentiments, portraying the Chinese both abroad and at home as committed to education and knowledge, 'quite as moral as the ordinary run of whites', peaceful, anti-imperialistic, relatively well off and attached to the land and their families.[86] During his 1907 'Scamper Round the World', reported extensively in the *Labour Leader*, Keir Hardie found the Chinese of Vancouver to be 'truly … a wonderful people', if also 'inveterate gamblers' and suffering from overcrowded housing and living conditions.[87] In his lecture, 'On Life in China', also reported in the *Labour Leader*, Edward Carpenter declared the Chinese to be 'certainly a very remarkable people … acute, intelligent, observant, accurate, industrious, very kindly and polite one to another'.[88]

Finally, Japan won widespread and impressive plaudits from many sections of western society. Westerners increasingly saw Japan, especially after the defeat of

Russia in 1904-5, as the rising power in the Orient, or, as *Justice* put it, 'The Hope of Asia'.[89] British socialists used a variety of favourable adjectives to describe the Japanese people, the most common being 'efficient' (especially, and typically, by the Fabians), 'highly civilised and intelligent' (*Justice*), and 'the bravest, most athletic, the most loyal and patriotic, the daintiest and most modest people in the world' (*Clarion*).[90] For Robert Blatchford, who 'naturally' held the Japanese 'in high honour' and regarded them as 'my brothers', the 'genius of the Japanese' resided in 'the genius of common sense'. Having studied western civilisation, the Japanese, according to Blatchford, 'took from it what was sound and rejected what was rotten', including a rejection of the West's love of 'Mammon'.[91] Accordingly, the British socialist press took a keen interest in the nature and development of socialism in Japan.[92]

In this section I have argued that British socialist portrayals of 'non-white' indigenous Africans, Asians, and migrant Chinese people were, on balance, far more positive and far less uniformly negative and hostile than the new consensus would suggest. In conclusion, it should be noted that the socialist attitudes towards race described above can only be properly understood when situated within the imperial contexts in which they arose.[93] Therefore, I will now turn to a discussion of socialist attitudes to the questions of empire and imperialism.

2. Attitudes to Empire and Imperialism

(a) Enlightened Imperialism

As suggested by proponents of the limited nature of British labour and socialist critiques of imperialism, many socialists often expressed, alongside radical Liberals and Fabian- and Liberal-Imperialists, support for an 'enlightened' or 'civilised' form of imperial policy and rule.[94] Socialist support was of two kinds: that based upon substantive imperial practice; and that which looked forward to a 'higher' imperial form and future. I will address them in turn.

First, a minority of socialists writing upon imperial matters within the pages of the *Clarion*, the *Labour Leader* and *Justice*, while fully acknowledging its past and present 'sins', were prepared to recognise and publicise the 'virtues' of British imperialism as compared with its European counterparts. Most prominent in this respect were Robert Blatchford and Alex Thompson at the *Clarion*. A declared 'patriot' who was opposed to the declaration of the South African War, to the 'expansion of the Empire' ('I am, and always have been, what is sarcastically called a "Little Englander"'), indeed to 'Imperialism' itself and its associated evils of 'Jingoism', 'Militarism' and 'War', Blatchford nevertheless declared it to be 'a fact' that, 'England is universally admitted to be the best colonising Power the world has known, and the gentlest and wisest ruler over subject races'.[95] Thompson's trip to the Far East in 1910 likewise convinced him that 'British rule is a blessing rather than an evil to the lands upon which it has imposed itself', and that 'the maintenance of the British Empire is a primary condition of human progress'.[96] There was, according to Blatchford, 'no country in Europe where the masses have as much freedom, as little oppression, as great a power (had they but sense to use it) as in England'.[97] By way of contrast, stood the 'rigid military controls', repression, authoritarianism, war-like aggression and lack of respect for domestic workers' and colonial natives' rights characteristic of the regimes of especially Germany and Russia, but also other European powers. As a result, reasoned both Blatchford and Thompson, English, indeed British workers as a whole and all British colonial subjects, had 'a great deal to lose' in the event of dismemberment of the British Empire and England being 'conquered by some foreign Power'. Among such considerable potential losses could be counted a general commitment to 'civilised' rule and standards, 'free speech, a free Press and free education' and the likely creation of 'a vassal State'. Moreover, if pro-Boer British socialists 'had said and done in Germany, or France, or Russia what they have said and done here', they would be ' dead, or in Siberia or on Devil's Island, long ago'. The final salutary lesson in defence of British liberty lay in fact that, 'if they strike for wages in Russia or Germany, in Italy or Austria, they are ridden over or shot down by their own soliders'.[98] In sum, warts and all, Britain and the British Empire were, for Blatchford, prized havens of liberty, civilisation and honest decency.

Elements of Blatchford's arguments can be found, often in less bald and more nuanced form, in the thinking of other prominent socialists. For example, while firmly opposed to predatory and expansionary imperialism, and while careful not to see patriotism and the attainment of civil, religious, legal and political freedoms as synonymous with, or the product of, British imperialism, Hyndman and Hardie did differentiate British imperialism, as the least offensive, from its allegedly more autocratic, insensitive, cruel and bellicose German and Russian variants.[99]

While straying beyond my chronological boundary of 1910, I must also take note of the important fact that between 1915 and the early 1920s a relatively small, but very prominent, group of Labour MPs, trade union leaders and (increasingly ex-) socialists, including Alex Thompson, Victor Fisher, Havelock Wilson, W. Abraham ('Mabon'), Stephen Walsh, J.A. Seddon, C.B. Stanton, H.G. Wells and John Hodge, were involved with Lord Milner in the pro-First World War and pro-imperialist activities of the British Workers' League.[100] Formed in 1916 out of the Socialist National Defence Committee, itself established in the previous year, and known in the 1918 general election as the National Democratic and Labour Party, the League saw closer imperial union, regulation and protection and a heightened sense of 'Imperial' or 'Commonwealth' citizenship and duty as the effective antidotes to discredited laissez-faire capitalism, continued German aggression in international affairs and the spreading 'class-war' doctrine of Bolshevism.[101]

Committed to a belief in 'the destiny' and 'protection' of the 'virility and vigour of the race', League members eulogised the British Empire as being 'the first

Empire in the records of mankind based on the (sic) popular sovereignty'.[102] In marked contrast to the 'mailed fist', 'cruelty', 'greed', 'rapacity' and 'aggressive capitalist imperialism' characteristic of the 'junkered bullies' of Germany, the British had, according to the League's journal, the *British Citizen and Empire Worker*, traditionally brought 'peace', 'understanding and care', 'civilisation', 'higher standards' and a true appreciation of 'moderation' and 'gradual progress' to the 'native races' under their rule. The solution for the unresolved grievances of the 'child-like' 'natives' of India and elsewhere lay, accordingly, not in immediate, premature and potentially disastrous demands for independence and Home Rule, but patience and trust in continued British maternal care and wisdom. Continuing to live 'safely and happily under the Union Jack', the peoples of India and other 'coloured' colonies, would eventually achieve that 'moderate and reasoned' position of independence – already bestowed upon the 'more advanced' white-settler colonies – which constituted 'true liberty'.[103]

Beyond the shores of Britain, in those self same 'more advanced' white-settler colonies, there also were to be found tenacious, if simultaneously very complex, and somewhat ambiguous and contested, personal, familial and wider social forms of allegiance to continued imperial ties with the beneficent, but also self-interested, 'mother country'. Thus, notwithstanding the presence of anti-capitalist and anti-imperialist socialist and labourist ideas in both South Africa and Australia, and continuing socialist and labour links with comrades 'at home', positive identifications with Britain and the more 'enlightened' aspects of the British 'imperial idea', remained strong in domestic labour movement and socialist circles.

Like their counterparts in Britain, socialists in Australia opposed the aggressive imperialism of the Boer -War type. The South African War was seen by most Australian socialists and many in the labour movement to have resulted from the 'machinations' of capitalist mine owners and financiers for higher profits and cheap labour: the 'Jingo monomaniacs' and 'Stock Exchange blood-suckers' and 'Rhodes and his chartered Scoundrelism' who had cynically and disastrously dictated British policy in South Africa.[104] As seen in chapter two, the same socialists and labourites also eagerly grasped the opportunity to construct a 'new Australia', a 'workman's paradise', free from the 'monarchical' and 'aristocratic' privileges and snobbery, and the naked capitalist exploitation and glaring class-based distinctions and poverty which were believed to characterise Britain.[105] Moreover, they incorporated their radical, but gendered, egalitarianism of practical and pragmatic 'mateness', 'Equal Rights' and class consciousness into what it meant to be an Australian, into the very fabric of an Australian nationalism rooted in 'local, as opposed to British imperial, patriotism'.[106] Republicanism constituted an important, but not dominant, part of this class-conscious radical nationalism.[107] However, mainly as a result of continued personal and familial ties, Britain still constituted a part of 'home' for many Australians, including a significant number of those on the Left. Furthermore, and notwithstanding the 'betrayal' of the 'responsible' and 'civilised' imperial tradition by 'Rhodes and his capitalist gang', some Australian socialists praised Britain as 'by far the greatest and best power in the world', a power which was perceived to have delivered very important direct and indirect rewards to large sections of the Australian people.[108] It is to a brief consideration of these rewards and Australians' gains that I now turn.

As Terry Irving has observed of the nineteenth-century Anglo-Australian relationship, it had been as early as the mid-Victorian years that 'the liberal aspects of the colonial state were put in place'.[109] These aspects included the concession by the British government of the right to 'frame their own constitutions to the colonies of New South Wales, Victoria, Tasmania and South Australia', and the achievement by adult males in these colonies of 'access to the state through enfranchisement, the secret ballot and equal electoral districts'. Of crucial importance in terms of our imperial framework of reference was the new colonial parliaments' enactment of these rights of male political citizenship prior to their enactment in Britain. Equally significant was the general absence of conflict and hostility between Australia and Britain at mid century. Thus,

> In terms of nation building the critical aspects of the transfer of state power to the new colonial governments were that it happened without bloodshed, and that it was delayed until the new societies could support a diversifying economy and a liberal polity. *The absence of bloodshed meant that no tradition of national political or cultural resistance to the mother country was established.*[110] (emphasis added)

As a result of the federation of the six colonies, the new Commonwealth of Australia was formed in 1901. Resting upon the '"three pillars" of white Australia, New Protection, and compulsory arbitration', the infant Commonwealth represented the climax of the process of nation building.[111] Significantly, the creation of the Commonwealth met with the full approval of the British imperial 'mother'.

As Irving further observes, at the heart of the paradox that 'Australia would become a nation without a national movement', stood colonial businessmen who 'were not a native bourgeoisie formed by an anti-imperialist logic, but a regional sub-set of the imperial ruling class'. Similarly, and notwithstanding their growing class consciousness and 'awareness of separate interests within the empire', stood workers who looked to Britain for their trade union model and often defended 'work practices that had been fashioned in Britain'.[112]

Finally, as noted earlier, within 'this regional variation of British imperialism', the imperially-fashioned ties of race and racism proved to be of major importance. Above all, race 'operated as a powerful unifying symbol in the nationalist project' of the 1900s. Not only did the demands for racial purity and cultural homogeneity centrally inform the process of class reconciliation embodied in the National Settlement of the new Commonwealth, but they also rallied many of the warring workers and employers of the previous decade behind the demand for a 'White Australia'. The imperial dimension of race was a central component of the latter.

As Myra Willard concluded in the 1920s,

> Australians have adopted the White Australia policy because they believe it to be necessary for their existence *as a nation of the British type*. Unrestricted immigration of non-European peoples … would, in their opinion, result … in a mixture of races which would radically alter the *British characteristics of the Australian people and, therefore, be just as fatal to the present Australian nationality*.[113] (emphasis added.)

Two examples may be cited to demonstrate the continuing, indeed in some ways strengthened, importance of the imperial tie, complete with its familial and racial dimensions, to Australian labour. First, in 1911 Andrew Fisher, Labour Prime Minister of the New Commonwealth, and former Ayrshire miner, returned home from the Imperial Conference in London convinced that the enhanced consultative powers gained by his country on imperial matters signalled both her entry into the 'inner family circle', and his labour movement's duty to carry on 'the Government of Empire with the single aim and object of securing the peace and prosperity of all mankind'.[114] Second, in 1916 William Morris Hughes, another Australian Labour Prime Minister and a 'true patriot' and 'apostle of Empire', accepted the invitation to be the main speaker at the inaugural meeting of the British Workers' League in London.[115]

In South Africa socialists also considered the Boer War to be 'capitalist' and 'imperialist' in character. They saw the war as a 'capitalist dodge' to obtain cheap, and as matters transpired, especially Chinese, labour in order to depress the wages, job opportunities and living standards of white and, to a much lesser extent in socialist perception, black African workers.[116] I have already noted that there were divisions among socialists concerning the rights and 'places' of black South Africans, with the majority opinion in favour of white privilege and domination over the 'uncivilised natives'. Furthermore, in the aftermath of the War and up to and beyond the 1910 Act of Union, relations between 'white' workers – the mainly craft-unionist British and the poorer and anti-British Afrikaners who were largely excluded from the unions and who were used as strike breakers in 1907 – were often tense. Simultaneously, there was, however, growing, if very uneven, evidence of 'white' worker solidarity in the face of competition from 'cheap' black workers and employer and state hostility and repression.[117] As Tim Moldram informs us, the experience of the First World War – with the official support of the Union government for the British Empire and English-speaking miners 'flocking to enlist in the army' standing in marked contrast to the 'strong republican ideals' and anti-Britishness of many Afrikaner workers – 'was a serious blow' to the South African Labour Party's attempt 'at uniting a white working class'.[118]

As illustrated by the miners' actions, many white British emigrant workers to South Africa, including socialists, thus retained a strong attachment to the Empire. Indeed, given the substantial and often pressing indentured Indian, Afrikaner, black South African and, albeit short-lived, 'forced' Chinese presence – as contrasted with the official post-1901 position in Australia of 'non-white' 'absence' and, more continuously, aboriginal 'virtual absence' or 'separation' – this sense of imperial attachment was probably stronger and more sustained in South Africa than in Australia. Notwithstanding the continued presence among South African socialists of anti-capitalist and anti-imperialist sentiments, many white British South African workers drew very positive lessons from their imperial experience. Above all, the latter delivered substantial material and non-material rewards. By the First World War period these 'wages of whiteness' included segregated labour markets, housing and patterns of residence, relatively high wage levels and living standards, strong political clout, and assumed cultural and psychological superiority over both the 'natives' and Afrikaners.[119] Furthermore, the 1914-1918 experience greatly strengthened, in South Africa and elsewhere, the idea of an enlightened, democratic and tolerant British Empire fighting manfully against cruel, autocratic and intolerant 'Kaiserism'.[120]

Finally, in terms of the wider imperial context, the strong development during this period of time of a racialised sense of 'family' between Britain and the 'white-settler' colonies further strengthened the white imperial tie. As Pat Thane has argued,

> When some of the British began to imagine the empire as a racial rather than a political unity, as a 'family' with an assumed common genetic inheritance, all members of a British 'imperial race', a barrier was raised between the colonies of white settlement … and those … which were not.
> At the same time, in the early years of the twentieth century the elites of the white dominions were evolving national identities of their own which blended association with Britain with a sense of the distinctiveness of their South African, Australian, and other identities, while excluding from those identities groups such as the black inhabitants of South Africa, Aboriginals in Australia, and the Inuit in Canada.[121]

Second, in addition to their defences of existing aspects of imperial practice, socialists expressed the desire for a more enlightened and increasingly socialist (i.e. collectivist and fully democratic) imperial form and future. This desire was set against both the predatory and irresponsible imperialism of the Boer War, and the individualist and hierarchical, if more enlightened and responsible, radical Liberal view of empire. Indeed, the sentiment in favour of a 'higher' imperial form was far more marked and widespread, especially among British socialists, than the defence of aspects of substantive imperial practice.

Examples of the socialist desire for a more enlightened imperial future abound in the socialist press. For example, in response to the 'gravity of the present situation in Zululand' in 1907, F.W. Pethick-Lawrence urged socialists to put pressure on the Imperial Government to act responsibly and fairly with regard to the claims of the Zulus to be the victims of state repression and violence in Natal rather than the wilful instigators of riot and rebellion. It was, declared Pethwick-Lawrence, imperative to 'prevent the Natal Government from acting contrary to justice in regard to the Zulus', for 'the foundations of British justice and the *whole future of the British Empire* depend upon its decision'.[122] In a similar vein, Margaret MacDonald appealed in the same year to socialists to prod the Liberal government into effecting 'justice between black and white' in Swaziland in the form of allowing the Swazis to live in peace on their land rather than to be tricked out of it by the white settlers. MacDonald's desired outcome would aid the 'helpless natives' and satisfy the Swazi chiefs who had travelled to Britain 'on a mission to get *fair play* for their country'.[123]

A lament for missed opportunities and hopes for a brighter future constituted a recurrent feature of socialist argument. In opposition to the repulsive and wasteful domination, subjection and exploitation integral to 'capitalist imperialism', Hyndman, the SDF and Hardie supported the demand for 'a democratic federation', a 'voluntary association of free peoples'. Led by the economically, politically and socially 'most advanced' English-speaking societies of Britain, the USA and the white-settler colonies, the federation would form the basis for 'true' international solidarity, 'the first real socialistic combination' against 'the plutocratic oligarchy' and for 'the advancement of humanity'.[124]

On a more specific level, Hyndman, perhaps the most authoritative and, along with Hardie, outspoken socialist critic of the exploitative and parasitic nature of British imperialism in India – with 'our upper and middle classes' constantly 'draining millions' out of that country – nevertheless, believed that matters might have been very different. As he declared in an interview with a *Clarion* reporter in 1907,

> If we had established the native rulers under the (sic) British hegemony and introduced needful reforms in a spirit of helpfulness, we should never have witnessed this outburst of so-called 'sedition'.[125]

While at times expressing the view that 'it may be that the people of India are not yet fit for the Colonial form of self-government', Hardie also combined criticism of existing policy in India with a strong reformist desire for future improvement. As he wrote in 1908,

> between self-government,... and the present soul-less bureaucracy there are many degrees of expansion in the direction of modifying bureaucratic power and enlarging the rights and liberties of the people. Sooner or later a beginning must be made towards enfranchising the masses and opening up the way for the educated native to fill the higher and better paid positions.

The attainment of the 'many degrees of expansion' was deemed to be absolutely vital 'if India is to be pacified and kept loyal to the British Raj'.[126]

Advocacy of reformist means of imperial improvement, furthermore, was widespread among socialists and within the labour movement. Notwithstanding the charge of racism, as directed by Jay Winter against the Webbs, there is no doubt that many Fabians sought the creation of not only an efficient and collectivist empire, built upon a 'true' programme of social reform, but also an empire run in 'a lofty and public-spirited' way', as being 'beneficial' 'to the interests of those alien races under its sway'.[127] Indeed, Bernard Porter has gone so far as to argue that,

> The Empire of the Fabians' dreams was not the Empire of ruler and ruled, of white overlords and coloured subjects, but what Shaw called a 'partnership' between the races, and what Sydney Webb was later to term a 'Commonwealth'.[128]

Ramsay MacDonald's belief in the adoption and widespread application of an 'Imperial' or 'International' 'Standard', was rooted in assumptions of imperial paternalism (the role of the 'affectionate father', as exemplified by British rule in the Cape Colony), responsibility, and 'justice being done to all subject races'. 'As Imperial subjects', argued MacDonald, 'you must accept the notion of justice and of the administration of law which cannot be dissociated from the rule of that empire'.[129] Furthermore,

> Such a standard might do much to preserve native races and elevate them into the position of self-governing citizens. Every Socialist and Labour MP in Britain was helping to do something in that direction with respect to India and other dependencies.[130]

Similarly, the demand for the application an 'imperial standard' to the future conduct of industrial relations, in order to bring about 'fairness', 'due reward' and class reconciliation, was strongly made by Blatchford, Thompson and the *Clarion* at the beginning of the First World War.[131] Later, this demand was taken up, unsurprisingly, by the British Workers' League in which, as noted earlier, Thompson was a leading figure. And it became an important part of the League's and the National Democratic and Labour Party's wider vision of civilised and transformed 'Imperial CITIZENSHIP': of 'Patriotism without Jingoism, of faith in the Destiny of the Race without Imperialistic Aggression; of adequate Empire Defence, economic and military, without Militarism'.[132] Or, as Councillor Willie Dyson, official of the Workers' Union and National Democratic and Labour Party parliamentary candidate for Nuneaton in 1918, put it:

> His imperialism is the dominance of no sect or class, but an imperialism the warp and woof of whose fabric is a commercial inter-dependence that is all the stouter because inter-defensive.

Designed to create 'a stronger, a greater, and a happier British community', Dyson's 'Britainism' contained 'no race prejudice'.[133] Rather, the overriding need, as expressed by the *British Citizen and Empire Worker*, was to develop to the full the resources of the Empire 'in the interests of the whole people'.[134]

Finally, in anticipation of the increasingly dominant reformist element within the Labour Party's colonial policy, many British socialists frequently argued between 1900 and 1910 that hopes for imperial justice and 'fair play', and the effective divorce of imperial policy from its capitalist associations and its gradual 'socialist' transformation could only be effectively met and managed by a socialist-influenced Labour Party. Two examples will suffice to support this argument. First, as part of his criticism of the decision not to appoint a 'coloured man' to a seat on the Inter-Colonial Commission on Native Affairs in South Africa, Haden Guest declared in 1905 that,

> Neither the South African nor the Imperial Government can be relied on to deal with the race problem, and it is necessary that the Labour Party should take the subject up and thoroughly discuss it.

There was also a pressing need to consider with 'the leaders of coloured opinion' what should be done.[135] Second, MacDonald's 'Imperial standard', framed partly as a criticism of the report of the Milner Native Commission and the putative policies of the mine owners and the authorities in Natal to criminalise and proletarianise the 'natives', was offered as a vital part of an alternative socialist colonial policy. In the absence of such an alternative, declared MacDonald, 'the Imperialists will inevitably hold the ground'.[136]

In conclusion, as suggested specifically by Macdonald's argument and more generally by the discussion of defences of substantive aspects of imperial policy and suggestions for future improvement, the words 'imperial' and 'imperialism' thus lent themselves to a plurality of usages and meanings within late Victorian and Edwardian society: they signified contestation as well as consensus.[137] This important point has immediate relevance for the attempt accurately to pinpoint the 'true' character of imperialism in the eyes of British socialists. I now turn to this matter of 'true' definition.

(b) Imperialism: A System of Class and Race Domination

As noted earlier, it is axiomatic of the new consensus that it was the 'enlightened' form of imperialism that characterised the latter's 'real' essence. Conversely, the aggressive and irresponsible imperialism of the South African War is seen as 'aberrant'. While it is certainly true, as further suggested by the new orthodoxy, that most British socialists and labour movement activists in the post-Boer War years desired neither the expansion nor the immediate dissolution or abandonment of the British Empire and that their prescriptions were predominantly reformist in character,[138] it by no means necessarily follows that an enlightened form of imperial rule constituted, for these very same socialists and activists, *the* defining feature of imperialism *itself.* Indeed, I offer the counter argument that, notwithstanding genuine reformist socialist desires for imperial policy to move in a more enlightened direction, *actually-existing* imperialism signified to the vast majority of British socialists expressing themselves in the pages of the *Clarion,* the *Labour Leader* and *Justice,* a *thoroughgoing capitalist system of class and race domination and exploitation.* Moreover, these socialists saw the Boer War as a necessary, if extreme, example of this system of imperialism, rather than a deviation from a more enlightened norm.

It is also the case that many socialists shared with radical Liberals a long-standing tradition of humanitarian and moral opposition both to chattel slavery and to indentured or 'forced' labour in general (effective 'slavery' masquerading as 'freedom'). Often rooted in religious nonconformity, this tradition manifested itself in the abolitionist movement and in support for the North during the American Civil War. Radicals had also traditionally championed the causes of civil liberty and political freedom, and opposed the 'unfair' (i.e. 'excessive') exactions of 'dishonourable' employers, financiers and landowners.[139] However, in further opposition to the new consensus, I strongly argue that it is wrong simply to subsume the socialist critique of imperialism presented in the pages of the socialist press, under the heading of an inter-class tradition of popular radicalism, as manifested specifically in radical Liberalism. To do so is improperly to ignore important points of difference and conflict between socialists and radical Liberals. Above all, as I will document below, socialists identified capitalist imperialism *itself,* rather than its 'unacceptable face' – the latter in the form of Rhodes and other 'scoundrels' and 'financial adventurers' – as the 'true' exploiter of workers of whatever colour, point of origin and place of residence. Moreover, inheriting and further developing that tradition of class-based radicalism characteristic of Chartism and other independent working-class movements, socialists, unlike most radical Liberals, registered their opposition to the very fact of 'wage-slavery', as well as to chattel slavery, indentured labour and other more transparent forms of exploitation.[140] The ills of capitalism were not confined to its 'dishonourable' members. Finally, socialists maintained that under the expanding system of capitalist imperialism, complete with the incessant search for new sources of cheap labour, class-based exploitation assumed an increasingly racialized character.

In sum, I present two general theses antithetical to those of the new consensus. First, the socialist critique of capitalist imperialism was fundamental and challenging rather than 'limited'. Second, it possessed a sufficiency of distinctive class-based features, including a racialized notion of class, clearly to differentiate it from the more moderate critique of imperialism offered by the radical Liberals. Two related theses may be added. While the observed socialist critique may have lacked the intellectual sophistication and precision of those of Hobson, Lenin, and leading members of German Social Democracy, it carried great *political* force and conviction.[141] Furthermore, largely masked by the new liberal revisionism, the very existence of the socialist critique pointed to an important aspect of the continued *independence* and vitality of a tradition of popular radicalism dating back to the early nineteenth century. As with the socialist critique of imperialism, this tradition cannot be seen as simply one part of a continuous, consensual and wider tradition of radical liberalism and Liberalism. Rather, there continued to exist predominantly class-based tensions and conflicts within 'the British radical tradition' which the socialist critique of imperialism further exposed and nourished.[142]

In seeking to substantiate these theses, I must offer the prefatory observation that the late nineteenth-century socialist belief that imperial policies had become subservient to both the articulated and unspoken needs and interests of capitalists who were generally antagonistic to popular radicalism, was by no means new. For example, it had constituted part of the wider Chartist critique of coercive British 'aristocratic' and 'class' rule in Ireland and support for universal manhood suffrage and self determination for the Irish people. Significantly, these measures of support were not advocated by Daniel O'Connell and most English middle-class radicals.[143] As most recently shown by Margot Finn, this belief had also been a feature of radical working-class support for internationalism and nationalist and democratic causes in the post-Chartist years. This support had also often provided a continuing source of conflict and tension with mid-Victorian middle-class Liberals.[144] During these years, furthermore, Ernest Jones, arguably the leading figure in late Chartism, had been one of the most outspoken critics of British colonialism per se, especially its adverse effects upon 'native' peoples and its denial of the fundamental right of republican self government. As he declared in his *Notes to The People* in the early 1850s,

> Men of America! thank heaven! (thank your own strong arms) for having escaped from the corrupt legislation of this island ... On its colonies the sun never sets, but the blood never dries...
> Its commerce touches every shore, but their ports have been opened by artillery, and are held by murder.

And,

> The entire system of colonial government is an error ... England would derive more benefit from a free state of Hindostan, a free republic of Australia, than she does from abject, crouching, or rebelling nations – and she would no longer stand before the world as a sanctimonious murderess, painting the profaned cross with the blood of every nation she is strong enough to massacre.[145]

As observed in the 'old' historiography of Porter and Pelling, the belief that a capitalist search for higher profits and cheaper sources of labour underpinned the South African War, was widespread in British labour movement and socialist circles during the late nineteenth- and early twentieth-centuries.[146] Porter also referred very briefly to the socialist belief in the racialized dimension of British imperialist exploitation.[147] In what follows I build upon and extend the foundations laid by Porter and Pelling in order to substantiate the central argument that, in the opinion of the socialist press, race and class domination and exploitation constituted *the* defining characteristics of British imperialism, both in the case of the South African War and in general, during the years between 1899 and 1910.

The evidence supporting my case may be presented in the following way. First, the socialist weeklies expressed a common belief in imperialism as a system of domination. As such, they identified a fundamental incompatibility between practical imperialism and liberty. This purported incompatibility was of a general rather than a specific character. In the opinion of the *Labour Leader*, British imperialism, whether in India or South Africa, was 'all the time oppressive and burdensome'.[148] Similarly for *Justice* a basic contradiction existed between 'Imperium et Libertas'. 'Empire is a denial of liberty', declared an editorial in *Justice* in 1900,

> Empire means *domination*, and we should as vigorously resist Anglo-Saxon domination, as that of the Celt, the Teuton, or the Sclav (sic). *All this talk of the British Empire, of imperial federation, is a fraud, a delusion, and a snare. It only means the enslavement of the people here at home so that they may be tools for the subjugation and enslavement of the people of other lands.*[149] (emphasis added.)

The 'talk' referred to was that of the Prince of Wales, Lord Salisbury, Chamberlain and other prominent figures in the British Empire League. It was diametrically opposed to Hyndman's and the Social Democratic Federation's language of 'true' federation, of a democratic union of self-governing peoples aspiring to socialism.

As a means of domination and subjugation the 'new imperialism' was seen to have nothing in common with the free-trading and peace-loving ideals of mid-nineteenth century Cobdenite Liberalism. Reflecting upon his great intellectual and moral debt to Cobden, Gladstone and Bright, Keir Hardie argued that the 'real' liberalism of commerce and internationalism and the Imperialism of force, conquest and general militarism 'were antagonistic and mutually destructive'. Yet Hardie was forced to conclude that the 'bogus imperialism' of 'Militarism' had, in practice, triumphed over 'Commercialism'. For example, in South and West Africa and in the Sudan there was abundant evidence of Imperial government military support for the chartered companies' attempts to 'exterminate negroes ... and Arabs', and 'all in the interests of the chartered libertines and robbers'.[150]

Lacking Hardie's sense of profound debt, nevertheless, *Justice*, and indeed at times the *Labour Leader*,[151] likewise noted the passing of the 'Manchester School of Old', and the widespread upsurge of aggressive, competitive and warring imperialism(s) 'with its feverish haste to appropriate the earth's surface'.[152] 'The wars of today', claimed *Justice*, are commercial wars, waged to extend markets, open up fresh fields for exploitation, to force the shoddy products of our too prolific factories on the unwilling inhabitants of far distant climes, even at the bayonet's point. *This is the new imperialism.*[153] (emphasis added.)

In addition to their support for the 'honest', 'decent' and 'loyal' British 'Tommy' during the South African War, Blatchford and the *Clarion* also remained forceful and consistent in their opposition to imperialist 'Militarism' and 'Jingoism' and, along with the rest of the socialist press, became increasingly alarmed at the prospect of a general imperialist war, with the autocratic and bullying 'Prussian Goth' being identified as the main threat to world peace.[154]

Many of the socialists' criticisms of aggressive, domineering and reactionary imperialism were summed up in a resolution moved by the ILPer, Joseph Burgess, at the Labour Party's 1901 Annual Conference. The resolution read,

> modern Imperialism with its attendant *militarism* is a reversion to one of the worst phases of *barbarism*, is inimical to social reform and disastrous to trade and commerce, a fruitful cause of *war*, *destructive of freedom*, fraught with menace to representative institutions at home and abroad, and must end in the *destruction of democracy* ... (emphases added)

Socialists, accordingly, had a duty to combat 'this dangerous and barbaric development in all its manifestations'.[155] The conference unanimously adopted the resolution.

Second, the domination socialists regarded as necessary to the prevalent system of imperialism, was also seen by them to be class specific rather than amorphous and general in character. They believed imperial policy more or less directly mirrored the interests not only of finance capital, but also, as explained in the *Clarion*, 'landlords and employers'.[156] Consciously, cynically and hypocritically exploiting the 'people's' senses of decency, patriotism and imperial duty, these capitalists and their allies in government, the state, the press and other positions in the vast British imperial network, attempted to whip up frenzies of jingoism, nationalism and race hatred. This was done in order to realise their 'true' goals of higher profits and returns on investment, reduced costs and new 'spheres of influence' with respect to economics, politics and the spread of 'civilisation'.[157] As *Justice* declared, war in South Africa signified,

> not the success of the British nation, but the success of the plunderers of the British nation. It is for Rhodes, Chamberlain, Rothschild ... and the rest of the capitalist class, that Tommy Atkins is fighting in South Africa, not for the British nation as a whole, or for the British flag. *The flag is only a cloak to cover the nefarious designs of the exploiting class.*[158] (emphasis added)

The socialist *Blackburn Labour Journal* was in full accord, the war having been brought about by 'a swindling horde of home and foreign exploiters of labour for their own ends', with 'no national interest' being 'at stake'.[159]

Contrary to the 'populist' and 'traditional-radical' interpretation offered by Kenneth Morgan, Keir Hardie's explanation of the South African War was also a class-based and socialist one.[160] Hardie directed his fire not only, as claimed by Morgan, against 'specific capitalist conspirators on the Rand', but also against the capitalists and their puppets at home. These combined, if at times fractious, forces were attempting to mask their 'real' interests in the acquisition of the highly profitable mines, the land, and the cheap labour supply of the Transvaal and the Orange Free State, and the creation of a political system more responsive than that of the Boers to their immediate and long term goals.[161] This was done by raising for popular consumption the 'spurious pretext' of the extension of the franchise to the Outlanders in the Boer republics.[162] 'We are told it is to spread freedom and to extend the rights and liberties of the common people', declared Hardie. In truth, however,

> The war is a capitalist war. The British merchant hopes to secure markets for his goods, the investor an outlay for his capital, the speculator more fools out of whom to make money, and the mining companies cheaper labour and increased dividends'.[163]

The South African War was an awful feature of Imperialism – 'the bane of progress' supported by pathetic, 'underfed wretches'.[164]

As the 'bane of progress', aggressive and domineering capitalist imperialism was by no means confined to South Africa. India and the Far East, for example, were also 'fair game' for continued capitalist ambition and expansion. As briefly noted earlier, both Hyndman and Hardie were prominent critics of British rule in India, and especially the latter's parasitical nature which was perceived to have exacted a dreadful toll in terms of misery and death among the indigenous people. *Justice* ran frequent articles on British rule in India as the 'Greatest Crime of All the Centuries' and a 'Curse to Mankind'.[165] The financial exactions of British 'Old Corruption' – the drain upon the purchasing power of the masses of the Indian population and the consequent 'manufacture of permanent famine' – met with repeated and outraged comment in the British socialist press. For example, observing in January 1900 that 'In India – our great and glorious Empire in the East – millions of people are literally dying of famine', *Justice* attributed the latter phenomenon, 'not really' to 'a scarcity of food', but to,

> a scarcity of means of buying food due entirely to the continual drain upon India of the Imperial Government and its hangers-on. India, as our comrade Hyndman pointed out years ago, is being steadily and persistently bled to death.

In reality, 'the dominant classes of England are plundering and starving the people of India', just as they 'are furiously eager to plunder the Boers'.[166]

Somewhat more regretful than *Justice* and the SDF for the past 'mistakes' and holding out more hope for a 'change of heart' on the part of British rule in India, the *Labour Leader* and Hardie, nevertheless, were equally outraged by, and withering in their critique of the effects of such rule. For example, in 1900 the *Labour Leader* condemned unreservedly the failure of the authorities to take effective measures against recurring famine and the excessive levels of taxation and land rent borne by the Indian masses. The 'poorest and most miserable people in the world', concluded the *Labour Leader,* were being 'ground down by a burden of taxation to maintain an Empire which oppresses them'.[167] Six years later in the House of Commons Hardie 'fiercely attacked' 'conditions in India – the rising death rate, the almost total exclusion of native Indians from local government, the low wages that prevailed in Indian textile factories'.[168] These, and other attacks, were delivered at first hand when Hardie's 'Scamper Round the World' took him to an India 'seething with unrest and political conflict' in 1907. Notwithstanding the 'good intentions' of some of those in power and authority, British rule in India was declared to be 'a huge soulless bureaucracy', regarding 'every form of popular rights' as 'a menace to the stability of the Empire', and totally lacking in necessary decentralisation and popular control. 'Harsh and exacting in all its relations towards the people', the central goal of policy was not 'the improvement of the condition of the people', but 'the increase of the sources from which revenue can be drawn'.[169] Much of the British press predictably accused Hardie of 'making inflammatory speeches and stirring up sedition among the Indian people'.[170]

In terms of the Far East, the early twentieth-century designs of 'greedy capitalists' and 'impertinent' British and European 'intruders' upon parts of China were roundly criticised by all three socialist organs. 'Having saved the wind in South Africa', declared *Justice* in 1900, 'we appear to be reaping the whirlwind in the Far East'. Despite the undisputed barbarism and cruelty' of some of the Chinese 'methods of warfare', socialists everywhere were exhorted to oppose Russian or 'Muscovite despotism's' bid 'to become one of the paramount powers in the Far East', and the British government's desired 'annexation of part of the territory of the Celestial Empire'. Its sympathy lying 'wholly with the Chinese', *Justice* staunchly defended the former's right to self-government, 'free from European interference in their own territory'.[171] The *Labour Leader* likewise condemned the proposed 'butchery' and imperialist partition of China on the part of 'civilised Imperialists', complete with their arrogant, unfounded and hypocritical desire to 'introduce the leaven of enlightened Christian civilisation into the dark mass of Asiatic barbarism'. Notwithstanding 'legitimate' commitments to trade and other forms of economic exchange, Britain's 'true' goals were seen to reside in base motivations. As Hardie unsentimentally declared, '… we are in China, as we are in the Transvaal – for what we can get out of it for our commercial and ruling classes'.[172] In the opinion of a *Clarion* correspondent, William L. Hare, the comparison extended to India, Britain's capitalist imperialists being about to 'ruin the Chinese as they have ruined and starved the Hindoos' (sic).[173]

Finally, for Hubert Parris, a 'Native West Indian Reformer', writing in *Labour Leader* on the subject of 'The Transvaal and the British West Indies: Comparisons and Contrasts', racist exploitation and oppression were endemic throughout the British Empire. Passivity, inferiority, and resignation to one's meagre physical and spiritual lot were the expected 'virtues' of black people under imperialism. As Parris acutely and mockingly observed,

> ... against John Bull and his God the black man dares not protest, for the one will give him hell here, and the other complacently plans the completion of his misery in hell hereafter. The only hope is to bow our heads to the decrees of an apparently grim fatality, which knows nothing of justice or equality where we are concerned, and chant a dolorous A-a-a-men![174]

Third, as a means of class-based domination, socialists perceived imperialism as extracting a heavy price from its main object of exploitation and oppression, the working class. Of particular relevance to us is the fact that all three socialist organs saw the working class as comprising workers throughout the British Empire, 'white' as well as 'coloured', and 'native' as well as 'non-native'. All these workers were subjected to capitalism's ceaseless and increasingly globalized drive to maximise profits, cut costs, and to 'hold the workers of all countries in universal, social, and economic servitude'.[175]

For example, *Justice* argued that it was in the interest of British imperialism that 'proletarians, black, brown or white are plundered and slaughtered', and that,

> The Imperialist Tory, the Imperialist Unionist, and the Imperialist Liberal are all at heart convinced that the dominance of the white race abroad, and the servile subjection of the white workers at home, should be supported by force wherever it is threatened.[176]

Whether in India, Egypt, South Africa or Britain, Keir Hardie likewise identified British imperialism's international common denominator of class-based oppression. In 'our wars on native races', declared Hardie,

> we see the manifestations of that class antagonism of which the workers here are equally the victims with the ryots of India, the fellaheen of Egypt, and the Kaffir boys of the Cape.[177]

Hardie's emphasis upon the intersection of class- and race- based oppression and exploitation was in turn echoed and developed within both the socialist press and the socialist movement. Thus, in the opinion of the *Labour Leader*, 'the capitalist exploiter is the economic foe of both black men and white, and this vital fact the leaders of native opinion in Africa have thoroughly grasped'.[178] And, as the SDF declared in its 1901 Manifesto,

The same aristocrats and plutocrats who butcher the Boer in Africa and gleefully starve your luckless fellow-subjects in India deliberately deprive you of any control over the products of your own labour at home.[179]

The grievances of workers under the 'new imperialism', moreover, embraced not only lack of control, but also poverty, hunger, poor housing, unemployment, overwork, insecurity, the heavy financial and human costs incurred in supporting aggressive and competing states, and lack of the general means to acquire a civilised life. Significantly, none of our selected socialists identified, in the manner of Lenin, an 'aristocracy of labour' as a privileged white beneficiary of imperialism. Rather, the emphasis lay overwhelmingly upon the adverse effects of imperialism upon workers, both at home and abroad. As Hugh Rainsford sarcastically noted in the *Clarion,*

We may be starved and sweated, plundered and degraded, to heap up profit and grind out pleasure for our betters. But if we can rise to the spiritual frenzy of the inspired and perspiring scribe of the 'Daily Mail' our own suffering and squalor will vanish before the effulgent radiance of the Imperial Idea.[180]

As noted at various points throughout this essay, specific socialist concern rested with the 'new imperialism's' increasingly world-wide search for sources of cheap and proletarianised labour, both 'free' and 'unfree', and its aim to reduce costs by means of enhanced labour market competition and flexibility and the successful negation or reduction of organised labour's influence at the workplace and beyond. The employment of 'slave' Chinese labour in the Transvaal, and attempts both to 'liberate' black workers from the land in South Africa and employ them in the mines as cheap labour, constituted conspicuous examples of capitalist cost cutting labour market strategy.[181] As the *Labour Leader* claimed in 1908, 'Land robbery and the exploitation of the natives – that is the inner meaning of racial supremacy in South Africa at the present time'.[182]

Fourth, in terms of both its general characteristics and its specific concerns with labour, capitalist imperialism was, as implied above, identified as a system not only of class-, but also race-based domination and exploitation. In its general manifestation, the notion of 'race domination' was everywhere in evidence in the socialist press. For 'Chufff', one of the South African socialist correspondents to the *Clarion,* British colonial policy was 'one of spoliation', with blacks as 'the conquered race'.[183] In the opinion of Haden Guest, writing in the *Clarion* in relation to the rebellion in Natal in 1906, it was 'the mission of the Caucasian to exploit the negro for his temporal and eternal welfare'.[184] For Bandele Omoniyi, whose article, 'The Regeneration of Africa', appeared in the *Labour Leader* in 1907, the 'history of

British rule in Africa' amounted to 'the universal subjugation of the native African people by the white races'.[185] Writing in the same socialist organ, Edward Carpenter claimed that it was imperialist greed which 'places the ... material interests of the white races before all else', and 'fear of the growing power, rights and political education of the blacks'.[186] The *Labour Leader*, itself, declared it to be 'evident beyond the shadow of a doubt that',

> the race problem is of the white man's creating (sic). It is due chiefly to obtuseness, lordliness and cupidity. It is due to the desire to rule and to exploit, to keep the coloured man in social subjection.[187]

And *Justice* was typically forthright in its claim that the European powers 'have parcelled up the black man's countries everywhere and at every opportunity'.[188]

More specifically, race domination was closely associated with the various attempts of white capitalists and their political allies to coerce 'coloured' labour into submission to capital's will. These attempts were, in the period of time and geographical context under scrutiny, commonly identified by British socialists with three systems. First, there was the indentured or contract labour system, operating most prominently and notoriously with respect to the Indians of Natal and to the Transvaal's importation and employment, between 1903 and 1907, of some 60,000 Chinese to work the mines as a substitute for black labour. Second, there was the credit-ticket system of labour organisation and recruitment whereby the formally 'free' migrants were beholden to their creditors, predominantly merchants, in order to repay the debt incurred in the passage from home to place of work. This second system pertained to the majority of Chinese migrants to North America and Australasia, with many of the immigrant Chinese suffering not only from 'debt bondage' to their creditor merchant capitalists at home, but also from close supervision and control of their daily conditions and terms of work by Chinese merchant houses and their agent bosses in the 'host' country.[189] Third, there was the system at work in South Africa whereby employers and the state machinery, often with direct or indirect support from the Imperial government, sought, by the imposition of the hut tax and other punitive devices, to proletarianise and employ nominally free black rural dwellers and migrants as cheap labour in the gold mines.

While concerned mainly with the operation of the first and third systems, nevertheless, our British socialists did at times pass judgement on the second system as practised in Australia. Moreover, they were at pains to highlight and substantiate the claim that all three, increasingly racialized, labour systems had key common characteristics. These were seen to reside in various degrees of unfreedom and capitalist 'tyranny'; the 'slave-like' victimisation of the 'free' labourers involved and the cheapness of their labour power; the resulting general inability of these labourers to achieve a civilised standard of work and life, 'manly' independence and sustained collective labour organisation; and the very real threat posed by these systems to the conditions of work, life and collective organisation achieved by workers with 'higher capacities' in competing or other labour market situations, both at home and abroad.

References to these characteristics abound in the socialist press and the wider movement. Our purpose here is to provide the reader with selected examples rather than a comprehensive picture. In terms of the first system, Haden Guest was expressing a common socialist viewpoint in declaring there to be a fundamental incompatibility between indentured or contract and 'free' labour. Although not formally owned, as in the condition of the slave, the indentured or contracted labourer, nevertheless, was seen to share many of the tyrannies, indignities and unfreedoms imposed upon the slave. For example, freedom of choice and action and the capacity for change to one's terms and conditions of work were highly circumscribed, and at times totally negated, by the fixed terms of the contract. For Guest indenture constituted,

> an inhuman and purely mechanical relationship; the binding force is the club of the policeman, the whip of the boss, and the rifle of the manager.

Furthermore, if contracted workers in South Africa and elsewhere were allowed to 'behave like inhuman machines', and if we 'justify them on the grounds of the necessities of capital', continued Guest, then,

> we shall have the same tendencies expressing themselves in England as self-justified, and the elaborate moral-legal foundation of the rights of labour in England will vanish in a series of Taff Vale decisions.[190]

In his article, 'Undisguised Slavery in Natal', published in the *Labour Leader* in January 1901, Keir Hardie reinforced and developed many of the arguments made by Guest. In a view shared by Gandhi, Hardie maintained that the 65,000 indentured Indians working in Natal at the turn of the century were 'slaves' in terms of their restricted geographical mobility, their lack of the vote, and legislation which imposed curfews, and outlawed their engagement in trade and their right to walk on the sidewalk. 'Slavery' also permeated the Indians' supposedly free contractual rights and obligations. 'Of course, it may be said', observed Hardie,

> that this is a contract freely entered into by the Indians, and is therefore different from slavery. But the difference is in name only. *No* Indian may enter Natal save with the indenture; when there he is not free to hire himself to whom he pleases for what wage he pleases. At the end of his ten years' indenture he is liable to be shipped back whence he came. *He may not vote, nor own property, nor do any of the things a free man would do. Whatever he may be in name, he is in fact a slave.* (emphasis added.)

'It was this kind of freedom' contended Hardie, 'which we are sacrificing 250 lives and nearly two millions sterling in money every week to establish in the Transvaal'. Yet the 'war-mongers' still 'have the insolence to assert that one of their objects is to free the black man!'[191]

Many of the same anti-slavery arguments were directed by British and some South African socialists against the Transvaal's 'Chinese Labour Experiment'. Their recruitment negotiated by the Imperial state, the male and predominantly single labourers were housed in compounds, and subjected to 'freely contracted' long, hard and poorly paid hours of work, with virtually no opportunity to improve their conditions of 'service'. Their period of residence in South Africa fixed by the terms of contract, and banned from working outside mining, indeed their assigned mine, the Chinese labourers' lives were closely policed by authoritarian and racist employers and the state. And, as Shula Marks and Stanley Trapido note, 'The greater coercion provided by the new state as well as the inability of the Chinese workers to find refuge beyond the purpose-built mine compounds, meant that they had little alternative but to remain at their place of work'.[192] In the face of considerable opposition to 'Chinese slavery', both in Britain and South Africa, and growing instances of dissatisfaction and even rebellion among the contracted Chinese,[193] the 'Experiment' was brought to a close in 1907. Indian indentured servitude in Natal ceased in 1913.

Socialists entertained no doubts concerning the victimised, cheap, and slave-like status of the Chinese and the extreme threat posed to trade unionism and the organised labour movement of South Africa by their presence. Declaring that 'compulsory labour, however disguised, means slavery', the Labour Leader warned as early as January 1903 that 'the experiment of employing white labour has proved too costly', and that the mine owners of the Transvaal were accordingly seeking alternative 'coloured' sources of labour. At that point in time 'coloured' was equated with 'native', but by 1904 had been extended to include the incoming 'cheap' Chinese. In any event, substance had been given to the Labour Leader's earlier claim that, 'The chances are ... that this country is now committed to a policy of slavery in South Africa in the interest of the goldbags of Johannesburg'.[194] Indeed, 'the madness of the war had been followed by a thorough disillusionment ... The foundation of the new Colony had been laid on the bodies of 25,000 brave soldiers, but the superstructure was Chinese slavery'.[195]

The Labour Leader's view of the Chinese as the poor, unwitting dupes of capitalist greed and brutality was echoed in socialist circles in South Africa as well as, more widely, in Britain. For example, in 1905 J. Erasmus, secretary of the Cape Town branch of the SDF, wrote a report for Justice in which he combined support for 'vigorous agitation' on behalf of the unemployed of South Africa with strong protest against the introduction of the Chinese 'for the benefit of the mine owners'. The employment of the Chinese constituted,

an assertion of capital's tyranny over the people of this country, a direct deprivation of this country's right of self-government and a warning that freedom to work
out our own salvation is limited by the demands of the mine owners ... the desire to
cut up trade unionism by the roots.

Recognising both the 'injustice to these Chinese' and 'conditions of slavery' which
'in many respects' were 'more dishonouring to the people tolerating such in their
midst than the Chinese', Erasmus went on to argue for collective ownership of the
mines as the only true solution for labour's ills.[196]

Erasmus's carefully chosen strategy of attacking the conditions under which they
were compelled to labour rather than the Chinese labourers themselves, found
significant, if limited, support among socialists in South Africa. While some socialists did adopt negative racial stereotypes of the Chinese and claimed that they
were 'better housed and fed' than white workers,[197] others were quick to debunk
such notions and to express the 'true' socialist viewpoint of empathy, solidarity
and criticism of the awful conditions and harsh and violent regime, involving floggings, under which the Chinese lived in the compounds.[198] Yet another, perhaps
the majority socialist group, expressed a mixture of arguments which were at once
sectional, class conscious and racist in character. For example, John F. Back could
declare in 1906 that, 'We of the Johannesburg (Clarion) Fellowship are opposed to
Chinese labour on the Rand; but we are not opposed to Chinamen'. Back was opposed to 'imported contract labour of any kind', whether white or yellow, because
of its strong tendency to 'cut down the wages of those already there. It produces
an army of unemployed, and thus strengthens the hands of employers in the economic struggle'. Yet at the same time 'Asiatics' were condemned for 'their filthy
habits' ('Much of the scum of China has been enlisted for mine work here'), being
seen as 'a constant menace to the health and comfort of the whites'. 'The Socialist',
according to Back,

> does not stand primarily for the improvement of the Chinaman's conditions, but for
> his repatriation (as does the trade unionist); the observance of humane conditions
> while he is here, and the extension of the same State care to the white man that his
> yellow brother now enjoys.[199]

The situation in Britain, at least with respect to the attitudes of most socialists and
Labour party activists, was less complex than in South Africa. Notwithstanding undoubted instances of popular racism,[200] it was the *Labour Leader*'s class-conscious
approach to the Chinese miners in South Africa which prevailed.[201] For example,
at the Labour Party's 1904 Annual Conference it was far more the detrimental economic effects of the introduction of the Chinese into the Transvaal, rather than the
Chinese themselves, which met with forthright and overwhelming condemnation.
During the following year's conference David Shackleton denounced the playing
of the race card by the mine owners in order to reduce labour costs and negate the

power of organised white labour. Thus the owners did not want to employ whites as they would,

> desire similar conditions of citizenship and rights of combination through their Trade Unions as they had enjoyed in the colonies and in the mother country.

'This, we may assume', continued Shackleton,

> has been the real reason that has led these mine owners and alien capitalists to lower the flag of British freedom and to tarnish the good name of our country.[202]

With respect to the third system, as seen in the situation of black people in South Africa, the vast majority of British socialists were united in their denunciation of the coercion and intimidation employed by most whites and the state towards nominally free people. It is interesting to note in this context that, in opposition to Hardie, both Hyndman and Blatchford did not trust the Boers to treat black people any more decently than the British. Indeed, characterised by Hyndman as being 'for the most part, a coarse, ignorant, cruel, and bigoted set', the Boers were perceived to 'treat the natives more cruelly and slave-drive them more relentlessly even than our people do'.[203] More generally, the *Clarion*, the *Labour Leader* and *Justice* all denounced the 'white slave-drivers" attempts, supported by coercive political forces, to poll tax, rack-rent and seize the land of rural blacks in order to force them into becoming a 'cheap proletariat' and 'a mere blackleg agency'.[204] Moreover, as Marks informs us, this was a black African proletariat whose bargaining power, notwithstanding the early twentieth century shortages of labour in the mines and elsewhere, 'was removed by direct state intervention at the very time that they were in a relatively strong position to exert it'. 'Revitalised and re-formulated' Pass laws, racialised labour market segregation, the criminal penalties for breach of contract under 'newly designed' Master and Servant laws, and the 'tightening up' of urban racial segregation – these were the key means and features of that process of coercive removal.[205]

At times of crisis there was also the resort to official violence. In the wake of the 'dastardly shooting of natives' by the forces of the Natal government in 1906, *Justice* was moved to declare that, 'The suppression of the rising has been carried out in the most savage and ruthless fashion', and, with biting sarcasm,

> It is to be hoped that the Kaffirs will learn and profit by the lessons in Christian civilisation they are now being taught.[206]

In sum, the liberty of black South Africans was mythical. As Guest observed, the object of official policy lay in 'retaining the blacks as a servile caste, free in name, but debarred from all hope of rising from the lowest grades of work'. Furthermore,

In Africa the conditions are infinitely more unfavourable to the blacks than they ever were to the working classes in this country, owing to the impossibility of their making their voices heard.

It was the duty of British socialists to 'press in Parliament the claims for fair treatment of the coloured races in South Africa'.[207]

Finally, the credit-ticket system, as relating to much of the Chinese migration to Australia, also attracted adverse comment from socialists, who saw this system as denying freedom to the labourer in the form of the latter's 'debt bondage' and more or less total control by capital. In addition, in its general 'cheapness', Chinese migrant labour, whether still part of the credit-ticket system or not, was assumed to constitute an 'unfair' means of competition with unionised labour. As we will see in more detail below, openly racist arguments were also present, indeed dominant, in the attitudes of late nineteenth- and early twentieth-century Australian labour activists and socialists towards the Chinese in Australia.[208] However, most British socialists avoided the racist trap. As *Justice* declared, the Chinese in Australia generally constituted victimised 'cheap labour for capitalist exploiters', and should be welcomed into the labour movement. Instead of practising 'the universal brotherhood of man preached by Socialists all the world over', and 'instead of accentuating the class war at present raging on every hand', anti-Asiatic Australians were criticised by *Justice* for 'only creating a race war by dividing mankind into castes of colour'.[209] Even within Australia there had been 'a measure of toleration' for the mid-century Chinese immigrants to the goldfields. The passage of time did see a hardening of attitudes, with increasingly racist slurs being added to fears of economic downgrading. Yet even in the wake of the introduction of the White Australia Policy in 1901, white racism was not all pervasive. Thus Tom Mann and likeminded comrades grouped around the Melbourne-based journal, the *Socialist*, continued to appeal for 'the brotherhood of all nations, black or white'. According to Graeme Osborne, Mann was,

> careful to point out that he did not wish to see underpaid coloured workers lower Australian living standards. But he added that *this was not a racially-based view*. He bore no ill feeling toward Kanakas or Chinese.[210] (emphasis added.)

Fifth, notwithstanding the fact that our socialists critiqued capitalist imperialism as a system of race- as well as class-based domination and exploitation, they afforded primacy to the latter rather than the former. In structural terms, class was seen to prevail over race. It was a case of class-based economic exploitation assuming, in some contexts, a racialized form, rather than a dominant system of 'ethnicity', 'race' or 'race relations' being, in some instances, 'classed'. 'To a thorough socialist', declared *Justice*, 'class is much more than race'.[211] And in relation to the specific and most pressing issues of labour supply and potential competition and conflict between 'white' and 'coloured' workers, Guest expressed the prevailing view among British socialists that 'colour is, from the labour point of view, only of secondary importance', or, at times, more baldly, that 'colour is unimportant'.[212]

For Guest, the essential task lay in devising a labour market strategy which would successfully unite, rather than divide, workers of different *capacities* – of varying expectations, standards and 'needs' in relation to conditions of life and work. Neither immutable nor race-specific, Guest nevertheless saw high levels of capacity as predominating among 'white' workers in the economically, socially and politically more 'advanced' western capitalist countries. As a corollary, low capacities were to be found mainly among 'coloureds' in Africa, India and parts of the Far East. In Guest's opinion,

> There is, in essentials, no 'coloured' labour problem; only a labour problem. The coloured man is not essentially different because he is coloured, but only because he represents a certain grade of capacity. The real problem is the problem of regulating the competition between great numbers of men of (a) low grade capacity and (a) low standard of life, and men (chiefly white men) of (a) comparatively high grade and high standard of life.

And,

> It is, therefore, necessary for Labour to find a policy which shall enable coloured and white to work side by side, and shall ensure that the competition of products in the world market injures neither one nor the other.[213]

The reader will observe that in Guest's analysis we again encounter that blend of cultural superiority and desire for unity and cooperation between black and white workers which we have found to be characteristic of British socialist attitudes towards race during this period of time. Yet it should also be observed that the two overriding emphases to be found in the writing of Guest and other socialists, were upon the historically/environmentally – rather than biologically – conditioned nature of 'capacities', including the ability to move from one level to another; and, whenever circumstances realistically permitted, upon the development of inclusive class-based rather than exclusive, race-based, labour market policies.[214]

Accordingly it was beholden upon socialists to avoid both unnecessary labour market divisions and conflicts, and the racist snares and delusions to be encountered in the nationalistic, jingoistic and racialised imperialist policies dangled before the 'masses' by the ruling class. In submitting the issue of labour market inclusion versus exclusion to 'the thoughtful consideration of British Socialists', Alex Thompson referred to the proclamation made by 'A Hindoo long resident in America' that, 'if the whites drive out the yellow from the West, the yellow will retaliate by driving the white trade out of the East'. Yet, unlike many of his contemporaries, Thompson did not regard this 'Monroe doctrine of the Orient' to be a foregone conclusion. Rather, it was the responsibility of socialists, of 'white statesmanship', to 'avert the inevitable' by taking the lead in building interracial economic, political and civil bridges in order to fashion, regulate and civilise labour markets in the interests of as many as possible of the workers involved. In so doing, not only would the majority of workers benefit economically, but also the potentially huge conflicts of a highly racialized global labour market would be kept to a minimum.[215] According to *Justice*, 'This race prejudice', was both 'nonsense' and 'mischevious', being 'readily ... made use of by our masters' in an attempt to divide workers on a worldwide basis.[216] By way of contrast, Social Democracy, as an 'international working-class movement', 'free from the prejudices of nationality', 'eliminates distinctions of race and colour and creed, and recognises that the real conflict of to-day is not one of race but of class'.[217]

It is to a closer examination of the nature, strengths and limitations of the British socialists' attempt to develop inclusive policies and strategies in order to demonstrate the 'supremacy of class over race' that we must now turn.

3. The Class-Based Response

A) SOCIALIST RACISM?

I have already marshalled a strong body of evidence in this essay – especially in those sections entitled *Portrayals of "Non-White" Indigenous Peoples and Migrant Workers* and *Imperialism: A System of Class and Race Domination* – to support the thesis that socialist opinion, as expressed mainly in the *Clarion*, the *Labour Leader* and *Justice*, constituted an example of 'the supremacy of class over race'. The purpose of this section is to introduce new material further to substantiate, indeed to clinch, this thesis. This material relates predominantly to the attitudes and actions of British socialists. I will later incorporate more substantially the views of South African and Australian socialists into our discussion.

It is the case that the impressive class consciousness of British socialists did not signify the complete absence of racism in their thoughts and deeds. For example, we should add, to Alex Thompson's mixed portrayal of Chinese people quoted in the 'Portrayals' section, his frequent references to actual and potential conflicts between the European 'workers of civilisation' and 'those teeming and hungry semi-barbarians of the East'.[218] Similarly, in addition to Beatrice Webbs' general racism, we must cite Sidney Webbs' specific allegation, made while on tour in Australia, that the Chinese in Victoria 'did not understand the Factory Acts, and they simply ignored and escaped them'.[219] Furthermore, South African socialists and trade unionists' frequent cry during the early- and mid-1900s that the Chinese and black Africans were being employed at the expense of increasingly impoverished and unemployed white workers, did find a ready echo in British labour movement circles. For example, in May 1904 the Blackburn Trades Council called a meeting of the town's citizenry to denounce 'the ordinance respecting the introduction of Chinese labour in South Africa' in order to employ 'cheap yellow labour to lower the standard of comfort among the working-class population of South Africa'. Notwithstanding their representation as the 'cheap' victims of capitalism, the Chinese and the black Africans were also presented in Blackburn and elsewhere as increasingly the *conscious* competitors and underbidders of white labour. According to a piece which appeared in the *Blackburn Labour Journal* in the following month,

> We fought the Boers in order that the South African capitalists might import cheap labour. Already the Chinamen are on their way to the Transvaal. They will eventually supersede the whites. You English workers so starve, unless you will come down to the Chinese price. The Ching-chungs are even underbidding the Kaffirs.[220]

Finally, while denying that they were 'activated by race prejudice', both Harry Quelch's and Hyndman's savage attacks on Jewish financiers, as supposed prime movers of the South African War, and Jews, as 'rousing the patriotism of the people by waving the union jack and hounding us to slaughter the Boers', met with outraged responses and charges of anti-semitism among some of *Justice's* correspondents during the latter months of 1899.[221]

However, these instances of British socialist racism were more than outweighed by examples to the contrary. For example, we can usefully recall that it was the *Labour Leader's* non-racist and class-based opposition to 'unfree' labour, whether Indian, Chinese or black African, which effectively set the tone and standard of British socialist debate about racism in Africa. For example, with reference to the debate about 'Chinese slavery', *Justice*, in the manner of the *Labour Leader*, expressed its opposition not to the Chinese 'as a man and a brother', but as 'slaves in everything but name'. Thus,

> We have no objection whatsoever to the Chinaman as Chinaman. The Chinese people have an equal right with the other peoples of the earth to work out their own salvation. All that we object to is the Chinaman being made use of and his lower standard of life being exploited in the interests of capitalism and to the injury of white labour and the degradation of the general standard of life.

The latter state of affairs, concluded *Justice*, was certainly the case in South Africa where the Chinaman had been 'imported as a mere chattel', to 'debase the whole conditions of existence, and to make life impossible to the white man, simply in the interest of an exploiting class'.[222] Haden Guest also argued that 'we must strenuously denounce the injustice of the conditions' under which 'cheap' 'coloured' workers, whether Chinese or black African, laboured in the mines of South Africa. 'But, continued Guest,

> we must even more strenuously denounce the evil of the introduction of these un-

conscious blacklegs (… from … different language, religion and custom. They are quite unaware of what they are doing).[223]

In terms of the situation of the Chinese in Australia, Guest was not in agreement with the 'somewhat violent policy' of the Australian Labor Party.[224] And Hyndman, on the basis of his experience of having employing Chinese 'coolies' in mines in both the USA and Australia, and having written for the *Melbourne Argus* at a time of intense debate about Chinese exclusion, could not fault 'the coolies themselves'. 'I have', declared Hyndman in 1904,

> no sympathy with the opium and immorality cry. My experience is that if you treat them well they are very decent folk, as they are naturally not by any means the best of the Chinese nation, I think that is remarkable.[225]

In keeping with the views of *Justice* and Tom Mann, Hyndman was critical of the exclusionary racism of Australian labour while simultaneously opposing the effects of cheap Chinese labour. At a lecture entitled, 'Social-Democracy, Anti-Semitism and the Transvaal', delivered in London in 1899, Hyndman informed his audience that 'personally he liked the Chinese, but he would oppose by every means their introduction into this country to lower the standard of living among the workers'.[226]

The nagging charge of anti-semitism, levelled by contemporaries against the SDF, has been repeated in the historiography of the organisation.[227] As noted earlier, the issue of racism came prominently to the fore in the late 1890s when Hyndman and some of the other SDF leaders highlighted the alleged role of Jewish capitalists in instigating the South African War. Furthermore, 'while hatred of the Jew as Jew was shameful', declared Hyndman in *Justice* in November 1899, 'they were bound to admit that there were elements in the Jew which it was impossible to like'.[228] However, such negative statements were more than counterbalanced by positive representations. For example, *Justice* was unambiguous and unwavering in its opposition to 'unsocialistic race antipathy'; while Hyndman both denounced anti-semitism, 'pure and simple', as being 'wrong and abominable', and declared that, 'He had never denounced Jews any more than he had his own countrymen as men'.[229] Simultaneously both *Justice* and Hyndman were as uncompromising and unrepentant in their attacks upon Jewish capitalists as they were in relation to capitalists in general, irrespective of their colour, creed or nationality. Within the context of the outbreak of the Boer War, Hyndman contended that Jewish capitalists 'formed an international combination all over the world which … was a political danger'.[230] In company with Hyndman, Harry Quelch, another leading SDFer, branded the Boer War a 'Jew-capitalist war', on account of 'the prominent part Jew capitalists have taken in the Johannesburg agitation, and seeing their intimate relations with Cabinet Ministers here at home'. The villainous cast included 'the Beits, Ecksteins, Wernhess, Joels, and other Jew and Gentile owners of the gold mining properties on the Rand'. Quelch concluded that just as 'The Boer farmers and the British working class are the sufferers from their villainy today', so 'the Jew proletarian may suffer tomorrow'.[231]

The question of labour and socialist attitudes to Jews also became a matter of great significance between 1904 and 1906 when the subject of 'alien' or 'pauper' immigration into Britain was hotly debated. Many immigrants were poverty-stricken Jews, fleeing from religious and political persecution in central and eastern Europe, especially in Russia. Strongly concentrated in the cities of Leeds and Manchester and London's East End, the newly arrived immigrants encountered considerable public hostility, on both economic and openly racist grounds. In terms of the former, the poor Jews were accused of having a deleterious effects on wages and living standards, with the issues of 'sweating', overcrowding and sanitary conditions to the fore. In terms of the latter, public attention was directed towards their supposedly 'alien' racial characteristics.[232]

There is no doubt that anti-Jewish voices, predominantly of the economic but also of the racist kind, can be detected within the British labour and socialist movements. The importation, or even 'free', arrival of 'cheap' or 'pauper' im-migrant labour met with strong trade union and TUC disapproval.[233] According to Logie Barrow, while Robert Blatchford worried throughout the period under review about the adverse economic effects of the general, rather than specifically Jewish, 'infusion of so much alien blood into the British stock', nevertheless, in the context of the debate about 'alien' immigration and its restriction under the 1905 Aliens Act, economic and environmental fears slipped into becoming 'racialistic' in character.[234] There were voices in the socialist press simultaneously expressing concern and sympathy for the 'plight of persecuted Russian Jews', and question-ing the latter's capacities to 'assimilate' and move beyond the 'cheapness' of the 'sweating dens'.[235]

Once again, however, it is significant that the vast majority of socialists, while seriously concerned about the potentially adverse economic effects of 'pauper' and 'blackleg' immigration and importation,[236] did *not* erect racist barriers against the Jews. Indeed, they were quick both to defend the political and civil rights of the im-migrants, and to denounce the restrictionist 'Anti-Alien Humbug' peddled by the *Daily Mail* and others of the 'mad dog Fleet Street'.[237] Thus *Justice* ridiculed the 'ab-surdly exaggerated statistics' concerning immigration produced by the pro-restric-tionists, saw the poor Jews as the victims of poverty, persecution and oppression, denied vehemently that they caused sweating, and resolutely upheld their 'Right of Asylum'. Apart from its characterisation of the Russian Poles – 'a people who have been degraded to the lowest depths of poverty and dirt by their oppressors in a vain attempt to stamp out their nationality' – *Justice* stoutly defended the character and motivations of the immigrants. Thus,

The popular idea of the alien is that he is an individual whose sole aim in life is to come to England to work double the hours of the Englishman for half the pay, so that he may live in an overcrowded tenement in some slum. Now this is entirely errone-ous. Most aliens, 'strangers within our gates', were, cleaner in their habits than the lower class of Irish or English living in our great city slums; and as far as their opin-ions of the matters of working and housing are concerned, they are quite as sound as those of the average Englishman.[238]

The *Labour Leader* likewise presented a very positive image, the 'alien' being 'for the most part a sober, industrious, highly-educated and law-abiding person'.[239] Furthermore, the 'brotherhood of man, the internationalism of labour and the comradeship of Socialism', England's long and distinguished tradition of providing a safe haven for those fleeing religious and political persecution, and the rich and positive contribution made by generations of immigrants to 'the science, art and industry of the British' – all these factors demanded that the hand of support and friendship be offered to the Jewish immigrant.[240] Immigration restriction could only be defended only 'as a last resort', on the grounds of 'grave national hardship or peril'. But for Bruce Glasier, Keir Hardie and other contributors to the *Labour Leader*, no such national crisis existed. There were problems of overcrowding, poverty, sweating and poor sanitation in the cities, especially in London. But these were, at root, the results of capitalist 'disorder' and exploitation rather than immi-gration. As such they demanded in the immediate term the stricter enforcement of existing legislation and ultimately socialist solutions, rather than racist stereotyp-ing, exclusion and restriction.[241]

The *Clarion*, notwithstanding its more mixed overall portrayal of both the new immigrants and Jewish people in general, was also keen to avoid a uniformly nega-tive and racist approach. In the opinion of the *Clarion*, there were 'Jews and Jews'. On the one hand, there were 'the devoted, fearless, heroic band of Jewish Socialists', characterised by, for example, Marx and 'those currently involved in the revolu-tionary movement in Russia'. On the other stood, 'the Shylocks of Johannesburg and Park Lane, the insatiable war-making Emperors of International Finance', and 'the ignorantly fanatical sweater's slaves of Whitechapel'. On a general level there was no doubting 'the intelligence, the reforming ardour and heroism, and the gen-ius of the Jewish people'.[242]

Finally, as Joseph Buckman and Bill Williams have clearly demonstrated, there *was* significant 'new' Jewish-immigrant involvement in trade unionism in tailor-ing and elsewhere, and at times close cooperation between Jewish and non-Jewish workers and trade unionists. In sum, class could, and at times did, provide an important counterweight to 'ethnicity'. [243] On a wider canvas, the very complexity and shifting nature of its component attitudes and practices towards race meant that the British labour movement, both in this period and beyond, equally did not lend itself to a charge of fixed and blanket racism.[244]

(B) CAPACITIES, COOPERATION AND COMRADESHIP

Denouncing racism, our socialists set out both to cultivate and support, much in the manner of Chartist and post-Chartist independent radicalism, a global spirit of national self-determination and internationalism and 'brotherhood' among the 'people', the 'producers', the 'working class(es)'.[245] Of particular importance in terms of our late nineteenth-century and early twentieth-century focus, was the development of socialist support mechanisms for, and comradely ties with, 'our black brethren'. The means by which these aims were to be achieved and their form and substance occupy our attentions in this section. Once again, socialist attitudes and practices were informed by a blend of superiority, egalitarianism and cooperation.

At the heart of the socialist project of class-based interracial unity lay the emphasis upon inclusiveness. Thus Guest, 'We cannot exclude the coloured man from taking part in our Western civilisation. Indeed, our civilisation opens its arms to him.[246] This was, of course, inclusiveness upon elitist western terms. But, as seen earlier, for Guest and many other socialists respect for the potentially anti-capitalist features of 'primitive' societies and opposition to the greed, poverty, aggression and rampant individualism and competitiveness engendered by western capitalism, co-existed with a belief in the overall superiority of 'Western civilisation' over other forms. But even in terms of the latter belief, there emerged questioning socialist voices. For example, Hyndman had a very healthy respect for Japan – 'in future' to be 'reckoned with as a great power and as the champion of the yellow races' – and China – which 'will shortly awaken herself in earnest' – and urged British and Asian socialists to cooperate rather than engage in destructive competition.[247]

As a first step towards the realisation of interracial unity it was vital, Guest believed, to assess, and where necessary raise, the capacities, of 'coloureds'. Thus, British socialists should 'make an estimate' concerning 'any coloured race's capacity and standard of life', so that the latter might not be 'unloosened on the labour market' cheaply and indiscriminately.[248] 'We must bend our energies', declared Guest, 'to maintaining the standard of life of the white men and raising that of the coloured'. 'True' equality, however, would await the triumph of socialism.[249]

In keeping with this system of estimation, Guest proposed the adoption of a number of measures. These were at once elitist and judgmental, comradely, pragmatic, useful and carried far-reaching material, democratic and even revolutionary implications for existing structures of class and race domination and exploitation. At the most general level 'coloureds' were to be encouraged further to develop a cluster of 'capacities', rooted in self-respect, independence and 'manliness', conducive to the growth of trade unionism and socialism. More specifically, a system of 'sound elementary education' should be made compulsory 'for all coloured persons born within or permanently residing within the boundaries of white states', and technical institutions established to which 'suitable coloured persons may be drafted'.[250] In order successfully to challenge racial inequality within the labour market and at the workplace, Guest proposed 'equal economic rights' for 'coloureds' and 'whites', and the abolition of 'the iniquitous dual standard of wages and conditions of life'. Towards these ends support was given to interracial labour market cooperation, to 'coloured' trade unionism and workplace struggles, to a minimum wage and a 'minimum standard of life' for all, and to 'white wages' for 'coloureds who does (sic) as good work as the white man'.[251] British socialists were further urged to give their unqualified support to the South African 'native's' continued rights to land and communal ownership, and to the abolition of the differential system of taxation imposed on blacks and whites in that country. 'In co-operation with all the native races in South Africa', the British Labour party was exhorted to call a conference to 'discuss in a friendly way the whole native question'.[252]

Guest's proposals for enhanced 'coloured' educational and economic capacities and black and white cooperation met with strong endorsement among British socialists. Attention has earlier been drawn to Sydney Olivier's strong advocacy of 'race fusion', especially in the form of intermarriage between black and white. Keir Hardie, albeit much to the outrage of most white South Africans, proposed in a speech at Durban 'opening trade unions to coloured men'.[253] Expressing an increasingly minority viewpoint among his fellow South African socialists and trade unionists, David Donald of East Griqualand, nevertheless, wrote to the *Clarion* to urge white support for black rights and economic improvement. Thus, 'when labour gets on top of capital', wrote Donald,

> let us see to it that our coloured brother labourer gets more than a 'bunk, blanket and a plate of rice' – a little freedom, for instance – or retribution will overtake us as surely as it is overtaking the Capitalist.[254]

Some socialists also extended the notion of enhanced capacities to embrace 'unfree' and 'cheap' Chinese migrant labour. Guest, himself, writing in the *Clarion* in 1904, expressed the view that, once having escaped from the shackles imposed on them by capital and the secret societies to become 'established' and 'free', Chinese workers 'will insist on higher wages and any other terms – say rights of citizenship – that may be thought desirable'.[255] In the following year the *Labour Leader* voiced both its opposition to the floggings and other indignities suffered by the Chinese miners on the Rand, and its support for their acts of stubborn resistance against capitalist exploitation, including strikes for better pay and against increased workloads. 'It is the old story', commented the *Labour Leader,* 'the capitalist wants to force as much out of the Chinese coolie as possible ... the coolie refuses to be coerced into killing himself for the capitalist'. The Chinese possessed 'the spirit, if they have not the form, of trade unions. More power to the Chinese elbow, say we!'[256] Finally, an article critical of the White Australia policy, penned by Harold de Gackowski in

Justice, counselled Australian labour activists to introduce the minimum wage and 'educate the disciple of Confucius': 'Teach him to organise and act in co-operation with his white brothers against the octopus of capitalism.'[257]

White socialist support for enhanced 'coloured' capacities embraced not only economic, but also wider civil and political liberties and rights. As Guest declared of South Africa, 'we must recognise that the natives are human beings to whom we must give equal citizen (sic) rights and equal economic rights.'[258] For the *Labour Leader*, the 'domination of the white over the black is unjust and criminal', and black people were 'in every respect the equal, and in some respects the superior of their white brother.'[259] The *Blackburn Labour Journal* expressed the common viewpoint within the movement that, 'As Socialists we stand for freedom – politically and economically – for all races.'[260]

In practical terms, commitment to Equal Rights meant, according to Guest, making 'men equal before an equal law', framing and extending the political franchise to 'enable men of all colours to participate in the democratic rights of their own country', and generally guaranteeing equality of opportunity and status for black and white alike.[261] With particular reference to South Africa, socialists directly challenged the system of white supremacy, complete with its desire to 'keep the Nigger in his proper place'. Indeed, Hyndman and *Justice* articulated a view of long term black power and self-determination, with South Africa being 'a black man's country than a white man's', and the 'future of South Africa is ... to the Black man'.[262] Guest, Hardie, Hyndman and many other British socialists argued that South African blacks be 'allowed to vote and own property' rather than 'be treated as being part wild beast and part child'. Some socialists, including Hardie, did support limited educational and property qualifications for the franchise for blacks and/or black and white alike (the 'Cape model'). However, they were virtually unanimous both in their opposition to segregation and, as we will see below, in their strenuous defence of black rights during the 1906 'troubles' in Natal and black exclusion from political representation – 'the erection of the colour bar' – in the Union parliament during the establishment of the Union of South Africa.[263]

The principles of 'coloured' political representation and self-determination were also upheld in relation to India. Notwithstanding continuing debates concerning the extent of Keir Hardie's commitment to the cause of complete independence for India, there is no doubt that he did express considerable enthusiasm not only for 'the social emancipation of the downtrodden masses of India',[264] but also for the self-government of that country. What was at issue was less the principle than the timing of the process whereby the 'coloured' would follow the 'white' colonies in the achievement of self-determination. As Morgan has observed, 'Hardie did not argue for the immediate withdrawal of the British from India, but only for a gradual extension of self-government as had recently been implemented in Australia and South Africa.'[265] Hyndman and *Justice* were similarly attracted to the principle of self-determination for the black colonies, but were increasingly more urgent and unrestrained than Hardie in their cry of 'India for the Indians', albeit within the framework of 'some kind of continued British supervision'.[266] By way of stark contrast, Blatchford believed that home rule for India would be followed by a disastrous 'reversion to internecine chaos' and occupation by another, less 'civilised' imperial power than Britain. His preferred option was a continued period of enlightened imperial rule, increasingly of a socialist type.[267]

In sum, we may argue that the 'Class-based Response' offered by many British socialists was far less 'Little Englander' and far more genuinely internationalist in character,[268] racially inclusive and mindful of the plight of 'the native' than the current historiographical wisdom suggests. To be sure, the responses and prescriptions of our selected socialists did not amount to a totally coherent and fully comprehensive policy. Neither, as witnessed by Blatchford's thoughts on India, was there undivided socialist agreement on matters of substance and purpose. From the standpoint of socialism, the overall response was more reformist than revolutionary in character. However, in relation both to their diagnosis of imperialism as a system of class and race domination and their strategic response to that system, they offered a far more fundamental, challenging and class conscious, inclusive perspective than the adjectives, 'liberal', 'limited' and 'racist' would suggest.

(c) LIMITATIONS, BOUNDARIES AND EXCLUSIONS

Yet a response rooted in inclusive internationalism and class consciousness did not constitute the whole story. Indeed, we would be guilty of insufficient attention to the historical evidence to end our story on a starry-eyed and unblemished note of class unity. For, as we have observed throughout the essay, boundaries, ambiguities and exclusions were not absent from 'The rule of class'. Indeed, the reader will already have noted that the 'languages of socialism' identified in this essay were predominantly male in character and orientation. British socialists did allude to the predicaments and purposes of 'coloured people'. Among British and South African socialists there did exist, at least in principle, some support for the notion of adult suffrage, of extending the vote in both countries to 'all adult citizens fit to exercise it, irrespective of race, sex, colour or creed'.[269] And socialist women's voices could be heard in favour of votes for women. As Isabella Ford wrote in 1906 in relation to the issue of women's suffrage in South Africa,

> We have committed many injustices in South Africa, and one of the very gravest of which we have been guilty is the entire omission of women from the new constitution in the Transvaal.[270]

For the most part, however, our socialists' dominant points of reference were 'coloured' and 'white' men. Women tended either to be invisible or to be referred to in decorative and supportive ways. In sum, as Karen Hunt has acutely observed, the language of socialism, as a means of universal emancipation, was 'bounded', fractured and diminished by its gendered limitations.[271]

In addition, the economic and racial inclusiveness of Guest and other socialists was conditional in character. If 'coloureds' failed to attain the necessary level of 'capacity' to work efficiently and in harmony with 'whites' – if they continued to be a source of 'forced' and/or 'cheap' labour effectively beyond the 'improving' reach of the institutions of the labour movement; and if they continued to constitute a 'residuum' – then they were to be excluded from 'white' labour markets. As we have seen, such was the case with much socialist opposition to 'Chinese slavery' in South Africa and support for their repatriation.[272] As Guest declared, 'Labour's watchword must be, neglecting any question of mere colour', 'the competition of the efficient, safeguarded by a minimum line'. 'Coloureds' would be economically segmented, 'until it can be shown that the labour coming from them will compete not below a reasonable minimum of capacity and standard of life'.[273]

Tocsin, the independent Melbourne labour paper expressed the matter thus:

> From the strictly Labour point of view it is immaterial of what race, colour, or language men may be; the essential thing is that they should be MEN according to the Australian workers' standard of manhood, and not human CATTLE, capable of being used by the capitalist to supplant MEN.[274]

Similarly gendered notions were at play in Britain to denote 'manliness' and independence which were the very antithesis of 'cheapness' and cowering fear or deference. Moreover, it was this line of reasoning which led Guest, notwithstanding his opposition to its 'violent', short-sighted and geographically specific character, to support the White Australia policy as 'the most sensible' on offer for Australia – 'being thoroughly thought out by the people who are the only serious politicians – that is, working men'.[275] And it was the same line of argument, along with a desire not 'unnecessarily' to antagonise fellow socialists, many of them hailing from the 'old country', which persuaded Keir Hardie and other British socialists visiting Australia to 'wait and see' in relation to the fortunes of 'White Australia'.[276]

Finally, in some contexts 'coloured' exclusion from 'white' labour markets was accompanied either by physical exclusion from the country in question, or internal political exclusion and structured inequality and segregation in all walks of life. The former was the case in terms of Asiatics in post-1901 Australia, and the latter the case for most of the twentieth-century history of South Africa. Indeed, it is to a consideration of the 1900s contexts of South Africa and Australia that we must turn in the final part of the essay in order to impress upon the reader the ways in which racism in these colonies did, albeit in contested ways, turn the tables upon our the British socialists' 'rule of class'.

The considerable appeal and power of racism within the labour movement of South Africa has been demonstrated with reference to attitudes towards the employment of the Chinese. Branded 'unfree' and 'cheap', the Chinese were also

subjected, if far more so by South African trade unionists than socialists, to growing negative stereotyping as carriers of disease and crime, and although confined
to the compounds, a potential threat to the sexual purity and overall decency of
the 'white race'.[277]

Following the Liberals' electoral victory in Britain in early 1906, the future of
'Chinese slavery' in South Africa was effectively doomed. However, the 'native
question' rapidly assumed the pre-eminent position so recently occupied by the
'Chinese experiment'. Three developments underpinned this return to pre-emi-
nence. First, in 1906, new constitutions were drawn up for the ex-Boer republics.
And, as Shula Marks informs us, while granting 'self-government based on adult
male suffrage', the issue of vote for blacks in the ex-republics 'was not even subject
to debate'.[278] Second, between February and August of 1906 the 'Bambatha rebellion' occurred in Natal. The rebellion, or more accurately, a series of acts of black
resistance during 1906 and 1907 directed mainly against the imposition of a new
£1 Poll Tax on all adult males in the multi-racial colony, involved the killing of two
white police officers and an uncompromising response on the part of the authorities. The latter imposed martial law 'over the entire colony', sent the Natal militia
to the areas of unrest – 'burning crops and kraals, confiscating cattle, and deposing
chiefs'- and court-martialled and shot twelve of those involved in the earlier, fatal
affray with the police. Notwithstanding further conflict, indeed the continuation
of the disturbances into 1907, the 'last tribal revolt on South African soil' had effectively been bloodily defeated by mid-summer, 1906. As Marks has written in the
definitive account of the rebellion,

> By mid July all active resistance was over, although what were termed 'mopping up'
> operations continued into August, and martial law was only lifted a month later. It
> is estimated that between 3,500 and 4,000 Africans lost their lives during the dis-
> turbances. Some two dozen whites including about half a dozen civilians were also
> killed, although no white women or children were harmed in any way and white
> property remained relatively unscathed.[279]

Third, following the Bambatha Rebellion and the 'politicisation and mass unioni-
sation of the white working class' during and in the wake of the 1907 mine strike,
unification of the South African colonies became the burning political issue. A
national convention, 'representing most white political opinion', formulated a
constitution in 1908-9 which in turn formed the basis for the Act of Union of 1910.
Under the terms of the latter the Cape managed to retain its 'non-racial, class-based
franchise', rooted in educational and property-based qualifications. However,
'elsewhere white adult male suffrage obtained'. And African and Coloured opposition to the 'colour bar' of the new Union, including representation to the British
government, proved to be in vain. As Marks concludes,

> Most British politicians were convinced of the need for unification in the interests

of economic development, and euphoric about the great reconciliation which had taken place between the white 'races'. The few lonely voices raised against the dangers of a constitution which excluded the vast majority of the population from the political community, were ignored in the atmosphere of mutual congratulation.[280]

A marked lack of sympathy, and in some cases open and unrepentant racism, constituted the dominant responses of the South African labour and socialist movements to the worsening position of black people in their country. For example, in 1905, 'Hugo', in correspondence with the *Labour Leader*, acted as a mouthpiece for much indigenous white opinion in dismissing as 'utterly impracticable', the suggestion of British socialists that a conference be called between 'the leaders of native opinion' and Labour party leaders in South Africa to discuss the 'native question' in general and the issue of black enfranchisement in particular. 'Hugo' accused British socialists of being hopelessly out of touch with conditions in South Africa. In turn black South Africans were dismissed as 'infants', 'children' or 'misgrown' children and, more offensively, as 'savages', completely unfit in their existing state to exercise the vote. 'Give him time', counselled 'Hugo',

> educate him, civilise him by wise and gentle methods and generation after generation will become more intelligent, but for the present please remember that he is an infant.[281]

During the following year, the unfolding events of the Bambatha rebellion and especially British and some South African socialists' condemnation of the brutal treatment of the protesters by the authorities in Natal, brought forth an angry racist response from white South African socialists and trade-unionists. For example, Ramsay MacDonald's charge that the authorities and many white Natalians had acted in a 'bloodthirsty' manner, and had been keen to provoke black unrest in order to force them off their land and into the mines as cheap proletarian victims of the owners, triggered off a storm of protest and much acrimonious debate in the pages of the *Clarion*.[282] 'Pufff', in denying Macdonald's charge, justified the methods adopted by the authorities as being 'for the safety of the state' and 'the best for future peace', and launched into a typically racist defence of 'natural' white superiority and a diatribe against 'native' 'savagery' and 'violence'. 'In your Northern Isles', fumed 'Pufff', 'you have only the black dog of poverty to fight; we have, in addition, the black hordes of semi-savages.[283]

Others of a similar frame of mind within the South African labour movement followed suit. The list and tenor of their allegations and defences was long, loud and both aggressive and insecure in character. The South Africans accused Macdonald, Hardie and British socialists in general of lacking in 'patriotism', and of being woefully ignorant of the 'real' state of affairs in South Africa. Their defence of the rights of black people was seen as harmful to the South African labour and socialist causes. Furthermore, black men were alleged to be incapable of understanding politics, to have 'got out of hand from too lenient treatment', and to be 'lazy' and content to live off the labours of their wives. The Chinese in the Transvaal were similarly accused of an 'easy', most un-slave like existence.[284] To its credit, the *Clarion*, in the person of Alex Thompson, debunked such notions, and further endorsed MacDonald's and Hardie's indictment of the white 'rack-renting and labour-sweating' of the 'natives' in Natal. According to Thompson, the 'whole policy of the squatter tyrants of Natal consisted of,

> Unjust taxation to provoke discontent; bombardment of villages to provoke insurrection; insurrection to obtain confiscated land and cheap labour.[285]

The period preceding the Act of Union also witnessed massive white working-class opposition in South Africa to black political citizenship. The adult suffrage demanded by the Transvaal Political Labour League should be confined to 'the white British population'.[286] In 1909, the *Labour Leader* declared that, 'To their eternal shame the Trade Unionists of South Africa, influenced by Australian labour leaders, are anti-native to a man'.[287] M. Lucas, a member of the late Transvaal ILP agreed: with the exception of 'a few men with humanitarian instincts' and 'a few socialists', 'not a voice is lifted' in opposition to plans to deprive black people of the rights enjoyed in the Cape Colony.[288] 'Pufff', predictably went further, declaring 'not a single colonist' to be 'in favour of the amalgamation of the two races'.[289] One year later, with the formal creation of the Union and the political exclusion of black Africans, the same correspondent pronounced 'racialism' to be 'a sorry fact in this coloured land'. Furthermore, there was 'No use hiding it nor blinding the fact'.[290] 'Pufff's' pronouncement carried with it an awful sense of finality, of racist closure. Indeed in 1910 the curtain came down on the attempts of Hardie and other socialists to keep alive the dream of equal rights and opportunities in South Africa.

The formal introduction of the White Australia policy, in 1901, had also occasioned a sense of pessimism, albeit of a less profound type than in the South African case, on the part of many British socialists. Yet the vast majority of Australian trade unionists and socialists eagerly embraced 'White Australia' as an integral part of the construction of a 'workman's paradise' under the new Commonwealth of Australia.[291]

In retreat for much of the depressed 1890s, the labour movement 'began to lengthen its list of undesirable races' to include Afghans, Syrians, Japanese, Indians and Southern Europeans as well as the more familiar targets of the Chinese and, albeit far more recently, the indentured Melanesians or 'Kanakas' imported into Queensland's sugar plantations. In turn aborigines were, to quote Verity Burgman, 'despised and neglected rather than resented and feared'.[292] During the 1890s there developed strong support within the labour movement for the 'total exclusion of all non-whites', and, as noted by Ray Markey, 'White Australia became the foremost policy' of the Australian Labor Party.[293] As C.H. Adam, of Queenstown, Australia, declared in his letter, 'Australia for the Whites', published in the *Clarion* in 1908, 'Our objections to coloured races are economic, racial and moral'. Identifying 'white' as 'first' and standing for 'the highest ideals', the aim was to realise,

> the ideal we have set ourselves of a White Socialistic Commonwealth open to all of our own race to reside in, and open to all the world to take lessons from.[294]

Probably most pronounced in the labour movement in Queensland,[295] racism, nevertheless, affected all sectors of organised labour in Australia. Thus *Tocsin*, generally in the vanguard of progressive ideas, carried articles which portrayed the 'Kanakas' in the most negative and racist ways, and White Australia as 'not a Labour matter, but a White Man's matter', a 'family matter': 'an animal instinct of a natural kind', lying beyond the scope of argument'.[296] Instances of 'coloured' rebellion, in the form of strikes and union organisation, might prove that 'organisation is possible among them'. However, as seen in the cases of the Melanesians in the Queensland sugar industry and the Chinese in furniture making in Melbourne, such instances did not lead the white labour movement to preach interracial trade unionism and the inclusion of 'coloureds' in its ranks.[297] Prominent in the extended debate on racism held by Tom Mann's the *Socialist* in 1907 was the argument that only when socialism won the class war in Australia would it be both possible and morally defensible to admit 'our Eastern friends'. Prior to that victory, and given the existing fine balance of class forces and class struggle in Australia, argued Dr. T. F. MacDonald, it would be both economically ruinous and racially 'suicidal' to admit 'our primitive brothers' – 'alien peoples' of allegedly low capacities who 'blackleg unconsciously' against trade unionists and 'our democratic institutions'.[298]

In terms of the wider society, the 'cultivation of an Australian sentiment based upon the maintenance of racial purity ...', observes Markey, 'became the first federal objective'.[299] As a piece on 'A White Australia' in the Sixth Annual Report of the British Immigration League of Australia (dedicated 'with all diligence to build up a greater Britain from British stock') declared:

> the purity of the race is the one thing to be maintained above all others – especially if one studies ... the conditions of the Southern States of America, with their thirteen million negroes, the South African Union, with its vast numbers of coloured people, the Philippines, and the Islands of the North Pacific ... our federal statesmen have shown wisdom ... in seeking to keep this great Continent white. This, however, can only be done by adhering to the Imperial idea, with the Imperial Navy to keep off foes from without.[300]

Once again, the sense of racist closure was palpable.

Yet neither in South Africa nor in Australia did racism prevail in blanket and totally uncontested ways. In terms of the former country, British socialists continued throughout the late 1900s to express opposition to black exclusion from the franchise and to racist inequality, oppression and exploitation. For example, in 1906 Hardie, Guest, Hyndman and many other socialists fully endorsed MacDonald's criticisms of the racist brutality of the authorities in Natal.[301] Similarly, during the same year the racist outpourings of 'Pufff' and others in the pages of the *Clarion* were more than counterbalanced by articles and letters, from *both* British and South African socialists, fully supporting the cause of the 'Bambatha' rebels and denouncing racism in Natal and elsewhere.[302] Notwithstanding the growing and increasingly despairing realisation that in all probability black Africans would be excluded from the projected new Federation or Union of South African states, con-tributors to the *Clarion*, the *Labour Leader* and *Justice* continued between 1907 and 1909 to voice the demand that either the limited Cape – or the full, adult franchise should constitute the basis of the federal or union franchise.[303] These contributors, however, were far more British than South African in character.

Finally, in the Australian case opposition to white racism was admittedly far more muted. Reference has already been made to the British socialists' condemna-tion of White Australia. But within the Australian labour and socialist movements themselves, opposition was weak. Even in this case, however, as demonstrated by Andrew Markus, Bruce Scates and Frank Bongiorno, racism was *not* an all pervasive and unchanging force. There was more socialist debate and opposition surround-ing White Australia than the conventional Australian historiographical wisdom would allow.[304] Beyond our chosen period of time, both the Industrial Workers of the World and the Communist Party would promote anti-racist views.[305]

Conclusion

This chapter has argued that late nineteenth and early twentieth-century British socialists presented a critique of imperialism and attitudes towards 'coloured' in-digenous and migrant peoples which, respectively, were far more searching and anti-racist than suggested in much of the recent literature. Indeed, interrogation of our main source of evidence, the socialist weekly press, reveals that the dominant socialist viewpoint to emerge in the pages of the *Clarion*, the *Labour Leader* and *Justice* was, notwithstanding the widespread desire for a reformed and more en-lightened empire, one which denounced existing imperialism as a thoroughgoing and potentially divisive system of class and race domination and exploitation. As a counter to capitalist imperialism, socialists asserted the primacy of class over race. They exhorted workers worldwide to bury their racialised and other differences in the causes of international class unity, struggle and the eventual achievement of socialism. Both their diagnosis and prescription of capitalist imperialism owed less to an enduring tradition of inter-class radical liberalism than to a class-based tradition of independent popular radicalism.

However, the 'rule of class' was not unlimited. In addition to their gendered limitations and exclusions, socialists in Britain, Australia and South Africa routinely adopted a superior pose towards 'uncivilised' people of colour. Moreover, the support offered by the former to the latter was frequently conditional upon their attainment of enhanced labour market and other 'capacities'. Some socialists in all three countries denied racism while simultaneously adopting an exclusionary stance towards 'cheap' and predominantly 'non-white' labour. Another strand of socialist argument in Australia and South Africa was that the successful resolution of the 'race problem' was secondary to, and necessarily attendant upon, the achievement of socialism. Only with the attainment of the latter could the excluded 'coloured other' become a 'true' insider. Finally, in contrast to the majority opinion of their British comrades, as expressed in the socialist weeklies, and notwithstanding continuing internal debates and differences of opinion, most South African and Australian socialists were openly and unrepentantly racist in their desire to protect and extend the 'wages of whiteness'.

In sum, while our British socialists did demonstrate the 'supremacy of class over race' in both their attitudes and actions, in South Africa and Australia the very opposite was generally the case. The 'white-settler' positions of Australia and South Africa within the British imperial network, combined with other national 'peculiarities', largely accounted for their dominant socialist racism. Future research could usefully both further tease out the similarities and differences among the socialist voices identified in this essay, and more firmly relate these voices to their locations within the network of empire.

Notes

* Versions of this essay have benefited immensely from the comments made by Tony Zurbrugg of Merlin Press and participants in seminars at the Australian National University, the University of New South Wales, the University of Sydney, Manchester Metropolitan University and the International Centre for Labour Studies, University of Manchester. I am particularly indebted to the detailed and searching criticisms and suggestions made by Rick Halpern, David Montgomery, Paul Pickering and John Walton. I am, of course, solely responsible for the final outcome.

1. Edward P. Thompson, 'The Peculiarities of the English', in his *The Poverty of Theory and Other Essays* (London, 1979), 66-7.
2. Kenneth Lunn, 'A Racialized Hierarchy of Labour? Race, Immigration and the British Labour Movement, 1880-1950', in Alexander and Halpern, *Racializing Class*, 110.
3. 'Socialism and the Chinese Question', *Labour Leader*, 23 April, 1904.
4. For studies dealing entirely or in part with organised labour that have traditionally have gone against the domestic grain see, for example, Bernard Porter, *Critics of Empire: British Radical Attitudes to Colonialism in Africa 1895-1914* (London, 1968), Chapter 4; Richard Price, *An Imperial War and the British Working Class* (London, 1972); Partha Sarathi Gupta, *Imperialism and the British Labour Movement 1914-1964* (New York, 1975). More recently see, for example, John Saville, *The Politics of Continuity: British Foreign Policy and the Labour Government 1945-46* (London, 1993). For the question of class see Kirk, *Change*, Introduction; Lawrence, *Speaking*, Chapter 1.
5. See, for example, Alexander and Halpern, *Racializing Class*; Dorothy Thompson, *Outsiders: Class Gender and Nation* (London, 1993); Lunn, 'A Racialized Hierarchy'; Laura Tabili, 'We Ask for British Justice': Workers and Racial Difference in Late Imperial Britain* (New York, 1994); Lawrence, *Speaking*,

3-5, Chapter 6; Michael Savage, 'Space, Networks and Class Formation', in Neville Kirk (ed), *Social Class and Marxism: Defences and Challenges* (Aldershot, 1996), 58-86.

6. Berger and Smith, *Nationalism Labour and Ethnicity*, Chapter 1; Gyan Prakash, 'Subaltern Studies as Postcolonial Criticism', *American Historical Review*, 99,5 (Dec. 1994), 1475-1490; K. Sivaramakrishnan, 'Situating the Subaltern: History and Anthropology in the Subaltern Studies Project', *Journal Historical Sociology* 8,4 (Dec. 1995), 395- 429.

7. For this consensus see Karen Hunt, 'Fractured Universality: The Language of British Socialism before the First World War', in John Belchem and Neville Kirk (eds), *Languages of Labour* (Aldershot, 1997), 65-80; Berger and Smith, *Nationalism*, 17,24-25; Preben Kaarsholm, 'The South African War and the Response of the International Socialist Community to Imperialism between 1896 and 1908', in Frits van Holthoon and Marcel van der Linden (eds), *Internationalism in the Labour Movement 1830-1940* (Leiden, 1988), 42-67; idem, 'Pro-Boers', in Raphael Samuel (ed), *Patriotism: The Making and Unmaking of British National Identity: Volume 1:History and Politics* (London, 1989), 110-126; Logie Barrow, 'White Solidarity in 1914', in Samuel, *Patriotism*, vol. 1, 275-287; idem, 'The Socialism of Robert Blatchford and the "Clarion" 1889-1918', unpubd. PhD thesis, Univ. London 1975, especially 421-440; Jonathan Hyslop, 'The Imperial Working Class Makes itself 'White': White Labourism in Britain, Australia and South Africa before the First World War', *Journal Historical Sociology*, 12,4 (Dec. 1999), 398- 421; Stephen Howe, *Anticolonialism in British Politics: The Left and the End of Empire 1918-1964* (Oxford, 1993), Chapter 2; Lawrence, *Speaking*, 109-10, 185-6, 223-4, Conclusion; Alastair Bonnett, 'How the British Working Class Became White: The Symbolic (Re)formation of Racialized Capitalism', *Journal of Historical Sociology*, 11,3 (Sept. 1998), 316-340. See Lunn, 'A Racialized Hierarchy', 104-121, for a critique of the dominant approach which presents British labour's attitudes to 'race' and immigration as ones of more or less fixed and uniform 'negativity, of opposition and of hostility'. For similarly nuanced and convincing observations on the debates surrounding 'whiteness' and racism on the part of US labour see Eric Arnesen's contribution to the *International Labor and Working Class History* roundtable at the American Historical Association's meeting in Chicago, January 2000, on the H-Labor e-mail network, 27 Jan., 2000 (forwarded by Michael Hanagan).

8. Thompson, 'Peculiarities', 66-7; Halpern, 'Labour and the Empire'. See Marcel van der Linden's very welcome appeal to labour historians to broaden and deepen their horizons, in terms of geographical and chronological scope. Made at the *AHA's* Jan. 2000 *ILWCH* roundtable, van der Linden's appeal can be found on the H-Labor e-mail network, 22 Jan., 2000 (forwarded by Michael Hanagan); Stephen Howe, 'The Slow Death and Strange Rebirths of Imperial History', *Jnl. Imperial and Commonwealth History*, 29, 2 (May 2001), 131-41.

9. Hobsbawm, *Age of Empire*, Chap. 3.

10. For examples of the treatment of aboriginals in recent Australian labour historiography see, for example, Raelene Frances, Bruce Scates and Ann McGrath, 'Broken Silences? Labour History and Aboriginal Workers', in Terry Irving (ed.), *Challenges to Labour History* (Sydney, Univ. New South Wales Press, 1994), Chapter 12; Frank Bongiorno, 'Aboriginality and Historical Consciousness: Bernard O'Dowd and the Creation of an Australian National Imaginary', *Aboriginal History*, (2000). I am grateful to the author for a copy of his article.

11. For examples of mainly reports of lectures and book reviews dealing with the issues of race and empire see *Fabian News*, VIII,1, March 1898 (lecture by J. McKillop), X,4, June 1900 (lecture by Gilbert Murray), XVII,5, April 1907 (Leslie Guest's review of Sydney Olivier's *White Capital and Coloured Labour*), XXII,8, July 1911 (lecture by Annie Besant).

12. Porter, *Critics*, 101 (n.3).

13. Although *Fabian News* carried regular features entitled, 'What Members are Doing' and 'Local Fabian Societies', these were mainly brief and organisational reports. Little sense of the active life, debate and personnel of local Fabianism is conveyed.

14. I am grateful to Paul Pickering for making this comparison. For the *Northern Star* see Stephen Roberts, 'Who Wrote to the *Northern Star*', in Owen Ashton, Robert Fyson and Stephen Roberts (eds.), *The Duty of Discontent: Essays for Dorothy Thompson* (London, Mansell, 1995), 55-70.

15. Hobsbawm, *Empire*, 72.

16. See, for example, Price, *Imperial War*; Porter, *Critics*, Chapter 4; Howe, *Anticolonialism*, 35-8; Kaarsholm, 'The South African War',49-51; Henry Pelling, *Popular Politics and Society in Late Victorian Britain* (1979, London), Chapter 5, 'British Labour and British Imperialism', 82-100.

17. Miles Taylor, 'Imperium et Libertas? Rethinking the Radical Critique of Imperialism during the Nineteenth Century', *Journal Imperial and Commonwealth History*,19,1 (Jan. 1991), 14.

18. For the popular republican and revolutionary tradition – in relation to the attitudes of English Chartists towards Ireland and radical traditions both on the mainland and in Ireland – see Thompson, *Outsiders*, Chapters 4,5, and Paul A. Pickering, '"Repeal and the Suffrage": Feargus O'Connor's Irish "Mission", 1849-50', in Owen Ashton, Robert Fyson and Stephen Roberts (eds), *The Chartist Legacy* (Rendlesham, Suffolk, Merlin Press, 1999), 119- 146. For continuing tensions between independent popular radicalism and Liberalism in the mid-and late- Victorian periods see Margot Finn, *After Chartism: Class and Nation in English Radical Politics 1848-1874* (Cambridge, 1993), and Antony Taylor, 'Commemorisation, Memorialisation and Political Memory in Post-Chartist Radicalism: The Halifax Chartist Reunion in Context', in *The Chartist Legacy*, 255-285. For 'Little Englander', anti- imperialist Radicalism see Taylor, 'Imperium et Libertas?'

19. For the variety of working-class attitudes towards empire and imperialism see Porter, *Critics*, 95-7; Pelling, 'British Labour and British Imperialism', 82-3, 85-7, 99- 100; Price, *Imperial War*, 239-42; Lawrence, *Speaking*, 109- 110; John M. MacKenzie (ed.) *Imperialism and Popular Culture* (Manchester, 1986), Introduction. In terms of the socialist movement, the majority support offered by the Fabian Society to both the Boer War and social-imperialism was an exception to the norm. However, even in the Fabian case there did exist significant differences of opinion – amounting to splits and resignations over the War – in relation to imperialism. There was also majority support for 'true' or 'enlightened, as opposed to 'aggressive', imperialism among Fabians. For these matters see Bernard Semmel, *Imperialism and Social Reform: English Social- Imperial Thought 1895-1914* (New York, Anchor Books, 1968), Chapters III, VI; A.M. McBriar, *Fabian Socialism and English Politics 1884-1918* (Cambridge, 1966), Chapter V; Miles Taylor, 'Imperium et Libertas?', 16; Porter, *Critics*, 109-23; Royden J. Harrison, *The Life and Times of Sidney and Beatrice Webb 1858-1905: The Formative Years* (London, 2000), Chapter 8, especially 321-9.

20. Andrew Markus, 'Explaining the Treatment of non-European Immigrants in Nineteenth-Century Australia', *Labour History*, 48 (May 1985), 86-91; Tim Moldram, 'Treading the Diverse Paths of Modernity: Labour, Ethnicity and Nationalism in South Africa', in Berger and Smith, *Nationalism*, 215-241.

21. While Lunn's focus rests upon the local and national level in Britain, it is suggested that his conclusions can accurately be applied to British labour movement and socialist attitudes to indig-enous peoples and migrants in an international context.

22. Throughout this essay I follow Robert Miles's usage of the term racialization to 'refer to a process of signification in which human beings are categorized into "races" by reference to real or imagined phenotypical or genetic differences'. I also endorse Miles's argument that we need to go beyond the 'race relations' problematic by linking, in non-reductionist and non-functional ways, processes of racialization and 'the social relations necessarily established in the course of material production'. In so constructing a political economy of 'race', importance is attached to the contingent and chang-ing nature of the processes and meanings of racialization. See Robert Miles, *Capitalism and Unfree Labour: Anomaly or Necessity?* (London, 1987), 7; David Montgomery, 'Empire, Race and Working-Class Mobilizations', in Alexander and Halpern, *Racializing Class*, 3,14-15; Tabili, *British Justice*, 1-14; Lunn, 'A Racialized Hierarchy', 111-113.

23. For the United States see Andrew Gyory, *Closing the Gate: Race Politics and the Chinese Exclusion Act* (London, 1998); Alexander Saxton, *The Rise and Fall of the White Republic: Class Politics and Mass Culture in Nineteenth Century America* (London, 1990); David R. Roediger, *The Wages of Whiteness: Race and the Making of the American Working Class* (London, 1991); Herbert Hill, 'The Problem of Race in American Labor History', *Reviews in American History*, 24,2 (1996).For the white-settler colonies see Robert A. Huttenback, *Racism and Empire: White Settlers and Colored Immigrants in the*

British Self-Governing Colonies 1830-1910 (London, 1976); Persia Crawford Campbell, *Chinese Coolie Emigration to Countries within the British Empire* (London, 1923).

24. Campbell, *Chinese Coolie Emigration*, Chapter IV; Shula Marks, 'Southern and Central Africa,1886-1910', in Roland Oliver and G.N. Sanderson (eds), *The Cambridge History of Africa, vol. 6: From 1870-1905* (Cambridge, 1985), 484-5; P. Richardson, *Chinese Mine Labour in the Transvaal* (London, 1982); Montgomery, 'Empire, Race', 5.

25. Berger and Smith, *Nationalism*, 26.

26. Jonathan Hyslop's sweeping claim rests upon very insubstantial empirical foundations. See Jonathan Hyslop, 'The Imperial Working Class Makes Itself "White": White Labourism in Britain, Australia and South Africa before the First World War', *Journal Historical Sociology*, 12,4 (Dec. 1999), 398-421

27. Taylor, 'Imperium et Libertas?', 14-15; Nicholas Owen, 'Critics of Empire in Britain', in Judith M. Brown and William R. Lewis (eds), *The Oxford History of the British Empire, Vol. IV, The Twentieth Century* (Oxford, 1999), esp. 188-92. See also Andrew S. Thompson, 'The Language of Imperialism and the Meanings of Empire: Imperial Discourse in British Politics, 1895-1914', *Journal of British Studies*, 36,2 (April 1997), 147-177, for the Fabian idea of 'sane imperialism'. It is important to note that the notion, or more accurately notions, of 'true' or 'enlightened' imperialism received the support not only of many anti-Boer War radicals and critics of 'aggressive' imperialism, but also of pro-War Fabians and Liberal- Imperialists. See, for example, Taylor, 'Imperium et Libertas?, 14-16; Porter, *Critics*, 62-3, 88; Semmel, *Imperialism*, 52-3, 58; Julian Townsend, 'J.A. Hobson: Anti-Imperialist?', *International Review of History and Political Science*, 19 (1982), 28-41; H.C.G. Matthew, *The Liberal- Imperialists: The Ideas and Politics of a Post Gladstonian Elite* (Oxford, 1973). For socialist and labour attitudes to 'enlightened' imperialism see below, 166-174.

28. Taylor, 'Imperium et Libertas?', 15; Thompson, 'The Language', 165-170 for a discussion of the notion of 'trusteeship'; Porter, *Critics*, 84-93.

29. Howe, *Anticolonialism*, 45-6.

30. Loc. cit.; Partha Sarathi Gupta, 'Imperialism and the Labour Government of 1945-51', in J.M. Winter (ed), *The Working Class in Modern British History: Essays in Honour of Henry Pelling* (Cambridge, 1983), 99-124.

31. Kaarsholm, 'Pro-Boers', 120.

32. For illuminating studies of these prevailing ideas see Victor Kiernan, *The Lords of Human Kind: European Attitudes to Other Cultures in the Imperial Age* (London, 1995); Christine Bolt, *Victorian Attitudes to Race* (London, 1971).

33. Kaarsholm, 'The South African War', 62-3.

34. See, for example, Hyslop, 'The Imperial Working Class'; Howe, *Anticolonialism*, 44-52. See also Logie Barrow, 'The Origins of Robert Blatchford's Social Imperialism', and Robin Page Arnot's comments on Barrow's paper in *Society for the Study of Labour History Bulletin*, 19 (1969), 9-12. Notwithstanding his attention to the ambiguities of the evidence, Barrow's overall conclusion is one of socialist hostility and racism. See also Barrow's 'White Solidarity' and 'The Socialism', 421-38.

35. *Labour Leader*, 2 April, 1904.

36. Montgomery, 'Empire', 3,14; Shula Marks, *Reluctant Rebellion: The 1906-8 Disturbances in Natal* (Oxford, 1970), Chapter 1.

37. The *Worker's* comments were reported in *Justice*, 28 May, 1904. The Amalgamated Shearers' Union and the General Labourers' Union amalgamated to form the AWU in 1894. In 1904 the Queensland Workers' Union amalgamated with the AWU. See Ray Markey, 'New Unionism in Australia, 1880-1900', *Labour History*, 48 (May 1985), 15-28; Patmore, *Australian Labour History*, 60-176-7.

38. *Labour Leader*, 30 June, 1905. 'Kopjes' was referring not to indentured Chinese labourers in South Africa working on set contracts and confined to non-skilled and increasingly non- white sections of mining, but to 'all other Asiatics' who 'are free to do as they choose'. See also Kennedy, *A Tale of Two Mining Cities*, Ch. 1.

39. *Labour Leader*, 25 Aug., 1905.

40. *Clarion*, 26 Oct., 1906.

41. *Clarion*, 6 July, 1906. See also Margaret MacDonald's article in the *Labour Leader*, 15 Feb., 1907 for the 'native' as 'exotic'.

42. *Clarion*, 17 Nov., 1905, Aug. 31, 1906. See also two articles on this evolutionary theme by Tom Swain, *Labour Leader*, 14, 21 Feb., 1903; Barrow, 'The Socialism', 421-5.

43. See John Saville's entry on Guest in Joyce Bellamy and John Saville (eds), *Dictionary of Labour Biography*, vol. 8 (London, 1987), 88-91; *Fabian News*, XV,1 (Jan. 1905).

44. Haden Guest, 'A Labour View of the Coloured Labour Problem', *Clarion*, 22,29 July, 1904.

45. By this point in time most of the US labour movement supported Asian exclusion. Furthermore, the case in favour of the latter was routinely made on racist as well as economic grounds – 'not only to preserve our civilization, our standard of living, but our race'. Asiatics were said to be 'alien in race, in religion, in their mode and manner of thought and action, and with their highly developed race consciousness, they come here not to be absorbed but to absorb'. For these and similar comments see American Federation of Labor, *Proceedings*, (1906), 179-80.

46. *Clarion*, 30 June, 1900. See also Jonathan Spence, *The Search for Modern China* (New York, 1991), Chapters 10, 11.

47. John M. MacKenzie, *Orientalism: History, Theory and the Arts* (Manchester, 1995), 214.

48. Colin Holmes, *John Bull's Island: Immigration and British Society 1871-1971* (London, 1988), 84-5.

49. Sydney Olivier, *White Capital and Coloured Labour* (London, Independent Labour Party, 1906), 12, 17.

50. *Clarion*, 18 Jan., 1907.

51. *Labour Leader*, 21 April, 23 June, 1905.

52. *Labour Leader*, 5 Oct., 1906.

53. *Labour Leader*, 2 June, 1905.

54. *Labour Leader*, 5 Oct., 1906. See also the review of Olivier's *White Capital and Coloured Labour*, in *Labour Leader*, 7 Dec., 1906.

55. *Labour Leader*, 5 Oct., 1906.

56. *Labour Leader*, 2 June, 1905.

57. *Labour Leader*, 1 Sept., 1905. See also the article by Dr. Rudolf Broda in *Labour Leader*, 12 May, 1905.

58. See, for example, Chris Waters, ' "Dark Strangers" in our Midst: Discourses of Race and Nation in Britain, 1947-1963', *Journal British Studies*, 36,2 (April 1997), 224-5.

59. *Labour Leader*, 5 Oct., 1906. See also, *Justice*, 3 Nov., 1906.

60. *Labour Leader*, 23 June, 1905, 5 Oct., 1906.

61. *Labour Leader*, 1 Sept., 1905.

62. *Labour Leader*, 2 June, 1905. See also *Labour Leader*, 8 Nov., 1907.

63. *Labour Leader*, 14 Dec., 1906.

64. *Labour Leader*, 22 May, 1908, 13 Aug., 1909; *Tom Mann Papers*, Modern Records Centre, University of Warwick, MSS 334/7/2, 8,12,13,49-50,51-4,59,64,75-6,78-9,89.

65. See, for example, *Clarion*, 27 April, 1, 15, 29 June, 20 July, 3, 10, 24, 31 Aug., 1906 for a sense of the sharp conflict of opinion among socialists concerning black Natalians and responsibility for the rebellion in Natal. For socialist attitudes to race in South Africa see also Allison Drew, *Discordant Comrades: Identities and Loyalties on the South African Left* (Aldershot, 2000), Chapter 2.

66. Henry M. Hyndman, *England for All: The Text Book of Democracy* (1881) (Brighton, 1973), xxv of the introduction by Chushichi Tsuzuki. See Graham Johnson's entry on Hyndman in Vol. X of the *Dictionary Labour Biography* (London, 2000), 101-111.

67. Olivier, *White Capital*, especially Chapters III, IV; idem, *Fabian News*, XIV,12 (Dec. 1904) for a report of Olivier's lecture on the 'American Negro Question', XVII, 5 (April 1907) for Guest's review of Olivier's book; Peter Clarke, *Liberals and Social Democrats* (Cambridge, 1978), 56,83; See also John Saville's entry on Olivier in Vol. VIII of the *Dictionary Labour Biography* (London, 1987), 181-7.

68. *Justice*, 2 June, 1906.

69. *Justice*, 16 June, 1900.

70. *Justice*, 20 Aug., 1904.

71. *Labour Leader*, 16 Aug., 1907, 8 Nov., 1907.

72. *Labour Leader*, 14, 21 Sept., and 15 Sept., 1905 for the review of DuBois's *The Souls of Black Folk*.

73. *Labour Leader*, 21 April, 1 Sept., 1905.

74. *Labour Leader*, 17 March, 1, 22 Sept., 6 Oct., 3 Nov. 1905.

75. *Clarion*, 18 Jan., 1907.

76. Edward W. Said, *Orientalism* (London, 1985), 3,8.

77. See John MacKenzie's (*Orientalism*, 215) convincing critique of the 'procrustean' and 'mono-lithic and binary vision of the past' presented by 'the modern critics of Orientalism'. Mackenzie *Orientalism*, 215.

78. *Clarion*, 24 Oct., 1904.

79. Lawrence, *Speaking*, 223-4; Jay M. Winter, 'The Webbs and the Non-White World: A Case of Socialist Racialism', *Journal Contemporary History*, 9,1 (Jan. 1974), 181-192. Winter notes (p. 192) that the Webbs' beliefs in inequality and paternalism, and the 'natural outcome' of 'racialism', were directed towards the ('white') 'British working class as well as "lower races".

80. For the Chinese as victims, see, for example, *Labour Leader*, 9 April, 1904, 11 May, 1906, Porter, *Critics*, 132- 3. According to Andrew Gyory (*Closing the Gate*, Chapter 2, 246-259) opposition to the 'forced' or 'unfree', and, as a corollary, cheap character of Chinese labour in the United States, rather than to the Chinese as a racial group, constituted the main basis of organised labour's concern in the period preceding the passage of the Chinese Exclusion Act in 1882. Attempts to highlight, often on the basis of very limited evidence, the racist nature of socialist opposition in Britain to 'Chinese la-bour', are not convincing. See, for example, Barrow, 'White Solidarity', 277, 'The Socialism', 432-5.

81. *Clarion*, 24 Oct., 1904.

82. For further discussion of this topic see below191-199.

83. *Clarion*, 30 June, 1900, 23 Nov., 1906.

84. See, for example, the comments by a Boxer, resident in London, in *Blackburn Labour Journal*, July 1900. See also *Justice*, 30 June, 1900 for a reported conversation with a Boxer.

85. *Justice*, 30 June, 1900.

86. See, for example, *Labour Leader*, 7 July, 18 Aug., 1900, 24 Feb., 1905.

87. *Labour Leader*, 8 Nov., 1907.

88. *Labour Leader*, 15 Nov., 1902.

89. *Justice*, 3,17 June, 1905. Hyndman wrote to Tom Mann in the following glowing terms: 'This success of Japan against Russia is to my mind the greatest event in all modern history, perhaps the greatest event in the history of the human race'. Letter dated 25 Feb. 1905 in the *Tom Mann Papers*, National Museum of Labour History, Manchester, CP/IND/TORR/08/06.

90. Winter, 'The Webbs', 185-6; *Justice*, 4 March, 1905; *Clarion*, 30 June, 1905.

91. *Clarion*, 30 June, 1905.

92. See, for example, *Labour Leader*, 4 Oct., 1907. In his letter to Tom Mann, dated 25 Feb. 1905 (see note 80 above), Hyndman expressed the view that 'our Party in Japan will make great headway after the war' (against Russia).

93. For a stimulating study of the interconnections of discourses of race, sexuality, empire and power – with particular reference to Foucault's *History of Sexuality* – see Ann Laura Stoler, *Race and the Education of Desire* (London, Duke University Press, 1995).

94. Semmel, *Imperialism*, 52, 58; Harrison, *Sidney and Beatrice Webb*, 329-332; Taylor, 'Imperium et Libertas?', 14-16.

95. While continuing to disapprove of the Boer War, Blatchford nevertheless came to see that 'there were faults on both sides' and that, as a 'patriot', 'I would not attack my own country while she was at war'. Support for the British 'bottom dog', the gallant 'Tommy Atkins' fighting for his country's interests in distant South Africa, became of overriding concern to him. See *Clarion*, 13 July, 1901, 15 Sept., 1905. See also, the entry on Blatchford by Judith Fincher Laird and John Saville in Bellamy and Saville (eds), *Dictionary Labour Biography*, vol. 1V (London, 1977), 34-42; Semmel, 214-225. *Clarion*,

13 July, 1901, 15 Sept., 1905, 12 Oct., 1906; Barrow, 'The Socialism', 391.

96. *Clarion*, 29 April, 1910.

97. *Clarion*, 13 July, 1901; Barrow, 'The Socialism', 390.

98. *Clarion*, 13 July, 1901, 30 Sept., 1904.

99. For Hyndman see the Introduction to *England for All*, xxviii. For Hardie see *Labour Leader*, 27 Dec., 1907; Fred Reid, *Keir Hardie: The Making of a Socialist* (London, 1978), 124. It is important to note that both Hyndman and Blatchford, along with Alex Thompson, John Hodge and H.G. Wells were involved in the Socialist National Defence Committee, formed in 1915. The leading light in the SNDC was Victor Fisher. A member of the Fabian Society, the Social Democratic Federation and the British Socialist Party, Fisher had resigned from the latter 'because of its pacifist leanings'. See Roy Douglas, 'The National Democratic Party and the British Workers' League', *The Historical Journal*, XV,3 (1972), 533-52; J.O. Stubbs, 'Lord Milner and Patriotic Labour', *The English Historical Review*, LXXXVII (Oct. 1972), 717-754. For Hodge, Steelsmelters' leader and Labour MP see the entry by David Howell and John Saville in Bellamy and Saville (eds), *Dictionary*, vol. III (1976), 109-115.

100. For the activities and philosophy of the BWL see Stubbs, 'Lord Milner', Douglas, 'The National'.

101. *British Citizen and Empire Worker*, 26 Jan., 4, 11 May, 1918.

102. *British Citizen and Empire Worker*, 7, 14 Oct., 1916.

103. *British Citizen and Empire Worker*, 5, 12 Jan., 20 April, 1918, 3, 10, 17 April, 1919.

104. See *Tocsin*, Melbourne's main 1890s labour newspaper, 3, 10 Aug., 21 Sept., 1899. As in Britain, these capitalist 'machinations' were sometimes expressed in racialized ways by Australian socialists. For example, on May 8 1908, the Melbourne-based *The Socialist* referred to the Boer War as 'largely the result of the machinations of the mining Jew and his British-Gentile imitators'. A bound volume of *The Socialist* (April 1906- Feb. 1909) is to be found in the *Tom Mann Papers*, CP/IND/TORR/08/05. See also material under the *Socialist Racism?* heading in *The Class-Based Responses* section below. For Australians and the Boer War see C.N. Connolly, 'Class, Birthplace, Loyalty: Australian Attitudes to the Boer War', *Historical Studies*, 18,71 (Oct. 1978), 210-232.

105. Scates, *A New Australia*; Metin, *Socialism Without Doctrine*; Buckley and Wheelwright *No Paradise for Workers*. See also the essays by Ross Shanahan, Martin Shanahan and Glenn Giles in Palmer, Shanahan and Shanahan, *Australian Labour History Reconsidered*, Part IV.

106. Metin, *Socialism*; Ward, *Australian Legend* ; idem, 'The Australian Legend Re-Visited', *Historical Studies*, 18,71 (Oct. 1978), 171-190.

107. Ray A. Markey, 'The 1890s as The Turning Point in Australian Labor History', *ILWCH*, 31 (Spring 1987), 77-88.

108. *Tocsin*, 5 Oct., 1899.

109. Terry Irving, 'Labour, State and Nation Building in Australia', in Berger and Smith, *Nationalism*, 195.

110. Irving, 'Labour', 196.

111. See the papers presented by Ray Markey ('Federation and the Labour Movement') and Stuart Macintyre ('Federation and Labour') to the Working Life and Federation conference, organised by the Australian Society for the Study of Labour History, Univ. Sydney, 28 April 2000. See also Stuart Macintyre, 'The Making of the Australian Working Class: An Historiographical Survey', *Historical Studies*, 18,71 (Oct. 1978), 233-253.

112. Irving, 'Labour', 198.

113. Willard, *History of The White Australia Policy*, 201.

114. *Labour Leader*, 2,9 June, 22 Sept., 1911.

115. Stubbs, 'Lord Milner', 730. See also *British Citizen and Empire Worker*, 22 Sept. 1916

116. See, for example, the report on the Transvaal elections in *The Socialist*, 27 April, 1907. *Labour Leader*, 9,16,30 June, 1905.

117. Moldram, 'Treading', 230-2; Shula Marks and Stanley Trapido, 'Lord Milner and the South African State', *History Workshop Journal*, 8 (Autumn 1979), 73.

118. Moldram, 'Treading', 233

119. Robert Gregg, 'Apropos Exceptionalism: Imperial Location and Comparative Histories of South Africa and the United States', in Halpern and Morris (eds.), *American Exceptionalism*, Chapter 12.

120. Moldram 'Treading', 238-41; Marks, 'Southern and Central Africa', 485-8; A.P. Walshe and Andrew Roberts, 'Southern Africa', in A.D. Roberts (ed.), *The Cambridge History of Africa*, vol. 7, *From 1905 to 1940* (Cambridge, 1986) Chapter 11, especially pp. 545-56, 560-3.

121. Pat Thane, 'Introduction', *Journal British Studies*, 36,2 (April 1997), 143. For the 'imperialism of race and civilisation' see David Nicholls, *The Lost Prime Minister: A Life of Sir Charles Dilke* (London, 1995), 25-9; Paul A. Kramer, 'The Blood of Government: Race, Empire and Democracy at the Anglo-Saxon Fin-De-Siecle', paper presented at Maryland University, April 1999.

122. *Labour Leader*, 13 Dec., 1907 (emphasis added).

123. Loc. cit. (emphasis added).

124. For Hyndman and the SDF see Graham Johnson, 'British Social Democracy and Imperialism, 1881-1911', unpublished paper, March 2000, especially 37-40; idem, *Social Democratic Politics in Britain 1881-1911* (Lampeter, 2002), Ch. 4. See also Hyndman, *England*, Ch. VII. For Hardie see, for example, *Labour Leader*, 17 Feb., 1900.

125. *Clarion*, 11 Oct., 1907.

126. *Labour Leader*, 31 Jan., 1908. See also *Labour Leader*, 3, 10, 17 Jan., 1908 for Hardie's further thoughts on India in his 'A Scamper Round the World'.

127. Semmel, *Imperialism*, 56,58; Porter, *Critics*, 115; Thompson, 'The Language', 157.

128. Porter, *Critics*, 115. See also Anna Davin, 'Imperialism and Motherhood', *History Workshop Journal*, 5 (Spring 1978),18.

129. *Clarion*, 15 June, 1906.

130. *Labour Leader*, 30 Aug., 1907.

131. Barrow, 'White Solidarity', 283.

132. *British Citizen and Empire Worker*, 8 Sept., 1916.

133. *British Citizen and Empire Worker*, 15 June, 1918.

134. *British Citizen and Empire Worker*, 7 Oct., 1916.

135. *Labour Leader*, 23 June, 1905.

136. *Clarion*, 15 June, 1906; *Labour Leader*, Aug. 30, 1907.

137. See Andrew Thompson, 'The Language'.

138. See, for example, *Labour Leader*, 12, 19 Aug., 1904; MacKenzie, *Imperialism and Popular Culture*, 7.

139. Biagini and Reid, *Currents of Radicalism*; E.F. Biagini, *Liberty Retrenchment and Reform: Popular Liberalism in the Age of Gladstone 1860-1880* (Cambridge, 1992); Gareth Stedman Jones, 'Rethinking Chartism', in his *Languages of Class: Studies in English Working Class History 1832-1982* (Cambridge, 1983), especially 116-17, 122-3, 134- 7, 153-8; Seymour Drescher, *Capitalism and Antislavery: British Mobilization in Comparative Perspective* (London, 1986), 144- 161; David Northrup, *Indentured Labour in the Age of Imperialism 1834-1922* (Cambridge, 1995).

140. Many Chartists had condemned the 'hypocrisy' of John Bright and other radical Liberals who opposed chattel slavery while upholding 'wage-slavery'. See Neville Kirk, 'In Defence of Class: A Critique of Recent Revisionist Writing Upon the Nineteenth-Century English Working Class', *International Review of Social History*, XXXII (1987), 2-47; Janet Toole, 'Workers and Slaves: Class Relations in South Lancashire in the Time of the Cotton Famine', *Labour History Review*, 63,2 (1998), especially 165-6, 173-8; Patricia Hollis,' Anti-slavery and British Working-Class Radicalism in the Years of Reform', in Christine Bolt and Seymour Drescher (eds.), *Anti-Slavery Religion and Reform* (Folkestone, 1980), 294-315.

141. See Johnson, 'British Social Democracy'.

142. For the tensions between popular radicalism and liberalism see Kirk, *Change Continuity and Class*, Introduction.

143. Thompson, *Outsiders*, Chapter 4.

144. Finn, *After Chartism*, Introduction, Chapter 2.

145. Ernest Jones (ed), *Notes to The People*, vol. I, May 1851-May 1852 (Merlin Press, London, 1967),

1,135. See also 144, 172.

146. Porter, *Critics*, Chapter 4; Pelling, 'British Labour and British Imperialism', 82-7.

147. Porter, *Critics*, 104, 132

148. *Labour Leader*, 3 August, 1900.

149. *Justice*, 5 May, 1900. See also Johnson, *Social Democratic Politics*, Chapter 4, and Barrow (*SSLHB*, 19 (1969), 11) for the SDF's fundamental anti-imperialism.

150. *Labour Leader*, 3, 24 Nov., 1900.

151. The *Labour Leader*, nevertheless, tended to eschew sentiment in favour of 'balance' and context in its assessment of Cobden. The latter was seen as a product of his times whose progressive reforming sentiments were, perhaps more than, counterbalanced by his commitment to 'individualism'. See, for example, *Labour Leader*, 10, 24 June, 1904.

152. *Justice*, 25 Aug., 1900.

153. *Justice*, 2 June, 1900.

154. *Clarion*, 13 July, 1901, 15 Sept., 1905. See also Hyndman, *England for All*, xxvii.

155. *Labour Party Conference Reports 1900-1905* (Hammersmith Reprints of Scarce Documents no. 3, London 1967), 44.

156. *Clarion*, 26 Aug., 1904.

157. See, for example, Barrow, 'The Socialism', 391; *Labour Party Conference Reports*, 44; *Justice*, Nov. 11, Dec. 9, 30 1899, 6 Jan. 1900; *Labour Leader*, 14 Feb., 1908.

158. *Justice*, 2 June, 1900.

159. *Blackburn Labour Journal*, Jan. 1900.

160. Kenneth O. Morgan, *Keir Hardie: Radical and Socialist* (London, 1975), 106.

161. For a first-rate discussion of these capitalist interests in South Africa see Marks and Trapido, 'Lord Milner'.

162. For continuing historiographical debates about the origins and causes of the South African War see Shula Marks, 'Southern and Central Africa'; idem, 'Scrambling for Africa', *Journal of African History*, 23 (1982); Marks and Trapido, 'Lord Milner'; Iain R. Smith, 'The Origins of the South African War (1899-1902): A Re-Appraisal', *South African Historical Journal*, 22 (1990), 24-60; Peter J. Cain and A.G. Hopkins, *British Imperialism: Innovation and Expansion 1688-1914* (London, 1997), 369-81

163. *Labour Leader*, 6 Jan., 1900. For similar sentiments see *Justice*, Nov. 11, Dec. 9, 30 1899, 6 Jan. 1900.

164. *Labour Leader*, 6 Jan. 1900.

165. See, for example, *Justice*, 20 Jan., 10 March, 12 May 1900, 27 Feb., 1904.

166. *Justice*, 6 Jan., 1900.

167. *Labour Leader*, 28 April, 4 Aug., 1900.

168. Morgan, *Keir Hardie*, 191.

169. Loc. cit.; *Labour Leader*, 31 Jan.,7, 14, 21 Feb., 1908; Emrys Hughes, *Keir Hardie* (London, 1956), Chapter 15.

170. Hughes, *Keir Hardie*, 148-58 ; Morgan, *Keir Hardie*, 191-4

171. *Justice*, 16, 23, 30 June, 1900.

172. *Labour Leader*, 28 July, 4 Aug., 27 Oct., 1900.

173. *Clarion*, 21 July, 1900.

174. *Labour Leader*, 30 Dec., 1899.

175. Porter, *Critics*, 132.

176. *Justice*, 14 July, 4, 11 Aug., 1906.

177. *Justice*, 14 July 1906.

178. *Labour Leader*, 8 Nov., 1907.

179. *Blackburn Labour Journal*, June 1901.

180. *Clarion*, 27 May, 1910. For the expression of similar sentiments see, for example, *Labour Party Conference Reports*, 1901, 44; *Report of the Thirty Second Annual Trades Union Congress*, Plymouth 1899, 85-7; the comments of British fraternal delegate, Allen Gee, at the 1906 American Federation

of Labor's convention, AF of L, *Procs.*, 123,127; *Justice*, 20 Jan., 1900; *Labour Leader*, 17 Feb., 1900, 14 Feb., 1908.

181. Miles, *Capitalism*, Chapter 6; Marks, 'Southern and Central Africa', 465-485; Marks and Trapido, 'Lord Milner', 64-72.

182. *Labour Leader*, 14 Feb., 1908.

183. *Clarion*, 18 Jan., 1907.

184. *Clarion*, 27 April, 1906.

185. *Labour Leader*, 16 Aug., 1907.

186. *Labour Leader*, 27 Aug., 1909.

187. *Labour Leader*, 7 Dec., 1906.

188. *Justice*, 16 June, 1900

189. For the credit-ticket system see Campbell, *Chinese Coolie Emigration.*

190. *Labour Leader*, 17 March, 1905.

191. *Labour Leader*, 19 Jan., 1901.

192. Marks and Trapido, 'Lord Milner', 65.

193. Campbell, *Chinese Coolie Emigration*, Chapter IV.

194. *Labour Leader*, 24 Jan., 1903.

195. *Labour Leader*, 9 April, 1904.

196. *Justice*, 14 Jan., 1905.

197. See, for example, *Clarion*, 23 June, 31 July 1905.

198. *Clarion*, 25 Aug., 1905, 24 Aug., 1906.

199. *Clarion*, 12 Oct., 1906.

200. Lawrence, *Speaking*, 223-4; Pelling, 'British Labour and British Imperialism', 98-9.

201. *Labour Leader*, 9, 23 April, 13 May 1904.

202. *Labour Party Conference Reports* (1904), 173, (1905), 218-19.

203. Hyndman, *England for All*, xxv; *Justice*, 7 Oct., 1899.

204. *Clarion*, 27 April, 1 June, 1906; *Labour Leader*, 6 April, 20 July, 1906; *Justice*, 15 Sept., 1900, 24 March, 28 April, 1906.

205. Marks, 'Southern and Central Africa', 466, 484.

206. *Justice*, 14 April, 28 July, 1906.

207. *Labour Leader*, 20 July, 1906.

208. For the dominant racism of Australian labour see Verity Burgmann, 'Revolutionaries and Racists: Australian Socialism and the Problem of Racism, 1887-1917', unpublished PhD thesis, Australian National University, July 1980; Ann Curthoys and Andrew Markus (eds), *Who are our Enemies? Racism and the Australian Working Class* (Neutral Bay, NSW, 1978); Bruce Scates, *A New Australia*, 5,25, 160-2.

209. *Justice*, 18 Aug., 1906. See also *Justice*, 4 March, 1905.

210. Osborne, 'Tom Mann', 103-4. For mid-century attitudes to the Chinese see Markus, *Fear and Hatred*, 19-43; Paul Pickering, 'The Finger of God'.

211. *Justice*, 13 Jan. 1900.

212. *Clarion*, 22, 29 July, 1904; *Labour Leader*, 7 July, 1905. See also the comments by Alex Thompson, giving priority to the 'economic' over issues of 'race or colour prejudice' in the *Clarion*, 13 Dec., 1907.

213. *Clarion*, 22, 29 July, 1904.

214. See, for example, Alex Thompson's criticisms of Australian labour's hostility and exclusion towards the Japanese and other people of Asia, to be found in the *Clarion*, 13 Dec., 1907.

215. Loc.cit.

216. *Justice*, 13 Jan., 1900, 14 July, 1906.

217. *Justice*, 13 Jan., 1900.

218. *Clarion*, 30 June, 1900.

219. *Labour Leader*, 26 Aug., 1899.

220. *Blackburn Labour Journal*, June 1904. For similar sentiments see also, *Clarion*, 11 March, 29

April, 17 June, 1904, 28 July, 1905; *Labour Leader*, 11, 18 July, 1903.

221. See, for example, *Justice*, 7, 21, 28 Oct., 4, 11 Nov., 1899.

222. *Justice*, 13 Feb., 27 Feb., 1904.

223. *Labour Leader*, 17 March, 1905.

224. Loc.cit.

225. *Justice*, 27 Feb., 1904.

226. *Justice*, 11 Nov., 1899.

227. See, for example, Hunt, 'Fractured Universality', 74-8. See also Paul Ward, *Red Flag and Union Jack: Englishness Patriotism and the British Left 1881-1924* (Woodbridge, Suffolk, 1998), 67-8.

228. *Justice*, 11 Nov., 1899.

229. *Justice*, 28 Oct., 11 Nov., 1899. As Johnson observes of the SDF (*Social Democratic Politics*, p. 114): 'Jewish activists were praised, the much abused Jewish immigrants in Britain were defended, and sympathy was expressed with the sufferings of Jews mistreated and discriminated against by foreign governments. It was when the Jew also happened to be a capitalist that SDF support was less forthcoming'.

230. *Justice*, 28 Oct., 11 Nov., 1899.

231. *Justice*, 4 Nov., 1899.

232. Colin Holmes, *Anti Semitism in British Society 1879-1939* (London, 1979), Chapter 2; Joseph Buckman, 'Alien Working-Class Response: The Leeds Jewish Tailors, 1890-1914', in Kenneth Lunn (ed), *Hosts Immigrants and Minorities: Historical Responses to Newcomers in British Society 1870-1914* (Folkestone, 1980), 222-262; Panikos Panayi, *Immigration Ethnicity and Racism in Britain 1815-1945* (Manchester, 1994); David Feldman, *Englishmen and Jews: Social Relations and Political Culture 1840-1914* (New Haven, 1994).

233. Holmes, *Anti Semitism*, Chapter 2; Lunn, Introduction, Chapter 11 ('Reactions to Lithuanian and Polish Immigrants in the Lanarkshire Coalfield 1880-1914') in *Hosts*; *Report of The Twenty-Eighth Annual TUC*, Cardiff 1895, 45; *Labour Leader*, 19 March, 1904.

234. Barrow, 'The Socialism', 431, 437-40.

235. See, for example, *Clarion*, 24 Aug., 1906 (M.D. Eder); *Clarion*, 28 July, 1905 (T. Hunt).

236. Keir Hardie attempted to introduce an amendment to the Aliens Bill against the introduction by employers of 'blackleg labour from abroad during strikes and lock outs'. *Clarion*, 28 July, 1905.

237. *Clarion*, 1 September, 1905.

238. *Justice*, 22 April, 6 May, 1905.

239. *Labour Leader*, 23 April, 1904.

240. *Labour Leader*, 30 April, 1904.

241. *Labour Leader*, 30 April, May 13, 1904; 21 July, 1905; Morgan, *Keir Hardie*, 179-80.

242. *Clarion*, 13 July, 1906.

243. Buckman, 'Alien Working-Class Response'; Bill Williams, 'The Beginnings of Jewish Trade Unionism in Manchester, 1889-1891', in Lunn, *Hosts*, especially 295-8.

244. Lunn, 'Reactions', 323, 326-7, 332-3; idem, 'A Racialized Hierarchy of Labour?'; Tabili, *We Ask for British Justice*; Satnam Virdee, 'Racism and Resistance in British Trade Unions, 1948-79', in Alexander and Halpern, *Racializing Class*, 122-149.

245. *Labour Leader*, 1 Sept., 1905.

246. *Labour Leader*, 21 April, 1905.

247. Hyndman to Tom Mann, 25 Feb., 1905. *Tom Mann Papers*, CP/IND/TORR/08/06; H.M. Hyndman, 'The Awakening of Asia', *Fortnightly Review*, 100 (Oct. 1916), 677-90.

248. *Clarion*, 29 July, 1904.

249. *Labour Leader*, 7 July, 1905.

250. *Clarion*, 29 July, 1904.

251. *Labour Leader*, 29 July, 1904, 7 July, 1905, 16 March, 1906.

252. *Clarion*, 27 April, 1906.

253. Morgan, *Keir Hardie*, 197.

254. *Clarion*, 29 June, 1906. Also *Justice*, 18 Aug., 1906.

255. *Clarion,* 22 July, 1904.

256. *Labour Leader,* 14 April, 16 June, 1905.

257. *Justice,* 18 Aug., 1906.

258. *Labour Leader,* 16 March, 1906.

259. *Labour Leader,* 4 Aug., 1900.

260. *Blackburn Labour Journal,* Sept., 1901.

261. *Labour Leader,* 16 March, Dec. 7, 1906; *Clarion,* 27 April, 1906

262. *Justice,* 27 Feb., 1904; Johnson, 'British Social Democracy'.

263. *Labour Leader,* 8, 22 May, 1908, 23 April, 13, 27, Aug., 1909; *Justice,* 13 Jan., 17 Feb., 5 May, 2, 9 June, 1900, 27 Feb., 1904, 24 July, 28 August 1909. See also *Justice,* 16, 23 April, 18, 25 June 1910 for opposition to 'Kaffir slavery', as the successor to 'Chinese slavery', on the Rand.

264. *Labour Leader,* 25 Oct., 1907. See also *Labour Leader,* 20 Oct., 3 Nov., 1905 for growing unrest in India.

265. Morgan, *Keir Hardie,* 192-5; *Labour Leader,* 29 Nov., 20, 27 Dec., 1907, 3,10,17,31 Jan., 1908; Howe, *Anticolonialism,* 45-6.

266. Johnson, 'British Social Democracy'; *Justice,* 17 Feb., 1900, 2 Jan., 1904, 1, 22 April, 13 May, 1905. In an interview in 1907 Hyndman was reported as declaring, 'We have got to leave India', and 'it is our duty to help forward the day of (Indian) emancipation with all our strength'. See the *Clarion,* 11 Oct., 1907; Hyndman, *England for All,* 130. Of related interest see the article, 'Home Rule for Egypt', in *Justice,* 23 Sept., 1905.

267. Barrow, 'The Socialism', 391,425.

268. Chris Wrigley, 'Widening Horizons? British Labour and the Second International', *Labour History Review,* 58,1 (Spring 1993), 12.

269. In practice, however, some 'coloured people' in South Africa, were deemed 'unfit' for *immediate* enfranchisement. See, for example, the views of the Johannesburg branch of the ILP reported in the *Labour Leader,* 23 April, 1909.

270. *Labour Leader,* 10 Aug., 1906.

271. Hunt, 'Fractured Universality'.

272. *Clarion,* 12 Oct., 1906.

273. *Clarion,* 29 July, 1904.

274. *Tocsin,* 3 Oct., 1901.

275. By way of qualification, Guest believed that a 'white Australia' was 'not a final answer for Australia, and is not applicable to either America or South Africa'. See the *Clarion,* 22, 29 July, 1904.

276. For the strong presence of circumspection and diplomacy on the part of British socialists towards Australian labour's White Australia policy see Morgan, *Keir Hardie,* 196; *Clarion,* 6 May, 1904, 30 June, 1905; *Labour Leader,* 23 Nov., 1906, 28 Feb., 6, 13, 20 March, 10 April, 1908.

277. *Clarion,* 7 April, 23 June, 28 July, 4 Aug., 1905, 12 Oct., 1906; *Labour Leader,* 27 Dec., 1902. For 'the sensationalized and sexualized image of white working women as victims of competition from Chinese male workers', and 'anxieties over femininity, motherhood, and racial and sexual purity … endemic to historical discussions of Chinese immigration' in California see, Martha Mabie Gardner, 'Working on White Womanhood: White Working Women in the San Francisco Anti-Chinese Movement, 1877-1890', *Journal Social History,* 33,1 (Fall 1999), 73-95.

278. Marks, 'Southern and Central Africa', 488.

279. Marks, *Reluctant Rebellion,* xvi.

280. Marks, 'Southern and Central Africa', 491.

281. *Labour Leader,* 25 Aug., 13 Oct., 1905.

282. For MacDonald's criticisms and his defence of the 'enlightened' form of imperial rule practised in the Cape Colony see *Clarion,* 15 June, 1906.

283. For examples of 'Pufff's' racist outpourings see *Clarion,* 25 May, 1 June, 20 July, 3, 24, 31 Aug., 26 Oct., 1906, 12 April, 1907.

284. For the expression of such views see *Clarion,* 1 June, 10, 17 Aug., 14 Sept., 1906, 22 March, 1907.

285. *Clarion*, 1 June, 26 Oct., 1906.

286. *Labour Leader*, 29 Sept., 1905, 13 April, 1906.

287. *Labour Leader*, 16 July, 1909. For the same, if contested claim, see *Clarion*, 22 May, 17 July, 1908.

288. *Labour Leader*, 16 July, 1909.

289. *Clarion*, 28 May, 1909; idem, 29 March, 12 April, 1907.

290. *Clarion*, 16 Sept., 1910. See also the Clarion, 18 Oct. 1911, for a letter from the editor of the *Pretoria News*, Vere Stent, condemning 'Pufff's' hypocritical advocacy of both socialism and racism in South Africa. The Chair of the South African Labour Party, H.W. Simpson, an early member of the British ILP, supported both segregation ('The black races in South Africa do not assimilate with the white and are merely being exploited by the employers to the detriment of the white. They have a different standard of morality, a different sense of justice, different customs, different instincts, different ideals.') and black self- government and ownership of the land 'stolen from them'. In addition, Simpson saw black South Africans as possessing an 'extraordinary capacity for advance', being, for example, in many instances the equal of whites in skilled work. See the *Labour Leader*, 30 June, 1911. For the rule of race over class in the 1900s South African labour movement see also Kennedy, *A Tale of Two Mining Cities*, Ch.1.

291. In addition to the references listed in notes 105,107 and 114, see Ray Markey, 'Populist Politics: Racism and Labor in NSW, 1880- 1900', in Curthoys and Markus (eds.), *Who are our Enemies?*, 66-79.

292. Burgmann, 'Revolutionaries',93-8; Markey, 'Populist Politics', 72-3.

293. Markey, 'Populist Politics', 75-7.

294. *Clarion*, 27 March, 1908.

295. It is significant that William Lane – English emigrant, socialist, racist, and leader of the Australians who set out to create a socialist utopia in Paraguay – settled for a time in Brisbane and edited the socialist and racist Queensland *Worker*. See Whitehead, *Paradise Mislaid*.

296. *Tocsin*, 14, 21, 28 July, 1898, 7 May, Oct. 3, 1901.

297. *Tocsin*, 21 July, 1898; Kay Saunders, 'Masters and Servants: The Queensland Sugar Workers' Strike 1911', in Curthoys and Markus (eds.), *Who are our Enemies*, 96-111; Markus, *Fear and Hatred*, 92-3, 122-4, 132, 154, 164-8.

298. *The Socialist*, 29 June, 1907; Graeme Osborne, 'A Socialist Dilemma: Racism and Internationalism in the Victorian Socialist Party, 1905-21', in Curthoys and Markus (eds.), *Who are our Enemies?*, 112-128.

299. Markey, 'Populist Politics', 77.

300. *Sixth Annual Report of the British Immigration League of Australia, 1910-11*, 4,26. This report is to be found in the records of the *British Immigration League: New South Wales Branch, 1905-1943* in the Mitchell Library, Sydney, Australia, MLMSS 302, Box 6. While disclaiming any 'aversion' to the 'law abiding, industrious, thrifty and peaceable' Chinese people 'settled in this country', Sir Henry Parkes similarly declared that 'it is our duty to preserve the type of the British nation'. The Chinese constituted 'an alien race, out of tone with us in faith, in law, in traditions, in everything that endears life'. See Sir Henry Parkes, 'The Chinese in Australia', in *Speeches of Sir Henry Parkes, Prime Minister of New South Wales* (Sydney, 1888), pamphlet held in the Mitchell Library, especially 5-7.

301. See, for example, *Labour Leader*, 6 April, 18 May, 1 June, 24 Aug., 2 Nov., 1906; *Justice*, 28 April, 1906.

302. See, for example, *Clarion*, 29 June, 10, 24 Aug., 14 Sept., 26 Oct., 2, 9 Nov., 1906; W.P. Visser, 'Workers' Strife: Socialists and the South African Labour Party, 1910-1924 – An Uneasy Relationship', Paper presented to the Seventh National Labour History Conference, ANU, Canberra, Australia, April 19-21, 2001. I am grateful to the author for a copy of his paper.

303. See, for example, *Labour Leader*, 3 Jan., 8, 22 May, 1908, 23 April, 13, 27 Aug., 1909; Morgan, *Keir Hardie*, 198; *Clarion*, 17 July, 1908; *Justice*, 22 Dec., 1906, 28 Aug 1909. See also the British Labour Party's opposition to the 'regrettable feature' and 'retrograde provision' of the 'colour bar' in the South Africa Bill. *Report of the Tenth Annual Conference of the Labour Party*, February 9-11

Newport 1910, London, p. 20.

304. Markus, *Fear and Hatred*; *idem*, 'Explaining the treatment of non-European immigrants', 86-91; Scates, *New Australia*, 160-2; Frank Bongiorno, 'Bernard O'Dowd and the "Problem" of Race', in *Labour and Community*, Proceedings of the Sixth National Conference of the Australian Society for the Study of Labour History, edited by Robert Hood and Ray Markey. I am grateful to Bruce Scates for a copy of his book and to Frank Bongiorno for a copy of his article. See also McQueen, *A New Britannia*.

305. Burgmann, *Revolutionary Industrial Unionism*; Julia Martinez, 'Questioning "White Australia": Unionism and "Coloured" Labour, 1911-37', *Labour History*, 76 (May 1999), 1-19.

Conclusion

Were my predominantly white and male British, American and Australian subjects, as suggested by the title of this book, indeed comrades as well as cousins across the oceans? Did they not only share personal and familial ties, but also develop common transatlantic and imperial labour movement methods and goals? Or did nationally-based and other differences outweigh cross-national similarities and 'customs in common'? In responding to these questions, the conclusion briefly offers both a summary of, and a critical judgement upon many of the key themes and issues that have arisen in the course of this study.

The increasingly global ambitions and reach of late nineteenth-century industrial capitalism – complete with its 'new imperialist' rivalries and its intensified attempts to reduce labour costs, maximise profits and ensure the more unlimited formal and inform control of capital over labour – presented new challenges and opportunities for labour movements, both nationally and internationally. The formation of the Second International constituted organised labour's main cross-national institutional response to the international spread of capital and capitalism. The focus of this study, however, has rested not upon the International, but upon both the responses and initiatives of selected individuals, groups and institutions within the national labour movements of Britain, the USA and Australia and upon cross-national labour-movement links and representations.

In terms of the latter, an attempt has been made to highlight the substantial interest displayed by selected labour-movement activists in all three countries in corresponding movements abroad, their increasing awareness and critical appraisal of these movements, and their visits to brothers, sisters and comrades overseas. They were keen to learn, exchange ideas, strengthen or establish formal links – such as the fraternal delegate system between the AF of L and the TUC – and, wherever possible, formulate similar and common strategies and tactics. We have seen that, notwithstanding differences and disagreements, they were commonly influenced by the structures and feelings of class, and were substantively and morally committed to regulating, taming, civilising, and in some cases transforming, capitalism in the interests of working people. The vast majority of them also unreservedly condemned the 'new imperialist' face of capitalism. Furthermore, they shared a fundamental commitment to building 'the movement'. Comprising like-minded and proudly independent men and women, it was the collective labour movement that constituted the means whereby the emancipation of 'the people', the 'producers', the 'working class' or the 'working classes', both nationally and internationally, was to be achieved. Organised workers, accordingly, were expected to subordinate individual self-interest, ambition and ideological preference to the greater good and demands of their movement. Finally, labour's spreading bonds of solidarity and its internationally 'moving frontier of radicalism', were set against the backcloth of, and derived great nourishment from, the mass migrations of people seeking work under conditions of expanding industrialization. In these ways the notion of international comradeship was grounded not only in ideas, but also in the developing political economy of capitalism itself.

However, and setting aside personal differences and rivalries, the consciousness of our labour movement subjects in all three countries was very strongly, indeed primarily, informed by nationally-based concerns and interests. For example, while both Sam Gompers and Andrew Fisher readily acknowledged their heavy debt to the nineteenth-century British labour-movement pioneer, they were keen to adjust 'the British model' to suit the 'peculiarities' of their own countries, and, increasingly, to strike out in their own 'American' and 'Australian' ways. Indeed, by the end of the 1900s both Gompers and Fisher were broadcasting the 'superiority' of their chosen national labour movement paths. In the American case this revolved around the primacy of 'craft' trade unionism, anti-statism and increasingly anti-socialism and 'the defence of democracy'; while the Australian movement adopted a combination of statist Labor politics, mass unionism and workerist nationalism. The British movement – as pioneering inspiration, and as global supplier of both labour-movement personnel and an ideological mixture of voluntarism and collectivism, craft and general unionism, liberalism, labourism and socialism – continued to occupy a 'special place' in the hearts and minds of many Australian and some American labour movement activists. However, the British movement was increasingly regarded as too 'traditional' by its increasingly assertive, forward-looking, independent-minded and nationalistic American and Australian cousins. Herein, lay a pointer to much of the future tension between hegemonic nationalism and subordinate, yet often heroic, internationalism during the course of international labour's twentieth-century history.

Furthermore, the very universalism of our labourist, trade unionist and socialist subjects was often limited, disfigured and diminished by racism. We have observed that unapologetic racism was most pronounced on the part of the Australian labour movement, including most socialists within that movement. Australian labour had much in common with its counterpart in South Africa. Notwithstanding its traditional support for 'free' immigrants, the American labour movement overwhelmingly shared the exclusionary sentiments displayed by the country as a whole towards 'Orientals'. In addition, most

African-Americans and many 'new' immigrants from southern and south-east-ern Europe were not welcomed into the 'white' ranks of mainstream American labour.[1] In contrast, British socialists generally asserted the primacy of class over race. Notwithstanding their minority numerical standing within the ranks of the British labour movement as a whole, these socialists attempted, however imper-fectly, to develop and spread anti-racist ideas and actions.

The degree of comradeship preached and practised by our three labour move-ments was also limited by the issue of gender. While women were involved in all three labour movements, they appear for the most part as supportive and often marginal figures. Gender constituted an important basis of difference and divi-sion not only within the labour movements, but also within the wider working classes of Britain, the USA and Australia. Therefore, the internationalist and universalist sentiments of our comrades and cousins were simultaneously, and often severely, limited by the influences of nation, race and gender.

In turning to a brief consideration of the implications of this study for organ-ised labour's role in the current period of globalization, it is necessary to strike a cautionary note. It is very difficult to draw clear, unambiguous and mean-ingful conclusions from the past and apply them to the very different context of the present. This task becomes even more hazardous when conclusions are expressed in the form of hard-and-fast 'lessons' or 'rules'. The latter are all too often expressed by politicians and other interested parties in one-dimensional or partial, and largely predetermined and ideological ways which pay scant justice to the complexities and nuances of both the past and the present. However, as reasoned by many British socialists a century ago, the essays in this study do lend themselves to the argument that labour in the twenty-first century has most to gain from a strategy of inclusiveness under conditions of capitalist globalization. Moreover, I would argue that this inclusive aim must be pursued not only as a counter to the divisive effects of globalization in national and international la-bour markets – in setting 'white' against 'black' and 'coloured', 'skilled' against 'non-skilled', men against women, and workers of the 'developed' world against those of the 'developing' and 'undeveloped' – but in all aspects of life. For, in truth, the 'utopian' principles of inclusivity, equality, democracy and respect for genuine diversity and choice have pragmatically assumed the utmost urgency in the face of increasing global inequality, chronic mass poverty, and the barbarism currently being visited upon the world by arrogant, intolerant and unashamedly imperialist capitalist 'crusaders' and religious fundamentalists.

Finally, this study has merely scratched the surface in terms of the develop-ment of a comprehensive account of workers' and labour movements' attitudes and actions towards class and race across the Atlantic and throughout the British Empire in the globalized era of 'new imperialism'. For example, the practical constraints of time, resources, linguistic ability, source availability and energy, in addition to the fact that Britain, the USA and Australia so readily lent themselves to the kind of comparison envisaged from the very outset of my project, restricted my geographical focus to the selected experiences of three countries. As such, all three essays in my book could usefully benefit from further national points of comparison and contrast within the chosen transatlantic and imperial frameworks of reference. Furthermore, it has not been my purpose to examine the thoughts and actions of those Jewish and other immigrants to Britain, and those African-American, black South African, Indian, Chinese and aboriginal people who were so often the objects of the discourses of class, race, nation and empire practised by my British, US, Australian and South African labour activists. A complete account, of course, must pay careful attention to their 'voices'[2] – including their powers of agency as well as their positions of powerlessness and subordination – and their complex, shifting, and classed, gendered and racialized relations and engagements with the 'white other'. However, this study has hopefully made a contribution towards setting some of the substantive, methodological and conceptual foundations upon which this future work will build. For the further development of cross-national comparative studies in labour history, and especially those of a transatlantic and imperial kind, can only redound to the future health and excitement of our subject area. They may even productively feed into political debate concerning labour's role in the globalized world of the new millennium.

Notes

1. For debates concerning the 'whiteness' of American labour see Eric Arnesen, 'Whiteness and the Historians' Imagination', *ILWCH* 60 (Fall 2001), 3-32, and the responses in the same issue of *ILWCH* by James R. Barrett, David Brody, Barbara J. Fields, Eric Foner, Victoria C. Hattam and Adolph Reed Jr. See also Judith Stein's introduction, in *ILWCH* 60, to this 'Scholarly Controversy' and Arnesen's reply to the responses. For an effective critique of 'whiteness', in the form of largely unchanging 'racial homogeneity', as applied to Britain, see Laura Tabili, 'Labour Migration, Racial Formation and Class Identity. Some Reflections on the British Case', in *Journal of the North West Labour History Group – The Black Presence in the North West*, 20 (1995), 16-35.
2. For examples of attention to such 'voices' see the references in note 1 above. See also Tabili, '*We Ask for British Justice*'; Roediger, *Wages of Whiteness*; Prakash, 'Subaltern Studies'; Sivaramakrishnan, 'Situating the Subaltern'; Hill, 'The Problem of Race'; Feldman, *Englishmen and Jews*; Virdee, 'Racism and Resistance'; Diane Frost, 'Ambiguous Identities: Constructing and De-Constructing Black and White "Scouse" Identities in Twentieth-Century Liverpool', in Neville Kirk (ed.), *Northern Identities: Historical Interpretations of 'The North' and 'Northernness'* (Aldershot, 2000), 195-217; idem, 'West Africans, Black Scousers and the Colour Problem in inter-war Liverpool', *Jnl. North West Lab. Hist. Group*, 20 (1995), 50-57; Mark Christian, 'Black Struggle for Historical Recognition in Liverpool', in ibid., 58-66; Marika Sherwood, *Manchester and the 1945 Pan-African Congress* (London, 1995).

Index